T. He...

LOGIC AND LA...

A. G. N. FLEW is Professor of Philosophy at the University of Keele, in England. He was formerly Lecturer at Christ Church, Oxford, and also at King's College, Aberdeen. Among his other books published in the United States are *Essays in Conceptual Analysis, Hume's Philosophy of Belief,* and, with Alasdair Macintyre, *New Essays in Philosophical Theology.*

Logic and Language

(FIRST AND SECOND SERIES)

EDITED WITH INTRODUCTIONS BY
Antony Flew

ANCHOR BOOKS
DOUBLEDAY & COMPANY, INC.
GARDEN CITY, NEW YORK

Logic and Language was originally published
in two volumes by Basil Blackwell, Oxford,
the First Series in 1951 and the Second Series in 1953.
The Anchor edition is
published by arrangement with Basil Blackwell.

Anchor edition: 1965

ACKNOWLEDGMENTS

Chapters II, V, VIII, IX, and X of the First Series originally appeared in the *Proceedings of the Aristotelian Society* for 1931/2, 1937/8, 1948/9, 1940/1, and 1944/5, respectively. Chapters VI and VII were first included in Supplementary Volumes XV (1936) and XIX (1945) of the same *Proceedings*. Chapters III and IV were published originally in the *Australasian Journal of Psychology and Philosophy* for 1941 and in *Mind* for 1949, respectively. The Second Series included two papers, Chapters VI and VII, published there for the first time. Of the remaining chapters, IV, V, VIII, and X first appeared in the *Proceedings of the Aristotelian Society* for 1938/9 and in the Supplementary Volumes XV (1939), XX (1946), and XXI (1947), respectively. Chapters II and IX were originally published in *Mind* 1946 and *Mind* 1950. Chapter III was an article in the *Philosophical Quarterly* for 1951; Chapter XI in the *Australasian Journal of Psychology and Philosophy* for 1940; and Chapter XII in *Philosophy and Phenomenological Research* for 1951. The Editor and the Publishers wish to thank here all the authors, societies, and editors concerned.

EDITOR'S PREFACE

TO THE DOUBLEDAY ANCHOR EDITION

In this first paperback edition the two Series of *Essays in Logic and Language* are bound together in a single volume substantially as they originally appeared in hardcover. Since, for technical reasons, it unfortunately proved impossible to preserve the pagination, original page numbers have been indicated in the headlines. Even the two separate Introductions have been kept as they first appeared, save for the acknowledgments, which have been consolidated and transferred to the front papers. The main reasons for not attempting to conflate the two Introductions are: first, that any such operation would have been bound to result in something possibly better than but certainly very different from the originals—and that too something too like other pieces already published elsewhere; and, second, that the period flavour of those originals should serve to underline the warnings, now more than ever necessary, that the papers printed here must not automatically be presumed to represent the present views of their authors.

It remains simply to welcome the initiative of Doubleday Anchor in making these two sets of papers thus still more widely and easily available.

Antony Flew

University of Keele,
Staffordshire, England.
March 17, 1964

CONTENTS

SECOND SERIES

First Series

Perhaps if ideas and words were distinctly weighed and duly considered, they would afford us another sort of logic and critic than what we have hitherto been acquainted with.

JOHN LOCKE,
An Essay concerning Human Understanding.

I

Introduction

A. G. N. FLEW

'Perhaps if ideas and words were distinctly weighed and duly
considered, they would afford us another sort of logic and
critic than what we have hitherto been acquainted with'
(John Locke, *An Essay concerning Human Understanding*,
Bk. IV, Chap. 21, § 4). It is this new sort of 'logic and critic',
foreseen over two centuries ago by John Locke, which philosophers of the movement represented in this collection of
essays have been working to produce. This movement of
philosophic opinion has been taking shape and growing in
influence in the universities of the British Isles since the beginning of this century. It has gained momentum until now it
dominates the philosophy faculties of Oxford, Cambridge,
and London, is powerfully represented elsewhere in the
United Kingdom, and even has outposts overseas, especially
in Australasia and the United States. But in spite of this
steady progress inside the philosophic world, almost nothing
is known of these developments by that general educated and
interested public which has no direct contact with academic
philosophy. This isolation is certainly the responsibility,
though not perhaps the fault, of the professional philosophers. For those of them who have been in touch with the
new developments have been so engrossed in the exciting
work of following up their fresh insights that they have for
the most part written little or even nothing at all: and what
has been written has been in the form of articles which have
been published only in technical journals which are not read,
and are usually not even accessible, outside professional philosophic circles.

In compiling this collection of articles we had two purposes in view: first, we wanted to do something to end this isolation by making some of these articles available in book form to the lay public, so that they could examine examples of this new kind of philosophizing; second, we wanted to make it possible for people studying philosophy to buy and to own some of the important articles which previously they could only borrow from those few libraries which take the journals in which they originally appeared. In the attempt to achieve these two purposes simultaneously we have had to apply complex multiple principles of selection. In one way this has made the job of selection easier. For, since to choose is always to exclude, the more necessary criteria there are which have to be satisfied by any candidate, the more possible grounds are there upon which otherwise eligible candidates may be reasonably excluded. But in another way the demands of this dual purpose have made the job of selection harder. For articles which would have been ideal for one purpose have had to be excluded because their inclusion would have obstructed the other purpose. Inevitably any editor who has had reluctantly to omit so many first-rate articles must hope that the reception of the present volume will make it possible to produce further similar collections in the near future. Equally inevitably no one other than he will be satisfied with the selection finally made. Perhaps some of the unavoidable regrets over the omission of favourite articles may be softened if we say something more about the criteria of selection which we have tried to apply. And then perhaps something needs also to be said about the origins and character of the philosophic movement from the work of which these essays have been selected.

We have tried to compile a collection of articles which would as far as possible satisfy a multiple set of criteria. Firstly, they had to be immediately readable by and intelligible to the layman. All symbolism was therefore excluded. This was easily achieved, for the protagonists of this movement in England, unlike those of the similar and parallel philosophic tendencies of Logical Positivism and Semanticism on the Continent and in the United States, strive to write in plain untechnical and unsymbolic English. And in this they stand squarely in the British tradition of Thomas

Hobbes and John Locke, of Bishop Berkeley and David Hume. It was Berkeley who proclaimed in the first draft of the Introduction to his *Principles of Human Knowledge* that 'I shall throughout endeavour to express myself in the clearest, plainest, and most familiar manner, abstaining from all hard and unusual terms which are pretended by those that use them to cover a sense abstracted and sublime'. Secondly, the collection had to contain the maximum number of those articles which are most constantly recommended by tutors to their pupils: and thus the claims of Mr. Paul's contribution were irresistible, even in spite of his own protests that, taken out of its context, it might give a wrong impression of the discussions from which it emerged. Thirdly, the essays selected had preferably to be ones which were not, and were not likely to become, available elsewhere in book form. But the claims of Mr. Wisdom's 'Gods' were too strong to be passed over, even though this article should shortly appear again in a volume of his collected papers. Fourthly, an effort was made to select articles representative of as many as possible of the major problems and branches of philosophy. Mr. Edwards, Professor Findlay, and Miss Macdonald deal with aspects of the complexes of problems which are loosely and confusingly dubbed the problems of Induction, Time, and Substance; articles by Mr. Hart, Miss Macdonald, and Mr. Wisdom represent moral philosophy, political philosophy, and the philosophy of religion, respectively. Fifthly, the articles included had to contain patterns of argument which would be stimulating, and suggestive of further developments and applications in other parts of philosophy. Dr. Waismann's conception of 'open texture', for example, could be used to illuminate those fascinating and perplexing legal and quasi-legal dilemmas in which a grammatically interrogative sentence is used to express something which is logically not so much a question asking for an answer as a demand requiring a decision. When we raise the problem 'Is a flying-boat a ship?' we may not be asking for information about flying-boats or ships nor yet even for linguistic information about the present and proper use of the words 'ship' and 'flying-boat'. The problem arises just because the concept of 'ship' does have this 'open texture', and just because we are here

faced with one of the situations in which there is no established correct usage. We have no linguistic rules ready to tell
us whether a flying-boat is or is not properly describable as a
ship. And so the problem has to be taken to the courts for
decision. It was so taken by the case of *Polpen Shipping Co.*
v. *Commercial Union Assurance Co.*, [1943] K.B.161, and
the court decided that the answer was to be in the negative.
But this solution to the problem was, of course, not an answer
to a question as to what proper usage was, for there was no
pre-existing proper usage to be discovered, but a decision as
to what proper usage was to be, for now in law at least proper
usage is usage which accords with this decision.

Similarly, again, Mr. Wisdom's parable of the dispute
about the interventions of a hypothetical gardener, which he
offers in order to illuminate problems of the philosophy of
religion, might also be exploited as a paradigm of the scientific debates about animal spirits or the ether. For in these
debates claims which started their careers as genuine and respectable hypotheses, risking falsification in the hope of
achieving verification, degenerated through successive stages
of qualification until they were abandoned as idle and scientifically worthless. Like Mr. Wisdom's gardener hypothesis,
they were never strictly speaking disproved. They were never
disproved because, whenever counter evidence was produced,
their protagonists added further qualifications: if the entities
could never be seen, that was because they were invisible;
if they could never be touched that was because they were
intangible; if they could never be weighed that was because
they had the unusual property of having no weight; and so on.
And there came a time when the scientists abandoned the
search for the unfindable animal spirits and the forever elusive ether: not because they had proved that there were no
such things but because it had become clear that they never
could prove this. These sometime hypotheses had thus degenerated into what was, scientifically considered, mere idle
talk. A scientific hypothesis is only valuable so long as it is
not in fact proved to be false, but it is only a scientific hypothesis at all so long as it is in principle falsifiable.

It would be possible to go on for a long time pointing out
possible developments and applications of things said by the

authors of these articles, but this is all that is necessary to
illustrate our fifth principle of selection. Perhaps it would be
as well to stress here both that the authors are responsible
solely for their own contributions and that many of these
were first written several years ago: it must not be assumed
that any author necessarily agrees with anything written by
any other contributor or by the Editor; nor yet that all the
contributors would still wish to stand by everything they said
when they originally wrote these articles. The final main principle of selection was that the collection taken together had
to present a picture of this modern movement in British philosophy which should be as far as possible self-explanatory.
It therefore opens with Professor Gilbert Ryle's first powerful
plain manifesto, 'Systematically Misleading Expressions'.
These six are not all the principles of selection which were
employed, and the reasons given are by no means the only
reasons for the inclusion of each of the articles mentioned.
But enough may have been said to explain, if not perhaps
to excuse, the most flagrant omissions.

Perhaps something needs to be said about the nature and
the history of the philosophic developments which this volume tries to represent. A few remarks on this subject might
help to initiate the uninitiated: though this is neither the
time nor the place to write the history of these developments,
and actual examples of this sort of philosophizing will show
its nature better than any description could hope to do. We
have already shown by quotations that these developments
are in the main British philosophic tradition: Berkeley was
expressing a traditional aspiration when he claimed credit for
his good, plain, untechnical English; John Locke was expressing what has been an almost traditional insight when he foresaw that a new sort of logic and critic might arise from the
study of ideas and words. Before either Locke or Berkeley
wrote, Thomas Hobbes in his *Leviathan* had combined these
two aspects of the tradition in his protest that 'the Writings
of Schoole-Divines, are nothing else for the most part, but
insignificant Traines of strange and barbarous words, or
words otherwise used, than in the common use of the Latine
tongue; such as would pose Cicero, and Varro, and all the
Grammarians of ancient Rome. Which if any man would see

proved, let him (as I have said once before) see whether he
can translate any Schoole-Divine into any of the Modern
tongues, as French, English, or any other copious language:
for that which cannot in most of these be made Intelligible,
is not Intelligible in the Latine. Which Insignificancy of language, though I cannot note it for false Philosophy; yet it
hath a quality, not only to hide the Truth, but also to make
men think they have it, and desist from further search.' (This
passage comes in Chapter 46 which, like the similar Chapters 1–12, seems to have been almost entirely neglected:
Hobbes is still generally supposed to be a political philosopher only.) Passages such as these occur again and again,
notably in Book III of Locke's *Essay concerning Human Understanding* and in Berkeley's attacks on the doctrine of abstract ideas, in *The Principles of Human Knowledge* and in
Book VII of *Alciphron, or the Minute Philosopher*. But
though the classical British philosophers realized that the distortion of and departure from plain, common English was a
prime source of philosophical befuddlement and nonsensical
construction, and sometimes even, like Locke in the passage
quoted at the beginning of this Introduction, foresaw that a
new sort of 'logic and critic' might be evoked from the study
of ideas and words, they never realized quite how important
these insights were, and they consequently failed to follow
them up by developing this new sort of 'logic and critic'. This
task was left for the philosophers of this and future centuries.

It is almost twenty years since Gilbert Ryle, now Wayn-
flete Professor of Metaphysical Philosophy in the University
of Oxford, first proclaimed to the Aristotelian Society his reluctant conversion to the view that the main if not the only
proper business of philosophy is 'the detection of the sources
in linguistic idioms of recurrent misconstructions and absurd
theories'. This proclamation was made at the end of the paper
which is reprinted as the first item in this collection. Ten
years earlier, Dr. Ludwig Wittgenstein, who was later to become Professor of Philosophy in the University of Cambridge, had claimed in his apocalyptic *Tractatus Logico-
Philosophicus* (Kegan Paul, 1922) that 'Most propositions
and questions, that have been written about philosophical
matters, are not false but senseless. We cannot, therefore,

answer questions of this kind at all, but only state their sense-lessness. Most questions and propositions of the philosophers result from the fact that we do not understand the logic of our language'. And he went on to assert that 'All philosophy is "Critique of language" . . . Russell's merit is to have shown that the apparent logical form of the proposition need not be its real form'. (These sentences come in theses 4.003 and 4.0031.) It is this discovery, which Professor Wittgenstein here credits to his teacher, Bertrand Russell, which is most central and most fundamental to modern British philosophy, or rather to the dominant tendency in modern British philosophizing. Professor Wittgenstein and Professor Ryle were both expressing in their very different ways what was substantially the same insight. To-day they would no doubt wish to put it all very differently, not placing the stress in the same places. But nevertheless it remains true that it is from this and upon this central and fundamental discovery that all the other characteristic doctrines and assumptions of modern British philosophy have been developed and founded. It has been realized that expressions may be grammatically similar and yet logically different. We might say that 'This is past' and 'This is red', 'It goes on to London' and 'It goes on to Infinity', and 'Nobody came' and 'Somebody came' are pairs of grammatically similar expressions. But the members of all these pairs of grammatically similar expressions are logically very different. That is to say that nothing but nonsense and paradox will result if we ask questions about one assertion which are only appropriate and significant when asked about the other. It would be absurd, but it would also be easy, to be misled by the grammatical similarity of 'It goes on to London' to 'It goes on to Infinity' into the misconception that 'Infinity' like 'London' refers to a place, albeit a very queer and very inaccessible place. It is absurd, but to some people it is also easy, to be misled by the grammatical similarity of 'Somebody came' to 'Nobody came' into the misconception that 'Nobody' refers to a person just as does 'Somebody'. It was this misconception of the logic of the word 'Nobody' which Lewis Carroll exploited in *Through the Looking Glass*:

' "I see nobody on the road," said Alice.

' "I only wish *I* had such eyes," the King remarked in a fretful tone. "To be able to see Nobody! And at that distance too! Why, it's as much as *I* can do to see real people, by this light!" '

These are very simple and rather hackneyed examples of the sort of thing which philosophers have been pointing out when they have distinguished between logical and grammatical form, between logical and grammatical resemblance. And when they have talked of misunderstanding the logic of our language they have been alluding to the mistakes made by people who are misled by grammatical similarities or dissimilarities into overlooking logical dissimilarities or similarities. Such is the mistake of the King who treats 'Nobody' as if it had the logic of 'Somebody', as if 'Nobody' referred to somebody, albeit a rather insubstantial somebody. Such, in a slightly more subtle form, is the mistake of the person who fails to appreciate the fact, which we pointed out earlier, that the grammatically interrogative sentence 'Is a flying-boat a ship?' may be used to express something which is not logically interrogative at all. It may be used not as, or to express, a question asking for information but rather to raise a dilemma demanding a decision. Such in ever more subtle forms are the mistakes about the logic of 'defeasible' concepts which Mr. Hart exposes in his paper on 'The Ascription of Responsibility and Rights', the mistakes and perplexities arising from the question 'What is Time?' which Professor Findlay disentangles in his 'Time: a Treatment of some Puzzles'. Such in an even more subtle form still is the mistake about the logic of 'invisible and intangible gardeners', which Mr. Wisdom suggests in the parable of the gardener in his 'Gods': though 'invisible and intangible gardener' is grammatically very similar to 'irritable and irascible gardener', it seems that logically the two expressions are very different indeed; while the latter refers to a particular and not uncommon kind of gardener, the former expression seems logically to be embarrassingly similar to 'no gardener at all'.

It is from this first fundamental insight, that grammatical resemblances and dissimilarities may be logically misleading, that the new sort of logical criticism of language represented in this volume has been developed. It was this discovery that led on to the realization that grammatically respectable sentences might be logically disreputable, that sentences which appear to be good English, which contain no grammatical errors, may logically speaking be nonsense, but specious just because they do resemble grammatically other sentences which are logically quite in order.

And this realization made it easier to appreciate the point and the necessity of the contribution of that apostle of common-sense and linguistic propriety, Professor G. E. Moore. For it has been Professor Moore who has made philosophers see how easy it is to slip into nonsense by even apparently trivial deviations from standard English, how easy it is to use sentences which look all right, which have a close grammatical resemblance to sentences which are indeed proper, but which are nevertheless logically disreputable, which are deviations from standard English to which no sense has been attached.

As such discoveries have been developed and applied in field after field, enterprises of metaphysical construction have seemed less and less practicable, less and less respectable. For anyone who has seen how much muddle and perplexity, how much paradox and absurdity, has already been traced back to its tainted sources in misleading idiom, or in unexplained and unnoticed distortions of standard English, must suspect that any further metaphysical construction which he might be tempted to erect would soon meet with a similar humiliating and embarrassing débâcle under the assaults of the new 'logic and critic'.

We have already said enough to suggest that this new sort of 'logic and critic' has strong, deep, traditional roots. Locke foresaw that it was possible to develop it. Hobbes realized how much philosophic absurdity might be dissolved by translating or trying to translate into plain English. Hobbes, Locke, Berkeley, and Hume all realized how too easy it was to be misled by words. Others before Professor G. E. Moore had seen, though unsteadily, how philosophic error could arise from unnoticed distortions of proper language: Locke for instance (in the *Essay*, Bk. II, Chap. 21, § 21) wrote 'I think the question is not proper, *whether the will be free*, but *whether a man be free*'. Others before Bertrand Russell had seen, though dimly, that grammatical similarity might conceal logical dissimilarity: Plato for instance pointed out that 'barbarian', though it looked like a positive term such as 'Persian', was logically a negative term, that is to say that barbarians were so called not in virtue of some positive common quality they shared, but in virtue of the fact that none of them possessed the positive quality of being Greek. (The modern English parallel would be the mistake of thinking that foreigners must have something positive, and perhaps positively perverse, in common in virtue of which they are all properly called foreigners.) These and innumerable other points made by previous philosophers will be brought into attention when the history of this modern movement in British philosophy comes to be written. But however much may have been seen by predecessors it remains true that it was left to our contemporaries to develop these flashes of foresight and insight into the new logical criticism of language represented in this volume.[1]

Finally we think that all who have been associated with this book and with the philosophic developments which it tries to represent would wish to acknowledge their debt to the genius of one man above all. Though his name is almost unknown outside the world of academic philosophy, everyone who belongs to that world will see throughout this volume marks of the enormous influence, direct and indirect, of the oral teachings of Professor Wittgenstein.

Christ Church,
March 1950.   Oxford.

[1] When I wrote this Introduction I had not yet read Frege's *Foundations of Arithmetic*. (Breslau, 1884; and recently reprinted with an English translation, Blackwell, 1950.) I should now be more hesitant about the attribution of the distinction between logical and grammatical form to Russell, especially in view of Frege's remarks about the difference between 'wise' and 'one' (pp. 39–40 of the new edition); and should therefore write this paragraph differently.

II

Systematically Misleading Expressions

PROFESSOR GILBERT RYLE

Philosophical arguments have always largely, if not entirely, consisted in attempts to thrash out 'what it means to say so and so'. It is observed that men in their ordinary discourse, the discourse, that is, that they employ when they are not philosophizing, use certain expressions, and philosophers fasten on to certain more or less radical types or classes of such expressions and raise their question about all expressions of a certain type and ask what they really mean.

Sometimes philosophers say that they are analysing or clarifying the 'concepts' which are embodied in the 'judgements' of the plain man or of the scientist, historian, artist, or who-not. But this seems to be only a gaseous way of saying that they are trying to discover what is meant by the general terms contained in the sentences which they pronounce or write. For, as we shall see, 'x is a concept' and 'y is a judgement' are themselves systematically misleading expressions.

But the whole procedure is very odd. For, if the expressions under consideration are intelligently used, their employers must already know what they mean and do not need the aid or admonition of philosophers before they can understand what they are saying. And if their hearers understand what they are being told, they too are in no such perplexity that they need to have this meaning philosophically 'analysed' or 'clarified' for them. And, at least, the philosopher himself must know what the expressions mean, since otherwise he could not know what it was that he was analysing.

Certainly it is often the case that expressions are not being intelligently used and to that extent their authors are just gabbling parrot-wise. But then it is obviously fruitless to ask what the expressions really mean. For there is no reason to suppose that they mean anything. It would not be mere gabbling if there was any such reason. And if the philosopher cares to ask what these expressions *would* mean *if* a rational man were using them, the only answer would be that they would mean what they would then mean. Understanding them would be enough, and that could be done by any reasonable listener. Philosophizing could not help him, and, in fact, the philosopher himself would not be able to begin unless he simply understood them in the ordinary way.

It seems, then, that if an expression can be understood, then it is already known in that understanding what the expression means. So there is no darkness present and no illumination required or possible.

And if it is suggested that the non-philosophical author of an expression (be he plain man, scientist, preacher, or artist) does know but only knows dimly or foggily or confusedly what his expression means, but that the philosopher at the end of his exploration knows clearly, distinctly, and definitely what it means, a two-fold answer seems inevitable. First, that if a speaker only knows confusedly what his expression means, then he is in that respect and to that extent just gabbling. And it is not the rôle—nor the achievement—of the philosopher to provide a medicine against that form of flux. And next, the philosopher is not *ex officio* concerned with ravings and ramblings: he studies expressions for what they mean when intelligently and intelligibly employed, and not as noises emitted by this idiot or that parrot.

Certainly expressions do occur for which better substitutes could be found and should be or should have been employed. (1) An expression may be a breach of, e.g., English or Latin grammar. (2) A word may be a foreign word, or a rare word or a technical or trade term for which there exists a familiar synonym. (3) A phrase or sentence may be clumsy or unfamiliar in its structure. (4) A word or phrase may be equivocal and so be an instrument of possible puns. (5) A word or phrase may be ill-chosen as being general where it should be specific, or allusive where the allusion is not known or not obvious. (6) Or a word may be a malapropism or a misnomer.

But the search for paraphrases which shall be more swiftly intelligible to a given audience or more idiomatic or stylish or more grammatically or etymologically correct is merely applied lexicography or philology—it is not philosophy.

We ought then to face the question: Is there such a thing as analysing or clarifying the meaning of the expressions which people use, except in the sense of substituting philologically better expressions for philologically worse ones? (We might have put the problem in the more misleading terminology of 'concepts' and asked: How can philosophizing so operate by analysis and clarification, upon the concepts used by the plain man, the scientist, or the artist, that after this operation the concepts are illumined where before they were dark? The same difficulties arise. For there can be no such thing as a confused concept, since either a man is conceiving, i.e. knowing the nature of his subject-matter, or he is failing to do so. If he is succeeding, no clarification is required or possible; and if he is failing, he must find out more or think more about the subject-matter, the apprehension of the nature of which we call his 'concept'. But this will not be philosophizing about the concept, but exploring further the nature of the thing, and so will be economics, perhaps, or astronomy or history. But as I think that it can be shown that it is not true in any natural sense that 'there are concepts', I shall adhere to the other method of stating the problem.)

The object of this paper is not to show what philosophy in general is investigating, but to show that there remains an important sense in which philosophers can and must discover and state what is really meant by expressions of this or that radical type, and none the less that these discoveries do not in the least imply that the naïve users of such expressions are in any doubt or confusion about what their expressions mean or in any way need the results of the philosophical analysis for them to continue to use intelligently their ordinary modes of expression or to use them so that they are intelligible to others.

The gist of what I want to establish is this. There are many expressions which occur in non-philosophical discourse which, though they are perfectly clearly understood by those who use them and those who hear or read them, are nevertheless couched in grammatical or syntactical forms which are in a demonstrable way *improper* to the states of affairs which they record (or the alleged states of affairs which they profess to record). Such expressions can be reformulated and for philosophy but *not* for non-philosophical discourse must be reformulated into expressions of which the syntactical form is proper to the facts recorded (or the alleged facts alleged to be recorded).

I use 'expression' to cover single words, phrases, and sentences. By 'statement' I mean a sentence in the indicative. When a statement is true, I say it 'records' a fact or state of affairs. False statements do not record. To know that a statement is true is to know that something is the case and that the statement records it. When I barely understand a statement I do not know that it records a fact, nor need I know the fact that it records, if it records one. But I know what state of affairs *would* obtain, if the statement recorded a state of affairs.

Every significant statement is a quasi-record, for it has both the requisite structure and constituents to be a record. But knowing these, we don't yet know that it is a record of a fact. False statements are pseudo-records and are no more records than pseudo-antiquities are antiquities. So the question, What do false statements state? is meaningless if 'state' means 'record'. If it means, What *would* they record if they recorded something being the case? the question contains its own answer.

When an expression is of such a syntactical form that it is improper to the fact recorded, it is systematically misleading in that it naturally suggests to some people—though not to 'ordinary' people—that the state of affairs recorded is quite a different sort of state of affairs from that which it in fact is.

I shall try to show what I am driving at by examples. I shall begin by considering a whole class of expressions of one type which occur and occur perfectly satisfactorily in ordinary discourse, but which are, I argue, *systematically misleading*, that is to say, that they are couched in a syntactical form improper to the facts recorded and proper to facts of quite another logical form than the facts recorded. (For simplicity's sake, I shall speak as if all the statements adduced as examples are true. For false statements are not formally different from true ones. Otherwise grammarians could become omniscient. And when I call a statement 'systematically misleading' I shall not mean that it is false, and certainly not that it is senseless. By 'systematically' I mean that all expressions of that grammatical form would be misleading in the same way and for the same reason.)

I. Quasi-ontological Statements

Since Kant, we have, most of us, paid lip service to the doctrine that 'existence is not a quality' and so we have rejected the pseudo-implication of the ontological argument; 'God is perfect, being perfect entails being existent, . . . God exists'. For if existence is not a quality, it is not the sort of thing that can be entailed by a quality.

But until fairly recently it was not noticed that if in 'God exists' 'exists' is not a predicate (save in grammar), then in the same statement 'God' cannot be (save in grammar) the subject of predication. The realization of this came from examining negative existential propositions like 'Satan does not exist' or 'unicorns are non-existent'. If there is no Satan, then the statement 'Satan does not exist' cannot be about Satan in the way in which 'I am sleepy' is about me. Despite appearances the word 'Satan' cannot be signifying a subject of attributes.

Philosophers have toyed with theories which would enable them to continue to say that 'Satan does not exist' is none the less still somehow about Satan, and that 'exists' still signifies some sort of attribute or character, although not a quality.

So some argued that the statement was about something described as 'the idea of Satan', others that it was about a subsistent but non-actual entity called 'Satan'. Both theories in effect try to show that something may *be* (whether as being 'merely mental' or as being in 'the realm of subsistents'), but not be in existence. But as we can say 'round squares do not exist', and 'real nonentities do not exist', this sort of inter-

pretation of negative existentials is bound to fill either the
realm of subsistents or the realm of ideas with walking self-
contradictions. So the theories had to be dropped and a new
analysis of existential propositions had to begin.

Suppose I assert of (apparently) the general subject 'carnivorous cows' that they 'do not exist', and my assertion is
true, I cannot really be talking about carnivorous cows, for
there are none. So it follows that the expression 'carnivorous
cows' is not really being used, though the grammatical appearances are to the contrary, to denote the thing or things
of which the predicate is being asserted. And in the same
way as the verb 'exists' is not signifying the character asserted,
although grammatically it looks as if it was, the real predicate
must be looked for elsewhere.

So the clue of the grammar has to be rejected and the
analysis has been suggested that 'carnivorous cows do not exist' means what is meant by 'no cows are carnivorous' or 'no
carnivorous beasts are cows'. But a further improvement
seems to be required.

'Unicorns do not exist' seems to mean what is meant by
'nothing is *both* a quadruped *and* herbivorous *and* the wearer
of one horn' (or whatever the marks of being an unicorn are).
And this does not seem to imply that there are some quad-
rupeds or herbivorous animals.

So 'carnivorous cows do not exist' ought to be rendered
'nothing is both a cow and carnivorous', which does not as it
stands imply that anything is either.

Take now an apparently singular subject as in 'God exists'
or 'Satan does not exist'. If the former analysis was right,
then here too 'God' and 'Satan' are in fact, despite grammatical appearance, predicative expressions. That is to say,
they are that element in the assertion that something has a
specified character, which signifies the character by which the
subject is being asserted to be characterized. 'God exists'
must mean what is meant by 'Something, and one thing only,
is omniscient, omnipotent, and infinitely good' (or whatever
else are the characters summed in the compound character
of being a god and the only god). And 'Satan does not exist'
must mean what is meant by 'nothing is both devilish and

alone in being devilish', or perhaps 'nothing is both devilish and called "Satan"', or even '"Satan" is not the proper name of anything'. To put it roughly, 'x exists' and 'x does not exist' do not assert or deny that a given subject of attributes x has the attribute of existing, but assert or deny the attribute of being x-ish or being an x of something not named in the statement.

Now I can show my hand. I say that expressions such as 'carnivorous cows do not exist' are systematically misleading and that the expressions by which we paraphrased them are not or are not in the same way or to the same extent systematically misleading. But they are not false, nor are they senseless. They are true, and they really do mean what their less systematically misleading paraphrases mean. Nor (save in a special class of cases) is the non-philosophical author of such expressions ignorant or doubtful of the nature of the state of affairs which his expression records. He is not a whit misled. There is a trap, however, in the form of his expression, but a trap which only threatens the man who has begun to generalize about sorts or types of states of affairs and assumes that every statement gives in its syntax a clue to the logical form of the fact that it records. I refer here not merely nor even primarily to the philosopher, but to any man who embarks on abstraction.

But before developing this theme I want to generalize the results of our examination of what we must now describe as 'so-called existential statements'. It is the more necessary in that, while most philosophers are now forewarned by Kant against the systematic misleadingness of 'God exists', few of them have observed that the same taint infects a whole host of other expressions.

If 'God exists' means what we have said it means, then patently 'God is an existent', 'God is an entity', 'God has being', or 'existence' require the same analysis. So '. . . is an existent', '. . . is an entity' are only bogus predicates, and that of which (in grammar) they are asserted is only a bogus subject.

And the same will be true of all the items in the following pair of lists.

Mr. Baldwin—	Mr. Pickwick—
is a being.	is a nonentity.
is real, or a reality.	is unreal or an unreality, or an appearance.
is a genuine entity.	is a bogus or sham entity.
is a substance.	is not a substance.
is an actual object or entity.	is an unreal object or entity.
is objective.	is not objective or is subjective.
is a concrete reality.	is a fiction or figment.
is an object.	is an imaginary object.
is.	is not.
	is a mere idea.
	is an abstraction.
	is a logical construction.

None of these statements is really about Mr. Pickwick. For if they are true, there is no such person for them to be about. Nor is any of them about Mr. Baldwin. For if they were false, there would be no one for them to be about. Nor in any of them is the grammatical predicate that element in the statement which signifies the character that is being asserted to be characterizing or not to be characterizing something.

I formulate the conclusion in this rather clumsy way. There is a class of statements of which the grammatical predicate *appears* to signify not the having of a specified character but the having (or not having) of a specified *status*. But in all such statements the appearance is a purely grammatical one, and what the statements really record can be stated in statements embodying no such quasi-ontological predicates.

And, again, in all such quasi-ontological statements the grammatical subject-word or phrase *appears* to denote or refer to something as that of which the quasi-ontological predicate is being predicated; but in fact the apparent subject term is a concealed predicative expression, and what is really recorded in such statements can be re-stated in statements no part of which even appears to refer to any such subject.

In a word, all quasi-ontological statements are systematically misleading. (If I am right in this, then the conclusion follows, which I accept, that those metaphysical philosophers are the greatest sinners, who, as if they were saying something of importance, make 'Reality' or 'Being' the subject of their propositions, or 'real' the predicate. For at best what they say is systematically misleading, which is the one thing which a philosopher's propositions have no right to be; and at worst it is meaningless.)

I must give warning again, that the naïve employer of such quasi-ontological expressions is not necessarily and not even probably misled. He has said what he wanted to say, and anyone who knew English would understand what he was saying. Moreover, I would add, in the cases that I have listed, the statements are not merely significant but true. Each of them records a real state of affairs. Nor *need* they mislead the philosopher. We, for instance, I hope are not misled. But the point is that anyone, the philosopher included, who abstracts and generalizes and so tries to consider what different facts of the same type (i.e. facts of the same type about different things) have in common, is compelled to use the common grammatical form of the statements of those facts as handles with which to grasp the common logical form of the facts themselves. For (what we shall see later) as the way in which a fact *ought* to be recorded in expressions *would* be a clue to the form of that fact, we jump to the assumption that the way in which a fact *is* recorded *is* such a clue. And very often the clue is misleading and suggests that the fact is of a different form from what really is its form. 'Satan is not a reality' from its grammatical form looks as if it recorded the same sort of fact as 'Capone is not a philosopher', and so was just as much denying a character of a somebody called 'Satan' as the latter does deny a character of a somebody called 'Capone'. But it turns out that the suggestion is a fraud; for the fact recorded would have been properly or less improperly recorded in the statement ' "Satan" is not a proper name' or 'No one is called "Satan" ' or 'No one is both called "Satan" and is infinitely malevolent, etc.', or perhaps 'Some people believe that someone is both called "Satan" and infinitely malevolent, but their belief is false'. And none of these statements even pretend to be 'about Satan'. Instead, they are and are patently about the noise 'Satan' or else about people who misuse it.

In the same way, while it is significant, true, and directly intelligible to say 'Mr. Pickwick is a fiction', it is a systematically misleading expression (i.e. an expression misleading in virtue of a formal property which it does or might share with other expressions); for it does not really record, as it appears to record, a fact of the same sort as is recorded in 'Mr. Baldwin is a statesman'. The world does not contain fictions in the way in which it contains statesmen. There is no subject of attributes of which we can say '*there* is a fiction'. What we can do is to say of Dickens '*there* is a story-teller', or of Pickwick Papers '*there* is a pack of lies'; or of a sentence in that novel, which contains the pseudo-name 'Mr. Pickwick' '*there* is a fable'. And when we say things of this sort we are recording just what we recorded when we said 'Mr. Pickwick is a fiction', only our new expressions do not suggest what our old one did that some subject of attributes has the two attributes of being called 'Mr. Pickwick' and of being a fiction, but instead that some subject of attributes has the attributes of being called Dickens and being a coiner of false propositions and pseudo-proper names, or, on the other analysis, of being a book or a sentence which could only be true or false *if* someone was called 'Mr. Pickwick'. The proposition 'Mr. Pickwick is a fiction' is really, despite its *prima facies*, about Dickens or else about Pickwick Papers. But the fact that it is so is concealed and not exhibited by the form of the expression in which it is said.

It must be noted that the sense in which such quasi-ontological statements are misleading is not that they are false and not even that any word in them is equivocal or vague, but only that they are formally improper to facts of the logical form which they are employed to record and proper to facts of quite another logical form. What the implications are of these notions of formal propriety or formal impropriety we shall see later on.

II. *Statements seemingly about Universals, or Quasi-Platonic Statements*

We often and with great convenience use expressions such as 'Unpunctuality is reprehensible' and 'Virtue is its own reward'. And at first sight these seem to be on all fours with 'Jones merits reproof' and 'Smith has given himself the prize'. So philosophers, taking it that what is meant by such statements as the former is precisely analogous to what is meant by such statements as the latter, have accepted the consequence that the world contains at least two sorts of objects, namely, particulars like Jones and Smith, and 'universals' like Unpunctuality and Virtue.

But absurdities soon crop up. It is obviously silly to speak of an universal meriting reproof. You can no more praise or blame an 'universal' than you can make holes in the Equator.

Nor when we say 'unpunctuality is reprehensible' do we really suppose that unpunctuality ought to be ashamed of itself.

What we do mean is what is also meant but better expressed by 'Whoever is unpunctual deserves that other people should reprove him for being unpunctual'. For it is unpunctual men and not unpunctuality who can and should be blamed, since they are, what it is not, moral agents. Now in the new expression 'whoever is unpunctual merits reproof' the word 'unpunctuality' has vanished in favour of the predicative expression '. . . is unpunctual'. So that while in the original expression 'unpunctuality' seemed to denote the subject of which an attribute was being asserted, it now turns out to signify the having of an attribute. And we are really saying that anyone who has that attribute, has the other.

Again, it is not literally true that Virtue is a recipient of rewards. What is true is that anyone who is virtuous is benefited thereby. Whoever is good, gains something by being good. So the original statement was not 'about Virtue' but about good men, and the grammatical subject-word 'Virtue' meant what is meant by '. . . is virtuous' and so was, what it pretended not to be, a predicative expression.

I need not amplify this much. It is not literally true that 'honesty compels me to state so and so', for 'honesty' is not the name of a coercive agency. What is true is more properly put 'because I am honest, or wish to be honest, I am bound to state so and so'. 'Colour involves extension' means what is meant by 'Whatever is coloured is extended'; 'hope deferred maketh the heart sick' means what is meant by 'whoever for a long time hopes for something without getting it becomes sick at heart'.

It is my own view that all statements which seem to be 'about universals' are analysable in the same way, and consequently that general terms are never really the names of subjects of attributes. So 'universals' are not objects in the way in which Mt. Everest is one, and therefore the age-old question what *sort* of objects they are is a bogus question. For general nouns, adjectives, etc., are not proper names, so we cannot speak of 'the objects called "equality", "justice", and "progress"'.

Platonic and anti-Platonic assertions, such as that 'equality is, or is not, a real entity', are, accordingly, alike misleading, and misleading in two ways at once; for they are both quasi-ontological statements and quasi-Platonic ones.

However, I do not wish to defend this general position here, but only to show that in *some* cases statements which from their grammatical form seem to be saying that 'honesty does so and so' or 'equality is such and such', are really saying in a formally improper way (though one which is readily understandable and idiomatically correct) 'anything which is equal to x is such and such' or 'whoever is honest, is so and so'. These statements state overtly, what the others stated covertly, that something's having one attribute necessitates its having the other.

Of course, the plain man who uses such quasi-Platonic expressions is not making a philosophical mistake. He is not philosophizing at all. He is not misled by and does not even notice the fraudulent pretence contained in such propositions that they are 'about Honesty' or 'about Progress'. He knows what he means and will, very likely, accept our more formally proper restatement of what he means as a fair paraphrase, but he will not have any motive for desiring the more proper form of expression, nor even any grounds for holding that it is more proper. For he is not attending to the form of the fact in abstraction from the special subject-matter that the fact is about. So for him the best way of expressing something is the way which is the most brief, the most elegant, or the most emphatic, whereas those who, like philosophers, must generalize about the *sorts* of statements that have to be made of *sorts* of facts about *sorts* of topics, cannot help treating as clues to the logical structures for which they are looking the grammatical forms of the common types of expressions in which these structures are recorded. And these clues are often misleading.

III. Descriptive Expressions and Quasi-descriptions

We all constantly use expressions of the form 'the so and so' as 'the Vice-Chancellor of Oxford University'. Very often we refer by means of such expressions to some one uniquely described individual. The phrases 'the present Vice-Chancellor of Oxford University' and 'the highest mountain in the world' have such a reference in such propositions as 'the present Vice-Chancellor of Oxford University is a tall man' and 'I have not seen the highest mountain in the world'.

There is nothing intrinsically misleading in the use of 'the'-phrases as unique descriptions, though there is a sense in which they are highly condensed or abbreviated. And philosophers can and do make mistakes in the accounts they give of what such descriptive phrases mean. What are misleading are, as we shall see, 'the'-phrases which behave grammatically as if they were unique descriptions referring to individuals, when in fact they are not referential phrases at all. But this class of systematically misleading expressions cannot be examined until we have considered how genuine unique descriptions do refer.

A descriptive phrase is not a proper name, and the way in which the subject of attributes which it denotes is denoted by it is not in that subject's being *called* 'the so and so', but in its possessing and being *ipso facto* the sole possessor of the idiosyncratic attribute which is what the descriptive phrase signifies. If Tommy is the eldest son of Jones, then 'the eldest son of Jones' denotes Tommy, not because someone or other *calls* him 'the eldest son of Jones', but because he is and no one else can be both a son of Jones and older than all the other sons of Jones. The descriptive phrase, that is, is not a proper name but a predicative expression signifying the joint characters of being a son of Jones and older than the other

sons of Jones. And it refers to Tommy only in the sense that
Tommy and Tommy alone has those characters.

The phrase does not in any sense *mean* Tommy. Such a
view would be, as we shall see, nonsensical. It means what
is meant by the predicative expression, '. . . is both a son of
Jones and older than his other sons', and so it is itself only
a predicative expression. By a 'predicative expression' I mean
that fragment of a statement in virtue of which the having
of a certain character or characters is expressed. And the having a certain character is not a subject of attributes but, so
to speak, the tail end of the facts that some subject of attributes has it and some others lack it. By itself it neither
names the subject which has the character nor records the
fact that any subject has it. It cannot indeed occur by itself,
but only as an element, namely, a predicative element in a
full statement.

So the full statement 'the eldest son of Jones was married
to-day' means what is meant by 'someone (namely, Tommy)
(1) is a son of Jones, (2) is older than the other sons of
Jones [this could be unpacked further] and (3) was married
to-day'.

The whole statement could not be true unless the three
or more component statements were true. But *that* there is
someone of whom both (1) and (2) are true is not guaranteed by their being stated. (No statement can guarantee its
own truth.) Consequently the characterizing expression
'. . . is the eldest son of Jones' does not *mean* Tommy either
in the sense of being his proper name or in the sense of being
an expression the understanding of which involves the knowledge that Tommy has this idiosyncratic character. It only
refers to Tommy in the sense that well-informed listeners will
know already, that Tommy and Tommy only has in fact this
idiosyncratic character. But this knowledge is not part of
what must be known in order to understand the statement,
'Jones' eldest son was married to-day'. For we could know
what it meant without knowing that Tommy was that eldest
son or was married to-day. All we must know is that someone
or other must be so characterized for the whole statement to
be true.

For understanding a statement or apprehending what a

statement means is not knowing that this statement records this fact, but knowing what *would* be the case if the statement *were* a record of fact.

There is no understanding or apprehending the meaning of an isolated proper name or of an isolated unique description. For *either* we know that someone in particular is called by that name by certain persons or else has the idiosyncratic characters signified by the descriptive phrase, which requires that we are acquainted both with the name or description and with the person named or described. *Or* we do not know these things, in which case we don't know that the quasi-name is a name at all or that the quasi-unique description describes anyone. But we can understand statements in which quasi-names or quasi-unique descriptions occur; for we can know what would be the case if someone were so called or so describable, and also had the other characters predicated in the predicates of the statements.

We see, then, that descriptive phrases are condensed predicative expressions, and so that their function is to be that element or (more often) one of those elements in statements (which as a whole record that something has a certain character or characters) in which the having of this or that character is expressed.

And this can easily be seen by another approach.

Take any 'the'-phrase which is naturally used referentially as the grammatical subject of a sentence, as 'The Vice-Chancellor of Oxford University' in 'The Vice-Chancellor of Oxford University is busy'. We can now take the descriptive phrase, lock, stock, and barrel, and use it non-referentially as the grammatical predicate in a series of statements and expressions, 'Who is the present Vice-Chancellor of Oxford University?' 'Mr. So-and-So is the present Vice-Chancellor of Oxford University', 'Georges Carpentier is not the present Vice-Chancellor of Oxford University', 'Mr. Such-and-Such is either the Vice-Chancellor of Oxford University or Senior Proctor', 'Whoever is Vice-Chancellor of Oxford University is overworked', etc. It is clear, anyhow, in the cases of the negative, hypothetical, and disjunctive statements containing this common predicative expression that it is not implied or even suggested that anyone does hold the office of Vice-Chancellor. So the 'the'-phrase is here quite non-referential, and does not even pretend to denote someone. It signifies an idiosyncratic character, but does not involve that anyone has it. This leads us back to our original conclusion that a descriptive phrase does not in any sense *mean* this person or that thing; or, to put it in another way, that we can understand a statement containing a descriptive phrase and still not know of this subject of attributes or of that one that the description fits it. (Indeed, we hardly need to argue the position. For no one with a respect for sense would dream of pointing to someone or something and saying 'that is the meaning of such and such an expression' or 'the meaning of yonder phrase is suffering from influenza'. 'Socrates is a meaning' is a nonsensical sentence. The whole pother about denoting seems to arise from the supposition that we could significantly describe an object as 'the meaning of the expression "*x*"' or 'what the expression "*x*" means'. Certainly a descriptive phrase can be said to *refer* to or *fit* this man or that mountain, and this man or that mountain can be described as that to which the expression '*x*' refers. But this is only to say that this man or that mountain has and is alone in having the characters the having of which is expressed in the predicative sentence-fragment '. . . is the so-and-so'.)

All this is only leading up to another class of systematically misleading expressions. But the 'the'-phrases which we have been studying, whether occurring as grammatical subjects or as predicates in statements, were not formally fraudulent. There was nothing in the grammatical form of the sentences adduced to suggest that the facts recorded were of a different logical form from that which they really had.

The previous argument was intended to be critical of certain actual or possible philosophical errors, but they were errors about descriptive expressions and not errors *due* to a trickiness in descriptive expressions as such. Roughly, the errors that I have been trying to dispel are the views (1) that descriptive phrases are proper names and (2) that the thing which a description describes is what the description means. I want now to come to my long-delayed muttons and discuss a farther class of systematically misleading expressions.

Systematically Misleading Quasi-referential 'The'-phrases

1. There frequently occur in ordinary discourse expressions which, though 'the'-phrases, are not unique descriptions at all, although from their grammatical form they look as if they are. The man who does not go in for abstraction and generalization uses them without peril or perplexity and knows quite well what he means by the sentences containing them. But the philosopher has to re-state them in a different and formally more proper arrangement of words if he is not to be trapped.

When a descriptive phrase is used as the grammatical subject of a sentence in a formally non-misleading way, as in 'the King went shooting to-day', we know that if the statement as a whole is true (or even false) then there must be in the world someone in particular to whom the description 'the King' refers or applies. And we could significantly ask 'Who is the King?' and 'Are the father of the Prince of Wales and the King one and the same person?'

But we shall see that there are in common use quasi-descriptive phrases of the form 'the so-and-so', in the cases of which there is in the world no one and nothing that could be described as that to which the phrase refers or applies, and thus that there is nothing and nobody about which or whom we could even ask 'Is it the so-and-so?' or 'Are he and the so-and-so one and the same person?'

It can happen in several ways. Take first the statement, which is true and clearly intelligible, 'Poincaré is not the King of France'. This at first sight looks formally analogous to 'Tommy Jones is not (i.e. is not identical with) the King of England'. But the difference soon shows itself. For whereas if the latter is true then its converse 'the King of England is not Tommy Jones' is true, it is neither true nor false to say 'The King of France is not Poincaré'. For there is no King of France and the phrase 'the King of France' does not fit anybody—nor did the plain man who said 'Poincaré is not the King of France' suppose the contrary. So 'the King of France' in this statement is not analogous to 'the King of England' in the others. It is not really being used referentially or as a unique description of somebody at all.

We can now redraft the contrasted propositions in forms of words which shall advertise the difference which the original propositions concealed between the forms of the facts recorded.

'Tommy Jones is not the same person as the King of England' means what is meant by '(1) Somebody and—of an unspecified circle—one person only is called Tommy Jones; (2) Somebody, and one person only has royal power in England; and (3) No one both is called Tommy Jones and is King of England'. The original statement could not be true unless (1) and (2) were true.

Take now 'Poincaré is not the King of France'. This means what is meant by '(1) Someone is called "Poincaré" and (2) Poincaré has not got the rank, being King of France'. And this does not imply that anyone has that rank.

Sometimes this twofold use, namely the referential and the non-referential use of 'the'-phrases, troubles us in the mere practice of ordinary discourse. 'Smith is not the only man who has ever climbed Mont Blanc' might easily be taken by some people to mean what is meant by 'One man and one man only has climbed Mont Blanc, but Smith is not he', and by others, 'Smith has climbed Mont Blanc but at least one other man has done so too'. But I am not interested in the occasional ambiguity of such expressions, but in the fact that an expression of this sort which is really being used in the non-referential way is apt to be construed as if it *must* be referentially used, or as if any 'the'-phrase was referentially used. Philosophers and others who have to abstract and generalize tend to be misled by the verbal similarity of 'the'-phrases of the one sort with 'the'-phrases of the other into 'coining entities' in order to be able to show to what a given 'the'-phrase refers.

Let us first consider the phrase 'the top of that tree' or 'the centre of that bush' as they occur in such statements as 'an owl is perched on the top of that tree', 'my arrow flew through the centre of the bush'. These statements are quite unambiguous, and convey clearly and correctly what they are intended to convey.

But as they are in syntax analogous to 'a man is sitting next to the Vice-Chancellor' and 'my arrow flew through the curtain', and as further an indefinite list could be drawn up of different statements having in common the 'the'-phrases, 'the top of that tree' and 'the centre of that bush', it is hard for people who generalize to escape the temptation of supposing or even believing that these 'the'-phrases refer to objects in the way in which 'the Vice-Chancellor' and 'the curtain' refer to objects. And this is to suppose or believe that the top of that tree is a genuine subject of attributes in just the same way as the Vice-Chancellor is.

But (save in the case where the expression is being misused for the expression 'the topmost branch' or 'the topmost leaf of the tree') 'the top of the tree' at once turns out not to be referring to any object. There is nothing in the world of which it is true (or even false) to say 'That is the top of such and such a tree'. It does not, for instance, refer to a bit of the tree, or it could be cut down and burned or put in a vase. 'The top of the tree' does not refer to anything, but it signifies an attribute, namely, the having of a relative position, when it occurs in statements of the form 'x is at or near or above or below the top of the tree'. To put it crudely, it does not refer to a thing but signifies a thing's being in a certain place, or else signifies not a thing but the site or locus of a thing such as of the bough or leaf which is higher than any of the other boughs or leaves on the tree. Accordingly it makes sense to say that now one bough and now another is at the top of the tree. But 'at the top of the tree' means no more than what is meant by 'higher than any other part of the tree', which latter phrase no one could take for a referential phrase like 'the present Vice-Chancellor'.

The place of a thing, or the whereabouts of a thing is not a thing but the tail end of the fact that something is there. 'Where the bee sucks, there suck I', but it is the clover flower that is there which holds the honey, and not the whereabouts of the flower. All that this amounts to is that though we can use quasi-descriptive phrases to enable us to state where something is, that the thing is there is a relational character of the thing and not itself a subject of characters.

I suspect that a lot of Cartesian and perhaps Newtonian blunders about Space and Time originate from the systematically misleading character of the 'the'-phrases which we use to date and locate things, such as 'the region occupied by *x*', 'the path followed by *y*', 'the moment or date at which *z* happened'. It was not seen that these are but hamstrung predicative expressions and are not and are not even ordinarily taken to be referentially used descriptive expressions, any more than 'the King of France' in 'Poincaré is not the King of France' is ordinarily treated as if it was a referentially used 'the'-phrase.

Take another case. 'Jones hates the thought of going to hospital', 'the idea of having a holiday has just occurred to me'. These quasi-descriptive phrases suggest that there is one object in the world which is what is referred to by the phrase 'the thought of going to hospital' and another which is what is referred to by 'the idea of having a holiday'. And anyhow partly through accepting the grammatical *prima facies* of such expressions, philosophers have believed as devoutly in the existence of 'ideas', 'conceptions' and 'thoughts' or 'judgements' as their predecessors did (from similar causes) in that of substantial forms or as children do (from similar causes) in that of the Equator, the sky, and the North Pole.

But if we re-state them, the expressions turn out to be no evidence whatsoever in favour of the Lockean demonology. For 'Jones hates the thought of going to hospital' only means what is meant by 'Jones feels distressed when he thinks of what he will undergo if he goes to hospital'. The phrase 'the thought of . . .' is transmuted into 'whenever he thinks of . . .', which does not even seem to contain a reference to any other entity than Jones and, perhaps, the hospital. For it to be true, the world must contain a Jones who is sometimes thinking and sometimes, say, sleeping; but it need no more contain both Jones and 'the thought or idea of so and so' than it need contain both someone called 'Jones' and something called 'Sleep'.

Similarly, the statement 'the idea of taking a holiday has just occurred to me' seems grammatically to be analogous to 'that dog has just bitten me'. And as, if the latter is true, the world must contain both me and the dog, so it would seem, if the former is true, the world must contain both me and the idea of taking a holiday. But the appearance is a delusion. For while I could not re-state my complaint against the dog in any sentence not containing a descriptive phrase referring to it, I can easily do so with the statement about 'the idea of taking a holiday', e.g. in the statement 'I have just been thinking that I might take a holiday'.

A host of errors of the same sort has been generated in logic itself and epistemology by the omission to analyse the quasi-descriptive phrase 'the meaning of the expression "x"'. I suspect that all the mistaken doctrines of concepts, ideas, terms, judgements, objective propositions, contents, objectives and the like derive from the same fallacy, namely, that there must be *something* referred to by such expressions as 'the meaning of the word (phrase or sentence) "x"', on all fours with the policeman who really is referred to by the descriptive phrase in 'our village policeman is fond of football'. And the way out of the confusion is to see that some 'the'-phrases are only similar in grammar and not similar in function to referentially-used descriptive phrases, e.g. in the case in point, 'the meaning of "x"' is like 'the King of France' in 'Poincaré is not the King of France', a predicative expression used non-referentially.

And, of course, the ordinary man does not pretend to himself or anyone else that when he makes statements containing such expressions as 'the meaning of "x"', he is referring to a queer new object: it does not cross his mind that his phrase might be misconstrued as a referentially used descriptive phrase. So he is not guilty of philosophical error or clumsiness. None the less, his form of words is systematically misleading. For an important difference of logical form is disguised by the complete similarity of grammatical form between 'the village policeman is reliable' and 'the meaning of "x" is doubtful' or again between 'I have just met the village policeman' and 'I have just grasped the meaning of "x"'.

(Consequently, as there is no object describable as that which is referred to by the expression 'the meaning of "x"', questions about the status of such objects are meaningless. It is as pointless to discuss whether word-meanings [i.e. 'concepts' or 'universals'] are subjective or objective, or whether sentence-meanings [i.e. 'judgements' or 'objectives'] are subjective or objective, as it would be to discuss whether the Equator or the sky is subjective or objective. For the questions themselves are not about anything.)

All this does not, of course, in the least prevent us from using intelligently and intelligibly sentences containing the expression 'the meaning of "*x*"' where this can be re-drafted as 'what "*x*" means'. For here the 'the'-phrase is being predicatively used and not as an unique description. 'The meaning of "*x*" is the same as the meaning of "*y*"' is equivalent to ' "*x*" means what "*y*" means', and that can be understood without any temptation to multiply entities.

But this argument is, after all, only about a very special case of the systematic misleadingness of quasi-descriptions.

2. There is another class of uses of 'the'-phrases which is also liable to engender philosophical misconstructions, though I am not sure that I can recall any good instances of actual mistakes which have occurred from this source.

Suppose I say, 'the defeat of the Labour Party has surprised me', what I say could be correctly paraphrased by 'the fact that the Labour Party was defeated, was a surprise to me' or 'the Labour Party has been defeated and I am surprised that it has been defeated'. Here the 'the'-phrase does not refer to a thing but is a condensed record of something's being the case. And this is a common and handy idiom. We can always say instead of 'because A is B, therefore C is D' 'the D-ness of C is due to the B-ness of A'. 'The severity of the winter is responsible for the high price of cabbages' means what is meant by 'Cabbages are expensive because the winter was severe'.

But if I say 'the defeat of the Labour Party occurred in 1931', my 'the'-phrase is referentially used to describe an event and not as a condensed record of a fact. For events have dates, but facts do not. So the facts recorded in the grammatically similar statements 'the defeat of the Labour Party has surprised me' and 'the defeat of the Labour Party occurred in 1931' are in logical form quite different. And both sorts of facts are formally quite different from this third fact which is recorded in 'the victory of the Labour Party would have surprised me'. For this neither refers to an event, nor records the fact that the Labour Party was victorious, but says 'if the Labour Party had won, I should have been surprised'. So here the 'the'-phrase is a protasis. And, once more, all these three uses of 'the'-phrases are different in their sort of significance from 'the defeat of the Conservative Party at the next election is probable', or 'possible', or 'impossible'. For these mean 'the available relevant data are in favour of' or 'not incompatible with' or 'incompatible with the Conservative Party being defeated at the next election'.

So there are at least these four different types of facts which can be and, in ordinary discourse, are conveniently and intelligibly recorded in statements containing grammatically indistinguishable 'the'-phrases. But they can be restated in forms of words which do exhibit in virtue of their special grammatical forms the several logical structures of the different sorts of facts recorded.

3. Lastly, I must just mention one further class of systematically misleading 'the'-phrase. 'The whale is not a fish but a mammal' and 'the true Englishman detests foul play' record facts, we may take it. But they are not about this whale or that Englishman, and they might be true even if there were no whales or no true Englishmen. These are, probably, disguised hypothetical statements. But all I wish to point out is that they are obviously disguised.

I have chosen these three main types of systematically misleading expressions because all alike are misleading in a certain direction. They all suggest the existence of new sorts of objects, or, to put it in another way, they are all temptations to us to 'multiply entities'. In each of them, the quasi-ontological, the quasi-Platonic and the quasi-descriptive expressions, an expression is misconstrued as a denoting expression which in fact does not denote, but only looks grammatically like expressions which are used to denote. Occam's prescription was, therefore, in my view, 'Do not treat all expressions which are grammatically like proper names or referentially used "the"-phrases, as if they were therefore proper names or referentially used "the"-phrases'.

But there are other types of systematically misleading expressions, of which I shall just mention a few that occur to me.

'Jones is an alleged murderer', or 'a suspected murderer', 'Smith is a possible or probable Lord Mayor', 'Robinson is an ostensible, or seeming or mock or sham or bogus hero', 'Brown is a future or a past Member of Parliament', etc. These suggest what they do not mean, that the subjects named are of a special kind of murderer, or Lord Mayor, or hero, or Member of Parliament. But being an alleged murderer does not entail being a murderer, nor does being a likely Lord Mayor entail being a Lord Mayor.

'Jones is popular' suggests that being popular is like being wise, a quality; but in fact it is a relational character, and one which does not directly characterize Jones, but the people who are fond of Jones, and so 'Jones is popular' means what is meant by 'Many people like Jones, and many more like him than either dislike him or are indifferent to him', or something of the sort.

But I have, I think, given enough instances to show in what sense expressions may seem to mean something quite different from what they are in fact used to mean; and therefore I have shown in what sense some expressions are systematically misleading.

So I am taking it as established (1) that what is expressed in one expression can often be expressed in expressions of quite different grammatical forms, and (2) that of two expressions, each meaning what the other means, which are of different grammatical forms, one is often more systematically misleading than the other.

And this means that while a fact or state of affairs *can* be recorded in an indefinite number of statements of widely differing grammatical forms, it is stated better in some than in others. The ideal, which may never be realized, is that it should be stated in a completely non-misleading form of words.

Now, when we call one form of expression better than another, we do not mean that it is more elegant or brief or familiar or more swiftly intelligible to the ordinary listener, but that in virtue of its grammatical form it exhibits, in a way in which the others fail to exhibit, the logical form of the state of affairs or fact that is being recorded. But this interest in the best way of exhibiting the logical form of facts is not for every man, but only for the philosopher.

I wish now to raise, but not to solve, some consequential problems which arise.

1. Given that an expression of a certain grammatical form is proper (or anyhow approximates to being proper) to facts of a certain logical form and to those facts only, is this relation of propriety of grammatical to logical form *natural* or *conventional*?

I cannot myself credit what seems to be the doctrine of Wittgenstein and the school of logical grammarians who owe allegiance to him, that what makes an expression formally proper to a fact is some real and non-conventional one-one picturing relation between the composition of the expression and that of the fact. For I do not see how, save in a small class of specially-chosen cases, a fact or state of affairs can be deemed like or even unlike in structure a sentence, gesture or diagram. For a fact is not a collection—even an arranged collection—of bits in the way in which a sentence is an arranged collection of noises or a map an arranged collection of scratches. A fact is not a thing and so is not even an arranged thing. Certainly a map may be like a country or a railway system, and in a more general, or looser, sense a sentence, as an ordered series of noises, might be a similar sort of series to a series of vehicles in a stream of traffic or the series of days in the week.

But in Socrates being angry or in the fact that either Socrates was wise or Plato was dishonest, I can see no concatenation of bits such that a concatenation of parts of speech could be held to be of the same general architectural plan as it. But this difficulty may be just denseness on my part.

On the other hand, it is not easy to accept what seems to be the alternative that it is just by convention that a given grammatical form is specially dedicated to facts of a given logical form. For, in fact, customary usage is perfectly tolerant of systematically misleading expressions. And, moreover, it is

hard to explain how in the genesis of languages our presumably non-philosophical forbears could have decided on
or happened on the dedication of a given grammatical form
to facts of a given logical form. For presumably the study of
abstract logical form is later than the entry into common
use of syntactical idioms.

It is, however, my present view that the propriety of
grammatical to logical forms is more nearly conventional than
natural: though I do not suppose it to be the effect of whim
or of deliberate plan.

2. The next question is: How are we to discover in particular cases whether an expression is systematically misleading or not? I suspect that the answer to this will be of this
sort. We meet with and understand and even believe a certain expression such as 'Mr. Pickwick is a fictitious person'
and 'the Equator encircles the globe'. And we know that if
these expressions are saying what they seem to be saying,
certain other propositions will follow. But it turns out that
the naturally consequential propositions 'Mr. Pickwick was
born in such and such a year' and 'the Equator is of such and
such a thickness' are not merely false but, on analysis, in contradiction with something in that from which they seemed
to be logical consequences. The only solution is to see that
being a fictitious person is not to be a person of a certain
sort, and that the sense in which the Equator girdles the
earth is not that of being any sort of a ring or ribbon en-
veloping the earth. And this is to see that the original propositions were not saying what they seemed on first analysis to
be saying. Paralogisms and antinomies are the evidence that
an expression is systematically misleading.

None the less, the systematically misleading expressions as
intended and as understood contain no contradictions. People do not really talk philosophical nonsense—unless they are
philosophizing or, what is quite a different thing, unless they
are being sententious. What they do is to use expressions
which, from whatever cause—generally the desire for brevity
and simplicity of discourse—disguise instead of exhibiting the
forms of the facts recorded. And it is to reveal these forms
that we abstract and generalize. These processes of abstraction and generalization occur before philosophical analysis

begins. It seems indeed that their results are the subject matter of philosophy. Pre-philosophical abstract thinking is always misled by systematically misleading expressions, and even philosophical abstract thinking, the proper function of which is to cure this disease, is actually one of its worst victims.

3. I do not know any way of classifying or giving an exhaustive list of the possible types of systematically misleading expressions. I fancy that the number is in principle unlimited, but that the number of prevalent and obsessing types is fairly small.

4. I do not know any way of proving that an expression contains no systematic misleadingness at all. The fact that antinomies have not yet been shown to arise is no proof that they never will arise. We can know that of two expressions 'x' and 'y' which record the same fact, 'x' is less misleading than 'y'; but not that 'x' cannot itself be improved upon.

5. Philosophy must then involve the exercise of systematic restatement. But this does not mean that it is a department of philology or literary criticism.

Its restatement is not the substitution of one noun for another or one verb for another. That is what lexicographers and translators excel in. Its restatements are transmutations of syntax, and transmutations of syntax controlled not by desire for elegance or stylistic correctness but by desire to exhibit the forms of the facts into which philosophy is the inquiry.

I conclude, then, that there is, after all, a sense in which we can properly inquire and even say 'what it really means to say so and so'. For we can ask what is the real form of the fact recorded when this is concealed or disguised and not duly exhibited by the expression in question. And we can often succeed in stating this fact in a new form of words which does exhibit what the other failed to exhibit. And I am for the present inclined to believe that this is what philosophical analysis is, and that this is the sole and whole function of philosophy. But I do not want to argue this point now.

But, as confession is good for the soul, I must admit that I do not very much relish the conclusions towards which these conclusions point. I would rather allot to philosophy a sublimer task than the detection of the sources in linguistic idioms of recurrent misconstructions and absurd theories. But that it is at least this I cannot feel any serious doubt.

III

Time: A Treatment of Some Puzzles

PROFESSOR J. N. FINDLAY

(This article was written in 1941. Though I still agree with its general approach, I am now inclined to attach rather more positive value and importance to the metaphysical perplexities and positions it deals with. It will be obvious that the basic ideas of this paper derive from Wittgenstein.)

The aim of this paper is to inquire into the causes of some of our persistent perplexities with regard to time and change. We do not propose to offer a solution for these difficulties, but rather to make clear how they have come to worry us. For we shall suggest that they have their origin, not in any genuine obscurity in our experience, but in our ways of thinking and talking, and we shall also suggest that the clear consciousness of this origin is the only way to cure them. It is plain that we do not, in any ordinary frame of mind, find time so hard to understand: we are in fact always competently dealing with what we may describe as 'temporal situations'. We are dealing with such situations whenever we say, without hesitation or confusion, that this lasted longer than that, that this took place at the same time as that, that this has just happened or that that will happen soon. We have no difficulty in showing other people what we mean by such forms of statement, nor in getting them to agree that we have used them truly and appropriately. Yet all these forms of statement, and the situations to which they refer, seem capable of creating the most intense perplexity in some people: people are led to say that time is 'paradoxical', 'contradictory', 'mysterious', and to ask how certain things are 'possible' whose actuality seems obvious. Thus it has been asked how it is 'possible' for anything to reach the end of a phase of continuous change, or how it is 'possible' for that which *is* the case ever to cease being the case, or how it is 'possible' for the duration of any happening to have a length and a measure. In all such cases it seems reasonable to say that the burden of proof that there *is* a genuine problem or difficulty is on the person who feels it, and not on the person who refuses to depart from ordinary ways of speaking. And it certainly does seem odd that people who have always had to deal with changing objects and situations, and whose whole language is perfectly adapted to dealing with them, should suddenly profess to find time so very strange. If time is so odd, we may very well ask, in terms of what things more familiar and understandable shall we proceed to explain it or to throw light on its possibility? We may indeed regard it as a strange disorder that people who have spent all their days 'in time', should suddenly elect to speak as if they were casual visitors from 'eternity'. And it must be our business to cure them of this disorder through a clear awareness of its causes. There is indeed 'a short way with puzzlers' who inquire into the 'possibility' of perfectly familiar and understandable situations: we may simply point to some instance of the kind that perplexes them and say: 'That's how it is possible for so-and-so to be the case'. Thus if a man were to ask me 'How is it possible that that which *is* the case should cease to be the case?', I might simply crook my finger and say 'Now my finger is crooked', then straighten it and say 'Now it has ceased to be crooked. And that's how it's possible for that which *is* the case to cease being the case.'[1] But such

[1] The example given and the general method indicated was suggested by Professor Moore's proof that external objects exist. He proves that there are such objects by proving that there are two human hands, the latter being proved 'by holding up his two hands, and saying as he makes a certain gesture with the right hand, "Here is one hand", and adding, as he makes a certain gesture with the left, "and here is another"' (*Proof of an External World*, p. 25). [Reprinted in *British Academy Proceedings*, Vol. 25 (1939).— EDITOR.]

an expedient, though perfectly proper in itself, and more than a man has a right to ask for in most cases, would not suffice to allay our questioner's perplexity, since he, presumably, is quite as familiar with ordinary usage as we are.

A treatment of the puzzles of time will also serve to illustrate a treatment which might be applied to many other questions and difficulties. For some people quite readily fall into a mood in which they feel that there is something mysterious and doubtful about things that they would normally regard as elementary and obvious. They are then led to ask questions which seem queer, because it is not in the least plain how one should set about answering them. Thus a man may wonder how it is possible for a number of distinct things to share in the same quality, or whether he really is the same person from year to year, or why *this* world exists rather than any other. Now in ordinary unreflective moods we should regard these questions as either unanswerable or not worth answering, but our questioner plainly wants an answer and he doesn't want an obvious answer. It is plain, in particular, that we couldn't remove our questioner's perplexity by 'appealing to experience', by pointing to anything that both he and we could observe. For he *has* all the kinds of experience that could throw light on his problem, and yet he is puzzled. It seems clear that, where the simplest and most familiar instances of something occasion profound perplexity, we cannot hope to remove such perplexity, or even to allay it, by indefinitely accumulating other instances of the same kind, some of which would be strange and others highly complex. We are accordingly brought back to our supposition that there are some questions which beset us, not because there is anything genuinely problematic in our experience, but because the ways in which we speak of that experience are lacking in harmony or are otherwise unsatisfactory. We are sometimes thrown into a mood of interrogation not because we are in quest of further facts, but because we are in quest of clearer, or less discordant, or merely different ways of verbally dealing with those facts. Such moods of questioning plainly have no answers, in any ordinary sense of 'answer'; we may nevertheless hope to relieve them by becoming clearly conscious of the underlying needs that prompt them, and by deliberately adopting ways of talking that provide appeasement for those needs.

There are other reasons why there is interest in our difficulties with regard to time. These difficulties form a relatively self-contained group of puzzles, which do not seem to share their entrails with too many other philosophical problems. We can find time difficult without finding anything else difficult, but we couldn't be puzzled by matter or mind or knowledge, without being puzzled by practically everything else. Hence we can deal more cleanly with these temporal puzzles than with other issues; they provide, accordingly, a simpler paradigm of method. These puzzles are also important in that philosophical difficulties seem to flourish more readily in the temporal field than in almost any other. It would be safe to say that rapid change and the 'nothingness of the past' are things which can always be relied on spontaneously to vex a large number of unsophisticated people, and so to constitute one of the standing mysteries of our universe. We have reason, of course, to suspect such generalizations; for we know nowadays that there is no way of ascertaining the philosophical reactions of unphilosophical common sense, except by testing and questioning large numbers of people.[2] But in the absence of such testing, vague experience certainly bears witness to the generality of such puzzlement.

We may now point to a circumstance which is certainly responsible for *some* of our difficulties with regard to time. This is the fact that it is possible to persuade a man, by an almost insensible process, to use certain familiar locutions in ways which become, on the one hand, steadily wider and more general, or, on the other hand, steadily narrower and stricter. This persuasive process is only one of the many processes by which an able dialectician can twist or stretch or shift or tear apart the web of words with which we overlay our world. In doing so, he relies on the fact that the boundaries of linguistic usage are seldom clear, that there are always

[2] See, e.g., Arne Ness's *Truth as conceived by those who are not professional philosophers*, Oslo, 1938. [In *Skrifter utgitt av Det Norske Videnskaps–Akademi i Oslo*, II. Hist.-Filos. Klasse, Vol. IV. —EDITOR.]

ranges of cases in which it is simply doubtful whether a given locution is or is not applicable, and that there are, in addition, a number of deep-seated tendencies in language which facilitate linguistic shifts in certain directions. In the particular case we are now considering there are, it is plain, words and phrases whose use very readily widens: it is easy to persuade a man that they really *ought* to be used in cases in which it has never before occurred to anyone to use them. And it is also plain that there are words and phrases whose use very readily narrows, so that we are easily persuaded to say that it was 'wrong' or 'improper' to use them in cases where we previously used them without hesitation. And it is possible for the adroit dialectician, by making repeated use of a big stick called 'consistency', on the one hand, and another big stick called 'strictness', on the other hand, to persuade us to use such forms of speech so widely that they apply to everything, or so narrowly that they apply to nothing: the result in either case is to turn a serviceable mode of speaking into one that is totally unserviceable. Good examples of these dialectical processes would be arguments which led us to use the term 'know' so widely, on the one hand, that we might be said, like the monads of Leibniz, always to know everything, or so narrowly, on the other hand, that we might never be said to know anything. There is, of course, nothing in such an exaggerated width or narrowness of reference which *necessarily* leads to paradoxes or problems. If we persuade a man to use words in new ways, we disorganize his linguistic habits for the time being, but there is no reason why he should not rapidly build up a new set of habits, which will enable him to talk of ordinary situations as plainly and as promptly as before. But the trouble is that such a sudden change of usage *may* produce a temporary disorientation, it is like a cerebral lesion from which an organism needs to recover, and in the interval before recovery sets in, and new connections take the place of the old, a man may readily become a prey to serious confusions. For even after a man has been persuaded to use certain phrases in totally new ways in certain contexts, he may still hark back to old uses in other contexts: he may even try to incorporate both uses in the same context, thus giving rise to statements and questions which cannot be interpreted in either way of speaking.

Now in regard to time it is plain that there is a strong tendency in language to use terms connected with the 'present' in an ever stricter manner, so that, if this tendency is carried to the limit, the terms in question cease to have *any* application, or, at best, a novel and artificial one. It is also plain that *some* of the problems of time are connected with this fact. We can readily be persuaded to use the present tense and the temporal adverb 'now' (as well as the imperfect past and imperfect future tenses and the words 'then', 'at that time', etc.) in stricter and stricter ways; and if we yield completely to such pressure, our normal habits of speech will be disorganized. Our use of the present tense and of the temporal adverb 'now' is not very strict in ordinary circumstances: we are prepared to say, even of happenings that last a considerable time, that they are happening *now*, e.g. we say 'The National Anthem is now being sung', 'The Derby is now being run', etc. Now the present tense and the temporal adverb 'now' *might* have been the sort of speech-form that we tended to use more and more widely, so that we might easily have been persuaded to say 'The history of England is now running its course', 'The heat death of the Universe is now taking place'. We might then have been persuaded to allow that, since a *whole* cannot be happening now, unless all its component *parts* are also happening now, John is now really signing Magna Carta, life on the earth is now really extinct, and so on. The problems that this way of speaking might occasion, would certainly be serious. The natural development of the speech-forms we are considering does not, however, lie in this direction. We tend rather, if pressed, to use the present tense and the temporal adverb 'now' more and more narrowly: thus if we had said that the National Anthem was being sung, and someone asked us 'But what are they singing *just now*?', we should not widen our reference to cover the whole evening's concert, but narrow it to apply to some line or phrase or word or note of the National Anthem. Now since our tendencies lie in *this* direction, we can readily be persuaded to give up saying that anything which takes an appreciable time is happening now. We can be bul-

lied into admitting that this is a 'loose' and 'inaccurate' way
of talking. And it is possible to force us to grant that the
really strict speaker would not use these forms of speech in
the case of anything but a happening which was so short that
it took *no time at all*. Thus we might force a man first to
admit that nothing which was *past*, nothing which was *no
longer there*, could possibly be said to be happening now.
We might then press him to admit the additional principle
that nothing of which a *part* lay in the past could properly
be said to be happening now. We might then persuade him
to grant, with regard to any happening that 'takes time', that
it doesn't happen 'all at once', but that it has parts which
happen one after the other, and that, when any *one* of these
parts *is* happening, all the *other* parts either *have* happened
or *will* happen. It then becomes easy to prove that no happening which takes time can properly be said to *be* taking place,
and that the only parts of it of which such a thing could ever
be rightly said, would be parts that took *no time at all*.[3]

[3] The typical historical case of this argument is Augustine, *Confessions* (Book XI: 19, 20): 'Are an hundred years, when present,
a long time? See first, whether an hundred years can be present. For
if the first of these be now current, it is present, but the other ninety
and nine are to come, and therefore are not yet, but if the second
year be current, one is now past, another present, the rest to come.
And so, if we assume any middle year of this hundred to be present,
all before it are past; all after it to come; wherefore an hundred years
cannot be present. But see at least whether that one which is now
current itself is present; for if the current month be its first, the rest
are to come; if the second, the first is already past, and the rest are
not yet. Therefore neither is the year now current present; and if not
present as a whole, then is not the year present. For twelve months
are a year; of which, whatever be the current month is present; the
rest past, or to come. Although neither is that current month present; but one day only; the rest being to come, if it be the first; past,
if the last; if any of the middle, then amid past and to come. See
how the present time which alone we found could be called long, is
abridged to the length scarce of one day. But let us examine that
also; because neither is one day present as a whole. For it is made up
of four and twenty hours of night and day: of which the first hath
the rest to come; the last hath them past; and any of the middle
hath those before it past, those behind it to come. Yea, that one
hour passeth away in flying particles. Whatsoever of it hath flown
away is past; whatever remaineth is to come. If an instant of time

In all these arguments we are being persuaded to apply linguistic principles which are established in the case of happenings of *fairly long duration*, to happenings of very short duration; we are not obliged, but can be readily pressed, to be 'consistent' in this manner since there are no clear lines between the long and the short. But the result of yielding to this pressure is to turn a serviceable way of talking into one that has no use. For it is obvious that all the happenings that we can point to (in any ordinary sense of 'point to') take time, and that pointing itself takes time, so that if the only happenings of which we may say 'This is happening now' are happenings which take no time, there are no happenings which we can point to, of which we may say 'This is happening now'. Now this does not, of course, imply that a clear and useful meaning cannot be given to phrases and sentences which mention happenings that take no time: it is plain, in fact, that very clear and useful meanings *have* been given to them by a long succession of mathematicians and philosophers. But it is also plain that these new forms of diction may, at first, merely serve to disorganize existing speech-habits, and that, while this lasts, we may fail to give any clear or serviceable meaning to 'happenings which take no time'; we may tend to talk of them as if they were happenings we could point to, in the same sense in which we can point to happenings which *do* take time, and we may further credit them unthinkingly with many of the properties of happenings which *do* take time. Such ways of talking, it is plain, must lead to many quite unanswerable questions.

After this preliminary consideration of *one* source of our temporal difficulties, we may turn to Augustine's problem in the eleventh book of the *Confessions*. This we may phrase as follows: 'How can we say of anything that it lasts a long time or a short time? How can a time have length? And how can

---

be conceived which cannot be divided into the smallest particles of moments, that alone is it, which may be called present, which yet flies with such speed from future to past, as not to be lengthened out with the least stay. For if it be, it is divided into past and future. The present hath no space. Where, then, is the time which we may call long?'

that length be measured?'[4] What was it, we may ask, that
Augustine found so difficult in the length and measure of
time? We may perhaps distinguish three aspects of his bewilderment, which might be grounds for anyone's bewilderment. He found it difficult, in the first place (we may suppose), to see how happenings which take *no* time could ever
be 'added up' to make the happenings which *do* take time.[5]
This difficulty is not peculiar to our thought of time, but
applies to space as well. It seems absurd to say that an accumulation of events, the duration of each of which is zero,
should have, together, a duration that is more than zero. The
matter might be put more strongly. We are inclined to say
that, if the duration of events were reduced to zero, 'there
would be nothing left of them', they would 'just be nothing',
and we obviously could not hope to make something out of
an accumulation of nothings.[6] We may regard this as one
side of the Augustinian problem. A second slightly different
side consists in the fact that the stages of any happening that
takes time are never there *together*. Now it seems absurd to
say of a number of things which are never together, but always apart, that they can ever *amount* to anything, or form a
whole of any kind: it would be as if one were to try to build
a house with bricks that repelled each other, so that each
one moved away when the next one was brought up to it. At
such a rate, it would seem, one could build no house and no
interval of time.[7] But Augustine's problem has a third side
which seems to have worried him particularly: that if we
measure an interval of time, we must be measuring something
of which a vanishing section only has reality: all the other
sections of it, which give it breadth and bulk, are either *not
yet there* or *not there any longer*. Now it is hard to grasp

[4] The interest in Augustine as a case of philosophical puzzlement
is due to Wittgenstein.
[5] Augustine: 'The present hath no space. Where then is the time
which we may call long?' See above.
[6] Augustine: 'If time present . . . only cometh into existence because it passeth into time past, how can we say that either this is,
whose cause of being is that it shall not be' (XI, 17).
[7] Augustine: 'Therefore neither is the year now current present;
and if not present *as a whole* (our italics) then is not the year present.' See above.

how we can measure something which is no longer there, which is 'past and gone', of which we are tempted to say that it is 'simply nothing'. And it is also hard to grasp how we can measure something which is not yet there, which is merely expected, which we are likewise tempted to describe as 'nothing'. It would be like trying to measure a building of which all but the tiniest fragment had been blasted by a bomb, or existed merely in a builder's blue-print. In such a situation we should have no building to measure, and it seems we should be in the same position with regard to lengths of time.[8]

We shall now briefly point to some ways—there are an indefinite number of such ways—in which we might avoid these Augustinian perplexities. We might, first of all, evade the whole argument by which we have been bludgeoned into saying that there are some events that take no time, and that only these are ever truly present. We might refuse to say, of certain happenings which are very short, that any of their parts lie in the past or future; we do not normally, in fact, make use of the past and future tenses in speaking of the parts of very short events contemporary with our utterance. Alternatively we might say that some sufficiently short events can be 'present as wholes', though most of their parts are past or future; this too agrees with ordinary usage, for we say that many fairly long events *are* happening, though we should talk in the past or future tense of some of their remoter parts. Or again we might deny—as Whitehead in his doctrine of epochal durations has denied—that certain very brief events come into being *part by part*.[9] There is, in fact, no plain empirical meaning to be given to the supposition that all events come into being part by part, since there must necessarily be a

[8] Augustine: 'In what space then do we measure time passing? In the future, whence it passeth through? But what is not yet we measure not. Or in the present by which it passes? But no space we do not measure. Or in the past to which it passes? But neither do we measure that, which now is not' (XI, 27).

[9] 'Accordingly we must not proceed to conceive time as another form of extensiveness. Time is sheer succession of epochal durations. . . . The epochal duration is not realized *via* its *successive* divisible parts, but is given *with* its parts' (*Science and the Modern World*, p. 158).

limit to the division of events by human judgements or instruments. Or again we might choose to follow certain other
trends of language, and to say, of certain very brief events,
that they 'took no time at all', thereby excluding from the
start the whole issue of divisibility into successive parts.[10]
It does not, in fact, matter, in all this choice of diction, *what*
we say, provided only that we truly please ourselves: the facts
are there, we can see and show them, and it is for us to talk
of them in ways which will neither perplex nor embarrass us.
It is desirable, in our choice of words, that we should be
consistent, but it is not desirable that we should make a fetish
of consistency. Consistency in language is most necessary if it
means that we shall not, in a given context, fall victims to
linguistic conflicts, that we shall not try to say something,
while striving at the same time to unsay it.[11] Consistency is
also very desirable if it means that we shall be guided by the
analogies of things in what we say in *different* contexts; in
the absence of *some* degree of such consistency, all language
would be arbitrary and communication impossible. But consistency is wholly undesirable if it becomes a bogey, if it
makes us say something in one context merely because we
have said it in some other, more or less analogous context,
and if it then leads us on to say further things which be-
wilder and confuse us. For the analogies of things are varied
and conflicting, and it is impossible, without disrupting human language, to do justice to them all.

So far we have pursued a line which shakes the dialectic on
which the Augustinian problem is founded. By so doing we
avoid giving a sense to the phrase 'events which take no
time', and are not obliged to say that these alone are truly
present. Suppose however we are moved by this dialectic, or
by some consideration of scientific convenience, to admit this
talk of 'momentary presents', how then shall we proceed to
deal with the various aspects of the Augustinian problem? As
regards the first aspect, the building of a whole which has size

[10] *How* brief the happenings must be, of which we say any of
these things, is of course a matter for arbitrary decision.

[11] Unless, indeed, a linguistic conflict is deliberately used to express some personal reaction to reality, as has been done by some
philosophers.

out of parts which have *no* size, we may simply point out that it mixes up the familiar sense in which a pile of money is built up out of coins, with the new sense in which a happening which takes time may be built up out of happenings which take no time. Because one couldn't amass a fortune out of zero contributions, one tends to think one couldn't make a measurable duration out of parts with no duration. But the situations are quite different; no one has witnessed a lapse of time being built up out of instants, as he can witness a pile of money being built up out of coins, nor can the former be imagined as the latter is imagined.[12] Hence if we wish to speak of 'happenings which take no time', we are quite free to fix what may be said of them, and this means that we may simply rule that events which take time *are* made up of events which take no time. And once misleading pictures are avoided, we shall find no problem in this. We may in the same way dispose of the difficulties which spring from the tendency to say that an event which took no time would 'just be nothing'. Either we must restrain this inclination—to which we are not in duty bound to yield—or be prepared to say that certain parts of real temporal wholes are simply nothing, and that mere nothing can at times have definite properties. This way of talking would no doubt do violence to our habits, and abound in dangerous suggestions, but we should not, with a little practice, find it difficult.

The second aspect of the Augustinian problem involves a similar confusion. Because it would be absurd to say of certain wholes—houses, mountains or libraries, for instance—that they existed and were measurable, although their parts were never together, we think it would be absurd to say the same thing of happenings. But the fact that we shouldn't say that *some* of the things we call parts could constitute the things we call their wholes, unless they were present together, does not oblige us to say this in the case of *other* things we also call parts and wholes. For the sense in which the parts were parts, and the wholes wholes, and the former made up the latter, might be ruled to be different in the two sets of cases:

[12] Though a sense might be invented in which we could be said to witness or imagine the former.

we might say we were dealing with two totally different *sorts* of parts and wholes. And we do in fact rule so; for we regard it as nonsense to say of an event that takes time, that its parts are present together. And we recognize the difference between the two sets of cases by talking of *coexistent* parts in the one set of cases, and of successive parts in the other: the successive parts of a whole are, in fact, just those parts of it that *don't* need to be together. But if we feel ourselves unconquerably opposed to calling something a whole whose parts are not together, we may simply rule that some things may have magnitude although they are not wholes. And other similar expedients will meet other possible difficulties.

As regards the third difficulty of Augustine, how we manage to measure something which is in part past, we may again suggest a number of alternatives. We might, in the first place, reject the analogy between the measurement of a co-existent whole like a house, which isn't there to be measured if any parts of it lie in the past, and the measurement of a successive whole like a happening, which *must* have parts in the past. Or we might follow certain other trends of language, and say that we have succession *in the present*, and that certain happenings which are not too long are able to be present as wholes and so to be measured directly. Other longer happenings might then be measured by means of the briefer and directly measurable happenings which entered into their remembered history. Or if it is the 'nothingness of the past' that troubles us, we must remember that we are not compelled to say that the past is nothing: we may, if we like, credit it with existence or subsistence or any other suitable status. For we are only worried by the 'nothingness of the past' because we think it will stop us from finding out any facts about the past, just as the nothingness of a bachelor's children stops us from asking for their ages or appearance. But there are so many clear and agreed ways of establishing what has happened in the immediate or remoter past, that it would be nonsense to put past events in the position of a bachelor's children. So that if we wish to say that they exist or subsist, there is no good reason why we should not do so. But if the 'existence' of the past is going to suggest to us that we could by some device revive or revisit the past, as we could revive a drowned man or revisit Palermo, then it is perhaps better to go on saying that the past is nothing, allowing meanwhile that there may be measurable wholes which have certain parts that are nothing.

The puzzles of Augustine lead on very naturally to the problems of Zeno, or rather to a certain very general difficulty which seems to be involved in every one of Zeno's paradoxes. This is our difficulty in seeing how anything can happen, if *before* it happens something else must happen, and *before* that happens something else must happen, and so on indefinitely. If we make time continuous and infinitely divisible, we also feel obliged to say that before any happening is completed, an infinity of prior happenings must have been completed, and this seems to mean that *no* happening can ever be completed. We seem to be in the plight of a runner in a torch-race, who wants to hand on his torch to another runner A, but is told by A that he will only take it from B, who tells him he will only take it from C, who tells him he will only take it from D, and so on indefinitely. Or in the plight of a man who wants to interview a Cabinet Minister, and who is informed by the Minister that he must first discuss his business with the Under-Secretary, who informs him he must first discuss it with the Chief Clerk, etc., etc. Our runner obviously will never get rid of his torch, and our harassed petitioner will obviously never see his Minister, and it looks as if all happenings involve the same hopeless difficulty. The difficulty we are presenting is, of course, not identical with any one of Zeno's historical puzzles: in all of these the difficulties of duration are complicated by the introduction of change and motion. But it is plain that all these puzzles could be so restated as to deal with happenings without regard to whether those happenings were changes or persistent states, and without regard to whether they involved motion or not. A plum continuing to hang on a tree for a certain period affords, less dramatically, the same species of philosophical perplexity as an arrow in its flight. Moreover, when we strip Zeno's problem of its spatial and other wrappings, its significance becomes clearer. For it is not, essentially, a problem of space or quantity, but solely one of time: it is only because all motion is *successive*, because an infinity of positions must be passed *before* any subsequent position, that the possibility of such motion seems so utterly ruled out. If the infinite stages of a motion could be there all at once, as the parts of a piece of space are, we should feel no problem in their infinite number. It is therefore foolish to imagine that we can meet Zeno's puzzles by the modern theory of the continuum or by the facts of infinite convergent numerical series.[13] And the problem assumes its most vexing form if we allow that ordinary happenings have ultimate parts that take no time. For of such parts it seems most natural to say that none can be next to any other,[14] and once this is said it is hard to understand how any ultimate part can ever pass away or be replaced by any other. For before such a part can be replaced by any other similar part, it must first have been replaced by an infinity of other similar parts. Our admission seems to leave us with a world immobilized and paralyzed, in which every object and process, like the arrow of Zeno, stands still in the instant, for the simple reason that it has no way of passing on to other instants.

As before, we may deal with our difficulties in several different ways. We might, in the first place, deny that very short happenings are divisible as fairly long ones are divisible: the divisibility of *all* happenings is in any case without a definite meaning. This is the line followed by Professor Whitehead, who makes time flow in indivisible drops, and says that it is 'sheer succession of epochal durations'.[15] But, far less drastically, we might give to all this talk of instants and of infinite divisibility a sense consistent with the obvious facts of our experience, that things happen and that phases are outlived, that the world is not immobilized, and that we seldom have to cast about for ways of passing on to novel stages. For the infinite happenings that must first occur before a given thing can happen, are not like ordinary happenings we can see and show, of which it would be absurd

[13] This point is clearly brought out by Whitehead. See *Process and Reality*, p. 95.

[14] Unless we choose to say that there is a finite number of ultimate parts in any happening, or other queerer things.

[15] *Science and the Modern World*, quoted above.

to say that an infinite number ever were completed. They are happenings of a new sort to which a meaning must be arbitrarily given. And since *we* have to give a meaning to these happenings, it is for us to see that they mean nothing which conflicts with our established ways of saying things. And once we strip them of pictorial vividness, we also strip them of their puzzling character. Our problem also vanishes when we note that even to be 'desperately immobilized', to 'cast about in vain for means to pass to other stages', would both, if they were anything, be states that lasted and took time. Our problem therefore takes for granted the very thing it finds so difficult.

We turn, in conclusion, from these Augustinian and Zenonian difficulties, to a different set of temporal puzzles, quite unconnected with our tendency to use the present tense in more exact and narrow ways. We shall consider briefly the very general wonderment which professes to find something 'unintelligible' or 'contradictory' in time and change. 'How is it possible', we sometimes like to ask, 'for all the solid objects and people around us to melt away into the past, and for a new order of objects and persons to emerge mysteriously from the future?' This kind of wonderment is most strongly stirred by processes of *rapid change*: we wonder at things which have no constant quality for any length of time however short, at things which only reach a state to leave it, and so forth. A similar perplexity besets us in regard to 'truths' or 'facts': we wonder how what *is* the case can ever cease to be the case, or how what was false *then* can come to be true *now*, and so on. This week the peaches in our garden are not ripe; next week we find them ripe; the following week they are no longer ripe, but rotten: in certain frames of mind we find this difficult. Our difficulty with regard to change may also be expressed in terms of 'happenings' and their 'properties' of 'pastness', 'presentness' and 'futurity', the form in which this problem was propounded by McTaggart. We wonder how it comes about that happenings which are at first remotely future, should steadily become more nearly future, how in the end they manage to be present, and how from being present they become past, and how they go on, ever afterwards, becoming more and more remotely past.

McTaggart has shown plainly that we cannot solve this problem (if it is a problem) by bringing in the 'different times' at which events are present, past and future, since these themselves (whatever we may mean by them) have also to be present, past and future, and so involve the very difficulty they are called in to remove.

Now it is hard to see, if we remain in any ordinary, unreflective state of mind, what is the problem that is being raised by those who say they can't see how what *is* the case at one time, is not the case at other times, or that they can't see how a happening that is future can ever come to be a happening that is past. As we observed at the beginning of this paper, it should be possible to remove such difficulties by pointing to some ordinary happening around us, a man diving, for instance, and saying, as it happened, 'Now he's not yet diving', 'Now he's diving', 'Now he is no longer diving', or other similar phrases. And if a man were really puzzled by our usage in such situations, it would not take him very long to master it. We do not ordinarily have difficulty in knowing what to say of happenings as they pass, nor any tendency both to say and not to say the same thing in a given context, a kind of inconsistency that is seldom desirable. Occasionally, where change is rapid, we may find ourselves at a loss to say whether something is or is not yellow, or whether it is or was yellow: we may also have a tendency to say that it is both or neither. But all this only means we lack a settled and satisfactory way of talking about very swiftly changing things. But in the case of changes which are less rapid, we find ourselves quite free from conflict or confusion. *Before* an event occurs we say, if we have evidence that it is not yet happening, that it hasn't yet happened, but that it will happen, while if it *is* happening we say that it is now happening, that it hasn't ceased happening and that it isn't about to happen, and *after* it has happened we say that it has happened, that it is no longer happening and that it is not going to happen. Stated in words these semantic rules might seem circular, but taught in connection with a concrete situation they are wholly clear. And our conventions with regard to tenses are so well worked out that we have practically the

materials in them for a formal calculus.[16] Where all is so
desirably definite, what room is there for puzzles or perplexities?

To give an answer to this question, we must point to a
certain aspiration which all our language to some extent ful-
fils, and which we are at times inclined to follow to unreasonable lengths. We desire to have in our language only
those kinds of statement that are *not* dependent, as regards
their truth or falsity, on any circumstance in which the statement happens to be made. We do not wish a statement which
we call 'correct' and 'justified by fact' when made by one
person, to be incorrect when made by another person, and
to have to be superseded by some other statement. In the
same way we do not wish a statement which we call 'correct'
when made in one place, to be incorrect when made in another place, and to have to be superseded by some other
statement. And there are occasions when we feel the same
sort of thing about the *time* at which a statement is made:
if we are right in saying something at a certain time, then,
we sometimes feel, we must be right in saying the same thing
at all other times. This means that we object, in certain
frames of mind, even to the easy, systematic changes of tense
which statements have to undergo when they are transmitted
from period to period. We might express our general aspiration by saying that we wish our statements to be independent
of 'extraneous circumstances' in regard to their truth or falsity: 'the facts' must settle whether what we say is true, and
nothing else must come into consideration. But such a way
of talking would be gravely question-begging, for it depends
on the sort of language we are speaking whether a circumstance is or is not extraneous. If we spoke a language in which
the statements permitted in one place differed systematically
from the statements permitted in another place, then it

[16] The calculus of tenses should have been included in the modern development of modal logics. It includes such obvious propositions as that

x present = (x present) present;

x future = (x future) present = (x present) future;

also such comparatively recondite propositions as that

(x). (x past) future; i.e. all events, past, present and future, *will*
be past.

wouldn't, in that language, be an extraneous circumstance, as regards the truth or falsity of a statement, whether that statement was made here or there. And those who used the language would protest quite legitimately that 'something was left out' by other languages which ignored all local circumstances of utterance. But the point is that we do *in part* say things which may be passed from man to man, or place to place, or time to time, without a change in their truth-value, and we look at things from *this* angle when we say that time, place and speaker are extraneous circumstances, and require our statements to ignore them.

Now the urge behind these austerities seems simply to be the urge towards more adequate communication, which is the fundamental impulse underlying language. We are prepared to sacrifice local and personal colour, or period flavour, in order that our statements may be handed on unaltered to other persons who are differently situated, or to ourselves in other situations. But it is not *this* sacrifice which gives rise to our perplexities: if we always spoke rigorously in the third person of everyone, ourselves included, if we avoided the adverbs 'here' and 'there', if we purged our language of tenses, and talked exclusively in terms of dates and tenseless participles, we should never be involved in difficulties. And for the purposes of science it is perhaps desirable that we should always talk in this manner. But our difficulty arises because we try to talk in this way but are also uneasy in doing so; we feel that something worth-while has been omitted, and try to combine our old way of talking with our new one. Thus McTaggart first offers us an order of events in which there are no differences of past, present and future, but only differences of earlier and later, in which every happening always stays the sort of happening it is, and always occupies the same position in the time-series: he then slides back into another way of talking in which events are present, past and future, and always *change* in these modalities. And his attempt to combine these ways of talking results in the unanswerable question: how can a single happening have the incompatible properties of being past and present and future? Whereas if we talk in the ordinary way we never have to say these things at once, and if we talk in an artificial, tenseless manner the question can't arise, since the modalities in question can't be mentioned. It is as if a man tried to retain the use of personal pronouns, such as 'I', 'you', 'he', etc., in a language in which everything that could truly be said by one man could be truly said by every other man, and were then led to ask: 'How can one and the same person be I and you and he?' And once we see the source of such perplexities, we should be easily rid of them.

IV

Bertrand Russell's Doubts about Induction

PAUL EDWARDS

I

A. In the celebrated chapter on induction in his *Problems of Philosophy*, Bertrand Russell asks the question: 'Have we any reason, assuming that they (laws like the law of gravitation) have always held in the past, to suppose that these laws will hold in the future?' (p. 100).[1] Earlier in the same chapter he raises the more specific question: 'Do *any* number of cases of a law being fulfilled in the past afford evidence that it will be fulfilled in the future?' (p. 96). We may reformulate these questions in a way which lends itself more easily to critical discussion as follows:

(1) Assuming that we possess n positive instances of a phenomenon, observed in extensively varied circumstances, and that we have not observed a single negative instance (where n is a large number), have we any reason to suppose that the $n + 1$st instance will also be positive?

[1] The references are to the original edition of *The Problems of Philosophy*, the pagination of which differs from that of the reset edition first published in 1946.

(2) Is there any number *n* of observed positive instances of a phenomenon which affords evidence that the *n* + 1st instance will also be positive?

It is clear that Russell uses 'reason' synonymously with 'good reason' and 'evidence' with 'sufficient evidence'. I shall follow the same procedure throughout this article.

Russell asserts that unless we appeal to a non-empirical principle which he calls the 'principle of induction', both of his questions must be answered in the negative. 'Those who emphasized the scope of induction', he writes, 'wished to maintain that all logic is empirical, and therefore could not be expected to realize that induction itself, their own darling, required a logical principle which obviously could not be proved inductively, and must therefore be *a priori* if it could be known at all' (*Our Knowledge of the External World* [2nd edition], p. 226). 'We must either accept the inductive principle on the ground of its intrinsic evidence or forgo all justification of our expectations about the future' (*Problems of Philosophy*, p. 106; also *Outline of Philosophy*, p. 286).

In conjunction with the inductive principle, on the other hand, question (1) at least, he contends, can be answered in the affirmative. 'Whether inferences from past to future are valid depends wholly, if our discussion has been sound, upon the inductive principle: if it is true, such inferences are valid' (*External World*, p. 226). Unfortunately Russell does not make it clear whether in his opinion the same is true about question (2).

As against Russell, I shall try to show in this article that question (1) can be answered in the affirmative without in any way appealing to a non-empirical principle. I shall also attempt to show that, without in any way invoking a non-empirical principle, numbers of observed positive instances do frequently afford us evidence that unobserved instances of the same phenomenon are also positive. At the outset, I shall concentrate on question (1) since this is the more general question. Once we have answered question (1) it will require little further effort to answer question (2).

I want to emphasize here that, to keep this paper within manageable bounds, I shall refrain from discussing, at any rate explicitly, the questions 'Are any inductive conclusions probable?' and 'Are any inductive conclusions certain?' I hope to fill in this gap on another occasion.

It will be well to conduct our discussion in terms of a concrete example. Supposing a man jumps from a window on the fiftieth floor of the Empire State Building. Is there any reason to suppose that his body will move in the direction of the street rather than say in the direction of the sky or in a flat plane? There can be no doubt that any ordinary person and any philosophically unsophisticated scientist, would answer this question in the affirmative without in any way appealing to a non-empirical principle. He would say that there is an excellent reason to suppose that the man's body will move towards the street. This excellent reason, he would say, consists in the fact that whenever in the past a human being jumped out of a window of the Empire State Building his body moved in a downward direction; that whenever any human being anywhere jumped out of a house he moved in the direction of the ground; that, more generally, whenever a human body jumped or was thrown off an elevated locality in the neighbourhood of the earth, it moved downwards and not either upwards or at an angle of 180°; that the only objects which have been observed to be capable of moving upwards by themselves possess certain special characteristics which human beings lack; and finally in all the other observed confirmations of the theory of gravitation.

B. The philosophers who reject common-sense answers like the one just described, have relied mainly on three arguments. Russell himself explicitly employs two of them and some of his remarks make it clear that he also approves of the third. These three arguments are as follows: (a) Defenders of common-sense point to the fact that many inferences to unobserved events were subsequently, by means of direct observation, found to have resulted in true conclusions. However, any such appeal to observed results of inductive inferences is irrelevant. For the question at stake is: Have we ever a reason, assuming that all the large number of observed instances of a phenomenon are positive, to suppose that an instance which is still unobserved is also positive? The question is not: Have we ever a reason for supposing that instances which have by now been observed but were at one time unobserved are positive? In Russell's own words: 'We have experience of past futures, but not of future futures, and the question is: Will future futures resemble past futures? This question is not to be answered by an argument which starts from past futures alone' (*Problems of Philosophy*, p. 100).

(*b*) Cases are known where at a certain time a large number of positive instances and not a single negative instance had been observed and where the next instance nevertheless turned out to be negative. 'We know that in spite of frequent repetitions there sometimes is a failure at the last' (*Problems of Philosophy*, p. 102). The man, for instance, 'who has fed the chicken every day throughout its life at last wrings its neck instead' (*Problems of Philosophy*, p. 98). Even in the case of the human being who is jumping out of the Empire State Building, 'we may be in no better position than the chicken which unexpectedly has its neck wrung' (*Problems of Philosophy*, p. 98).

(*c*) The number of positive and negative necessary conditions for the occurrence of any event is infinite or at any rate too large to be directly observed by a human being or indeed by all human beings put together. None of us, for example, has explored every corner of the universe to make sure that there nowhere exists a malicious but powerful individual who controls the movements of the sun by means of wires which are too fine to be detected by any of our microscopes. None of us can be sure that there is no such Controller who, in order to play a joke with the human race, will prevent the sun from rising to-morrow. Equally, none of us can be sure that there is nowhere a powerful individual who can, if he wishes, regulate the movement of human bodies by means of ropes which are too thin to be detected by any of our present instruments. None of us therefore can be sure that when a man jumps out of the Empire State Building he will not be drawn skyward by the Controller of Motion. Hence we have no reason to suppose that the man's body will move in the direction of the street and not in the direction of the sky.

In connection with the last of these three arguments attention ought to be drawn to a distinction which Russell makes between what he calls the 'interesting' and the 'uninteresting' doubt about induction (*Problems of Philosophy*, p. 95). The uninteresting doubt is doubt about the occurrence of a given event on the ground that not all the conditions which are known to be necessary are in fact known to be present. What Russell calls the interesting doubt is the doubt whether an event will take place although all the conditions known to be necessary are known to obtain. Russell's 'interesting doubt', if I am not mistaken, is identical with Donald Williams's 'tragic problem of induction' ('Induction and the Future', *Mind*, 1948, p. 227).

II

As I indicated above, it is my object in this article to defend the common-sense answers to both of Russell's questions. I propose to show, in other words, that, without in any way calling upon a non-empirical principle for assistance, we often have a reason for supposing that a generalization will be confirmed in the future as it has been confirmed in the past. I also propose to show that numbers 'of cases of a law being fulfilled in the past' do often afford evidence that it will be fulfilled in the future.

However, what I have to say in support of these answers is so exceedingly simple that I am afraid it will not impress the philosophers who are looking for elaborate and complicated theories to answer these questions. But I think I can make my case appear plausible even in the eyes of some of these philosophers if I describe at some length the general method of resolving philosophical puzzles which I shall apply to the problem of induction.

Let us consider a simple statement like 'there are several thousand physicians in New York'. We may call this a statement of common-sense, meaning thereby no more than that anybody above a certain very moderate level of instruction and intelligence would confidently give his assent to it.

The word 'physician', as ordinarily used, is not entirely free from ambiguity. At times it simply means 'person who possesses a medical degree from a recognized academic in-

stitution'. At other times, though less often, it means the
same as 'person who possesses what is by ordinary standards
a considerable skill in curing diseases'. On yet other occasions
when people say about somebody that he is a physician they
mean both that he has a medical degree and that he possesses
a skill in curing diseases which considerably exceeds that of
the average layman.

Let us suppose that in the common-sense statement 'there
are several thousand physicians in New York' the word 'physician' is used exclusively in the last-mentioned sense. This
assumption will simplify our discussion, but it is not at all
essential to any of the points I am about to make. It is essential, however, to realize that when somebody asserts in
ordinary life that there are several thousand physicians in
New York, he is using the word 'physician' in one or other of
the ordinary senses just listed. By 'physician' he does not
mean for example 'person who can speedily repair bicycles'
or 'person who can cure any conceivable illness in less than
two minutes'.

Now, supposing somebody were to say 'Really, there are
no physicians at all in New York', in the belief that he was
contradicting and refuting common-sense. Supposing that on
investigation it turns out that by 'physician' he does not
mean 'person who has a medical degree and who has considerably more skill in curing disease than the average layman'. It turns out that by 'physician' he means 'person who
has a medical degree and who can cure any conceivable illness
in less than two minutes'.

What would be an adequate reply to such an 'enemy of
common-sense'? Clearly it would be along the following lines:
'What you say is true. There are no physicians in New York
—in *your* sense of the word. There are no persons in New
York who can cure any conceivable disease in less than two
minutes. But this in no way contradicts the common-sense
view expressed by "there are several thousand physicians in
New York". For the latter asserts no more than that there
are several thousand people in New York who have a medical degree and who possess a skill in curing disease which
considerably exceeds that of the average layman. You are

guilty of *ignoratio elenchi* since the proposition you refute is different from the proposition you set out to refute.'

Our discussion from here on will be greatly simplified by introducing a few technical terms. Let us, firstly, call '*ignoratio elenchi* by *redefinition*' any instance of *ignoratio elenchi* in which (i) the same sentence expresses both the proposition which ought to be proved and the proposition which is confused with it and where (ii) in the latter employment of the sentence one or more of its parts are used in a sense which is different from their ordinary sense or senses. Secondly, let us refer to any redefinition of a word which includes all that the ordinary definition of the word includes but which includes something else as well as a '*high* redefinition'; and to the sense which is defined by a high redefinition we shall refer as a high sense of the word. Thus 'person who has a medical degree and who is capable of curing any conceivable disease in less than two minutes' is a high redefinition of 'physician' and anybody using the word in that fashion is using it in a high sense. Thirdly, we shall refer to a redefinition of a word which includes something but not all of what the ordinary definition includes and which includes nothing else as a '*low* redefinition'; and the sense which is defined by a low redefinition we shall call a low sense of the word. 'Person capable of giving first aid' or 'person who knows means of alleviating pain' would be low redefinitions of 'physician'. Finally, it will be convenient to call a statement in which a word is used in a high or in a low sense a *redefinitional statement*. If the word is used in a high sense we shall speak of a high-definitional statement; if it is used in a low sense we shall speak of a low-definitional statement.

A short while ago, I pointed out that the man who says 'there are no physicians in New York', meaning that there are no people in New York who have a medical degree and who can cure any conceivable illness in less than two minutes, is not really contradicting the common-sense view that there are physicians in New York. I pointed out that he would be guilty of what in our technical language is called an *ignoratio elenchi* by redefinition. Now, it seems to me that the relation between the assertion of various philosophers that past experience never constitutes a reason for prediction or generalization except perhaps in conjunction with a non-empirical principle and the common-sense view that past experience does often by itself constitute a reason for inferences to unobserved events has some striking resemblances to the relation between the redefinitional statement about physicians in New York and the common-sense view which this redefinitional statement fails to refute. And more generally, it strongly seems to me that almost all the bizarre pronouncements of philosophers—their 'paradoxes', their 'silly' theories—are in certain respects strikingly like the statement that there are no physicians in New York, made by one who means to assert that there are no people in New York who have medical degrees and who are capable of curing any conceivable disease in less than two minutes.

In making the last statement I do not mean to deny that there are also important differences between philosophical paradoxes and the high-definitional statement about physicians. There are three differences in particular which have to be mentioned if my subsequent remarks are not to be seriously misleading. Firstly, many of the philosophical paradoxes are not without some point; they do often draw attention to likenesses and differences which ordinary usage obscures. Secondly, the redefinitions which are implicit in philosophical paradoxes do quite often, though by no means always, receive a certain backing from ordinary usage. Frequently, that is to say, there is a secondary sense or trend in ordinary usage which corresponds to the philosophical redefinition, the 'real' sense of the word.[2] Thirdly, philosophical paradoxes are invariably ambiguous in a sense in which the high-definitional statement about the physicians is not ambiguous.[3]

Now, while fully admitting all these (and other) differences, I wish to insist on the great likenesses between philosophical paradoxes and the redefinitional statement about the

[2] Prominent instances of this phenomenon are 'real certainty', 'real knowledge', 'real sameness', 'real freedom', and 'really contemporaneous events'.

[3] The last of these points seems to me to be of enormous importance for understanding the phenomenon of philosophical paradoxes.

physicians. And in this article I am mainly concerned with the likenesses, not with the differences. My main object, of course, is to point out the likenesses between the high-definitional statement 'There are no physicians in New York' and the statement that past experience never by itself affords a reason for making inferences to unobserved events. However, my points there will be clearer if I first make them in connection with another celebrated paradox.

Following Plato, Berkeley[4] argued in favour of the view that heat and cold are not really 'in the object'. Ordinary people would unhesitatingly say that water of e.g. 50° C. is hot. Against this, Plato and Berkeley would point out that to a man who a moment before had held his hands in a jug of water with a temperature of 80° C., the water of 50° C. would appear cold. Similarly, to a race of individuals whose body-temperature was say 75° C., water of 50° would regularly appear cold. But the percepts of those to whom the water of 50° appears cold are just as genuine as the percepts of people to whom the water appears hot. Now, since it would be wrong to say that the water of 50° is really cold simply because of these genuine percepts of cold, it cannot any more rationally be said to be hot. The cold has 'just as good a right to be considered real' as the hot; and therefore, 'to avoid favouritism, we are compelled to deny that in itself'[5] the water is either hot or cold.

It is not difficult to show that this argument is a case of *ignoratio elenchi* by redefinition. When an ordinary person says that water of 50° C. is hot, all he means is that human beings, with their body-temperature being what it is, would in *all ordinary circumstances* have sense-impressions of heat on coming into contact with such water. In saying that water of 50° is hot, is *really* hot, an ordinary person in no way denies that under certain *special* conditions a human being would have genuine sense-impressions of cold. He also in no way denies that to a race of individuals whose body-temperature is 75° the water would genuinely appear cold. Point-

---

[4] *Three Dialogues between Hylas and Philonous,* p. 208 (Everyman edit.).

[5] The phrases are Russell's, used in a very similar context (*Problems,* p. 14).

ing to these facts does not therefore refute the ordinary man. Berkeley is clearly guilty of a high redefinition of 'hot' or 'really hot'. To him something is hot only if, in addition to appearing hot to human beings in ordinary circumstances, it also appears hot to them under special circumstances and if it appears hot to beings with a body-temperature which is much greater than the actual body-temperature of human beings.

However, this is not quite accurate since, like most other philosophical paradoxes, the paradox about heat and cold has a double meaning. It would be inaccurate simply to say that Berkeley is guilty of *ignoratio elenchi* by redefinition. On the other hand, without in any way being inaccurate, it can be said that Berkeley and Plato have laid themselves open to the following dilemma: 'Either you mean by "hot" what is ordinarily meant by it—if you do, then what you say is plainly false; or else you are using "hot" in a high sense—if so what you say is true, but in that case you are guilty of *ignoratio elenchi* by redefinition. In either event you have failed to refute common-sense.' Very similar answers can also be made to Berkeley's and Russell's arguments concerning colours, shapes, and the other qualities which common-sense believes to exist independently of being perceived.

At the same time it must be admitted that Berkeley's arguments have a certain value. In ordinary speech we make a fairly rigid distinction between 'real' and 'unreal' data. Among the unreal data we lump together both the percepts which we have under special conditions (and percepts which do and would appear to beings differently constituted from ourselves) and what we experience e.g. in dreams and hallucinations. 'Real' we call only those percepts which a normal observer has under certain standard conditions.

A classification of this sort obscures the many likenesses between the 'real' percepts and percepts appearing under special conditions, while also hiding the many differences between the latter and data which are experienced in dreams and hallucinations.

The situation becomes quite clear if we divide data into three and not merely into two groups, as follows:

the R-data: percepts appearing to a normal observer under standard conditions,

the A-data: percepts appearing to a normal observer under special conditions or to an abnormal observer in certain normal or special circumstances, and

the D-data: data appearing in dreams, hallucinations, etc.

It is unnecessary for our purposes to discuss exactly what are the likenesses between the R-data and the A-data. It is unnecessary, too, to discuss what exactly are the differences between the A-data and the D-data. It is sufficient to point out that while Berkeley is wrong in believing or suggesting that there are no differences between the R-data and the A-data, he is right in insisting that the differences between the R-data and the A-data are not nearly as great as ordinary speech suggests. In the case of colours, Berkeley's argument has the further merit of bringing out the fact that the expression 'X's real colour' has *two* perfectly proper senses. His argument helps one to realize that 'X's real colour' may mean 'the colour which X exhibits to a normal observer under certain standard conditions' *as well as* 'the colour which X exhibits to a normal observer under a finer instrument than the human eye, e.g. a microscope'.

III

A. Supposing a man, let us call him M, said to us 'I have not yet found any physicians in New York'. Suppose we take him to Park Avenue and introduce him to Brown, a man who has a medical degree and who has cured many people suffering from diseases of the ear. Brown admits, however, that he has not been able to cure *all* the patients who ever consulted him. He also admits that many of his cures took a long time, some as long as eight years. On hearing this, M says 'Brown certainly isn't a physician'.

Supposing we next take M to meet Black who has a medical degree and who can prove to M's and to our satisfaction that he has cured every patient who ever consulted him. Moreover, none of Black's cures took more than three years.

However, on hearing that some of Black's cures took as long as two years and ten months, M says 'Black certainly isn't a physician either'.

Finally we introduce M to White who has a medical degree and who has cured every one of his patients in less than six months. When M hears that some of White's cures took as long as five and a half months, he is adamant and exclaims 'White—what a ridiculous error to call him a physician!'

At this stage, if not much sooner, all of us would impatiently ask M: What on earth do you mean by 'physician'? And we would plainly be justified in adding: Whatever you may mean by 'physician', in any sense in which we ever use the word, Black and Brown and White are physicians and very excellent ones at that.

Let us return now to Russell's doubt about the sun's rising to-morrow or about what would happen to a man who jumps out of the Empire State Building. Let us consider what Russell would say in reply to the following question: Supposing that the observed confirmatory instances for the theory of gravitation were a million or ten million times as extensive as they now are and that they were drawn from a very much wider field; would we then have a reason to suppose that the man will fall into the street and not move up into the sky? It is obvious that Russell and anybody taking his view would say 'No'. He would reply that though our *expectation* that the man's body will move in the direction of the street would be even stronger then than it is at present, we would still be without a *reason*.

Next, let us imagine ourselves to be putting the following question to Russell: Supposing the world were such that no accumulation of more than five hundred observed positive instances of a phenomenon has ever been found to be followed by a negative instance; supposing, for instance, that all the chickens who have ever been fed by the same man for 501 days in succession or more are still alive and that all the men too are still alive feeding the chickens every day—would the observed confirmations of the law of gravity in that case be a reason to suppose that the man jumping out of the Empire State Building will move in the direction of the street and not in the direction of the sky? I am not quite sure what Russell would say in reply to this question. Let us assume he would once again answer 'No—past experience would not even then ever be a *reason*'.

Thirdly and finally, we have to consider what Russell would say to the following question: Supposing we had explored every corner of the universe with instruments millions of times as fine and accurate as any we now possess and that we had yet failed to discover any Controller of the movements of human bodies—would we then in our predictions about the man jumping out of the Empire State Building be in a better position than the chicken is in predicting its meals? Would our past observations then be a reason for our prediction? Whatever Russell would in fact say to this, it is clear that his remarks concerning the 'interesting' doubt about induction require him to answer our question in the negative. He would have to say something like this: 'Our *expectation* that the man's body will move in a downward direction will be even stronger than it is now. However, without invoking a non-empirical principle, we shall not *really* be in a better position than the chicken. We should still fail to possess a *reason*.'

As in the case of the man who refused to say that Brown, Black, and White were doctors, our natural response to all this will be to turn to Russell and say: What do you mean by 'being in a better position'? What on earth do you mean by 'a reason'? And, furthermore, why should anybody be interested in a reason in your sense of the word?

Russell's remarks about the need for a general principle like his principle of induction to serve as major premiss in every inductive argument make it clear what he means by a reason: like the Rationalists and Hume (in most places), he means by 'reason' a *logically conclusive* reason and by 'evidence' *deductively conclusive* evidence. When 'reason' is used in this sense, it must be admitted that past observations can never by themselves be a reason for any prediction whatsoever. But 'reason' is not used in this sense when, in science or in ordinary life, people claim to have a reason for a prediction.

So far as I can see, there are three different trends in the ordinary usage of 'reason for an inductive conclusion' and according to none of them does the word mean 'logically conclusive reason'. Among the three trends one is much more prominent than the others. It may fitly be called the main sense of the word. According to this main sense, what we mean when we claim that we have a reason for a prediction is that the past observations of this phenomenon or of analogical phenomena are of a certain kind: they are exclusively or predominantly positive, the number of the positive observations is at least fairly large, and they come from extensively varied sets of circumstances. This is, of course, a very crude formulation. But for the purposes of this article it is, I think, sufficient.[6]

Next, there is a number of trends according to which we mean very much less than this. Occasionally, for instance, we simply mean that it is *reasonable* to infer the inductive conclusion. And clearly it may be reasonable to infer an inductive conclusion for which we have no reason in the main sense. Thus let us suppose I know that Parker will meet Schroeder in a game in the near future and that it is imperative for me not to suspend my judgement but to come to a conclusion as to who will win. Supposing I know nothing about their present form and nothing also about the type of court on which the match is to be played. All I know is that Parker and Schroeder have in the previous two seasons met six times, Parker scoring four victories to Schroeder's two. In these circumstances it would be reasonable for me to predict that Parker will win and unreasonable to predict that Schroeder will win. Clearly, however, in the main sense of the word I have no reason for either prediction.

Again there is a trend according to which any positive instance of a phenomenon is *a* reason for concluding that the next instance of the phenomenon will be positive. Thus in the circumstances described in the preceding paragraph, it would be quite proper to say we have *more reason* for supposing that Parker will win than for predicting Schroeder's victory. It would be quite proper also to say that we have *some*

---

[6] I have so far left out one important element in the main sense of 'reason for an inductive conclusion'. I shall come to that in Section IV. In the meantime this omission will not affect any of my points.

reason for supposing that Schroeder will win. It would be proper to say this even if Schroeder had won only one of the six matches. To all these and similar trends in the ordinary usage of 'reason for an inductive conclusion' I shall from now on refer as the second ordinary sense of the word.

There can be no doubt that in both these ordinary senses of the word, we frequently have a reason for an inductive conclusion. In these senses we have an excellent reason for supposing that the man jumping out of the Empire State Building will move in the direction of the street, that the sun will rise to-morrow and that Stalin will die before the year 2000. The answer to question (1) is therefore a firm and clear 'Yes': in many domains we have a multitude of exclusively positive instances coming from extensively different circumstances.

The same is true if 'reason' is used in the third ordinary sense. However, I propose to reserve our discussion of that sense for Section v below. For the time being it will be convenient and, I think, not at all misleading to speak as if what I have called the main sense is the *only* ordinary sense of 'reason for an inductive conclusion'.

It should now be clear that, when Russell says that observed instances are never by themselves a reason for an inductive conclusion, he is guilty of an *ignoratio elenchi* by redefinition. His assertion that the premises of an inductive argument never by themselves constitute a *logically conclusive* reason for an inductive conclusion in no way contradicts the common-sense assertion that they frequently constitute a reason *in the ordinary sense of the word*. Russell's definition of 'reason' is indeed in one respect not a redefinition since in certain contexts we do use 'reason' to mean 'deductively conclusive reason'. However, it is a redefinition in that we never in ordinary life use 'reason' in Russell's sense when we are talking about inductive arguments.

Moreover, if 'reason' means 'deductively conclusive reason', Russell's questions are no more genuinely questions than e.g. the sentence 'Is a father a female parent?' For, since part of the definition of 'inductive inference' is inference from something observed to something unobserved, it is a *contradiction* to say that an inference is both inductive and at the same time in the same respect deductively conclusive. Russell's 'interesting' doubt, then, is no more sensible or interesting than the 'doubt' whether we shall ever see something invisible or find an object which is a father and also female or an object which is a man but not a human being.

In a similar fashion, Russell's remarks about the future future which we quoted in Section 1B constitute an *ignoratio elenchi* by redefinition.[7] If the word 'future' is used in its ordinary sense in the statement 'the future will resemble the past and the present in certain respects' then we have plenty of evidence to support it. For in the ordinary sense of the word, 'future' simply means 'period which has to the past and the present the relation of happening after it'. In its ordinary sense, 'future' does *not* mean 'period which has to the past and the present the relation of happening after it *and* which can never itself be experienced *as a present*'. The period which is referred to by 'future' in its ordinary sense may very well one day be experienced as a present.

In the ordinary sense of the word 'future' therefore, what Russell calls past futures *are* futures. They are futures in relation to certain other periods which preceded them. Now, the appeal to the fact that past futures resembled past pasts and past presents constitutes excellent inductive evidence for the conclusion that the future will resemble the past and the present. Stated fully, the argument is as follows: a period which has to the past and present the relation of happening after it will resemble the past and the present in certain respects because in the past periods which stood in the same temporal relation to other periods were found to resemble those periods in these respects.

It should be emphasized that in the conclusion of this argument 'future' means 'future future', as that phrase would normally be understood. It refers to a period which by the time at which the statement is made has not yet been experienced, i.e. has not yet become a present or a past.

The appeal to the resemblance between past futures and

[7] The paragraphs which follow are a summary in my own words of the main point of F. L. Will's delightful article 'Will the Future be like the Past?' (*Mind*, 1947, reprinted below, Second Series, Ch. II).

past pasts and presents is not to the point only if in the sentence 'the future will resemble the past and the present' the word 'future' means 'period which has to the present the relation of occurring after it *and* which can never be experienced as a present'. In that case, of course, past futures are not really futures. For, when they were experienced they were experienced as presents. However, anybody who in ordinary life or in science says or implies that the future will resemble the past and the present does not use 'future' in this sense. He means to assert something about a future which may one day be experienced as a present.

B. If Russell had answered in the affirmative any of the three questions which we imagined ourselves to be addressing to him, his question (1) would be a genuine question in the sense that it could then not be disposed of by an examination of definitions alone. But even then Russell would have been guilty of *ignoratio elenchi* by high redefinition. For in order to have a reason, in the ordinary sense of the word, for inferring that the next instance of a certain phenomenon is positive it is not necessary to observe all the positive and negative necessary conditions for the occurrence of this instance. Nor is it necessary that the collection of positive observed instances should be larger or taken from more extensively different circumstances than many we actually have. Nor, finally, is it necessary that breakdowns should never have occurred in *any* domain. All that is necessary in this connection is that there should have been no breakdowns in the same domain. Or, if any did occur in the same domain they must have proved capable of correlation with certain special features which are known not to be present in the subject of the prediction.

Anybody who takes the trouble to observe the ordinary usage of the word 'reason' in connection with inductive arguments can easily check up on these claims.

It may be interesting to return for a moment to the case of the chicken which finally had its neck wrung. If we had explored every corner of the universe with wonderfully fine instruments and failed to discover a Controller of human movements, then in any ordinary sense of 'being in a better position' we should undoubtedly be in a better position in the case of the man jumping out of the Empire State Building than the chicken in regard to its meals. If Russell even then denied that we are in a better position he is surely using the phrase 'being in a better position' in a strange sense. Or else he is asserting a very plain falsehood. For to say that possession of one set of observed facts, say P, puts one in a better position with regard to a certain inductive conclusion, say c, than possession of another set of observed facts, say Q, simply means that P is a reason for c while Q is not, or that P is a better reason than Q.

Moreover, even without having explored every corner of the universe, we *are* in a very much better position in the case of predicting the sun's rising or the movement of a man jumping from the Empire State Building than the chicken is regarding its meals. The truth is that Russell's analogy, although it is not wholly pointless, is very weak indeed. Its only merit consists in bringing out the fact that neither we nor the chicken have explored every corner of the universe. On the other hand, there are two important differences which Russell obscures when he says that even in the case of our most trusted scientific theories we may be in no better a position than the chicken. Firstly, the number of observed instances supporting our prediction in a case like the man's jumping from the Empire State Building is obviously much greater than the number of positive instances observed by the chicken. And secondly, although we cannot definitely say that there is nowhere a Controller of human motions, we certainly have no reason whatsoever to suppose that one exists. We have no reason whatsoever to suppose that a living individual, in any ordinary sense of 'control', controls the movements of human beings who jump out of a house. The chicken, on the other hand, if it knows anything, knows that it depends for its meals on another living object.

C. Let us now turn to question (2): Is there any number, n, of observed positive instances of a phenomenon which affords evidence that the $n + 1$st instance will also be positive? I have already mentioned the familiar fact that scientists as well as ordinary people of a certain level of intelligence do not rely for their inductive conclusions on the number of observed positive instances exclusively. However, it will be easier to discuss the question before us if we proceed on the assumption that according to common-sense the strength of past experience as evidence depends on the number of observed positive instances and on nothing else. All important points can be made more easily if we proceed on this assumption.

Now, in two senses the answer to question (2) must be admitted to be a clear 'No'. Firstly, even if there were in every domain or in some domains a number of observed positive instances which constitutes the dividing line between evidence and non-evidence or, as it is more commonly expressed, between sufficient and insufficient evidence, there is no reason whatsoever to suppose that the number would be the same for different domains. There is no reason to suppose that in the domain of animal learning, for example, the number is the same as in the domain of the movements of the heavenly bodies. But, secondly, there is no such number in *any* domain. For we are here clearly faced with a case of what is sometimes called 'continuous variation'. There is no more *a* number dividing sufficient from insufficient evidence than there is a number dividing bald people from those who are not bald or poor people from people who are not poor.

These facts, however, imply nothing against common-sense. For, from the fact that there is no rigid division between sufficient and insufficient evidence it does not follow that there are no cases of sufficient evidence. From the fact that there is no number which constitutes the borderline between adequate collections of positive instances and those which are not adequate it does not follow that no number of positive instances is adequate. Although we cannot point to a number which divides bald people from people who are not bald, we can without any hesitation say that a man without a single hair on his head is bald while one with a million hairs on his head is not bald.

Furthermore, just as we can say about many people that they are bald and about many others that they are not bald although we have not counted the number of hairs on their heads and just as we can say that Rockefeller is rich although we cannot even approximately say what is the dollar-equiva-

lent of his total possessions, so we can very often say *that* a
number of observed instances constitutes sufficient evidence
although we cannot say *what* this number is. The number of
instances supporting the theory of gravitation which human
beings have observed is for example more than sufficient
evidence—in any ordinary sense of the word—for supposing
that the man jumping out of the Empire State Building will
move in a downward direction. But nobody knows what this
number is. Human beings simply do not bother to keep records of all instances which confirm the law of gravity.

IV

A few words must now be said about the claim, made by
Russell, Ewing and others, that empiricism cannot provide a
justification of induction since any inductive or empirical
justification of induction would necessarily beg the question.
If the principle of induction 'is not true', to use Russell's
words, 'every attempt to arrive at general scientific laws from
particular observations is fallacious, and Hume's scepticism
is inescapable for an empiricist'. But 'the principle itself
cannot, without circularity, be inferred from observed uniformities, since it is required to justify any such inference'
(*History of Western Philosophy*, p. 699).

In the light of our remarks about redefinitions it is easy to
see that all claims of this nature are either mistaken or else
cases of *ignoratio elenchi* by redefinition. Before showing this,
it will be well to restate the principle of induction in a form
which is less confusing than that which Russell uses. Let us
try the following formulation:

'The greater the number of positive instances of a phenomenon which have been observed, assuming that no or
none except easily explicable negative instances have been
found, *and* the greater the number of kinds from which the
positive instances are drawn, the less often does it happen
that a new instance of the phenomenon turns out to be
negative.'[8]

I admit that this statement is rather vague and I also ad-

[8] Cf. Ernest Nagel, *Principles of the Theory of Probability*, p. 72.

mit that, unless one qualifies it so as to deprive it of all factual significance, one can find exceptions to it.

At the same time, it seems plain that the principle as here stated is very much closer to the truth than its contrary. Furthermore, whether or not it would be correct to regard the inductive principle as a *premiss* of all inductive arguments, it does seem to me part of the *reason* for every inductive conclusion. I mean by this that we would not apply 'reason' to a large number of positive and widely varied instances if the contrary of the inductive principle were true or nearer the truth than the inductive principle. Supposing, for example, it had been found in all domains that after 10,000 instances had been observed, all of them positive and gathered from very varied circumstances, chaos was found among the rest. After the 10,000th instance, in other words, predictions always became thoroughly unreliable. Supposing that in these circumstances we discover a new species of animal—let us call them grats. We want to find how long it takes the grats to solve a certain puzzle and find that all our first 10,000 subjects can solve it in less than an hour. Would we say, knowing what happened in all the many observed domains after the 10,000th instance, we had a reason for supposing that the 10,001st grat would also solve the puzzle in less than an hour? It seems clear that most of us would refuse to say this.

It is now apparent that my analysis in Section III of the main sense and also of the second ordinary sense of 'reason for an inductive conclusion' was incomplete. It will be sufficient here to indicate how my analysis requires to be supplemented in the case of the main sense. To say that p is a reason for an inductive conclusion, in the main sense of 'reason', is to say firstly that part of p asserts what I earlier claimed the whole of p to assert *and* secondly that the rest of p asserts the inductive principle. Part of p asserts the inductive principle at least in the sense of asserting that it is much closer the truth than its contrary.

Miss Ambrose, in her splendid article on induction, has tried to meet the charge of *petitio principii* by contending that the principle of induction is not a premiss of inductive arguments, but a principle of inference or substitution *ac-*

cording to which 'inductive inferences are made'.[9] But this seems to me an inadequate reply to the charge. For the enemies of common-sense might admit that what Miss Ambrose says is true of the principle as Russell is in the habit of formulating it. But they might then proceed to restate it in some such way as I have done, maintaining that in this sense it does form part of the reason for every inductive conclusion. At this stage they would undoubtedly renew their charge that the inductive argument cannot be supported by an inductive argument without begging the question.

And I want to show now that my admission that the inductive principle is part of the reason for every inductive conclusion implies nothing against common-sense or against empiricism. For this purpose it is necessary to distinguish two possible senses of any statement of the form 'All S are P'. Such a statement may either mean 'All *observed* S are P'; or it may mean 'All S *whatsoever* are P'. I propose to refer to statements of the first class as 'universal premisses' and to statements of the second class as 'universal conclusions'. Now, the charge of *petitio principii* could be sustained only if the inductive principle were meant as a universal *conclusion* when forming part of the evidence of inductive conclusions. But it is clear that when it forms part of the evidence of inductive conclusions, the inductive principle is or requires to be meant only as a universal *premiss*. We would refuse to regard a large collection of exclusively positive and widely varied instances of a phenomenon as a good reason for predicting that the next instance will also be positive if in all or most previous cases large collections of exclusively positive and widely varied instances turned out to be a thoroughly unreliable basis for prediction. However, given a large collection of exclusively positive and widely varied instances of a phenomenon, it would be sufficient for a correct application of 'reason' that in all or most *observed* cases large collections of exclusively positive and widely varied instances turned out

[9] 'The Problem of Justifying Inductive Inference', *Journal of Philosophy*, 1947, pp. 260 ff. Miss Ambrose's point is not actually made in order to answer the charge of *petitio principii*. However, if what she says were true of all possible forms of the inductive principle, the charge would have been implicitly disposed of.

to be a reliable basis for prediction. Any opinion to the contrary rests on the belief, exploded in the previous section, that according to ordinary usage 'reason for an inductive conclusion' means 'deductively conclusive reason for the inductive conclusion'.

V

I can well imagine that some people will not be moved by what I have said. Even if Russell himself were convinced, there are undoubtedly other philosophers who would take me to task for evading what they would declare to be the real issue. 'You may have shown,' it would be said, 'that in the ordinary sense of "reason" and "evidence" past observations do often constitute a good reason and sufficient evidence. But how do you know that what is a reason in the ordinary sense is *really a reason*? The fact that the sun has risen every day so far is admittedly a reason, in the ordinary sense, for supposing that it will again rise to-morrow. For to say this is simply to say that it has always risen in the past. But *can you predict* that the sun will again rise to-morrow simply because it has always risen in the past? The question, the interesting doubt about induction in this instance is not: Have we any reason in the ordinary sense for supposing that the sun will rise to-morrow? To this, we agree, the answer is 'Yes'. The real question is: Having a reason, in the ordinary sense, for believing that the sun will rise to-morrow, can we infer from this with any reliability that the sun will again rise to-morrow?

Before I take up this objection I should like to fill in a gap in my analysis of the ordinary usage of the phrase 'reason for an inductive conclusion'. It will be remembered that in Section III I distinguished between three trends in the ordinary usage of this phrase. Firstly there is what I called the main sense of the word; secondly there is a set of trends which I grouped together as the second sense of the word; and finally there is a trend or sense to which I alluded but which I have so far not attempted to analyse. According to both senses I analysed, '*p* constitutes a reason for *c*' (where *c* stands for some inductive conclusion) asserts the existence of *observed* events exclusively. Its truth need not at all be affected by the discovery that *c* is false.

Now, the third sense which I have not yet analysed is much less prominent than the main sense but, so far as I can see, much more prominent than the trends which I have grouped together as the second sense. When 'reason' is used in this third sense the observed facts referred to by 'reason' in the main sense are part of its referent, but they are not the whole of it. It is not indeed a necessary condition for the application of 'reason' (in this sense) to a set of propositions, say *p*, that the prediction based on *p* be *true*. But, where the prediction refers to a multitude of events, it is a necessary condition that it be considerably nearer the truth than its contrary. Where the prediction explicitly refers to a single event only, it is a necessary condition that a considerable majority of instantial predictions having the same relation to *p* be true. Thus, according to the third sense, we would have had a reason for believing that the man jumping out of the Empire State Building will move in a downward direction although subsequent observation shows him to move into the sky—provided that in most other cases, as yet unobserved at the time of making our prediction, human bodies did in similar circumstances move downwards. With our large collection of exclusively positive and widely varied past instances, we would have had a reason for believing that all men who will jump out of houses are going to move in a downward direction even if a few of them disappeared in the sky so long as *most* of them moved as we predicted. We would have had no reason in this third sense if in the case of a large proportion of subsequent jumps—approaching half the total number of new jumps—bodies failed to move in a downward direction.

It will be helpful to use different signs to distinguish between a reason in the main and a reason in the third sense. Let us use the sign 'reason *m*' to stand for reasons in the main sense and the sign 'reason *f*' to signify reasons in the third sense. Using this terminology, we may restate the objection outlined at the beginning of the present section as follows: 'You have shown that frequently people have reasons *m* for believing in inductive conclusions. However, the real question is whether, without appealing to a non-empirical principle, they ever have reasons f; and this you have not shown'. I could have stated this charge more easily by using the words 'probable' and 'certain'. But, as I explained earlier, an explicit discussion of the questions 'Are any inductive conclusions probable?' and 'Are any inductive conclusions certain?' is beyond my scope.

In reply to this charge, I wish to make two comments. The first of these is as follows: it simply is a fact that, given certain sets of observations, human beings can make true predictions. It simply is a fact that given reasons in the sense of reason m we very often also have reasons in the sense of reason f. This is a fact just as it is a fact that human beings can make genuine observations and just as it is a fact that certain objects have certain spatial relations to one another and that some events happen after other events. It is logically and also I think factually possible to have feelings of doubt and anxiety concerning the outcome of any prediction whatsoever. But it is also possible to have such doubts about the genuineness of observations at the present moment and about the reality of spatial and temporal relations. The possibility or the actual existence of such feelings no more implies that human beings cannot in certain circumstances make true predictions than it implies that they never make genuine observations or that there are no real relations in space and time.

Secondly, it seems to me that a person who has all the information which ordinary mortals have but who nevertheless asks, with an air of infinite puzzlement 'How can we now predict something which is not yet?' is tacitly confusing the statement 'c is true' with the statement 'c has been or is being directly verified'.[10] 'c can now be correctly predicted' does indeed imply 'c is true', but it does not imply 'c has been directly verified'. To say that we have a reason f for c does imply that c is at least probable. It does not imply that c has already been directly tested. Now, if 'correctly predict' is used in any ordinary sense, then the question 'How can we now predict an event which is not yet?' produces no cramps and can easily be answered by referring to the truth of past

[10] This distinction is brought out very lucidly by Sidney Hook in his *John Dewey*, p. 79.

predictions in certain circumstances. Questions like 'How can we now predict something which is not yet?' give rise to headaches only if '*c* can now be correctly predicted' is used in such a way as to imply '*c* has been directly verified'. Sentences like this then produce cramps and headaches because they are not really questions at all. They are like rhetorical questions. The sentence 'How can we now predict something which is not yet?' is then another way of *asserting the necessary* proposition that in the high sense of 'predict' in which '*c* can now be correctly predicted' implies '*c* has been directly verified', it is impossible ever to predict a future event. But this, of course, does not at all contradict the common-sense view that in the ordinary sense of 'predict' we can frequently predict future events. This objection, too, is therefore an *ignoratio elenchi* by redefinition.

To be more precise: the sentence 'How can we now predict something which is not yet?' produces a cramp if one believes oneself to be asking the (easy) question which the sentence expresses with every word in it used in its ordinary sense when one is in fact *asserting* the necessary proposition that in a certain high sense of 'predict' we can never predict anything at all.

Following Moore, Mr. J. N. Findlay has forcibly drawn attention to the queerness of the philosopher's doubt when he utters sentences like 'But how can any one set of facts furnish a valid basis for an inference concerning another set of facts?'[11] 'How do you know that one thing ever happens after another?' or 'How do you know that one thing is ever to the left of another?' Findlay suggests that we take a specific instance—e.g. what we would normally describe as a pencil lying to the left of a pen—, point it out to the doubting philosopher, and say 'This is how'.[12] In the case of predictions we could take a piece of chalk and call out 'I now predict that when I release this piece of chalk it will move in a downward direction'. We would then release it, and, as it

11 Williams, 'Induction and the Future', *Mind*, 1948, p. 227.
12 'Time: A Treatment of Some Puzzles', *Australasian Journal of Psychology and Philosophy*, 1941, p. 217 (reprinted as Chapter III above); cf. also Friedrich Waismann's introduction to Schlick's *Gesammelte Aufsätze*, pp. xxi ff.

falls in a downward direction, we would point to it and say
'This is how we can know in advance'. Since the philosopher
is just as familiar with these facts as we are and since he does
not, in one important sense at least, query any of them, it is
apparent that, without realizing it, he is using one or more of
his words in a strange sense.

V

The Philosopher's Use of Analogy

MARGARET MACDONALD

Views about the nature of philosophy and philosophical
method do not appear to permit of demonstration. As Mill
said of a similar topic, 'it is possible only to give considerations capable of determining the intellect either to give or
withhold its consent to the doctrine'. The method of science
is justified in practice. The scientist shows that he has the
correct method for discovering new facts by indisputably
presenting more and more of them. No one would dispute
that we know more about physics, chemistry, and psychology
than we did a hundred years ago. The philosopher has no
such means of conviction. For one of the points at issue is
whether he discovers any facts at all. He may recommend a
philosophical method, but whether he convinces will depend
as much on his audience and the general climate of opinion
as on his own reasoning. For there seems to be no accepted
criterion of when a philosophical question has been answered
and what satisfies one generation, it seems, does not satisfy
another. But everyone who was not satisfied that the problem
of combustion had, in essentials, been settled by Lavoisier
would rightly be considered incompetent or irrational. We
are not even sure whether this is because philosophical questions are more difficult than scientific questions or because

they are not questions at all. Certainly, we have not decided what sort of questions they are. I wish to invite, or strengthen, your consent to the view that philosophical propositions are not factual but verbal. That is itself a bald and misleading statement. I shall try to recommend it with the help of an example. Philosophical questions, it is suggested, arise from certain apparent peculiarities of ordinary statements. E.g., 'This is red' and 'That is red', yet they are not two colours but 'the same colour' (problem of universals); 'We have both got toothache but I can only feel my own' (problem of solipsism); 'That is a mirage though it looks exactly like an oasis' (problem of the existence of physical objects),[1] etc. We certainly understand these propositions and use them in ordinary conversation without any difficulty. Yet to the philosopher they appear queer and inconsistent. But, obviously, not in the sense in which 'He has gone out but is still at home' is inconsistent, for everyone would immediately agree that this was so. It is when, as we say, we reflect on statements of the first kind that they seem peculiar and puzzling. When we consider some of their implications and compare them with those of other statements. We consider, e.g., that two red flags may be in different places at the same time but that it would be nonsense to say of either of them that it could be in the same place and equal nonsense to say of their colour that it could not characterize at the same time many different objects in different places. 'What a peculiar thing a colour is', says the philosopher. 'How does it manage to multiply itself in a way impossible to coloured objects?' 'Perhaps it is like the day which is everywhere at once, or a very ethereal vapour which pervades visual space and becomes perceptible in different parts of it', etc. The same sort of remarks are made about the other statements. 'How queer that what we perceive now is exactly like what we have perceived when dreaming or deluded. Perhaps we are always deluded though some dreams and hallucinations last longer and are more coherent than others', etc. In making such remarks, what has the philosopher said? Does he make them as the result of a

[1] I wish only to suggest that these are of the type of statement which (among others) have caused these problems.

more profound study of the nature of colours and physical objects or has he analysed facts about them more carefully than the ordinary man? Has he discovered, e.g. a number of objects called *universals* with peculiar characteristics, signified by our use of general terms, of whose existence we were previously ignorant? Or has he (as the Nominalists supposed) discovered that since there *cannot* be general objects our use of general terms *must* refer only to groups of objects resembling each other? Is it his superior knowledge of human perceptions which makes him insist that since we *may* always be dreaming, drunk, or deluded whenever we perceive—however much we may protest on many particular occasions that we are not—we are for ever prevented from knowing whether physical objects exist? In other words, does he give us reason to believe that we always use ordinary language *wrongly*, or that all ordinary propositions are false, and, if so, what does he mean? Many philosophers have, I think, supposed that ordinary language is very inexact and misleading; that it needs to be refined, or a new, improved symbolism substituted for the purposes of philosophy. A symbolism which would express more accurately certain facts about the situations in which ordinary language is used and which that language either fails to express or expresses very loosely and vaguely. But this new and perfect language has never been achieved although the sciences bristle with technical terms for the expression of their discoveries. For a non-verbalist this ought to be somewhat surprising. But it would be a necessary consequence if the philosopher's puzzles which were generated by the known uses of words are capable only of a verbal solution. If philosophical questions, i.e. are never answered by producing more empirical facts but either by misusing words or by examining their already known, correct usage. The informative air, the plausibility and the paradoxes of most philosophical theories may not be due to any astonishing information acquired by the philosopher but to a curious practice of using words by analogy without giving the analogy any intelligible application. Philosophical theories which claim to state facts in much the same sense as physical theories will be found, I suggest, to appeal for evidence not to experience but to 'what we say' in certain relevant circumstances. They depend for their understanding, as scientific theories do not, *entirely* upon the known uses of ordinary words. They do not extend the use of these words but generally only misuse them. It is for this reason that such philosophical propositions have been called senseless. They try to operate with ordinary words when they have deprived them of their ordinary functions. They recombine known words in an unfamiliar way while trading on their familiar meanings. But these analogies lead to hopeless difficulties and so it seems that philosophical problems are never solved at all. Nor could they be solved, or even tackled satisfactorily, while the verbal character of both questions and answers was realized only half, or not at all. But if it is realized and is correct, then the only help we can get in tackling philosophical problems is from understanding the uses of words and their use and misuse by philosophers. But this conclusion certainly disgusts many philosophers. To be concerned 'merely with words' seems trivial and unimportant. Surely philosophy is not a branch of philology or grammar! Certainly it is not. Philology is an empirical science. Philologists formulate laws, e.g. Grimm's Law, from which they predict future forms of speech, etc. This is not philosophy. Nor does the philologist consider sentences of the form 'S is P' to elucidate the problem of substance. For the philologist or grammarian 'Substance is causa sui' is as good a grammatical sentence as 'St. Paul's is large', but for the philosopher they are very different. Yet it does not follow that philosophy is concerned with 'something more' than the uses of words. It is concerned with them differently and for a different purpose. Or rather, when it is said that philosophers study not words but *facts* it must be asked in what sense the word 'fact' is being used. In one of the commonest uses of 'fact' the empirical sciences state matters of fact. Consider therefore the difference between the introduction of a word like 'chromosome' and that of a phrase like 'sense-datum'. The first could not be completely defined, its use could not be wholly given, by other terms already in use. It could not be, we should say, because the biologists first gave a use to 'chromosome' by discovering chromosomes. But the philosophers did not similarly define 'sense-datum' as the result of discovering sense-data. They did not because 'sense datum' can be understood only in terms of words already used in describing what we perceive, viz., words and phrases like 'seeing', 'looking', 'looking as if', etc. As Mr. Paul and Professor Murphy have pointed out,[2] 'I am seeing an elliptical sense-datum of a penny' or 'I am seeing a tree-like sense-datum although there is no tree there' are, or can be considered as, only more misleading ways of saying 'That penny looks elliptical' or 'It looks as if there is a tree there but there isn't' and do not represent the discovery by the philosopher of an element in the perceptual situation as the use of the word 'chromosome' represents the discovery of a genetical element by the biologist. Again, consider the difference between what Lavoisier was doing when he discovered oxygen and the nature of combustion and when he reformulated the chemical vocabulary. The second involved defining new chemical terms and redefining old ones. It was wholly concerned with the uses of words and so far resembled philosophical activity. But it resulted from the first activity of empirical discovery which was not verbal. There is, I suggest, no such distinction in the activities of philosophers. Scientists use words to state facts. They do not consider, except in special circumstances, their uses. Philosophers use words entirely in order to make propositions about their uses however much their propositions seem to resemble scientific statements of fact. This is shown by the kind of assertions made and the reasons with which they are supported. The philosophers who dispute about universals, e.g., have not discovered that *red* or *redness* is or is not 'something more' than its instances. They have not discovered this in the sense in which Stalin is 'something more' than the whole collection of his photographs or 'Mrs. Harris' was 'nothing more' than the frequent references and descriptions of Mrs. Gamp. For if they had there would no longer be a dispute. But the Nominalist says: 'A universal cannot be something over and above its instances for (1) we use general

[2] Cf. 'Is There a Problem about Sense-data?' by G. A. Paul (*Proceedings of the Aristotelian Society*, Supp. Vol. XV, p. 61 *et seq.*), reprinted as Chapter VI, below.

'Two Versions of Critical Philosophy', by A. E. Murphy (*Proceedings of the Aristotelian Society*, 1937–38, p. 143 *et seq.*).

terms when we have been acquainted with instances of their application and (2) we commonly use the word "object" for something having unique spatio-temporal position and this is just how we do not use general terms. General terms, therefore, refer to classes of resembling instances.' The Realist asserts: 'A universal cannot be identical with the class of its instances for a universal term may be significant when it has no instances. If everything green disappeared "Leaves are green" would still be significant though false and though we might still "think of" green we should not be having green thoughts. Moreover, some univcrsals, e.g. *perfection,* may never have had instances and yet we can sometimes use the word "perfect" significantly. We must be referring to something. A universal must therefore be more than its instances and some universals are not even instantiated.' The dispute turns clearly on the uses of words and what must exist or not exist is deduced from these uses. And both disputants seem to be right, which would be impossible if they were in fact disputing the existence of something. For it is clearly true that we do not use general terms as we ordinarily use words for objects. They are indeed precisely those to which we oppose them. A tree is an object, a person is an object, a red patch is an object, but what is meant by saying that 'red' must name an object if it is used with none of the criteria with which the word 'object' is ordinarily used? But neither is a general term used for the class of its instances since it may have significance but no present application. The nominalist seems superficial since he stresses only part of the usage of general terms. The realist seems mystical because although he correctly emphasizes what the nominalist overlooks he combines this with a misuse of the word 'object' which causes more puzzles. Neither is content merely to describe for us the use of general terms, contrasting it with the use of words for objects, in the ordinary sense, but without offering pseudo-scientific explanations of these differences. Yet this may be the only business of the philosopher faced with the peculiar problems called philosophical.

Matter and Form

A similar account could be given of the problems of solip-sism and perceptual illusion, but I wish to take as my chief example of philosophical analogy and linguistic misusage the ancient antithesis of matter and form and especially its application by philosophers to the physical world. Material-ists have asserted and idealists denied the existence of matter or material substance. Both have assumed that the world must be made of *something*. For Thales the world was made of water; for Russell[3] events are the 'real stuff' of the world. To what questions are such peculiar statements the answer?

There seem to be three kinds of proposition which have puzzled philosophers into making such remarks. (1) Propo-sitions of the forms 'There is an x' or 'x exists', and (2) 'x has the property ϕ'. Or, in traditional language, propositions ascribing the essence of a thing, connoted by its class name, and those ascribing its accidental qualities. (3) Propositions asserting change.

The third problem is logically subsidiary to the first two, if not part of them, but since it has troubles of its own it is usually treated separately.

We say, then, 'That man is a millionaire' and 'That is a man'. A millionaire is a man having the quality of owning at least a million pounds. But whatever is a man must have certain qualities, e.g. human shape, reason, speech, etc. Even if we could not give a complete list of them which would cover all borderline cases we could say within very wide limits what they are. We can all recognize men and know how to use the word 'man'. Now 'being rich', says the philosopher, is predicated of a man. And 'man' also connotes a set of quali-ties. But of what are these predicated in the sense in which 'being rich' is, e.g., predicated of this man, viz., Lord Nuf-field? We can think of the quality of 'being rich' and imagine Lord Nuffield to be poor. We can 'abstract' the quality. We can also think of all the qualities which we generally mean by 'man'. But when we have abstracted them all, of what do

[3] Cf. *An Outline of Philosophy*, p. 291.

we think as having these qualities in the sense in which we think of Lord Nuffield as wealthy? This sounds extremely crude but I think it fairly represents what many philosophers have thought as the following highly respectable quotations may show. They could easily be multiplied.

'When all else is stripped off evidently nothing but matter remains . . . by matter I mean that which in itself is neither a particular thing nor of a certain quantity nor assigned to any of the other categories by which being is determined . . . for the predicates other than substance are predicated of substance while substance is predicated of matter.'[4]

'When I distinguish the wax from its exterior forms and when, as if I had stripped it of its vestments, I consider it quite naked . . . it is certain that nothing remains except something extended, flexible and movable . . . of which the perception is neither an act of sight, of touch, nor of imagination . . . but is simply an intuition of the mind.'[5]

This is surely a very curious proceeding. When its sensible qualities have been 'stripped' from a perceptual object nothing remains which could conceivably be perceived at all. When a man's hair is shorn he is left bald. How is he left when shorn of all qualities, we may ask. It may be objected that this is just stupid literalism. Of course, no one supposes that qualities are taken from objects as skins from an onion. They are simply abstracted, thought of apart from the objects, and that is perfectly possible. But I wish to concentrate on the metaphors for I believe they are important and have been very misleading. For the metaphor suggests and was undoubtedly intended to suggest that by abstraction an intellectual analysis of objects was performed which showed their composition in a way analogous to that in which a chemical analysis reveals their chemical composition. Thus it seemed plausible that an object should consist of perceived qualities attached to or 'informing' something logically imperceptible. For, by definition, for Aristotle, Descartes, Locke, and many other philosophers we cannot perceive the subject of all sensible qualities. We can know only that it *must* exist

4 Aristotle, *Metaphysics*, trans. Ross, 1029a, 10–20.
5 Descartes, *Meditation* 2, trans. Veitch.

as their substratum. But this analogy is an attempt to apply an ordinary use of the word 'analysis', viz., that in which a complex object, e.g. a machine, is decomposed or separated into its parts or a compound resolved into its elements. But for these operations we have sensible criteria for recognizing the whole, the process of separation and the parts when separated. It is logically impossible to apply any such criteria to the separation of matter from its qualities. The analogy, therefore, does not apply; it is not properly to be called an analogy at all and it gives a wholly wrong and misleading picture of the philosopher's problem and its solution. For when we 'abstract' red from this object we do not leave it colourless, nor when we think of all its properties do we leave it formless materia prima, intelligible extension or 'something we know not what'. To abstract qualities is to recognize that quality-words may be used in many different contexts. It is wrongly pictured as separating an element from a compound and then naming it, as if it resembled separating a gas from water and calling it oxygen. Such a picture gives the problem a pseudo-scientific air. But that it is not and does not resemble a scientific problem is shown by the admission that it would be logically impossible to verify the existence of material substance or of the abstracted qualities in the sense required and thus to apply the analogy of stripping, analysing, finding the 'base' of sensible qualities, which this language suggests. For the problem is not one of analysing objects or facts about them but of understanding the use of the subject term in certain propositions. This involves also examining the use of predicates or words for qualities. Moreover, since such propositions are used for what exists it is easy to confuse a scientific statement about what exists with a linguistic statement about the use of words for what exists, or to suppose that a proposition about what exists can be deduced from such a linguistic statement. That this is not so, again, can be seen by examining the use of the words in which such an alleged deduction is expressed. The linguistic nature of the problem was partly realized by Aristotle for he expressed it in terms of the categories. And the categories are forms of speech. True, they are, also, the clue to the nature of being, but since they appear to be the only clue, i.e.

nothing could be expressed about being except by a proposition in one of the categories, it is not clear in what sense problems about being are more than problems about the uses of the categories.

The solution is that existence propositions like 'That is a man', 'There are men', 'Men exist' are different from subject-predicate positions like 'That man is a millionaire', 'All men are gullible', and cannot be simply reduced to the subject-predicate form. It is quite clear that the category of substance does not ascribe a set of predicates to a subject other than a substance as Aristotle supposed. If we ask, 'What is called Bois Roussel and won the Derby in 1938?' the correct reply is 'a horse'. If we ask, 'What has the defining properties of a horse?' again the only sensible reply is 'a horse', not 'a piece of matter' or 'material substance'. But if we had asked, 'What horse won the Derby in 1938', the reply 'a horse' would have been absurd. Again, 'This piece of matter has the defining properties of a horse but is not itself a horse' is nonsense while 'This horse has a mane but is not itself a mane' is, I think, sensible and true. For propositions like 'This horse won the Derby', 'This man is wealthy' we have separate criteria for the use of the subject and predicate. We know how to distinguish a horse from its achievement of winning a race and a man from his possession of great wealth. But in one sense at least no such distinction is possible for existence propositions. To ascribe the defining properties of an object is to state what is correctly called by the name of that object. And whatever is correctly called, e.g. a man or a horse is just a man or a horse, not something else to which these properties are ascribed. For they are ascribed to men and horses and 'That is a man' or 'There are men' translated into the subject-predicate form would give the tautologies 'That man is a man' and 'Men are men'. Since existence propositions are never tautological it seems important to emphasize their difference from those which ascribe a predicate to a subject as well as for the reason that the denial of this difference has led philosophers to pseudo-theories of material substance. For matter is, on these views, the ultimate subject of all propositions about the physical world. But this is unintelligible. We must then recognize a difference between propositions which assert that an object of a certain sort exists and those which assert that such an object has various 'accidental' properties. Nothing is gained by denying their differences but something may be by understanding how they are significantly asserted.

This may sound platitudinous. Have we not been told by Kant and certainly by Russell of the difference in logical type between existence and subject-predicate propositions? We have certainly been told that existence is not a predicate, which is true. But I do not think we have been so clearly told how existence propositions ascribe predicates at all in the sense in which subject-predicate propositions, in the ordinary sense, do so. According to Russell,[6] 'There are men' or 'A man exists' means 'The property of being human belongs to something'[7] or 'x is human' is sometimes true, and that 'All horses neigh' means 'Whatever is equine neighs' or 'x is equine and x neighs' is always true. According to this they are similar in type though one is more complex than the other since it is a compound of two or more propositional functions. But we might be inclined to ask (assuming that 'man' here means 'man or woman, i.e. human being') what is the something that has the property of being human except a man? What is it that is equine except a horse which also neighs? That this view did lead to a more sophisticated attempt to find ultimate subjects for predicates seems to be shown by Russell's doctrine that the ultimate elements of facts are logical atoms named by logically proper names unadulterated by any description. The purified symbolism in which these objects were to be expressed does not, however, seem to have been formulated.

But although there seem to be important differences between existence propositions and those which ascribe predicates to subjects, in the ordinary sense, I do not myself profess to be able to state them adequately. I can indicate only what seem to be one or two marks of such differences. It might be said, e.g., that in order to know whether there are men we must make certain observations, viz., of human

6 *Introduction to Mathematical Philosophy*, pp. 171–2.
7 I think this is Prof. Moore's formulation.

shape and behaviour. To know whether men are tall and die we must make these plus other observations which verify 'being tall' and 'being mortal'. How then can it be said that although we observe that Mr. Chamberlain is tall and thin, we do not similarly observe that he has the property of being human, i.e. that he exists? For these seem to be similar activities. How then can they result in the assertion of two different types of proposition? The answer can be found only by considering further how we use these propositions, i.e. what else we say about them. We should say that to make human-ish observations is just the same thing as to observe that there are human beings; it is not to observe that there are objects which have the property of being human for that suggests that there are separate criteria for the use of the word 'object' in this connection. But observations of tallness and mortality would not be described as observation of the objects 'a tall man' and 'a mortal man'. For a tall man just is a man who is tall and a mortal man is one who will die. They are not different objects from men. But that men are tall and mortal does justify the assertion that certain properties belong to something, viz., mortality and exceptional height to men. Again, it would be true to say, pointing to Mr. Chamberlain, 'He (or "that man") might not have been so tall' and also 'He might not have existed' but it would, I think, be nonsense to say, 'He might not have been human'. So that in one sense 'A man exists' and 'x is human' do not mean the same since a true value for the propositional function would give a tautology while an existence proposition is never tautologous. This last statement may seem false. For we may, e.g., ask from a distance 'Is that a man or a tree?' and, on coming closer, remark, 'Yes, that is a man'. Of a monstrous birth we may decide that it is not human, etc. But we are not here doubtfully ascribing predicates to objects, as we might wonder whether a person's eyes are blue or brown; we are wondering whether they are certain objects, which is different. So that either, e.g. 'That has the property of being human' or 'x has the property of being human' simply means 'That man exists' or 'A man exists', for which it is a misleading reformulation, or it is a tautology which fails to give the meaning of an existence proposition. For it is not about the

existence of anything but about the meaning of a word, e.g.
'man'. Existence propositions do not ascribe their defining
properties to subjects and the search for such subjects by
philosophers is due to this typical confusion of propositions.
Nor does it follow that they have no subjects. Their subjects
are things which are asserted to exist.

The third class of proposition which has provoked philosophical theories of material substance is that of those asserting change. That change presupposes an unchangeable substance as its subject is asserted by many philosophers. It is
vehemently denied by others from Heraclitus to the Dialectical Materialists. Indeed, the word 'change' rouses the passions
of philosophers to a curious degree. For some change is a
shifty business to be shunned by searchers for eternal truth,
equated with logical certainty. For others it is the mysterious
source of novelty, incapable of prediction and therefore free
from the shackles of logic and reason. Both attitudes seem
absurd though it is not difficult to see the sort of propositions
which have tempted philosophers to make such remarks. But,
of course, propositions about change are not logically certain,
irrational nor non-rational. They are used with the criteria
of reasonable assertion appropriate to their type as a class of
contingent propositions, and that is all. Bergsonian eulogy
and platonic denunciation are both irrelevant.

It is clear that we frequently use in describing processes of
change the same subject in the same sense throughout. We
say, e.g., that this apple was green but has ripened and is now
red; that it has grown larger in the last six weeks; that it was
picked from that tree and placed in this bowl, etc. We should
say that it was 'the same apple' to which all these changes
occurred and we could give sensible criteria for determining
the respects in which it was the same and those in which it
had altered. In Aristotle's language, change can occur to a
substance in any of the categories except substance without
causing much philosophical trouble. The criteria may vary in
difficulty. An object which has changed its place only is more
easily recognized than one which has also changed its size,
shape, and colour, but as long as the same class name is applicable both before and after change the difficulties do not
seem insuperable or even very puzzling. I may not be sure

whether this is Smith whom I have not seen for twenty years
when he was young and is now old, but he is at least a man
of about the right age and I can find out whether he is
Smith. But we should scarcely ask of a heap of earth in the
churchyard whether it is Smith who has been dead for twenty
years. Yet Smith (or his body) dies and becomes ashes just
as he grows and becomes old. What is the surviving subject
of this change in the sense in which Smith recognizably survives all other changes which occur to him? How do we describe change of substance or the transformation of one object into another? A favourite answer of philosophers has
been: ' "X changes into Y" means "There is something called
'matter' or 'material substance' which at time t has or is informed by x qualities and at t^1 (later than t) has or is informed by y qualities. Matter itself does not change, neither
do the qualities, but change consists in the qualitative re-
shaping or re-forming of matter into different objects at
different times. Just as "this apple" is the subject when we
say "This apple was green and is now red and it is 'the same
apple' though it now has a different colour", so "matter" is
the subject when we say "The water that was in this bowl has
been changed into two gases" because this means "A certain
portion of matter had the qualities of water and now has
those of oxygen and hydrogen and it is the same piece of
matter although all its qualities are different".' But is this
suggested translation a proposition which we should ever
ordinarily assert and, if not, what does it mean? The following quotations illustrate this view, which is common to
many philosophers:

' "Matter", in the most proper sense of the term, is to be
identified with the *substratum* which is receptive of coming-
to-be and passing-away: but the *substratum* of the remaining
kinds of change is also, in a certain sense, "matter".'[8]

'Does the same wax remain after this change? It must be
admitted that it does remain; no one doubts it or judges
otherwise. What, then, was it I knew with so much distinct-
ness in the piece of wax? . . . It was perhaps . . . only a

[8] Aristotle, *De Generatione et Corruptione*, trans. Joachim, Oxford Press, § 320a.

body that a little before appeared to me conspicuous under these forms, and which now is perceived under others.'[9]

What is the significance of the words 'matter', 'material', 'stuff', etc., which are frequently used by philosophers of very different schools?

There are a number of propositions which we ordinarily make in which we distinguish a material or stuff, what is made of it, and the design or pattern according to which it is made. An architect examines the plans or specifications of a building and decides whether to build in brick or concrete. A dress pattern is made up in silk or cotton material. We choose 'exactly the same' ornament in platinum instead of gold, etc. Moreover, the material can be made into something else of a different form. The guinea is melted down and the gold re-made into a ring; souvenirs are made of wood from a famous ship, etc. In all these homely examples the distinction between what is matter and what is form is quite clear. We make it constantly and know how it is verified. When Aristotle wants an example of the distinction this is the kind of example he constantly gives. If we wished to teach a child the distinction we should do so by such examples. We know, too, from such examples, what it means to say that the material of a thing may remain unchanged though taking a different form and so becoming a different object. If the same gold is first a coin and then a ring we could say quite sensibly that one object has become another though its material has remained the same throughout these changes. We might describe this by saying 'This gold was a coin and is now a ring'. The use of the words 'matter' and 'material substance' is intended to suggest by analogy that an 'ultimate' *something* is related to different sets of 'essential' predicates at different times as a piece of gold is related to different shapes at different times. 'Being X' and 'being Y' are successively ascribed to a piece of matter as 'being coin-shaped' and 'being ring-shaped' are successively ascribed to a piece of gold. Further, matter is 'made into' different objects by its different predicates as gold is made into different objects by giving it different shapes. This is the analogy employed by all those philoso-

[9] Descartes, *loc. cit.*, p. 91.

phers who search for the 'ultimate stuff' of the physical world
or the nature of the 'ultimate' constituents of physical objects or of facts about them. This is true whether they call
what they have claimed to discover, materia prima, extension,
events, sense data or even mental states. The picture is that
of a material made into different objects as a roll of cloth is
made into different garments. It is important to state it thus
as crudely as possible. Philosophers who extol change like to
emphasize their denial that any permanent material substance
exists. But what are they denying and what are those who
assert it, asserting? They are not surely denying that we can
sometimes say truly, e.g. 'This is the same house although
it has been re-painted'? If so, they are denying that the word
'same' is significant in ordinary usage, which is absurd. For if
'same' has no significance neither has 'change'. To say that
something has changed is to say that it is not the same as it
was and this would be nonsensical if 'being the same' had *no*
meaning. If, however, they are denying the contention of
those philosophers who assert that an unchangeable matter
or substance is the ultimate material of the world, what is
the meaning of the assertion which is being denied? Where
are the verifiable distinctions which gave 'material' and 'design' their significance in ordinary usage? Since matter or
material substance is that which receives all forms or predicates and nothing which is known can be described except
by ascribing predicates, no description or knowledge of matter is possible. It is 'pure potentiality', 'something we know
not what'. We know only that it *must* exist as the subject of
all predicates and the material of all forms. Obviously, therefore, it is logically impossible to apply any sensible criteria
whatever for the distinction of material and design. But such
criteria are part of what we *mean* by such words; they give
the words their use and philosophers who attempt to apply
them by analogy without indicating similar criteria or, indeed, any sensible criteria whatever are not using an analogy
but simply misusing these ordinary words while trading on
the association of their ordinary meanings in appearing to
give some subtle information about the world where the
conditions of such information are absent.

But neither is the philosopher *merely* gibbering. To say

that such metaphysical assertions are nonsense is true but inadequate. They are not meaningless as a string of nonsense words is meaningless simply because they are or can be translated into syntactically correct arrangements of ordinary words of which we already know the meanings. Moreover, the propositions which tempt philosophers to make these assertions are themselves, as we have seen, perfectly ordinary propositions about the characters of things and their changes. What the philosopher does is to notice certain differences in our use of ordinary words which seem to require explanation by a theory about that to which the words are said to refer. But it may be that what is required is just a description of these different uses and their criteria. If this is to be called a 'theory', very well, but it must be noticed that this is a very different use of 'theory' from that employed by science and the C.I.D. or even in ordinary life when we contrast 'theory' and 'practice'. But it is in this second sense of 'theory' that philosophical doctrines of matter claim to be theories. For their authors and many other philosophers have thought that they gave at least a plausible account of what the facts *must* be even though we could never know them more directly and even when the account implied that all ordinary propositions must be false or, at least, very inexact and misleading. But if, as suggested, these doctrines are non-significant they cannot, in this sense, be plausible or unplausible theories for they cannot be theories at all.

I hope this illustration may have helped to make clear why and in what sense philosophical propositions are linguistic and not informative in the ordinary sense. It might, perhaps, be argued that the puzzle about change is not a genuine philosophical problem. It is a scientific problem which some philosophers have tried to solve without the necessary technique or for which others, e.g. Kant, have just adopted a solution from scientific practice. To ask for the substratum of substantial change is a queer way of asking for a connection between, e.g., the liquid state of water and the gaseous states of oxygen and hydrogen into which it is decomposed. Moreover, scientists do connect these by means of other bodies, molecules, atoms, etc., which function as the substratum of change and do assert that the quantity of matter remains constant throughout all changes. The difference is, of course, that propositions about the connection and prediction of changes, the existence of molecules, atoms, etc., are verifiable empirical statements, though the criteria for 'There are molecules' may be very different from those for 'There are apples' or even for 'There are chromosomes'. Similarly, to the truth of the law of the conservation of matter a large number of propositions asserting the equality of weight between substances before and after experiment is relevant. It certainly does not assert that a fixed amount of something which could never be weighed at all is preserved as the substratum of all equality of weight. And equality of weight itself cannot sensibly be called a *substance*. The law is, in fact, a compressed hypothetical proposition about physical operations and their results. But sensible observations and physical operations, as already shown, could never provide criteria for the meaning or use of the philosophical proposition that material substance exists.

The philosopher is not asking a scientific question, for of any scientific proposition it would be possible to ask similar questions about the use of the subject term and no propositions expressing sensible evidence would obviate this difficulty. Nor does the philosopher ever seek such evidence. The question, as we have seen, is asked in terms of categories which are forms of speech or forms of judgement. Aristotle knew as well as we do that much was yet to be sensibly discovered about the laws of physical changes but no such discovery, he thought, would settle the question of the subject of the category of substance. Descartes appeals only to the fact that 'we should all judge', or say, that it was 'the same wax' which remained after melting. The investigation of physical changes is a different undertaking from the investigation of philosophical puzzles which arise from the language used to describe such changes. These puzzles may differ with different terminologies used. They may sometimes be resolved by inventing a new terminology into which the propositions which suggested them can be translated, or by describing how these propositions are actually used. What is important is to notice the difference between this activity and that of the scientific investigation of changing objects.

For this difference is all that is meant by saying that philosophy is verbal and not factual.

That different predicates at different times can be ascribed to the same subject, i.e. that things remain recognizable after many changes, is true, and examples of this have been given from ordinary usage. Nor, in spite of Plato and Bergson and their followers, does it appear to be either more difficult or less rational to know that people grow old, apples turn red, and societies change their forms of government than to know that 2 + 2 = 4. But that all change *must* be ascribed to a permanent substance as subject in this sense is false if intended to describe our ordinary usage and, if not, is a linguistic recommendation by some philosophers which may or may not be accepted. It is certainly not a contingent proposition about what *exists* as the substratum of all change. Scientists may resolve gross bodies into microscopic ones in the course of investigating change and transformation, but no proposition about such scientific objects is, I think, part of what we mean by any ordinary propositions about change such as those responsible for the philosophical puzzles we are considering. Similarly, 'water' does not *mean* 'compound of oxygen and hydrogen', for if it did no one who did not know chemistry would know what water is, but we all do know what water is. And if we did not we could not come to know its composition.

No ordinary person has any difficulty with Aristotle's substantial change for the propositions describing it are used differently from those describing other kinds of change. They are used in different circumstances and with different verification. But grammatical similarities in expression may promote philosophical questions about the use of such expressions though this use itself is habitual and easy. What, then, is the difference in use between, e.g., 'The tree planted by the Mayor is taller than it was last year' and 'The tree planted by the Mayor was struck by lightning and it is now a heap of ashes'? One difference which may be indicated is that the descriptive phrase in the first example could be replaced by 'This' together with a pointing to a particular tree, viz., 'This tree was planted by the Mayor and is taller than it was last year'. A similar translation is not possible for the second exam-

ple, although we might, e.g., point to a photograph and say
'This is the tree which the Mayor planted and it was burned
last night'. The use of 'this' is clearly different from its use
in the first example. More usually one would say 'The tree
which stood here was planted by the Mayor and, etc.', or,
pointing to the ashes, 'This is all that remains of the tree
which was planted by the Mayor, etc.' The verification of the
second example is different from and more complicated than
that of the first. It is achieved not by searching for a permanent, imperceptible substance which survives change but by
recognizing location, environment, etc. These may remain
'the same' but they are not the subject of change in the sense
in which the tree is. There is not, in the ordinary usage,
something else which survives transformation as the tree survives growth. There are only different ways of verifying propositions which assert that objects have changed. It has been
supposed that the second example must have a different
subject which is first a tree and then ashes as the tree is first
2 ft. and then 6 ft. tall. But this is not so. The tree is as
much the subject of 'The tree has been burned' as it is of
'The tree has grown', but to verify whether it has grown
we look for *it* and measure *it*. To verify whether it has been
destroyed we do not look for it nor for something else which
had its characters and now has others, but we look for a number of different circumstances which are evidence that the
tree has been destroyed. That is to say, the propositions,
including their subject terms, are used differently and may
be said to be of different logical forms. For its destruction
is ascribed to a tree in a very different sense from that in
which its size is. It seems much too simple to suppose that
propositions asserting change ascribe different predicates to
subjects at different times as different coats of paint are applied to a wall at different times.

There seem to be other propositions about change which
do not ascribe predicates to any substance. If you watch a
green after-image, shut your eyes, and open them to find it
has disappeared or to find a blue flash succeeding a red, you
will certainly observe changes but not changes which would
properly be described as occurring to any substance which
remains in other respects unchanged. There just was a change

in your experience but not a change *of* anything. That all change *must* be ascribed to a substance, therefore, seems to be false, for very often it is, but sometimes it is not.

The obvious reply to this account of philosophical propositions may be a *tu quoque*. Philosophers are condemned for using analogies and yet this method constantly employs them. If an inquirer asks 'Do philosophical propositions give information?' he is not answered with a plain 'Yes' or 'No' but referred to other examples for comparison. 'Do they give information in the sense in which this proposition (e.g. a scientific proposition) does? If not, then if you wish to say that they give information you must be careful to specify the sense in which they do and you must compare your use of "giving information" with other uses, etc.' Does not this also apply to the statement 'Philosophical propositions are verbal or about the uses of words'? I think it does and that one must be careful to show by examples how philosophical propositions differ, e.g., from grammatical propositions and the statements of philologists, and, one might add, from the utterances of poets. I indicated one such difference at the beginning of this paper. Nor is the statement that philosophical propositions are verbal to be taken as a piece of brand new information about them as the composition of water was a piece of new information for eighteenth-century chemists. But it draws attention to the fact that the criteria for the truth or falsity of philosophical propositions are the uses of language. 'What we say' in certain circumstances is explicitly appealed to in the arguments of most philosophers although they often go on to try to deduce what must be the case from what we say. Since, however, these deductions are never empirically verifiable, we can test them only by considering how the words in which they are expressed are otherwise used and what uses of the propositions from which they are said to be derived have tempted philosophers to these alleged deductions.

I do not at all wish to disparage the making of comparisons and analogies which are often very useful. But as misused by philosophers in giving pseudo-scientific explanations of ordinary propositions they are non-significant. A comparison of propositions with a view to understanding the misuse of analogy and to resolving the puzzles which have caused it seems to me harmless for it does not attempt to re-define ordinary words. Most philosophers, on the contrary, seem to have supposed that they could correct and enlarge our ordinary and technical vocabularies. If, as suggested, they make no factual discoveries, it is not clear how this improvement is to be made. Indeed, the suggestion that anyone can prove that all ordinary language is incorrect and all ordinary propositions are false seems to be nonsense unless we are told how the improved language is to be understood. Philosophers who held this view seem only to have succeeded in misusing ordinary words. Against this, it is suggested that philosophical problems can be solved by understanding how language is ordinarily used, how certain uses of it have provoked these problems and how it has been misused in many alleged solutions.

VI

Is There a Problem about Sense-data?

G. A. PAUL

[That there must be sense-data had been suggested in, for example: 'The Ultimate Constituents of Matter', 'The Relation of Sense-data to Physics' and 'Knowledge by Acquaintance and Knowledge by Description' (in Bertrand Russell, *Mysticism and Logic*), 'On our Knowledge of the External World' and 'The World of Physics and the World of Sense' (in his *Our Knowledge of the External World*), 'The Refutation of Idealism', 'The Nature and Reality of Objects of Perception', 'The Status of Sense-Data', and 'Some Judgements of Perception' (in G. E. Moore, *Philosophical Studies*), 'A Defence of Common Sense' (by Moore in *Contemporary British Philosophy*, second series, ed. Muirhead, pp. 217 ff.), 'Sense-Perception and Matter' (in C. D. Broad, *The Mind and its Place in Nature*). 'The Given' (in H. H. Price, *Perception*), and A. J. Ayer, *Language, Truth and Logic*, passim.]

The problem with which we shall be principally concerned is 'Are there such things as sense-data?' We shall go on to consider also the questions, supposing there are such things, whether they are private, whether they can exist unsensed, and whether they can continue to exist throughout a period of time or are merely momentary.

About these last problems I shall perhaps be able to say something definite, but about the first I am unable to come to any decision. The difficulty about it is not that there is a problem which we can understand and to which we are unable to find the answer; the difficulty is on the contrary to find out clearly what the problem is itself. It is the difficulty of understanding what anyone is saying who says that there *are* such things as sense-data, and is due partly to the fact that not all the words used occur in everyday speech, a new technical term 'sense-datum' having been brought into use. It is not, however, due solely to the fact that a word is being introduced which has not been used before, for there are many cases in which this is done where there is no such difficulty. For example the physiologists who wished to introduce the word 'fovea' to describe a certain peculiarity of the structure of the eye can have encountered no such difficulty. They could say that they were using 'fovea' as a name for the slight depression in the retina diametrically opposite to the pupil, and by dissecting eyes could point to instances of this depression. When they had done this no one would have any difficulty in answering the question 'Are there such things as foveas?' This is the sort of question with which, because of its linguistic similarity, we are apt to compare our question 'Are there such things as sense-data?' and in case we should be misled by this similarity we require to point out the differences which also exist between them. Once we know that 'fovea' is being used to mean 'the slight depression in the retina diametrically opposite to the pupil' we can find the answer to Qf[1] by dissecting some eyes and finding in each case whether there is an object which answers to this description. Before we even start the experiment of dissecting we

---

[1] 'Qf' = 'the question "Are there such things as foveas?"'

have some idea of what it will be like to find such a depression and of what it will be like to be unable to find such a depression or to find that there is no such depression.

On the other hand if we are to find whether there are such things as sense-data we need make no experiment, and no experiment of any kind will help us. Sense-data, if there are such things, are objects which, so far from needing to seek by making an experiment, we cannot help seeing every time we see anything at all. It is sometimes said that we have only to inspect what happens whenever we have any visual experience of any kind to become aware that on such occasions we always do see an object of the sort which is being called the 'sense-datum' sort. For example, it is said, you know what it is to look from an angle at the top surface of a penny lying flat on a table; in such a case the surface which you can see of the penny is round but you see it by means of an object which is not round but elliptical. A great difference becomes quickly obvious between this and the answer to Qf, where the point of asking whether there were such things as foveas was that you would know what it was like to discover a retina which lacked a depression opposite to the lens, whereas in this case you do not know what it would be like to be seeing anything whatever and not be perceiving an object of the sort in question. It then seems that either there was no point in asking Qs[2] (since you can have no idea what it would be like for the answer to be 'No') or that the point of asking such a question is very different from the point of asking such a question as Qf. If this is not obvious, we can try to make it so by further consideration of the situation where you look at a penny from an angle. Sometimes in such a case it is true to say 'I see the round top surface of this penny, and I see that it is round, but it looks elliptical', and what some philosophers say is that you can become aware on inspection that it is true not only that you are seeing a round object but also that you are seeing an object which is elliptical (the elliptical object being related to the round object in a certain intimate way which we have expressed by saying that the round object is seen 'by means of it').

[2] 'Qs' = 'the question "Are there such things as sense-data?"'

Some people have claimed that they are unable to find such an object, and others have claimed that they do not understand how the existence of such an object can be doubted, which drives one to ask what it would be like to be unable to find such an object and what it is like to find one. A clue is given by the fact that the claim generally made is not what would sometimes be called the 'more moderate' one that whenever we see a physical object we do in fact see a sense-datum but the 'less moderate' claim that it is logically impossible that we should see a physical object and not see a sense-datum. To call one the 'more' and the other the 'less' moderate claim is misleading, for it obscures the fact that while the 'more' moderate would be a simple empirical statement the 'less' moderate is a statement that so and so is logically impossible, i.e., in this case, a statement about the way a certain expression is to be used, viz., that 'I saw a circular penny, and I saw an elliptical object (by means of which I saw it)' is to be another way of saying 'I saw a round penny, and it looked elliptical to me'.

Is there any test which would be relevant to whether it is true that in such a case there is an object which is round and also that there is an object which is elliptical?

This brings us to the question what it means to say of a sense-datum that it is an object. To say that there are such objects as foveas is to say that in eyes there is a shallow depression opposite to the lens; to say that a fovea is an object is to say that it is a physical object or at least a depression in a physical object, that it is the sort of thing that several people can see at once, and can be pointed to by, for example, placing a probe in it. It is not in the same way clear what is meant by saying of a *sense-datum* that it is an object, for people ask about it 'is it a physical part of a physical object?', 'is it private to one percipient?', 'is it the sort of thing one can point to?' Such questions have the usual empirical look, but if we consider what facts we should consider relevant to their truth or falsity we see that they are not asking for information about 'objects' but about the uses of words, viz., 'is "observed surface" of a physical object replaceable in all sentences in which it occurs by "corresponding sense-datum"?', 'does it mean anything to say "More than one person is seeing

the same sense-datum at the same time"?', 'is there anything
which is (to be) called "pointing to a sense-datum"?' In saying that the word 'fovea' is to stand for a *thing* of a certain
sort, meaning a *physical* thing, and at the same time *pointing*
to an instance of a fovea, we say a great deal about the way
the word is to be used—in fact we say all that any physiologist
requires in order to be able to use the word successfully, i.e.,
from our pointing only to one instance of a fovea and calling
it 'fovea' he knows at once what is meant by saying ever so
many things about foveas, e.g., that there are and have been
foveas which no one ever has or will see, that a given fovea is
the same one as we examined yesterday, that it continued to
exist overnight when no one was looking at it, that the person
standing beside me is looking at the same fovea as I am, that
it is turning a deeper yellow, and so on. This is a simple thing
to point out, but it is of importance here. All that seems to
happen is that someone points to an object, and says the name
of the object, whereupon by watching the behaviour of the
object we are enabled to make all sorts of true statements
about it. Similarly it seems in telling us what sense-data are,
someone refers to a situation with which we are all familiar,
viz., seeing a penny obliquely, and says 'the elliptical object
which is related in such and such a way to the observed surface of the penny is a sense-datum.' One is thereupon inclined to behave in the way one is justified in doing when
such a thing as a fovea is pointed out to one, viz., to suppose
that one knows what is to be meant by saying of such an object that, for example, objects of the same sort have existed
which no one ever has or will see, that this object is the same
one as I saw a short time ago, that it does or does not continue
to exist when no one is looking at the penny from this angle,
that it is turning a darker brown, and so on. That is, one is
inclined to go on and talk as if one had just learned the name
of some new kind of physical object which has just been
brought to light. We know in the case of physical objects
what it means to say '*this object* has such and such properties', and when someone tries to point out to us an object of
the sort that is to be called a 'sense-datum' we go on as if we
knew in the same way what it means to say '*this object* has
such and such properties', 'this sense-datum has such and

such properties'. But in fact the case is very different: the word 'fovea' was introduced as a name for a physical object, and we know how to use it in new cases because we know in general how words for physical objects are used in English. This statement is the crux of the present paper. There are certain general criteria which ordinarily enable us to decide whether a given physical object is the same object as we saw at a given previous time, whether it is the same object even though many of its properties are different, whether it is a different object from one we saw previously although it has very much the same properties, whether it is now changing its colour and shape, and so on. This being so, we are apt to think that all we have to do is to give a name to an object and then examine this object and watch its behaviour in order to be able to make up true statements about it in which this name occurs: we forget that the name-word is being brought into use as a member of a class of words whose use in certain contexts is already given. E.g., everyone can imagine circumstances in which it would be true to say 'He opened his eyes, saw a certain fovea, closed his eyes and did not see it for five seconds, opened them again and saw *the same fovea* again', and circumstances in which it would be false to say this (e.g. if during the five seconds someone cunningly replaced the eye-dissection he had been examining by another exactly similar). On the other hand, can anyone describe or imagine circumstances in which it would be true to say 'He saw a certain sense-datum, ceased to see it for five seconds, and then saw *the same sense-datum* again'? Would it be true to say this, for example, if it were true to say 'He saw a certain penny from a certain angle, and it looked elliptical to him, he closed his eyes and did not see it for five seconds, opened them again and saw the same penny looking exactly the same to him'? The answer is that no examination of such a situation will provide us with an answer: in the one case it seems that examination of the situation in question *will* provide an answer; in the other that it will not. It seems that in one case examination of the object in question will tell us whether it continued to exist throughout a period; but that in the other it will not. In a sense it does not do so in either case; but in the case where we introduce the word 'fovea' by pointing to

one or more foveas everyone does as a matter of fact know
under what conditions it is to be true to say that this is the
same fovea as I saw five seconds ago, this fovea has been on
this table for the last half-hour although no one has been in
the room, and so on. They know this because they know
under what circumstances it is true to say such things of other
physical objects; but it is not *necessary* that the word 'fovea'
should behave like other words for physical objects. We
might, for example, say 'No fovea lasts longer than a single
specious present' meaning this not as an empirical statement
but as a statement of how the word fovea is to be used. We
might have some good reason for adopting such a way of
speaking; e.g., suppose certain minute structures in the fovea
were, we discovered, annihilated and replaced every five minutes, then we might very well say 'During the last half-hour
I have observed five foveas succeed one another here, each
differing from the last one in respect of the minute structures
(M)' or 'During the last half-hour I have observed the same
fovea, the minute structures (M) in it being replaced every
five minutes' and mean the same by these two statements.

The word 'sense-datum' as people have employed it does
not fall into a fully-prepared scheme for its usage as a word
for a physical object does, but its usage is not purely arbitrary.
By this I mean that its use is connected with the use of certain words which *are* in ordinary language, e.g. 'looks', 'appears', 'appearance', and with certain uses of 'this', 'after-
image', and 'image'. We shall now consider some uses of
such words with which it is connected, and how it is connected with them.

We so use language that whenever it is true that I am seeing the round top surface of a penny, and know that it is
round, it is true to say that the penny *looks* (e.g.) elliptical
to me, in a sense in which this does not entail that I am in
any way deceived about the real shape of the penny. (I shall
indicate this sense by means of a suffix: 'looks*'.) The rule
which has generally been adopted is that the sense-datum is
correctly said to have whatever shape and colour-property
the corresponding surface of the physical object looks* to me
to have. E.g., suppose a red light is cast upon the penny as
I view it obliquely, then if it is true that the surface which

I see is round and brown, and looks* to be elliptical and red, then according to our rule it is true to say that the corresponding sense-datum *is* elliptical and red.

Those who have in practice used the word 'sense-datum' have not spoken as if what they were doing was introducing *merely* an alternative way of saying this same thing over again, but as if this new sentence which they substitute were in some way nearer to the facts. They have the idea that in some sense when a physical object looks* red to someone then something really is red, i.e., that there really are in such cases two *objects*, one which looks* red and one which *is* red, and that somehow the one which *is* red has generally been overlooked, and its existence has now for the first time been recognized. It is said that its existence cannot be doubted, for if we carefully inspect what happens when a physical object appears red to us we shall come to realize that we can see this object, and further that, while in every such case it is academically possible to doubt whether there really is a physical object which is appearing red, it is academically impossible to doubt that there is an object which *is* red. The point is that although I may have been mistaken in supposing that there was a round surface of a penny looking* elliptical to me, yet it is quite certain that there was an elliptical appearance (and that it is logically impossible that this appearance should merely have *looked* elliptical to me). I shall only point out that another way of describing the same situation is 'I thought I was seeing a round surface of a penny, which was looking elliptical to me, but in fact there was no penny there at all.' It is then asked: 'If there was no penny there at all, what was really happening? what were the elements of the situation?' and it is answered that what I was really seeing was a sense-datum which was elliptical, but was not a sense-datum 'of' a physical object (or at least not 'of' a penny). It is an equally good answer to say 'It only seemed to me as if there was a round penny which looked* elliptical. I was really not seeing anything at all.' This says just the same as the statement which contained the word 'sense-datum', and there is no question of the one saying it less or more adequately than the other.

Sometimes people explain how they are going to use 'sense-

datum' by taking the case when I have an after-image with
my eyes closed, in which case it is quite certain that there
is no external object which is appearing, say, red. They then
say that a sense-datum is any object which is seen in the
sense in which the after-image is seen, and ask us to notice
that whenever we see a physical object we see* an object (in
this sense, which I am going to call 'see*'). It is, however,
not at all clear what this means. For it is not certain that
whenever I see a physical object I see any *other* object in any
sense of see. What is certain is that, suppose the physical
object looks* red, there is nothing to prevent me from expressing that by saying that an object which is red corresponds
to the physical object, and nothing to prevent me from saying that I see* that object. Such a notation might be convenient for certain purposes, and is unlikely to mislead, because (1) it makes no sense to say of an after-image that it
looks different from what it really is, and we are not tempted
to say such a thing of a sense-datum, and certainly have not
given any meaning to saying it of a sense-datum, and (2) it
is possible, and may sometimes happen, that what we took to
be an after-image turns out to be an appearance of a physical
object, and vice versa. This way of talking at once suggests
that there really is in such a case an object (viz., a sense-
datum) about which it is doubtful whether it is an after-
image, or an appearance (sense-datum) of a physical object.

My intention has not been to deny that there are sense-
data, if by that is meant that (1) we can understand, to
some extent at least, how people wish to use the word 'sense-
datum' who have introduced it in philosophy, and that (2)
sometimes statements of a certain form containing the word
'sense-datum' are true, e.g., 'I am seeing* an elliptical sense-
datum "of" a round penny.' Nor do I wish to deny that the
introduction of this terminology may be useful in helping
to solve some philosophical problems about perception; but
I do wish to deny that there is any sense in which this terminology is nearer to reality than any other which may be
used to express the same facts; in particular I wish to deny
that in order to give a complete and accurate account of any
perceptual situation it is necessary to use a noun in the way

in which 'sense-datum' is used,[3] for this leads to the notion that there are entities of a curious sort over and above physical objects which can 'have' sensible properties but cannot 'appear to have' sensible properties which they have not got.

We shall consider now certain puzzles to which the use of 'sense-datum' has given rise.

There is first the idea of the sense-datum as a sort of barrier, an entity which gets between us and the physical object. In trying to overcome the idea of its being a barrier people ask 'Is the corresponding sense-datum identical with the observed surface of the physical object?' An answer to this question is relevant to many questions commonly asked, viz., are sense-data mental or physical, are they private or public, do they exist only when someone is seeing* them or can they exist while no one is seeing* them, are they merely momentary or can they continue to exist throughout a time? In order to be able to answer 'Yes' to it philosophers have even been prepared to alter their use of 'sense-datum' so that it makes sense to say that such and such a sense-datum appears to have sensible qualities it does not in fact have'[4]; for if the answer were 'Yes', not only would the idea of a barrier be overcome, but also the second of each of these alternatives would be true, for we should say that what is a part of the surface of a physical object in this sense is physical, and we know what it is for more than one person to see the same part of the surface of a physical object, and for such a part to exist while no one is perceiving it, and for it to continue to exist throughout a period of time. The question whether a given sense-datum is identical with the corresponding surface has the air of being a question about two objects (or about one object) which is to be settled by inspecting the object or objects. Actually it is to be settled by examining not an object but our use of the two words 'sense-datum' and 'surface'; if we find some sentence which says something true

---

[3] I.e., there are no facts of visual experience in order to express which it is necessary to use a noun functioning in the way 'sense-datum' does.

[4] E.g. John Wisdom, *Problems of Mind and Matter*, pp. 156–7, and Ch. IX passim.

about the sense-datum such that if the sentence which results from replacing the word 'sense-datum' in that sentence
by the word 'surface' is either false or meaningless, that is
what we shall call the sense-datum and the surface being not
identical. Thus if *ex hypothesi* the corresponding surface is
really round, and the sense-datum I see of it is elliptical, to
say 'the sense-datum is round' is either false or nonsense; and
so is 'the corresponding surface is elliptical'. This is what we
call the sense-datum and the surface being not identical.
Thus it is not true to say that in this case the sense-datum is
physical if we mean by that that it is a part of the surface of
a physical object in the sense in which the corresponding part
of the surface is a part of the surface of a physical object.

It is suggested that in certain favoured cases it may yet
be true that the sense-datum is identical with the corresponding surface. E.g., suppose I am looking at the penny in such
a way that it looks* to me the same shape as it really is, i.e.,
the corresponding surface is round and the sense-datum of it
is round. We have now to try and show a further difference
between the way the two words behave, and at this point the
most useful thing to consider is that future experience might
lead us to believe that the surface in question had not been
really round, whereas this same evidence would not lead us
to doubt that it had looked* round to me, i.e., that the sense-
datum I saw of it had been round. That is, what is evidence
in such a case against the truth of 'the surface is round' is
not evidence against the truth of 'the sense-datum is round'.

It is, however, not impossible to hold that in such a case
it is the same object which is being called 'round', but that
it is being called 'round' in two different senses, and that all
that has been shown is that it is not round in one sense but
may yet be round in the other.

This urges us to try to point out further differences in
usage between the two words, and so we come to a problem
which is thorny indeed. It is suggested that, say, a minute
ago the surface, in question, of the penny was in existence
but the sense-datum was not, that it only came into existence
when I looked at the penny. If one takes one's cue for the
use of 'sense-datum' from the use of 'looks*' this is the natural
thing to say. Suppose that a minute ago the penny was in

my pocket out of sight, then it is not true that 'the penny really was round and looked* ϕ to so and so', and we incline to say that if it was not looking* ϕ to anybody then there was no sense-datum of it. We ask 'How *can* there be a sense-datum which no one is seeing?' and get the answer 'A sense-datum is an object which you see. You know that other objects which you see exist while no one is seeing them. So why should not sense-data do so likewise?' We may then say: 'Sense-data are only products, which are made by certain physical processes involved in seeing. They can have no existence apart from such processes.' To this it will perhaps be answered 'There is no reason to suppose that sense-data are manufactured by these processes. We may suppose that our sense-data exist unsensed and that all that the processes involved in seeing do is to select from among those already there.' This sort of argument arises from considering sense-data as if they were a sort of physical objects. We know what it is for physical objects, which we see, to exist during times when we are not seeing them. We often do things which we call observing that a given physical object has continued to exist unperceived throughout a given period of time; but there is nothing which we similarly call observing that a given sense-datum has continued to exist unperceived throughout a given period of time. There are certain criteria which are ordinarily used as criteria for whether a physical object has gone on existing unperceived throughout a time; but there is nothing which is a criterion of this in the case of sense-data. We may if we care introduce such criteria, i.e., we may describe what we are going to call 'observing that a sense-datum has gone on existing unperceived throughout such and such a time'; but probably we are strongly disinclined to do so, because we incline to take our use of the word 'sense-datum' from that of 'looks*', 'appears', and 'appearance'.

It does not make sense to say that a sense-datum has existed unperceived; in giving the usage of the word we have not given a use to this, but it is open to us to do so if we care.

Perhaps it will be useful here to give an example of something which similarly does not make sense, but which we require to contemplate a little before we become quite clear that it doesn't. Whether rightly or wrongly, there is attributed to the President of this session the remark: 'It is not true that I sleep *more* than other people, I only sleep *more slowly*.' It takes just a moment or two to see that sleeping is not the sort of thing that one *can* do more slowly than other people, and perhaps another moment or two to see that this means that to say that one person sleeps more slowly than another is to say something which has no meaning. The world being as it is we are not inclined to give a use to this phrase; on the other hand it is easy to describe circumstances in which we would be so inclined. Suppose, for example, that human beings were clearly divided into two kinds, those who walked and ate slowly and required a long sleep to recover from a given amount of exercise, and those who walked and ate quickly and required only a short sleep to recover from a given amount of exercise, then we should be very inclined to say that people of the first kind slept more slowly than people of the second kind.

Similarly, to say that a sense-datum has existed unperceived is to say something to which no meaning is given, but to which in certain circumstances we might be strongly inclined to give meaning. It is worth pointing out, for example, that sometimes we speak of an 'appearance' of a thing which is not an appearance to anyone. E.g., 'What a fine sunset. It must present a wonderful appearance from the top of Mochrum hill' does not imply that there is anyone there to whom it would be presented. On the other hand, we frequently use 'appearance' in a different way. E.g., suppose I look at the round surface of the penny from a certain angle, then shut my eyes or go away for five minutes, then look at it again under similar conditions from the same place, we might describe this correctly by saying that 'I saw two different appearances of it which were exactly the same in shape and colour'. We do not describe it by saying that 'I saw twice the same appearance which continued to exist during the period when I was not seeing it'. Whether we are to say that in this case I saw numerically the same sense-datum twice or that I saw two sense-data which had the same qualities is a matter of indifference, and perhaps we will never require to use 'sense-datum' in such a case and so need never make any decision on the matter. The important point is that whatever we do is not demanded by the nature of objects which we are calling 'sense-data', but that we have a choice of different notations for describing the same observations, the choice being determined only by the greater convenience of one notation, or our personal inclination, or by tossing a coin.

Whether the sense-datum in question is to be said to have existed between the times when it was observed is also, as I have tried to show, a matter for the people who wish to use the terminology to decide, should occasion arise. What is important is that whatever criteria are laid down for the existence of a sense-datum during a time when it is unobserved, to say that since these criteria are fulfilled *therefore* it is the case that there is an object exactly like a sense-datum, only that it is unobserved, is misleading. That there is such an object is not a further fact inferred from them. It is better to say that these criteria being fulfilled is what we *call* a sense-datum's existing unobserved. This is particularly important in considering theories which say that an unsensed sense-datum exists at a certain place if an observer at that place would see a sense-datum answering to the given description. We may use the fact that if an observer were to be at a given place he would see a sense-datum of a given sort as a criterion for there existing an unsensed sense-datum of that sort; but if that is all we use, the fact that an observer at that place would see such and such a sense-datum is what we *call* a sense-datum of that sort's existing at that time. This is extremely important in considering the kind of view which tries to 'mitigate the severities of phenomenalism' by saying that physical objects are groups of actual and possible (or unsensed) sense-data. The attractiveness of such a view fades when one considers what is the criterion which is being used for the existence of unsensed sense-data, and what is the relation between the criterion and the object of whose existence it is a criterion.

It is also important in considering another thing which is said, viz., that sense-data are a sort of things which only one person can ever see, i.e. that it is impossible that you should ever see my sense-data, i.e. that you should ever see a sense-

datum which I see, and vice versa. People have the idea of
sense-data as sort of private physical objects which each person keeps behind a high wall, and that although two people
never see the same sense-datum the order in which I see my
sense-data is connected in a fortunate fashion with the order
in which you see yours and other people see theirs; but it is
with a feeling of regret that people say 'content can't be communicated, only structure can', and it is with a feeling of discomfort that they contemplate the possibility that although
when an object looks to me green, I have a green sense-datum,
yet it may always be the case that when an object looks to
you green you may have a red sense-datum, and so long as
the error is systematic it is undiscoverable.

In the first place we have to consider what is meant by
saying that 'content can't be communicated'. This suggests
that there is some process which we can describe but can't do,
viz., communicate content. It suggests that the walls between
our private collections of sense-data are so high that we can't
see over, but that it is not inconceivable that we should. That,
however, is misleading. It makes us feel 'If only I could
show you my sense-datum, we could decide whether we see
the same or not'. But in fact there is nothing I can't do. I
could show you all my sense-data if the words 'showing you
a sense-datum of mine' had any meaning. To say that content can't be communicated is to say that 'one person has
communicated the content of his sense-experiences to another'
means nothing at all. To suppose otherwise is to treat sense-
data as if they were a sort of physical objects, and so to assume that it makes sense to say that two people see the same
sense-datum.

Ingenious circumstances have been described in which we
should feel urged to say that one person was having another's
sense-datum; but I do not propose to give such an example
here. I wish to consider only two things: (1) suppose I look
over your shoulder at a gas fire some feet in front of us both,
and suppose that when I move my head into the position
where yours is there is no difference in the way the fire looks*
to me, and suppose when you move your head into the place
where mine was you say that there is no difference in the
way the fire looks* to you. Now suppose that we both have

good eyes and have shown no signs of abnormal colour-vision. Then it is true that the gas fire looks* the same to both of us, and there is a sense in which it is true that it presents the same appearance to both of us; but do we see the same sense-datum of the fire? I.e., numerically the same sense-datum of it? Most people who have used the term 'sense-datum' would with little hesitation say that the sense-datum you see is not identical with the sense-datum I see. Why? Not because they see something about the nature of such objects which shows that they are not numerically the same, but simply because no meaning is given to 'two people are seeing the same sense-datum'.

(2) This raises the problem, what is meant by saying of *someone else* that he is seeing a sense-datum of a certain sort? When we think of such a thing we all think of a sort of inner vision inside the man's head directed on an object which we picture as a sort of screen, the whole thing being cut off from the outside world by a high barrier. We think that a man's behaving or not behaving in such and such ways is a symptom of some inner condition, viz., whether he has in fact such an object before his inner eye behind the barrier, and we regard this thing of which his behaviour is a symptom as something which we can never directly observe, but as something which might conceivably not exist even if his behaviour were exactly what it is. Such imagery is pointless. If this entity which he alone sees did not exist and his behaviour were no different from what it is, the world would appear to us to go on just the same, except that he would never really see things as they are, but only appear to. This shows that we have made a mistake about the use of such a phrase as 'other people see sense-data similar to mine'. The mistake is, as before, the one about the relation between the criterion for a thing's existence and the thing's existence. What we call someone else's seeing a sense-datum is his behaving in certain ways in certain situations, his reacting in certain ways to certain stimuli. A man's being colour-blind is not his having pictures of *only* certain sorts in his private collection, at whose absence we can guess more or less reliably by certain tests. His being colour-blind is his behaving in certain ways. Similarly your seeing the

same colour as I do on looking at a certain object, or seeing a different colour when we should expect to see the same, is not my having in my collection a differently coloured picture from what you have in yours, but my behaving in a certain way. We could easily mention tests which would ordinarily be taken as tests for deciding whether people have the same (i.e., exactly similar) sense-data under such and such conditions. (E.g., colour-choosing tests for colour-blindness.)

I do not deal with *the* problem about sense-data, which gives point to the introduction of the word at all. I mean 'How are sense-data related to physical objects?' I.e., how does our use of the word 'sense-datum' compare with our use of our words for physical objects? and does the use of the word 'sense-datum' help to free us from any of the difficulties we get into about our use of words for physical objects?

And I have not touched upon how our use of the word 'sense-datum' is related to our use of the word 'sensation'.

All I have done is to consider a number of questions about the way 'sense-datum' is brought into use, which it seems to me must be considered before anything is said about the larger problems it was introduced to deal with.

VII

Verifiability

FRIEDRICH WAISMANN

[This paper was originally the second part of a Symposium in which the first symposiast was Mr. (now Professor) D. M. Mac-Kinnon. It therefore naturally contained several polemical references to Professor MacKinnon's contribution. In tearing the present paper from that context in order to reprint it in this collection, we tried to remove as many of these references as possible; but unfortunately it was not practicable to remove them all without re-writing the en-

tire paper. So we must apologize to Professor MacKinnon; and remind readers that in the interests of the unity of this book he has
been denied the right to speak in his own cause.]

I

When we reflect on such a sentence as 'The meaning of a
statement is the method of its verification', we should, first
of all, be quite clear as to what we mean by the term 'method
of verification'. From a logical point of view we are not interested in the various activities that are involved in verifying
a statement. What, then, is it we have in mind when we talk
of such things? Take an example. Suppose there is a metal
ball in front of me, and I have the task of finding out whether
the ball is charged with electricity. To do that I connect the
ball with an electroscope and watch whether the gold leaves
diverge. The statement 'The gold leaves of the instrument
diverge' (*s*) describes the verification of the statement 'The
ball is charged' (*p*). Now what exactly am I doing when I
describe the verification of the statement *p*? I establish a connection between two statements by declaring that the one
(*s*) is to follow from the other (*p*). In other words, I lay
down a *rule of inference* which allows me to pass from the
statement 'The ball is charged with electricity' to another
that describes an observable situation. By doing this I connect
the statement with another one, I make it part of a system
of operations, I incorporate it into language, in short, *I determine the way it is to be used*. In this sense giving the
verification of a statement is an important part of giving its
use, or, to put it differently, explaining its verification is a
contribution to its grammar.

In everyday life we understand sentences without bother-
ing much as to the way they are verified. We understand
them because we understand the single words which occur
in them and grasp the grammatical structure of the sentence
as a whole. The question of the verification arises only when
we come across a new sort of combination of words. If, for
instance, someone were to tell us that he owned a dog that
was able to think, we should at first not quite understand

what he was talking about and would ask him some further questions. Suppose he described to us in detail the dog's behaviour in certain circumstances, then we should say 'Ah, now we understand you, that's what you call thinking'. There is no need to inquire into the verification of such sentences as 'The dog barks', 'He runs', 'He is playful', and so on, as the words are then used as we may say in their *normal* way. But when we say 'The dog thinks', we create a new context, we step outside the boundaries of common speech, and then the question arises as to what is meant by such a word series. In such cases explaining the verification is explaining the meaning, and changing the verification is changing the meaning. Obviously meaning and verification *are* connected—so why say they are not?

But when I say that the statement p is connected with the statements $s_1, s_2 \ldots s_n$ which describe evidences for it, I do *not* say that p is *identical* with $s_1, s_2 \ldots s_n$ or their conjunction.[1] To say this would only be true if $s_1, s_2 \ldots s_n$ or their conjunction entailed p. Now is that so? There *may* be statements which are nothing more than abbreviations for all that which is unfolded in their verification. There are, however, other sorts of statements of which this is certainly not true. Recent discussions on phenomenalism, for example, tend to show that no conjunction or disjunction of sense-datum statements, however complex, entails the existence or the non-existence of a certain material object. If that is so, a material object statement, though it *is* connected with sense-datum statements, is not just an abbreviation for them, rather has it a logical status of its own, and is not equivalent to any truth-function of the latter ones. I think that the result of these discussions is essentially right, and I ask for permission, to make my point quite clear, to add one word more.

The failure of the phenomenalist to translate a material object statement into terms of sense-data is not, as has been suggested, due to the poverty of our language which lacks the

---

[1] This symbolism, and the other symbolism used in this article, is explained as it is introduced, and no knowledge of technical logic is required to understand it.—EDITOR.

vocabulary for describing all the minute details of sense experience, nor is it due to the difficulties inherent in producing an *infinite* combination of sense-datum statements though all these things may contribute to it. In the main it is due to a factor which, though it is very important and really quite obvious, has to my knowledge never been noticed —to the 'open texture'[2] of most of our empirical concepts. What I mean is this: Suppose I have to verify a statement such as 'There is a cat next door'; suppose I go over to the next room, open the door, look into it and actually see a cat. Is this enough to prove my statement? Or must I, in addition to it, touch the cat, pat him and induce him to purr? And supposing that I had done all these things, can I then be absolutely certain that my statement was true? Instantly we come up against the well-known battery of sceptical arguments mustered since ancient times. What, for instance, should I say when that creature later on grew to a gigantic size? Or if it showed some queer behaviour usually not to be found with cats, say, if, under certain conditions, it could be revived from death whereas normal cats could not? Shall I, in such a case, say that a new species has come into being? Or that it was a cat with extraordinary properties? Again, suppose I say 'There is my friend over there'. What if on drawing closer in order to shake hands with him he suddenly disappeared? 'Therefore it was not my friend but some delusion or other.' But suppose a few seconds later I saw him again, could grasp his hand, etc. What then? 'Therefore my friend was nevertheless there and his disappearance was some delusion or other.' But imagine after a while he disappeared again, or seemed to disappear—what shall I say now? Have we rules ready for all imaginable possibilities?

An example of the first sort tends to show that we can think of situations in which we couldn't be certain whether something was a cat or some other animal (or a *jinni*). An example of the second sort tends to show that we can consider circumstances in which we couldn't be certain whether something was real or a delusion. The fact that in many cases there is no such thing as a conclusive verification is con-

[2] I owe this term to Mr. Kneale who suggested it to me as a translation of *Porosität der Begriffe*, a term coined by me in German.

nected with the fact that most of our empirical concepts are not delimited in all possible directions. Suppose I come across a being that looks like a man, speaks like a man, behaves like a man, and is only one span tall—shall I say it *is* a man? Or what about the case of a person who is so old as to remember King Darius? Would you say he is an immortal? Is there anything like an exhaustive definition that finally and once for all sets our mind at rest? 'But are there not exact definitions at least in science?' Let's see. The notion of gold seems to be defined with absolute precision, say by the spectrum of gold with its characteristic lines. Now what would you say if a substance was discovered that looked like gold, satisfied all the chemical tests for gold, whilst it emitted a new sort of radiation? 'But such things do not happen.' Quite so; but they *might* happen, and that is enough to show that we can never exclude altogether the possibility of some unforeseen situation arising in which we shall have to modify our definition. Try as we may, no concept is limited in such a way that there is no room for any doubt. We introduce a concept and limit it in *some* directions; for instance, we define gold in contrast to some other metals such as alloys. This suffices for our present needs, and we do not probe any farther. We tend to *overlook* the fact that there are always other directions in which the concept has not been defined. And if we did, we could easily imagine conditions which would necessitate new limitations. In short, it is not possible to define a concept like gold with absolute precision, i.e. in such a way that every nook and cranny is blocked against entry of doubt. That is what is meant by the open texture of a concept.

Vagueness should be distinguished from *open texture*. A word which is actually used in a fluctuating way (such as 'heap' or 'pink') is said to be vague; a term like 'gold', though its actual use may not be vague, is non-exhaustive or of an open texture in that we can never fill up all the possible gaps through which a doubt may seep in. Open texture, then, is something like *possibility of vagueness*. Vagueness can be remedied by giving more accurate rules, open texture cannot. An alternative way of stating this would be to say that definitions of open terms are *always* corrigible or emendable.

Open texture is a very fundamental characteristic of most, though not of all, empirical concepts, and it is this texture which prevents us from verifying conclusively most of our empirical statements. Take any material object statement. The terms which occur in it are non-exhaustive; that means that we cannot foresee completely all possible conditions in which they are to be used; there will always remain a possibility, however faint, that we have not taken into account something or other that may be relevant to their usage; and that means that we cannot foresee completely all the possible circumstances in which the statement is true or in which it is false. There will always remain a margin of uncertainty. Thus the absence of a conclusive verification is directly due to the open texture of the terms concerned.

This has an important consequence. Phenomenalists have tried to translate what we mean by a material object statement into terms of sense experience. Now such a translation would be possible only if the terms of a material object statement were completely definable. For only then could we describe completely all the possible evidences which would make the statement true or false. As this condition is not fulfilled, the programme of phenomenalism falls flat, and in consequence the attempts at analysing chairs and tables into patterns of sense-data—which has become something of a national sport in this country—are doomed to fail. Similar remarks apply to certain psychological statements such as 'He is an intelligent person'; here again it is due to the open texture of a term like 'intelligent' that the statement cannot be reduced to a conjunction or disjunction of statements which specify the way a man would behave in such-and-such circumstances.

It may have been a dim awareness of this fact that induced Locke to insist on corporeal, and Berkeley on mental substance. Doing away with their metaphysical fog, we may restate what seems to be the grain of truth in their views by saying that a material object statement, or a psychological statement has a logic of its own, and for this reason cannot be reduced to the level of other statements.

But there is a deeper reason for all that, and this consists in what I venture to call the *essential incompleteness* of an

empirical description. To explain more fully: If I had to
describe the right hand of mine which I am now holding up,
I may say different things of it: I may state its size, its shape,
its colour, its tissue, the chemical compound of its bones, its
cells, and perhaps add some more particulars; but however
far I go, I shall never reach a point where my description
will be completed: logically speaking, it is always possible to
extend the description by adding some detail or other. Every
description stretches, as it were, into a horizon of open possibilities: however far I go, I shall always carry this horizon
with me. Contrast this case with others in which complete-
ness is attainable. If, in geometry, I describe a triangle, e.g.
by giving its three sides, the description is *complete*: nothing
can be added to it that is not included in, or at variance with,
the data. Again, there is a sense in which it may be said
that a melody is described completely in the musical notation (disregarding, for the moment, the question of its interpretation); a figure on a carpet, viewed as an ornament, may
be described in some geometrical notation; and in this case,
too, there is a sense in which the description may be called
complete. (I do not mean the *physical* carpet, but its pattern.) The same applies to a game of chess: it can be described, move by move, from the beginning to the end. Such
cases serve merely to set off the nature of an empirical description by the contrast: there is no such thing as complete-
ness in the case in which I describe my right hand, or the
character of a person; I can never exhaust all the details nor
foresee all possible circumstances which would make me modify or retract my statement. (This was already seen by Leibniz when he said that anything actual is always inexhaustible
in its properties and a true image of the Infinite Mind.)

The situation described has a direct bearing on the open
texture of concepts. A term is defined when the sort of situation is described in which it is to be used. Suppose for a
moment that we were able to describe situations completely
without omitting anything (as in chess), then we could produce an exhaustive list of all the circumstances in which the
term is to be used so that nothing is left to doubt; in other
words, we could construct a *complete definition*, i.e. a
thought model which anticipates and settles once for all ev-

ery possible question of usage. As, in fact, we can never eliminate the possibility of some unforeseen factor emerging, we can never be quite sure that we have included in our definition everything that should be included, and thus the process of defining and refining an idea will go on without ever reaching a final stage. In other words, every definition stretches into an open horizon. Try as we may, the situation will always remain the same: no definition of an empirical term will cover all possibilities. Thus the result is that the incompleteness of our verification is rooted in the incompleteness of the definition of the terms involved, and the incompleteness of the definition is rooted in the incompleteness of empirical description; that is one of the grounds why a material object statement p can *not* be verified conclusively, nor be resolved into statements $s_1, s_2 \ldots s_n$ which describe evidences for it. (In mathematics such a reduction is often possible: thus a statement about rational numbers *can*, without loss of meaning, be translated into statements about integers; but here you have complete description, complete definition and conclusive proof and refutation.)

One word more. Why is it that, as a rule, an experiential statement is not verifiable in a conclusive way? Is it because I can never exhaust the description of a material object or of a situation, since I may always add something to it—something that, in principle, can be foreseen? Or is it because something quite new and unforeseen may occur? In the first case, though I know all the tests, I may still be unable to perform them, say, for lack of time. In the second case I cannot even be sure that I know all the tests that may be required; in other words, the difficulty is to state completely what a verification would be in this case. (Can you foresee all circumstances which would turn a putative fact into a delusion?) Now the answer to the question is that *both factors combine* to prevent a verification from being conclusive. *But they play a very different part.* It is due to the first factor that, in verifying a statement, we can never finish the job. But it is the second that is responsible for the open texture of our terms which is so characteristic of all factual knowledge. To see this more clearly, compare the situation in mathematics: here a theorem, say Goldbach's hypothesis, which says that every even number can be represented as the sum of two primes, may be undecidable as we cannot go through all the integers in order to try it out. But this in no way detracts from the *closed* texture of the mathematical concepts. If there was no such thing as the (always present) possibility of the emergence of something new, there could be nothing like the open texture of concepts; and if there was no such thing as the open texture of concepts, verification would be incomplete only in the sense that it could never be finished (just as in the case of Goldbach).

To sum up: An experiential statement is, as a rule, not conclusively verifiable for two different reasons:

(1) because of the existence of an unlimited number of tests;

(2) because of the open texture of the terms involved.

These two reasons correspond to two different senses of 'incompleteness'. The first is related to the fact that I can never conclude the description of a material object, or of a situation. I may, for instance, look at my table from ever new points in space without ever exhausting all the possibilities. The second (and more exciting one) is due to the fact that our factual knowledge is incomplete in another dimension: there is always a chance that something unforeseen may occur. That again may mean two different things:

(*a*) that I should get acquainted with some totally new experience such as at present I cannot even imagine;

(*b*) that some new discovery was made which would affect our whole interpretation of certain facts.

An illustration of the first sort would be supplied by a man born blind who later obtained the experience of seeing. An illustration of the second sort would be the change brought about by the discovery of a new agent of nature, such as electricity. In this case we perceive that the data of observation are connected in a new and unforeseen way, that, as it were, new lines can now be traced through the field of experience. So we can say more exactly that the open texture of concepts is rooted in that particular incompleteness of our factual knowledge which I have just adumbrated.

What I have said modifies to a more or less extent the account I have given of verification. I said that in giving the method of verification we lay down a rule (or rules) of inference. We should, however, feel grave doubts whether that is so. If a material object statement were to entail a sense datum statement, to entail it in a strictly *logical* sense, then the premiss would be cancelled together with the conclusion: or, to put it differently, a single negative instance would suffice to refute the premiss. Suppose someone told me, 'Look, there is your friend, he is just crossing the street'. Now if I looked in the direction indicated, but failed to perceive the person who is my friend, would I say that the statement was refuted beyond the shadow of a doubt? There may be cases in which I may say that. But there are others in which I would certainly not think that the statement was refuted on the strength of such a single glance (for instance, when I was led to expect my friend at this hour, or received a letter from him saying that he will arrive at that time, and the like). A discrepancy between a material object statement and a single sense experience may always be explained away by some accessory assumption: I haven't looked thoroughly, my friend happened in this very second to be behind someone else, he just stepped into a doorway, and so on, not to mention more fanciful theories. I can never exclude the possibility that, though the evidence was against it, the statement may be true.

Whoever considers these facts with unbiassed eyes will, I trust, assent to the conclusion that a single sense experience, strictly speaking, never excludes a material object statement in the sense in which the negation of p excludes p. That means that no sense-datum statement s can ever come into *sharp logical conflict* with a material object statement p; in other words: $p . \sim s$ never represents a *contradiction* in the sense that $p . \sim p$ does. In the light of this we can no longer adhere to the view that p entails s. How, then, should we formulate the 'method of verification'—that is, the connection between a proposition p and the statements s_1, s_2 . . . s_n which are evidences for it? I propose to say that the evidences s_1, s_2 . . . s_n, *speak for* or *against* the proposition *p*, that they *strengthen* or *weaken* it, which does not mean that they prove or disprove it strictly.

There is a striking analogy to that in the relation that holds between a law of nature L and certain observational statements $s_1, s_2 \ldots s_n$, an analogy which may help to clarify the situation. It is often said that the statements of observation *follow* from the law (the latter being regarded as a sort of universal premiss). Since an unlimited number of consequences can be derived from a law, the ideal of complete verification is, of course, unattainable; whereas, on the other hand, a single counter observation seems to suffice to overthrow the law. From this it would follow that, while a law cannot be strictly verified, it can be strictly confuted; or that it can be decided only one way.[3] That is unrealistic. What astronomer would abandon Kepler's laws on the strength of a single observation? If, in fact, some anomaly in a planet's behaviour were detected, the most varied attempts at explaining the phenomenon would first be made (such as the presence of unknown heavy masses, friction with rarefied gases, etc.). Only if the edifice of hypotheses thus erected has too little support in experience, if it becomes too complex and artificial, if it no longer satisfies our demand for simplicity, or again if a better hypothesis presents itself to us, such as Einstein's theory, would we resolve to drop those laws. And even then the refutation would not be valid finally and once for all: it may still turn out that some circumstance had escaped our notice which, when taken into consideration, would cast a different light upon the whole. Indeed, the history of science exhibits cases (Olaf Römer, Leverrier) in which the apparent defeat of a theory later turned into complete victory. Who can say that such a situation will not repeat itself?

Here again the view suggests itself strongly that the relationship between a statement and what serves to verify it was too crudely represented in the past; that it was a mistake to describe it in logical terms such as 'entailment'; that a law is not a sort of universal statement from which particular statements follow; that its logic is still unexplored, and that

[3] See Karl Popper, *Logik der Forschung.*

it may possibly take the form of rules according to which the law's truth-weight—if I am allowed to use such a term—is increased or lessened by the data of observation. Be that as it may, the mere fact that a single counter observation $\sim s$ can always be reconciled with a general law L by some accessory assumption shows that the true relation between a law and the experiential evidence for it is much more complicated and only superficially in accord with the customary account.

It will be said that this is due to our representing the case in too simple a manner. In reality the observational statement s does not follow from L alone, but from L plus a number of further premisses which are often not expressly stated. So that, if the observation s which we expected fails to materialize, we may say that any of the other premisses is false.

Now this would be perfectly correct if the system of premisses could be stated accurately and completely in every single case. But can it? Can we ever be certain of knowing all, really all the conditions on which the result of even the simplest experiment depends? Plainly not; what is stated is only a *part* of the conditions, viz., those which, e.g., can be isolated in experimental technique and subjected to our will, or which can readily be surveyed, etc. The others merge into one indistinct mass: the vague supposition that 'a normal situation subsists', that 'no disturbing factors are present' or in whatever way we may hint at the possibility of intervention of some unforeseen conditions. The relation between L and s, then, when exactly stated, is this: Given such-and-such laws $L_1, L_2 \ldots L_m$, given such-and-such initial and boundary conditions $c_1, c_2 \ldots c_n$ and *no other disturbing factors being present*, so-and-so will happen. And here it must be stressed that behind the words italicized a presupposition is concealed which cannot be split up into clear, separate statements. When actually deducing a consequence from a physical law we never make use of this premiss: it never forms part of the body of premisses: it does not enter the process of deduction. But then it should not be termed a premiss at all; what a queer sort of premiss this is, which is never made use of! What is, in fact, conveyed by these

words is only that, in case of a conflict between theory and
observation, we shall *search* for disturbing factors whilst considering ourselves free to adhere to the theory. The question
at issue is *not* whether a certain system of assumption is
sufficiently comprehensive—that is a question of fact which
may be left to the expert; the question is rather whether
there is a *criterion* which assures us that a system of premisses is complete. To this there is no answer; nay, more,
we cannot even form any conception of such a criterion; we
cannot think of a situation in which a physicist would tell
us, 'Well, I have finished the job; now I have discovered the
last law of nature, and no more is to be found'. But if this
is devoid of meaning, there is no point in insisting, '*If* all
the conditions in the universe, and *if* all the laws governing
them were known to us, then—'. As the boundary regions of
our knowledge are always enveloped in a dust cloud—out of
which something new may emerge—we are left with the fact
that s is not a strict logical consequence of L together with
the initial conditions. Saying that the class of premisses is
not 'closed' and that *therefore* the conclusion is lacking in
stringency comes, in my view, to the same thing as saying
that s is *not* a logical consequence of the premisses as far
as they are stated. And that is all I wanted to say.

All this tends to suggest that the relation between a law
of nature and the evidences for it, or between a material
object statement and a sense-datum statement, or again between a psychological statement and the evidence concerning a person's behaviour is a looser one than had been hitherto imagined. If that is correct, the application of logic
seems to be limited in an important sense. We may say that
the known relations of logic can only hold between statements
which belong to a *homogeneous* domain; or that the deductive nexus never extends beyond the limits of such a domain.

Accordingly we may set ourselves the task of arranging the
statements of our language in distinct strata, grouping in
the same stratum all those statements linked by clearly apprehended logical relations. It is in this way, for instance,
that the theorems of mechanics are organized in a system
the elements of which stand in known logical relations with
one another and where it is always possible to decide of two

theorems in what logical relation they stand—whether one is a consequence of the other, whether they are equivalent, or independent of, or in contradiction with each other. In like manner the statements of a physicist in describing certain data of observation (such as the position of a pointer on his gauges) stand in exactly defined relations to one another. Thus a pointer on a scale cannot possibly be opposite 3 and 5 at the same time: here you have a relation of strict exclusion. On the other hand, no statement of mechanics can ever come into sharp logical conflict with a statement of observation, and this implies that between these two kinds of statements there exist no relations of the sort supplied to us by classical logic. So long as we move only among the statements of a single stratum, all the relations provided by logic remain valid. The real problem arises where two such strata make contact, so to speak; it is the problem of these planes of contact which to-day should claim the attention of the logician. We may, in this context, speak of the looseness of the chains or inference which lead from statements of one stratum to those of another; the connection is no longer coercive—owing to the incompleteness of all our data.

You will find that it is this fact to which the rise of philosophical troubles often can be traced. (Think of how confusing it is to assert or to dispute the statement, 'The floor is not solid', as it belongs to two quite distinct strata.) The fracture lines of the strata of language are marked by philosophical problems: the problem of perception, of verification, of induction, the problem of the relation between mind and body, and so on.

You will have noticed that I have used the term 'incompleteness' in very different senses. In one sense we may say of a description of a material object that it is incomplete; in another sense we may say that of our knowledge of the boundary conditions in a field of force. There is a sense in which we say that a list of laws of nature is always incomplete, and another sense in which even our knowledge of the agents of nature is so; and you may easily find more senses. They all combine, to a varying degree, to create what I have called the open texture of concepts and the looseness of inferences.

Incompleteness, in the senses referred to, is the mark of

empirical knowledge as opposed to *a priori* knowledge such as mathematics. In fact, it is the criterion by which we can distinguish perfectly *formalized* languages constructed by logicians from *natural* languages as used in describing reality. In a formalized system the use of each symbol is governed by a definite number of rules, and further, all the rules of inference and procedure can be stated completely. In view of the incompleteness which permeates empirical knowledge such a demand cannot be fulfilled by any language we may use to express it.

That there is a very close relation between content and verification is an important insight which has been brought to light by empiricists. Only one has to be very careful how to formulate it. Far from identifying the meaning of a statement with the evidences we have for it, the view I tried to sketch leads to a sort of many-level-theory of language in which 'every sort of statement has its own sort of logic'.

II

In the second part of his paper Mr. MacKinnon is anxious to relate the notions of reality and causality by admitting as real only those objects (or events, or processes) which satisfy the conditions of causality. What he says is 'that the manner of discursive thought . . . reveals itself as an obstinate resolve . . . to admit nothing as real that does not manifest some ground of its occurrence'. That is part of Kant's doctrine according to which nothing can ever become object of our knowledge which did not conform to certain *a priori* forms of our intuition and our understanding. Such an attempt, if it succeeded, would be of tremendous importance. Think how miraculous it would be, using this method, to deduce from it causality, premises of induction as well as other enjoyable things—I had almost said to *produce* them out of the conjuror's hat called the Transcendental Argument. How comforting would be the belief that we know the nature of space and time through and through so that we are able to enunciate the principles of geometry without fear of ever being defeated by experience. How reassuring it would be to say that nature *must* obey causal laws—and so on, you know the tune. The question is only whether Nature will conform to Kant. You will realize that such over-confidence is no longer permissible to-day, in the age of quantum mechanics. We are told by Mr. MacKinnon that 'we display an unwillingness to admit the completely random' (by the bye, what does he mean by that?) 'and discontinuous as objectively real'. But our protest, however strongly worded, would be of no avail if Nature was willing to baffle us. The words Mr. MacKinnon has been using state precisely the sort of situation with which we have come face to face in modern physics: things do happen without ground of their occurrence. May I be allowed to say a few words on this subject?

There are people who think that physicists have just not succeeded in discovering laws which tell us why things happen in the atomic world, in the cheerful hope that someone some day will have a brain-wave which will enable him to fill the gaps in wave mechanics; on this day the latter will turn into a completely deterministic theory. Let these people realize how wide the cleavage is that separates us from the good old days. The hope they cherish is based on an illusion: it has been proved[4] that the structure of quantum mechanics is such that no further laws can be added to it which would make the whole theory deterministic; for if we could, we should, owing to the uncertainty principle, get entangled in contradictions. (The situation is, in fact, more intricate, but this is not the place to go into it.) So we are faced with the dilemma that quantum mechanics is *either* self-consistent *or* deterministic: you can't have it both ways. The crack in the wall of Determinism is definitive, and there is no way out of the situation.

According to Kant causality is an inescapable form which the nature of our understanding imposes on any given material. If this were so, it would be inconceivable—against the conditions of possible experience—ever to come across any events which did not conform to the principle of causality. Quantum phenomena, however, have forced physicists to de-

---

[4] See, for instance, J. v. Neumann, *Mathematische Grundlagen der Quantenmechanik.*

part from this principle, or better, to *restrict* it, whilst a torso of it is retained. Though the fate of a single electron is not governed by causal laws, the particle being free to move about, for instance, to 'jump' in a collision with light waves however it pleases, the behaviour of millions of electrons is statistically predictable. Not exactly that quantum mechanics confronts us with a mathematician's dream of chaos come true. For, as I said, there is a causal aspect in the new theory, namely this: there are certain waves connected with the motion of particles, the de Broglie waves, which obey rigorous 'causal' laws. That is, the propagation of these waves is governed by a differential equation of the respectable old type such as you find in the classical physics of fields. Hence we can, given the initial conditions and the values over the boundary of a region during a certain interval of time, predict with absolute precision the propagation of the waves. That is exactly what any causal theory achieves. What is new, however, is the interpretation we must give to these waves: they are a sort of 'probability clouds' the density of which at each point signifies the probability of the occurrence of a particle. So what we can deduce from the theory are only *probability statements* regarding the presence of a particle in a given place at a given time. Such a statement can be tested, not by making a single experiment such as observing a single electron through a microscope, but by repeating the experiment a large number of times, or observing a large number of electrons and forming the mean value of all the data thus obtained. Therefore we cannot say where exactly a certain electron will be, but only with what probability, i.e. in what percentage of cases we may expect to find it at a certain place. In other words, the theory can be used only to predict the *average behaviour* of particles. That is the statistical aspect of the theory.

To sum up: quantum mechanics is neither a theory of the causal, deterministic type nor an indeterministic theory, whatever this may be taken to mean. The new physics combines deterministic and indeterministic features. What is deterministic is the law for the propagation of the de Broglie waves. That is, the propagation of these waves is *causally determined* in much the same way as, e.g., the propagation of electromagnetic waves is in the classical theories. What is indeterministic is the *interpretation* of these waves, that is, their connection with the facts of observation. Such an interpretation can only be given in statistical terms, and any attempt at interpreting it differently so as to reinstate causality would only lead to conflict with other well-established parts of the theory. Thus we have the curious result that causality holds for the de Broglie waves, which are no more than a purely symbolic and formal representation of certain probabilities, whereas the particles themselves obey no causal laws.

To bring home the last point let me add this: If it were possible to repeat exactly the same experiment and to bring about exactly the same conditions, the result would each time be a different one. Therefore the principle 'Like causes—like effects' no longer holds. *Lasciate ogni speranza . . .*

But may not quantum mechanics one day be superseded by a better theory that meets our demand for causal explanation? Certainly; no theory is sacrosanct and infallible. This, however, is not the point. What matters is, not whether quantum mechanics draws a true picture of reality, but only whether it draws a *permissible* one. About that there can be little doubt. Kant was of the opinion that if there was no such thing as causality science would simply break down. Now the important thing that has emerged is the *possibility* of constructing a theory along different lines, the *legitimacy* of departing from causality, while science has not died or committed suicide on that account. This suffices to disown any claim on the part of Kant to regard causality as an *indispensable* form of our knowledge of the world. Had he been right, we could not even *entertain* such views as physicists do today; to give up causality, even if in part, would mean robbing ourselves of the very condition for gaining knowledge; which could end in one result only, in complete confusion. But that is not so. Though causality has been severely limited, quantum mechanics is a useful tool. Kant did not foresee the possible forms of physical laws; by laying too much stress on the scheme of causality, by claiming for it an *a priori* status, he unduly narrowed the field of research.

The conclusion to be drawn for the preceding seems to me this: Even if quantum mechanics should one day be found wanting and be superseded by another theory, it still offers a *possible picture* of the material world. This picture is neither self-contradictory nor unintelligible, though it may not be the sort of picture to which we are accustomed; anyhow, it is a working hypothesis which serves its purpose in that it is fruitful, i.e. that it leads to new discoveries. Whether it contains the ultimate truth we cannot tell (nor can we in the case of the deterministic theories). It's only experience that can bring forward evidence against it. But the very fact that we *can* turn to experience is significant: in doing so we grant that quantum mechanics, and consequently the limits of causality, *can* be tested in experiment. Hence every attempt at raising the principle of causality to the status of a necessary truth is irreconcilable with the situation as it has emerged in science. No matter whether quantum mechanics will stand its ground or will have to undergo some modification or other, the mere fact that the construction of such a theory is legitimate should settle the dispute: it proves that Kant's argument is based on a fallacy.

It was indeed an important step when man learnt to ask, Why? But it was also a great step when he learnt to drop this question. But leaving quantum mechanics and turning to the common world of sense, I still fail to see any ground for accepting Kant's position. True, in order to get our bearings in the world we must presuppose that there is some sort of order in it so that we may anticipate the course of events and act accordingly. What I fail to see, however, is why this order should be a strictly *causal* one. Suppose, for the sake of argument, that the objects around us were, *on the average*, to display an orderly behaviour, then the world may still be a liveable place. Suppose, for instance, the behaviour of chairs and the support they give us could be foreseen with much the same accuracy as can the behaviour of Tory and Labour candidates in election times, may we then not make use of them just the same? Or suppose they were to conduct themselves as our best friends do—they won't let us down, no; still, you never know—then, as far as I can see, this would be quite enough for all our practical ends. And as to the theoretical ones—well, go to the scientist and you will hear a sorry tale of nature's trickery. I cannot see why such a world should not be possible.

This brings me to the topic in which Mr. MacKinnon is so much interested—are there any *necessary* conditions which must be fulfilled if we are to attain knowledge of the external world? I propose to drop for the moment the subject of causality and to tackle the problem from a broader angle. Let me begin with some observations on the terms 'reality' and 'knowledge'.

Mr. MacKinnon, in his paper, repeatedly speaks of 'the real', 'the reality', he asks, for instance, whether 'the completely random' can be admitted as 'objectively real'. He blames Berkeley for having omitted 'to face the question of the rules whereby the inclusion in or exclusion from reality was determined; in consequence of which', we are told, 'his theory of knowledge flags'. In another passage he speaks of 'the task of compelling the actual to disclose itself'. My impression is that he talks as if there was a clearly bounded domain called 'the real' or 'the actual' with the implication that it is one of the tasks of the philosopher to define it sharply. Unfortunately the belief that there is such a domain is very slender. Not that I deny for a minute that a word like 'reality' is a blessing; it definitely is. Look at such phrases as 'A tautology doesn't say anything about reality', 'Pure mathematics is not concerned with reality', 'In reality it was not Smith I saw but his brother'. It would be silly to put such a word on an *Index Prohibitorum Verborum* as though it were a sin to use it. It is very handy—if it were not in use, we should have to invent it. On the other hand, when a philosopher looks closely at it, tears it from the context and asks himself, 'Now what *is* reality?' he has successfully manœuvred himself into a fairly awkward position. For it is surprisingly easy to ask a number of questions which are more or less embarrassing; for instance, 'Is the elastic force present in a spring something real?' I suppose some people would answer Yes, some No. The fact is that there simply are no fixed rules that govern the use of the word. To go on—'Is a magnetic field something real?' 'Is energy? and entropy?' Again, I may ask, 'Is the power of my memory real?', 'Is the genius of a people, is the spirit of an age, is the beauty of a spring day real?' Now we begin to see how the idea is lost in indeterminacy. What we must understand is that such a word is used on many different levels and with many different shades of meaning. It has a *systematic ambiguity*. At the same time there is a sort of family likeness between all these uses, and it is that which makes us denote them by one word.

The same applies to a verb like 'to exist'. We use the word in many different senses: we may, for instance, say of a memory picture, an after-image, a mirror image, or again of a material object that it 'exists'; again, we may say of a wave-motion in a space of many dimensions, or of a law of nature, or of a number satisfying certain conditions that it 'exists'; and it is quite obvious that we do use the word in each case according to totally different criteria. So again we have a case of systematic ambiguity.

Next take the term 'knowledge'. Everyone is familiar with the distinction between knowledge by acquaintance and knowledge by description. This division is not fine enough. When I know something by acquaintance, I may know it in very different senses, as when I say 'I know sweetness' (meaning 'I am acquainted with the taste of sweetness'), 'I know misery', 'I know him', 'I know his writings'. In this series we go progressively farther away from simple acquaintance. In a case like 'I know his motives', it is doubtful whether I should say this unless I had experienced some such motive myself. Moreover, there are cases which fall under none of the two groups; so, for instance, when I say 'I know French', 'I know how to deal with that man'. Again, we may speak in different senses of knowledge by description. Compare the case of a reporter who gained knowledge of some hush-hush affair with that of a scientist who claims to possess knowledge of nature. Now is this knowledge in the same sense? And mark, in the latter case there are again subtle differences. Compare knowledge of the history of certain birds as based on observation with knowledge of the history of our solar system as based on some hypothesis; again knowledge of a natural law of the causal type with knowledge of a statistical law. Quantum mechanics, though it is based on the assumption of a randomness in the behaviour of electrons (and other particles), leads to a lot of predictions. On this ground physicists do not hesitate to honour the newly discovered laws by awarding them the degree of knowledge; whereas Mr. MacKinnon thinks 'that we do concede the title unintelligible to any field . . . where such (causal) lines have not been traced'. Well, I shall not argue about that; my sole object is to call attention to the fact that the actual usage is unsettled, that there are many different types of knowledge, and that, by talking of knowledge *in general*, we are liable to overlook the very important differences between them. Suppose that someone has a vague awareness of the direction in which history moves— shall, or shall I not call this knowledge? Can you draw a clear line to mark where such vague awareness ends and where true knowledge begins? Knowledge as supplied by quantum mechanics was unknown two or three decades ago. Who can tell what forms of knowledge may emerge in the future? Can you anticipate all possible cases in which you may wish to use that term? To say that knowledge is embodied in true propositions does not get you any farther; for there are many different structures that are called 'propositions'—different, because they are verified in different senses of the word and governed by different sets of logical rules. (Incidentally speaking, the failure to draw a clear line between the meaningful and the meaningless is due to the fact that these terms have themselves a systematic ambiguity, and so has the term 'verifiable'.)

There is a group of words such as 'fact', 'event', 'situation', 'case', 'circumstance', which display a queer sort of behaviour. One might say of such words that they serve as pegs: it's marvellous what a lot of things you can put on them ('the fact that—'). So far they are very handy; but as soon as one focusses on them and asks, e.g., 'What *is* a fact?' they betray a tendency of melting away. The peg-aspect is by far the most important of all. It's just as in the case of the word 'reality': in reality, e.g., 'in reality' is an adverb.

Again, there are many different types of fact; there are many different types of statement which are called 'empirical'; there are many different things which are called 'experience'; and there are many different senses of communication and clarity.

Now if I am to contribute to the main subject of this symposium, that is, to the question whether there are any *necessary conditions* for *gaining knowledge of reality*—what am I to reply? Knowledge of reality! Of *what* sort of reality, and *what* sort of knowledge? As a logician I am bound to say that the notions of reality and knowledge have a systematic ambiguity and, moreover, that they are on each level extremely vague and hazy. I am even not quite clear as to what a condition is, let alone a 'necessary condition'. How questionable all these ideas are! How can I be expected to answer a question which consists only of a series of question marks?

III

So far my criticism was mainly negative. In conclusion I should like to offer some constructive suggestions. Before doing so, I must warn you that I can't see any ground whatever for renouncing one of the most fundamental rights of man, the right of talking nonsense. And now I suppose I may go on.

People are inclined to think that there is a world of facts as opposed to a world of words which describe these facts. I am not too happy about that. Consider an example. We are accustomed to see colour as a 'quality' of objects. That is, colour cannot subsist by itself, but must inhere in a thing. This conception springs from the way we express ourselves. When colour is rendered by an adjective, colour is conceived as an attribute of things, i.e. as something that can have no independent existence. That, however, is not the only way of conceiving colour. There are languages such as Russian, German, Italian, which render colour by means of verbs. If we were to imitate this usage in English by allowing some such form as 'The sky blues', we should come face to face with the question, Do I mean the same fact when I say 'The sky blues' as when I say 'The sky is blue'? I don't think so. We say 'The sun shines', 'Jewels glitter', 'The river shimmers', 'Windows gleam', 'Stars twinkle', etc.; that is, in the case of phenomena of lustre we make use of a verbal mode of expression. Now in rendering colour phenomena by verbs we assimilate them more closely to the phenomena of lustre; and in doing so we alter not only our manner of speaking but our entire way of apprehending colour. We *see* the blue differently now—a hint that language affects our whole mode of apprehension. In the word 'blueing' we are clearly aware of an active, verbal element. On that account 'being blue' is not quite equivalent to 'blueing', since it lacks what is peculiar to the verbal mode of expression. The sky which 'blues' is seen as something that continually brings forth blueness—it radiates blueness, so to speak; blue does not inhere in it as a mere quality, rather is it felt as the vital pulse of the sky; there is a faint suggestion of the operating of some force behind the phenomenon. It's hard to get the feel of it in English; perhaps it may help you to liken this mode of expression to the impressionist way of painting which is at bottom a new way of seeing: the impressionist sees in colour an immediate manifestation of reality, a free agent no longer bound up with things.

There are, then, different linguistic means of rendering colour. When this is done by means of adjectives, colour is conceived as an attribute of things. The learning of such a language involves for everyone who speaks it his being habituated to see colour as a 'quality' of objects. This conception becomes thus incorporated into his picture of the world. The verbal mode of expression detaches colour from things: it enables us to see colour as a phenomenon with a life of its own. Adjective and verb thus represent two different worlds of thought.

There is also an adverbial way of talking about colour. Imagine a language with a wealth of expressions for all shades of lustre, but without adjectives for colours; colours, as a rule, are ignored; *when* they are expressed, this is done by adding an adverb to the word that specifies the sort of lustre. Thus the people who use this sort of language would say, 'The sea is glittering golden in the sunshine', 'The evening clouds glow redly', 'There in the depth a shadow greenly gleams'. In such phrases colour would lose the last trace of independence and be reduced to a mere modification of lustre. Just as we in our language cannot say 'That's very', but only some such thing as 'That's very brilliant', so in the language considered we could not say 'That's bluish', but only, e.g., 'That's shining bluishly'. There can be little doubt that, owing to this circumstance, the users of such language would find it very hard to see colour as a quality of things. For them it would not be the *things* that are coloured, rather colour would reside in the lustre as it glows and darkens and changes—evidence that they would see the world with different eyes.

'But isn't it still true to say that I have the same experience whenever I look up at the sky?' You would be less happy if you were asked, 'Do you have the same experience when you look at a picture puzzle and see a figure in it as before, when you didn't see it?' You may, perhaps, say you see the same lines, though each time in a different arrangement. Now what exactly corresponds to this different arrangement in the case when I look up at the sky? One might say: we are aware of the blue, but this awareness is itself tinged and coloured by the whole linguistic background which brings into prominence, or weakens and hides certain analogies. In this sense language does affect the whole manner in which we become aware of a fact: the fact articulates itself differently, so to speak. In urging that you *must* have the same experience whenever you look at the sky you forget that the term 'experience' is itself ambiguous: whether it is taken, e.g., to include or to exclude all the various analogies which a certain mode of expression calls up.

Again, consider this case: Suppose there is a number of languages A, B, C . . . in each of which a proposition is used according to a slightly different logic. Consequently a proposition in the language A is not a proposition in exactly the same sense as a proposition in the language B, etc. And not only this: what is described by a statement in the language A, i.e., if you like, the 'fact', is not a fact in the same sense as a fact described in the language B, etc.; which tends to show that what is called a fact depends on the linguistic medium through which we see it.

I have observed that when the clock strikes in the night and I, already half asleep, am too tired to count the strokes, I am seized by an impression that the sequence will never end —as though it would go on, stroke after stroke, in an unending measureless procession. The whole thing vanishes as soon as I *count*. Counting frees me, as it were, from the dark formlessness impending over me. (Is this not a parable of the rational?) It seems to me that one could say here that counting *alters* the quality of the experience. Now is it the same fact which I perceive when counting and when not counting?

Again, suppose there is a tribe whose members count 'one, two, three, a few, many'. Suppose a man of this tribe looking at a flock of birds said 'A few birds' whereas I should say 'Five birds'—is it the same fact for him as it is for me? If in such a case I pass to a language of a different structure, I can no longer describe 'the same' fact, but only another one more or less resembling the first. What, then, is the objective reality supposed to be described by language?

What rebels in us against such a suggestion is the feeling that the fact is there objectively no matter in which way we render it. I perceive something that exists and put it into words. From this it seems to follow that fact is something that exists independent of, and prior to language; language merely serves the end of communication. What we are liable to overlook here is that the way we see a fact—i.e. what we emphasize and what we disregard—is *our* work. 'The sunbeams trembling on the floating tides' (Pope). Here a fact is something that emerges out from, and takes shape against a background. The background may be, e.g., my visual field; something that rouses my attention detaches itself from this field, is brought into focus and apprehended linguistically; that is what we call a fact. A fact is noticed; and by being noticed it becomes a fact. 'Was it then no fact before you noticed it?' It was, if I *could* have noticed it. In a language in which there is only the number series 'one, two, three, a few, many', a fact such as 'There are five birds' is imperceptible.

To make my meaning still clearer consider a language in which description does not take the form of sentences. Examples of such a description would be supplied by a map, a picture language, a film, the musical notation. A map, for instance, should not be taken as a conjunction of single statements each of which describes a separate fact. For what, would you say, is the boundary of a fact? Where does the one end and the other begin? If we think of such types of description, we are no longer tempted to say that a country, or a story told in a film, or a melody must consist of 'facts'. Here we begin to see how confusing the idea is according to which the world is a cluster of facts—just as if it were a sort of mosaic made up of little coloured stones. Reality is undivided. What we may have in mind is perhaps that *language* contains units, viz. *sentences*. In describing reality, by using sentences, we draw, as it were, lines through it, limit a part and call what corresponds with such a sentence a fact. In other words, language is the knife with which we cut out facts. (This account is over-simplified as it doesn't take notice of *false* statements.)

Reality, then, is not made up of facts in the sense in which a plant is made up of cells, a house of bricks, a stone of molecules; rather, if you want a simile, a fact is present, in much the same sense in which a character manifests itself in a face. Not that I invent the character and read it into the face; no, the character is somehow written on the face but no one would on that account say that a face is 'made up' of features symbolic of such-and-such traits. Just as we have to interpret a face, so we have to interpret reality. The elements of such an interpretation, without our being aware of it, are already present in language—for instance, in such moulds as the notion of thinghood, of causality, of number, or again in the way we render colour, etc.

Noticing a fact may be likened to seeing a face in a cloud, or a figure in an arrangement of dots, or suddenly becoming aware of the solution of a picture puzzle: one views a complex of elements as one, reads a sort of unity into it, etc. Language supplies us with a means of comprehending and categorizing; and different languages categorize differently.

'But surely noticing a face in a cloud is not inventing it?' Certainly not; only you might not have noticed it unless you had already had the experience of human faces somewhere else. Does this not throw a light on what constitutes the noticing of facts? I would not dream for a moment of saying that I *invent* them; I might, however, be unable to perceive them if I had not certain moulds of comprehension ready at hand. These forms I borrow from language. Language, then, *contributes to the formation and participates in the constitution* of a fact; which, of course, does not mean that it *produces* the fact.

So far I have dealt with perceptual situations only. This, I am afraid, will not satisfy Mr. MacKinnon. What he wants to know is whether there are any *general* conditions of the possibility of factual knowledge. We have seen some of the fallacies involved in putting this question. Still we may ask ourselves whether there are any methodological rules which guide us in gaining knowledge. All I can hope to do here is to throw out some hints.

The empiricist has a let-the-facts-speak-for-themselves attitude. Well, this is his faith; what about his works? Remember, a scientific theory is never a slavish imitation of certain features of reality, a dead, passive replica. It is essentially a *construction* which to a more or less degree reflects our own activity. When, for instance, we represent a number of observations made in the laboratory by a corresponding number of dots and connect them by a graph, we assume, as a rule, that the curve is continuous and analytic. Such an assumption goes far beyond any possible experience. There will always be infinitely many other possible curves which accord with the facts equally well; the totality of these curves is included within a certain narrow strip. The ordinary mathematical treatment substitutes an exact law for the blurred data of observation and deduces from such laws strict mathematical conclusions. This shows that there is an element of convention inherent in the formulation of a law. The way we single out one particular law from infinitely many possible ones shows that in our theoretical construction of reality we are guided by certain principles—*regulative principles* as we may call them. If I were asked what these principles are, I should tentatively list the following:

(1) Simplicity or economy—the demand that the laws should be as simple as possible.

(2) Demands suggested by the requirements of the symbolism we use—for instance, that the graph should represent an analytic function so as to lend itself readily to the carrying out of certain mathematical operations such as differentiation.

(3) Aesthetic principles ('mathematical harmony' as envisaged by Pythagoras, Kepler, Einstein) though it is difficult to say what they are.

(4) A principle which so regulates the formation of our concepts that as many alternatives as possible become decidable. This tendency is embodied in the whole structure of Aristotelian logic, especially in the law of excluded middle.[5]

(5) There is a further factor elusive and most difficult to pin down: a mere tone of thought which, though not explicitly stated, permeates the air of a historical period and inspires its leading figures. It is a sort of field organizing and directing the ideas of an age. (The time from Descartes to Newton, for instance, was animated by an instinctive belief in an Order of Things accessible to the human mind. Though the thinkers of that time have tried to render this tone of thought into a rationalistic system, they failed: for that which is the living spark of rationalism is irrational.)

Such, I think, are some of the regulative principles. The formulation of some of them is very vague, and advisedly so: it wouldn't be good policy to reduce mathematical harmony, consonance with the whole background of an age, etc., to fixed rules. It's better to have them elastic. Principle (5) should perhaps better be described as a condition for making —and missing—discoveries.

Now none of these principles is *indispensable*, imposed on us by the nature of our understanding. Kant has tried to condense the tone of thought of the Newtonian age into strict rules—into *necessary conditions* of factual knowledge; with what success can be seen from the subsequent development: the belief in synthetic *a priori* judgements soon became something of a brake to research, discouraging such lines of approach as non-Euclidean geometry, and later non-causal laws in physics. Let this be a warning.

Writers on the history of philosophy are inclined to attend too exclusively to one aspect only—to the ideas explicitly stated, canvassing their fabric, but disregarding the tone of thought which gives them their impetus. The deeper significance of rationalism, for instance, lies in the fact that it cor-

[5] A more detailed account of this is given in my article on 'Alternative Logics' in *Proceedings of the Aristotelian Society*, 1945–6.

responds to what the scientist *does*, strengthening his belief that, if he only tries hard, he *can* get to the bottom of things. But slowly and gradually the mental climate changes, and then a philosophy may find itself out of tune with its time.

I do not think for a minute that what I have said is a conclusive refutation of Kant. On the other hand—you may confute and kill a scientific theory; a philosophy dies only of old age.

VIII

The Ascription of Responsibility and Rights

H. L. A. HART

There are in our ordinary language sentences whose primary function is not to describe things, events, or persons or anything else, nor to express or kindle feelings or emotions, but to do such things as claim rights ('This is mine'), recognize rights when claimed by others ('Very well, this is yours'), ascribe rights whether claimed or not ('This is his'), transfer rights ('This is now yours'), and also to admit or ascribe or make accusations of responsibility ('I did it', 'He did it', 'You did it'). My main purpose in this article is to suggest that the philosophical analysis of the concept of a human action has been inadequate and confusing, at least in part because sentences of the form 'He did it' have been traditionally regarded as primarily descriptive whereas their principal function is what I venture to call *ascriptive*, being quite literally to ascribe responsibility for actions much as the principal function of sentences of the form 'This is his' is to ascribe rights in property. Now ascriptive sentences and the other kinds of sentence quoted above, though they may form only a small part of our ordinary language, resemble in some important respects the formal statements of claim, the indictments, the admissions, the judgements, and the verdicts which constitute so large and so important a part of the language of lawyers; and the logical peculiarities which distinguish these kinds of sentences from descriptive sentences, or rather from the theoretical model of descriptive sentences with which philosophers often work, can best be grasped by considering certain characteristics of legal concepts, as these appear in the practice and procedure of the law rather than in the theoretical discussions of legal concepts by jurists who are apt to be influenced by philosophical theories. Accordingly, in the first part of this paper I attempt to bring out some of these characteristics of legal concepts; in the second, I attempt to show how sentences ascribing rights function in our ordinary language and also why their distinctive function is overlooked; and in the third part I attempt to make good my claim that sentences of the form 'He did it' are fundamentally ascriptive and that some at any rate of the philosophical puzzles concerning 'action' have resulted from inattention to this fact.

I

As everyone knows, the decisive stage in the proceedings of an English law court is normally a *judgement* given by the court to the effect that certain facts (Smith put arsenic in his wife's coffee and as a result she died) are true and that certain legal consequences (Smith is guilty of murder) are attached to those facts. Such a judgement is therefore a compound or blend of facts and law; and, of course, the claims and the indictments upon which law courts adjudicate are also blends of facts and law, though claims, indictments, and judgements are different from each other. Now there are several characteristics of the legal element in these compounds or blends which conspire to make the way in which facts support or fail to support legal conclusions, or refute or fail to refute them, unlike certain standard models of how one kind of statement supports or refutes another upon which philosophers are apt to concentrate attention. This is not apparent at once: for when the judge decides that on the facts which he has found there is a contract for sale between A and

B, or that B, a publican, is guilty of the offence[1] of supplying liquor to a constable on duty, or that B is liable for trespass because of what his horse has done on his neighbour's land, *it looks* from the terminology as if the law must consist of a set, if not a system, of legal concepts such as 'contract', 'the offence of supplying liquor to a constable on duty', 'trespass', invented and defined by the legislature or some other 'source', and as if the function of the judge was simply to say 'Yes' or 'No' to the question: 'Do the facts come within the scope of the formula defining the necessary and sufficient conditions of "contract", "trespass", or "the offence of supplying liquor to a constable on duty"?'

But this is for many reasons a disastrous over-simplification and indeed distortion, because there are characteristics of legal concepts which make it often absurd to use in connection with them the language of necessary and sufficient conditions. One important characteristic which I do not discuss in detail is no doubt vaguely familiar to most people. In England, the judge is not supplied with explicitly formulated general criteria defining 'contract', or 'trespass'; instead he has to decide by reference to past cases or precedents whether on the facts before him a contract has been made or a trespass committed; and in doing this he has a wide freedom, in judging whether the present case is sufficiently near to a past precedent, and also in determining what the past precedent in fact amounts to, or, as lawyers say, in identifying the *ratio decidendi* of past cases. This imports to legal concepts a vagueness of character very loosely controlled by judicial traditions of interpretation, and it has the consequence that usually the request for a definition of a legal concept—'What is a trespass?' 'What is a contract?'—cannot be answered by the provision of a verbal rule for the translation of a legal expression into other terms or one specifying a set of necessary and sufficient conditions. *Something* can be done in the way of providing an outline, in the form of a general statement of the effect of past cases, and that is how the student starts to learn the law. But beyond a point, answers to the questions 'What is trespass?', 'What is con-

[1] S. 16 of the Licensing Act, 1872.

tract?', if they are not to mislead, must take the form of references to the leading cases on the subject, coupled with the use of the word 'etcetera'.

But there is another characteristic of legal concepts, of more importance for my present purpose, which makes the word 'unless' as indispensable as the word 'etcetera' in any explanation or definition of them; and the necessity for this can be seen by examining the distinctive ways in which legal utterances can be challenged. For the accusations or claims upon which law courts adjudicate can usually be challenged or opposed in two ways. First, by a denial of the facts upon which they are based (technically called a traverse or joinder of issue) and secondly by something quite different, namely, a plea that although all the circumstances on which a claim could succeed are present, yet in the particular case, the claim or accusation should not succeed because other circumstances are present which brings the case under some recognized head of exception, the effect of which is either to defeat the claim or accusation altogether, or to 'reduce' it so that only a weaker claim can be sustained. Thus a plea of 'provocation' in murder cases, if successful, 'reduces' what would otherwise be murder to manslaughter; and so in a case of contract a defence that the defendant has been deceived by a material fraudulent misrepresentation made by the plaintiff entitles the defendant in certain cases to say that the contract is not valid as claimed, nor 'void', but 'voidable' at his option. In consequence, it is usually not possible to define a legal concept such as 'trespass' or 'contract' by specifying the necessary and sufficient conditions for its application. For any set of conditions may be adequate in some cases but not in others, and such concepts can only be explained with the aid of a list of exceptions or negative examples showing where the concept may not be applied or may only be applied in a weakened form.

This can be illustrated in detail from the law of contract. When the student has learnt that in English law there are positive conditions required for the existence of a valid contract, i.e. at least two *parties*, an *offer* by one, *acceptance* by the other, a *memorandum* in writing in some cases and *consideration*, his understanding of the legal concept of a contract is still incomplete, and remains so even if he has learnt the lawyers' technique for the interpretation of the technical but still vague terms, 'offer', 'acceptance', 'memorandum', 'consideration'. For these conditions, although necessary, are not always sufficient and he has still to learn what can *defeat* a claim that there is a valid contract, even though all these conditions are satisfied. That is the student has still to learn what can follow on the word 'unless', which should accompany the statement of these conditions. This characteristic of legal concepts is one for which no word exists in ordinary English. The words 'conditional' and 'negative' have the wrong implications, but the law has a word which with some hesitation I borrow and extend: this is the word '*defeasible*', used of a legal interest in property which is subject to termination or '*defeat*' in a number of different contingencies but remains intact if no such contingencies mature. In this sense, then, contract is a defeasible concept.

The list of defences with which an otherwise valid claim in contract can be met is worth a philosopher's inspection because it is here that reference to the factor that intrigues him—the mental factor—is mainly to be found. Thus the principal defences include the following:[2]

A. Defences which refer to the knowledge possessed by the defendant.
  i. Fraudulent misrepresentation.
  ii. Innocent misrepresentation.
  iii. Non-disclosure of material facts (in special cases, e.g. contracts of insurance, only).

B. Defences which refer to what may be called the will of the defendant.
  i. Duress.
  ii. Undue influence.

[2] This list, of course, is only a summary reference to the more important defences, sufficient to illustrate the point that the defeasible concept of contract cannot be defined by a set of necessary and always sufficient conditions. There are important omissions from this list, e.g. the disputed topic known to lawyers as 'Mistake'. Adequate discussion and illustration of these and other defences will be found in legal textbooks on contract, e.g. Cheshire and Fifoot, *Law of Contract*, Chap. IV.

C. Defences which may cover both knowledge and will.

    i. Lunacy.

    ii. Intoxication.

D. Defences which refer to the general policy of the law in discouraging certain types of contract, such as

    i. Contracts made for immoral purposes.

    ii. Contracts which restrain unreasonably the freedom of trade.

    iii. Contracts tending to pervert the course of justice.

E. The defence that the contract is rendered 'impossible of performance' or 'frustrated' by a fundamental and unexpected change of circumstance, e.g. the outbreak of a war.

F. The defence that the claim is barred by lapse of time.

Most of these defences are of general application to all contracts. Some of them, e.g. those made under (D), destroy altogether the claim that there is a contract, so that it is void *ab initio*; others, e.g. those under (B) or (C), have a weaker effect, rendering it merely 'voidable' at the option of the party concerned, and till this option is exercised the contract remains valid so that rights may be acquired by third parties under it; while the lapse of time mentioned in (F) merely extinguishes the right to institute legal proceedings, but does not otherwise affect the existence of the contract. It is plain, therefore, that no adequate characterization of the legal concept of a contract could be made without reference to these extremely heterogeneous defences and the manner in which they respectively serve to defeat or weaken claims in contract. The concept is irreducibly defeasible in character and to ignore this is to misrepresent it. But, of course, it is *possible* to obscure the character of such concepts by providing a general formula which seems to meet the demand often felt by the theorist for a definition in terms of a set of necessary and sufficient conditions; and since philosophers have, I think, obscured in precisely this way the defeasible character of the concept of an action, it is instructive to consider how such an obscuring general formula could be provided in the case of contract and to what it leads.

Thus the theorist bent on providing a general definition of contract could at any rate make a beginning by selecting the groups of defences (A), (B) and (C), which refer to the will and knowledge of the defendant, and by then arguing that the fact that these defences are admitted or allowed shows that the definition of contract requires as necessary conditions that the minds of the parties should be 'fully informed' and their wills 'free'. And, indeed, legal theorists and also on occasion judges do attempt to state the 'principles' of the law of contract much in this way. Thus Sir Frederick Pollock, writing[3] of the consent of the parties required for the constitution of a valid contract, says 'but we still require other conditions in order to make the consent binding on him who gives it. . . . The consent must be true, full and free'. Now, of course, this method of exposition of the law may be innocuous and indeed helpful as a summary of various types of defences which usefully stresses their universal application to all contracts, or emphasizes the similarities between them and so suggests analogies for the further development of the law or what can be called 'reasons' for that development. But unless most carefully qualified, such a general formula may be profoundly misleading; for the positive looking doctrine 'consent must be true, full and free' is only accurate as a statement of the law if treated as a compendious reference to the defences with which claims in contract may be weakened or met, whereas it suggests that there are certain psychological elements required by the law as necessary conditions of contract and that the defences are merely admitted as negative *evidence* of these. But the defence, e.g., that B entered into a contract with A as a result of the undue influence exerted upon him by A, is not evidence of the absence of a factor called 'true consent', but one of the multiple criteria for the use of the phrase 'no true consent'. To say that the law requires true consent is there-

[3] *Principles of the Law of Contract*, 10th edn., p. 442. The words omitted are 'though their absence in general is not to be assumed and the party seeking to enforce a contract is not expected to give affirmative proof that they have been satisfied'.

fore, in fact, to say that defences such as undue influence or coercion, and any others which should be grouped with them, are admitted. And the practice of the law (in which general phrases such as 'true consent' are of little importance) as distinct from the theoretical statement of it by jurists (in which general terms bulk largely) makes this clear; for no party attempting to enforce a contract is required to give evidence that there was 'true, full and free consent', though in special cases where some person in a fiduciary position seeks to enforce a bargain with the person in relation to whom he occupies that position, the onus lies upon him to prove that no influence was, in fact, exerted. But, of course, even here the proof consists simply in the exclusion of those facts which ordinarily constitute the defence of undue influence, though the onus in such cases is by exception cast on the plaintiff. Of course, the theorist could make irrefutable his theory that there are psychological elements ('full and free consent') required as necessary conditions of contract, by ascribing the actual procedure of the courts to the practical difficulties of proving 'mental facts'; and it is sometimes said that it is merely a matter of practical convenience that 'objective tests' of these elements have been adopted and that the onus of proof is usually upon the defendant to prove the nonexistence of these necessary elements. Such a doctrine is assisted by the ambiguity of the word 'test' as between evidence and criteria. But to insist on this as the 'real' explanation of the actual procedure of the courts in applying the defeasible concept of a contract would merely be to express obstinate loyalty to the persuasive but misleading logical ideal that all concepts must be capable of definition through a set of necessary and sufficient conditions. And, of course, even if this programme were carried through for the defences involving the 'mental' element it is difficult to see how it could be done for the other defences with which claims in contract can be met,[4] and, accordingly, the defeasible character of the concept would still remain.

---

[4] It could, of course, be done vacuously by specifying as the necessary and sufficient condition of contract, consent and other positive conditions and the negation of the disjunction of the various defences.

The principal field where jurists have, I think, created difficulties for themselves (in part under the influence of the traditional philosophical analysis of action) by ignoring the essentially defeasible character of the concepts they seek to clarify is the Criminal Law. There is a well-known maxim, '*actus non est reus nisi mens sit rea*', which has tempted jurists (and less often judges) to offer a general theory of 'the mental element' in crime (*mens rea*) of a type which is logically inappropriate just because the concepts involved are defeasible and are distorted by this form of definition. For in the case of crime, as in contract, it is possible to compile a list of the defences or exceptions with which different criminal charges may with differing effect be met, and to show that attempts to define in general terms 'the mental conditions' of liability, like the general theory of contract suggested in the last paragraph, are only not misleading if their positive and general terms are treated merely as a restatement or summary of the fact that various heterogeneous defences or exceptions are admitted. It is true that in crime the position is more complicated than in contract, since fewer defences apply to all crimes (there being notable differences between crimes created by statute and common-law crimes) and for some crimes proof of a specific intention is required. Further, it is necessary in the case of crime to speak of defences *or exceptions* because in some cases, e.g. murder, the onus of proof may be on the Prosecution to provide evidence that circumstances are not present which would, if present, defeat the accusation. Yet, none the less, what is meant by the mental element in criminal liability (*mens rea*) is only to be understood by considering certain defences or exceptions, such as Mistake of Fact, Accident, Coercion, Duress, Provocation, Insanity, Infancy,[5] most of which have come to be admitted in most crimes, and in some cases exclude liability altogether, and in others merely 'reduce' it. The fact that these are admitted as defences or exceptions constitutes the cash value of the maxim '*actus non est reus nisi mens sit rea*'. But in pursuit of the will-o'-the-wisp of a

[5] See for a detailed discussion of these and other defences or exceptions, Kenny: *Outline of Criminal Law*, Chap. IV.

general formula, legal theorists have sought to impose a spurious unity (as judges occasionally protest) upon these heterogeneous defences and exceptions, suggesting that they are admitted as merely evidence of the absence of some single element ('intention') or, in more recent theory, two elements ('foresight' and 'voluntariness') universally required as necessary conditions of criminal responsibility. And this is misleading because what the theorist misrepresents as evidence negativing the presence of necessary mental elements are, in fact, multiple criteria or grounds defeating the allegation of responsibility. But it is easy to succumb to the illusion that an accurate and satisfying 'definition' can be formulated with the aid of notions like 'voluntariness' because the logical character of words like 'voluntary' is anomalous and ill-understood. They are treated in such definitions as words having positive force, yet, as can be seen from Aristotle's discussion in Book III of the Nicomachean Ethics, the word 'voluntary' in fact serves to exclude a heterogeneous range of cases such as physical compulsion, coercion by threats, accidents, mistakes, etc., and not to designate a mental element or state; nor does 'involuntary' signify the absence of this mental element or state.[6] And so in a murder case it is a

[6] Thus Mr. J. W. C. Turner, in his well-known essay (in *The Modern Approach to Criminal Law. English Studies in Criminal Science*, Vol. I, p. 199) on the 'Mental Element in Crimes at Common Law' lays down two rules defining the mental element.

(First rule): 'It must be proved that the accused's conduct was voluntary.'

(Second rule): 'It must be proved that . . . he must have foreseen that certain consequences were likely to follow on his acts or omissions' (p. 199). Mr. Turner's view is indeed an improvement on previous attempts to 'define' the mental element in crime so far as it insists that there is not a single condition named *mens rea* and also in his statement on page 199 that the extent to which 'foresight of consequence' must have extended differs in the case of each specific crime. But none the less this procedure is one which really obscures the concepts it is meant to clarify, for the words 'voluntary' and 'involuntary' are used as if they refer to the presence and absence, respectively, in the agent of some single condition. Thus on page 204, Mr. Turner gives the same title of 'involuntary conduct' to cases of acts done under hypnotic suggestion or when sleepwalking, to 'pure' accidents, and to certain cases of insanity, drunkenness,

defence that the accused pulled the trigger reasonably but
mistakenly believing that the gun was unloaded; or that
there was an accident because the bullet unexpectedly
bounced off a tree; or that the accused was insane (within
the legal definition of insanity) or an infant; and it is a partial defence 'reducing' the charge from murder to manslaughter that the accused fired the shot in the heat of the
moment when he discovered his wife in adultery with the
victim. It is, of course, *possible* to represent the admission
of these different defences or exceptions as showing that
there is a single mental element ('voluntariness') or two elements ('voluntariness' and 'foresight') required as necessary
mental conditions (*mens rea*) of full criminal liability. But
in order to determine what 'foresight' and 'voluntariness' are
and how their presence and absence are established it is necessary to refer back to the various defences; and then these
general words assume merely the status of convenient but
sometimes misleading summaries expressing the absence of
all the various conditions referring to the agents' knowledge
or will which eliminate or reduce responsibility.

Consideration of the defeasible character of legal concepts
helps to explain how statements of fact support or refute
legal conclusions and thus to interpret the phrases used by
lawyers for the connection between fact and law when they
speak of 'the legal effect or consequences of the facts' or 'the
conclusions of law drawn from the facts' or 'consequences
attached to the facts'. In particular, it shows how wrong it
would be to succumb to the temptation, offered by modern
theories of meaning, to identify the meaning of a legal concept, say 'contract', with the statement of the conditions in
which contracts are held to exist; since, owing to the defeasible character of the concept, such a statement, though it
would express the necessary and sometimes sufficient conditions for the application of 'contract', could not express conditions which were always sufficient. But, of course, any
such theory of the meaning of legal concepts would fail for
far more fundamental reasons: for it could not convey the

---

and infancy, as well as to the case where B holds a weapon and A,
against B's will, seizes his hand and the weapon and therewith
stabs C.

composite character of these concepts nor allow for the distinctive features due to the fact that the elements in the compound are of distinct logical types.

Two of these distinctive features are of special relevance to the analysis of action and arise out of the truism that what a judge does is to judge; for this has two important consequences. First, the Judge's function is, e.g.,[7] in a case of contract to say whether there is or is not a valid contract, upon the claims and defences actually made and pleaded before him and the facts brought to his attention, and not on those which might have been made or pleaded. It is not his function to give an ideally correct legal interpretation of the facts, and if a party (who is *sui juris*) through bad advice or other causes fails to make a claim or plead a defence which he might have successfully made or pleaded, the judge in deciding in such a case, upon the claims and defences actually made, that a valid contract exists has given the right decision. The decision is not merely the best the judge can do under the circumstances, and it would be a misunderstanding of the judicial process to say of such a case that the parties were merely treated *as if* there were a contract. There *is* a contract in the timeless sense of 'is' appropriate to judicial decisions. Secondly, since the judge is literally deciding that on the facts before him a contract does or does not exist, and to do this is neither to describe the facts nor to make inductive or deductive inferences from the statement of facts, what he does may be either a *right* or a *wrong* decision or a *good* or *bad* judgement and can be either *affirmed* or *reversed* and (where he has no jurisdiction to decide the question) may be *quashed* or *discharged*. What cannot be said of it is that it is either *true* or *false*, logically necessary or absurd.

There is, perhaps, not much to tempt anyone to treat a judicial decision as a descriptive statement, or the facts as related to legal conclusions as being related as statements of fact may be to some descriptive statement they justify: though I think the tendency, which I have already mentioned, to regard the exceptions or defences which can defeat

[7] Different considerations may apply in criminal cases.

claims or accusations merely as evidence of the absence of some necessary condition required by the law in the full definition of a legal concept is in fact an attempt to assimilate a judicial decision to a theoretical model of a descriptive statement; for it is the expression of the feeling that cases where contracts are held not to exist 'must' be cases where some necessary condition, required in the definition of contract, is absent. But sometimes the law is cited as an example of a deductive system at work. 'Given the existing law,' it will be said, 'the statement of facts found by the judge entails the legal conclusion.' Of course, this could only be said in the simplest possible cases where no issue is raised at the trial except what common sense would call one of fact, i.e. where the parties are agreed that if the facts go one way the case falls within some legal rule and if they go another way it does not, and no question is raised about the meaning or interpretation of the legal rule. But even here it would be quite wrong to say that the judge was making a deductive inference; for the timeless conclusion of law (Smith is guilty of murder) is not entailed by the statements of temporal fact (Smith put arsenic in his wife's coffee on May 1st, 1944) which support it; and rules of law even when embodied in statutes are not linguistic or logical rules, but to a great extent rules for deciding.

II

If we step outside the law courts we shall find that there are many utterances in ordinary language which are similar in important respects, in spite of important differences, to the judicial blend of law and fact. But first some cases must be distinguished which are not instances of this phenomenon but are important because they help to explain why it has been overlooked.

A. First, we, of course, very often make use of legal concepts in descriptive and other sentences and the sentences in which we so use them may be statements and hence (unlike the judge's decision in which legal concepts are primarily used) they may be true or false. Examples of these are the obvious cases where we refer to persons or things by their known legal consequences, status or position. 'Who is that woman?' 'She is Robinson's wife and the adopted daughter of Smith, who inherited all his property.' 'What is that in the wastepaper basket?' 'My contract with John Smith.'

B. Secondly, we may refer to things, events and actions not by their known legal consequences, but by their intended or reputed legal consequence or position. 'What did your father do yesterday?' 'He made his will.' It should be noticed that this use may give rise to some curious difficulties if it is later found that the reputed or intended legal conclusion has not been established. What should we say of the sentence written in my diary that 'My father made his will yesterday' if it turns out that, since it was not witnessed and he was not domiciled in Scotland, the courts refuse to recognize it as a will? Is the sentence in my diary false? We should, I think, hesitate to say it is; on the other hand, we would not repeat the sentence after the court's decision is made. It should be noticed also that we may make use of our own legal system and its concepts for the purpose of describing things or persons not subject to it, as when we speak of the property of solitary persons who live on desert islands.

C. Thirdly, even outside the law courts we use the language of the law to make or reject claims. 'My father made his will yesterday' may indeed be a claim and not a pure descriptive statement, though it will, of course, carry some information with it, because with the claim is blended reference to some justifying facts. As a claim it may be later upheld or dismissed by the courts, but it is not true or false.

But in all these instances, though such sentences are uttered in ordinary life, the technical vocabulary of the law is used in them and so we are alert to the possibility that they may not function as descriptive sentences though very often they do. But consider now sentences where the words used derive their meaning from legal or social institutions, for example, from the institution of property, but are simple nontechnical words. Such are the simple indicative sentences in which the possessive terms 'mine', 'yours', 'his' appear as grammatical predicates. 'This is mine', 'This is yours', 'This is his' are primarily sentences for which lawyers have coined the expression 'operative words' and Mr. J. L. Austin the word 'performatory'.[8] By the utterance of such sentences, especially in the present tense, we often do not describe but actually perform or effect a transaction; with them we *claim* proprietary rights, *confer* or *transfer* such rights when they are claimed, *recognize* such rights or *ascribe* such rights whether claimed or not, and when these words are so used they are related to the facts that support them much in the same way as the judge's decision. But apart from this, these sentences, especially in past and future tenses, have a variety of other uses not altogether easy to disentangle from what I have called their primary use, and this may be shown by a sliding scale of increasing approximation to a pure descriptive use, as follows:

(*a*) First, the operative or performatory use. 'This is yours' said by a father handing over his gold watch to his son normally effects the transfer of the father's rights in the watch to the son; that is, makes a gift of it. But said by the elder son at the end of a dispute with his brother over the family possessions, the utterance of such a sentence constitutes a recognition of the rights of the younger son and abandons the claims of the elder. Of course, difficulties can arise in various ways over such cases analogous to the problems that confront the judge: we can ask whether the use of the words is a valid method of making gifts. If English law is the criterion, the answer is 'yes' in the example given; but it would be 'no' if what the father had pointed to was not his watch but his house, though in this case it may be that we would consider the son morally entitled to the house and the father morally bound to make it over to him. This shows that the rules which are in the background of such utterances are not necessarily legal rules. But the case to which I wish to draw attention is that where we use such sentences not to transfer or confer rights, but to ascribe or recognize them. For here, like a judge, the individual decides, *on* certain facts, that somebody else has certain rights, and his recognition is like a judgement, a blend of fact and rule if not of law.

[8] See his discussion of some cases in 'Other Minds', *Proceedings of the Aristotelian Society*, Suppl. Vol. XX, pp. 169–74, reprinted below, Second Series, Ch. VIII.

(*b*) Secondly, sentences like 'This is mine', 'This is yours', 'This is his' can be used simply as descriptive statements to describe things by reference to their owners. Taking visitors round my estate, I say, pointing to a field, 'This is mine' or 'I own this' purely by way of information.

(*c*) Thirdly, there is the more casual ascriptive use of these sentences in daily life which is difficult to classify. Suppose as we get up to go I see you have left a pen and give it to you, saying 'This is yours', or suppose I am walking in the street and notice as the man in front takes out his handkerchief a watch falls from his pocket. I pick it up and hand it back to him with the words 'This is yours'. We might be tempted to say that we are using the sentence here simply as a descriptive statement equivalent to 'You were carrying this and you dropped it or you left it'; but that this is not at any rate clearly so can be seen from the following considerations. If after we have handed back the watch the police drive up in a car and arrest the man for theft, I shall not willingly repeat the sentence and say it was true, though if it were 'descriptive' of the physical facts why should I not? On the other hand, I will not say of what I said that it was false. The position is, of course, that a very common good reason for recognizing that a person has some rights to the possession of a thing is that he is observed physically in the possession of it; and it is, of course, correct in such circumstances to ascribe such rights with the sentence 'This is yours' in the absence of any claim or special circumstance which may defeat them. But as individuals we are not in the position of a judge; our decision is not final, and when we have notice of new circumstances or new claims we have to decide in the light of them again. But in other respects the function of sentences of this simple and non-technical sort resembles that of judicial decisions. The concepts involved are defeasible concepts like those of the law and similarly related to supporting facts. It would be possible to take the heroic course of saying that sentences like 'This is his', 'This is yours' have acquired, like the word 'give', a purely descriptive sense to signify the normal physical facts on which it is customary to ascribe rights of possession; but this would not account for the peculiarity of our usage and would commit the mistake of ignoring their defeasible character and identifying the meaning of an expression with which we make decisions or ascriptions with the factual circumstances which, in the absence of other claims, are good reasons for them. With more plausibility it may be said that there is a sense of 'mine', 'yours', 'his' which is descriptive—the sense in which my teeth (as distinct from my *false* teeth) are mine or my thought and feelings are mine. But, of course, with regard to these we do not make and challenge utterances like 'This is mine', 'This is yours', 'This is his', and it is the logical character of these with which I am concerned.

III

So much for the ascription and recognition of rights which we effect with the simple utterances 'This is yours', 'This is his' and the associated or derivative descriptive use of these sentences. I now wish to defend the similar but perhaps more controversial thesis that the concept of a human action is an ascriptive and a defeasible one, and that many philosophical difficulties come from ignoring this and searching for its necessary and sufficient conditions. The sentences 'I did it', 'you did it', 'he did it' are, I suggest, primarily utterances with which we *confess* or *admit* liability, make accusations, or *ascribe* responsibility; and the sense in which our actions are ours is very much like that in which property is ours, though the connection is not necessarily a *vinculum juris*, a responsibility under positive law. Of course, like the utterances already examined, connected with the non-descriptive concept of property, the verb 'to do' and generally speaking the verbs of action, have an important descriptive use, especially in the present and future senses, their ascriptive use being mainly in the past tense, where the verb is often both timeless and genuinely refers to the past as distinguished from the present. Indeed, the descriptive use of verbs of action is so important as to obscure even more in their case than in the case of 'this is yours', 'this is his', etc., the non-descriptive use, but the logical character of the verbs of action is, I think, betrayed by the many features which sentences containing these verbs, in the past tense, have in common with sentences in the present tense using the possessive pronouns ('this is his', etc.), and so with judicial decisions by which legal consequences are attached to facts.

I can best bring out my point by contrasting it with what I think is the mistaken, but traditional philosophical analysis of the concept of an action. 'What distinguishes the physical movement of a human body from a human action?' is a famous question in philosophy. The old-fashioned answer was that the distinction lies in the occurrence before or simultaneously with the physical movement of a mental event related (it was hoped) to the physical movement as its psychological cause, which event we call 'having the intention' or 'setting ourselves' or 'willing' or 'desiring' to do the act in question. The modern answer is that to say that X performed an action is to assert a categorical proposition about the movement of his body, *and* a general hypothetical proposition or propositions to the effect that X would have responded in various ways to various stimuli, or that his body would not have moved as it did or some physical consequence would have been avoided, had he chosen differently, etc. Both these answers seem to me to be wrong or at least inadequate in many different ways, but both make the common error of supposing that an adequate analysis can be given of the concept of a human action in any combination of descriptive sentences, categorical or hypothetical, or any sentences concerned wholly with a single individual. To see this, compare with the traditional question about action the question 'What is the difference between a piece of earth and a piece of property?' Property is not a descriptive concept, and the difference between 'this is a piece of earth' or 'Smith is holding a piece of earth' on the one hand, and 'this is someone's property' and 'Smith owns a piece of property' on the other cannot be explained without reference to the non-descriptive utterances by means of which laws are promulgated and decisions made, or at the very least without reference to those by which rights are recognized. Nor, I suggest, can the difference between 'His body moved in violent contact with another's' and 'He did it' (e.g. 'He hit her') be explained without reference to the non-descriptive use of sentences by which liabilities or responsibility are ascribed. What is fundamentally wrong in both the old and the new version of the traditional analysis of action as a combination of physical and psychological events or a combination of categorical and hypothetical descriptive sentences, is its mistake in identifying the meaning of a non-descriptive utterance ascribing responsibility in stronger or weaker form, with the factual circumstances which support or are good reasons for the ascription. In other words, though of course not all the rules in accordance with which, in our society, we ascribe responsibility are reflected in our legal code nor vice versa, yet our concept of an action, like our concept of property, is a social concept and logically dependent on accepted rules of conduct. It is fundamentally not descriptive, but ascriptive in character; and it is a defeasible concept to be defined through exceptions and not by a set of necessary and sufficient conditions whether physical or psychological. This contention is supported by the following considerations:

First, when we say after observing the physical movements of a living person in conjunction with another, 'Smith hit her', or 'Smith did it' in answer to the question 'Who hit her?' or 'Who did it?' we surely do not treat this answer as a combined assertion that a physical movement of Smith's body took place, and that some inferred mental event occurred in Smith's mind (he set himself or intended to hit her); for we would be adding something to this answer if we made any such reference to psychological occurrences. Nor do we treat this answer as a combination of categorical or hypothetical sentences descriptive of a physical movement and of Smith's disposition or what would have happened had he chosen differently. On the contrary, saying 'He hit her' in these circumstances is, like saying 'That is his', a blend. It is an ascription of liability justified by the facts; for the observed physical movements of Smith's body are the circumstances which, in the absence of some defence, support, or are good reasons for the ascriptive sentence 'He did it'. But, of course, 'He did it' differs from 'That is his' for we are ascribing responsibility not rights.

Secondly, the sentence 'Smith hit her' can be challenged in the manner characteristic of defeasible legal utterances in two distinct ways. Smith or someone else can make a flat denial of the relevant statement of the physical facts, 'No, it was Jones, not Smith'. Alternatively (but since we are not in a law court, not also cumulatively), any of a vast array of defences can be pleaded by Smith or his friends which, though they do not destroy the charge altogether, soften it, or, as lawyers say, 'reduce' it.

Thus, to 'He did it' ('He hit her') it may be pleaded:

1. 'Accidentally' (she got in his way while he was hammering in a nail).

2. 'Inadvertently' (in the course of hammering in a nail, not looking at what he was doing).

3. 'By mistake for someone else' (he thought she was May, who had hit him).

4. 'In self defence' (she was about to hit him with a hammer).

5. 'Under great provocation' (she had just thrown the ink over him).

6. 'But he was forced to by a bully' (Jones said he would thrash him).

7. 'But he is mad, poor man.'

Thirdly. It is, of course, possible to take the heroic line and say that all these defences are just so many signs of the absence in each case of a common psychological element, 'intention', 'voluntariness', 'consciousness', required in a 'full' definition of an action, i.e. as one of its necessary and sufficient conditions, and that the concept is an ordinary descriptive concept after all. But to this, many objections can be made. These positive-looking words 'intention', etc., if put forward as necessary conditions of all action only succeed in posing as this if in fact they are a comprehensive and misleadingly positive-sounding reference to the absence of one or more of the defences, and are thus only understandable when interpreted in the light of the defences, and not vice versa. Again, when we are ascribing an action to a person, the question whether a psychological 'event' occurred does not come up in this suggested positive form at all, but in the form of an inquiry as to whether any of these extenuating defences cover the case. Further, when a more specific description of the alleged common mental element is given, it usually turns out to be something quite special, and characteristic only of a special kind of action, and by no means an essential element in all actions. This is plainly true of Professor H. A. Pritchard's[9] 'setting ourselves', which well describes some grim occurrences in our lives, but is surely not an essential ingredient in all cases where we recognize an action.

Fourthly. The older psychological criterion affords no explanation of the line we draw between what we still call an action though accidental and other cases. If I aim at a post and the wind carries my bullet so that it hits a man, I am said to have shot him accidentally, but if I aim at a post, hit it, and the bullet then ricochets off and hits a man, this would not be said to be my action at all. But in neither case have I intended, set myself to do, or wished what occurred.

Fifthly. The modern formula according to which to say that an action is voluntary is to say that the agent could have avoided it if he had chosen differently either ignores the heterogeneous character of our criteria qualifying 'He did it' when we use words like 'accidentally', 'by mistake', 'under coercion', etc., or only avoids this by leaving the meaning of the protasis 'If he had chosen differently' intolerably vague. Yet our actual criteria for qualifying 'He did it', though multiple and heterogeneous, are capable of being stated with some precision. Thus, if the suggested general formula is used to explain our refusal to say 'He did it' without qualification when a man's hand is forcibly moved by another, it is misleading to use the same formula in the very different cases of accident, mistake, coercion by threats or provocation. For in the first case the statement 'the agent could not have acted differently if he had chosen' is true in the sense that he had no control over his body and his decision was or would have been ineffective; whereas in, e.g., the case of accident the sense in which the statement is true (if at all) is that though having full control of his body the agent did not foresee the physical consequences of its movements. And, of course, our

[9] See *Duty and Ignorance of Fact*, p. 24 *et seq.* [Recently reprinted as Chapter II of his *Moral Obligation*, O.U.P., 1949.—EDITOR.]

qualification of 'He did it' in cases of coercion by threats or provocation (which have to be taken into account in any analysis of our usage of verbs of action) can only be comprehended under the suggested general formula if the protasis is used in still different senses so that its comfortable generality in the end evaporates; for there will be as many different senses as there are different types of defences, or qualifications of 'He did it'. Some seek to avoid this conclusion by saying that in cases where we qualify 'He did it', e.g. in a case of accident, there are, in fact, two elements of which one is *the genuine* action (firing the gun) and the other are its effects (the man being hit), and that our common usage whereby we say in such cases 'He shot him accidentally' is inaccurate or loose. 'Strictly', it is urged, we should say 'He fired the gun' (action in the strict sense) and 'the bullet hit the man'. But this line of thought, as well as supposing that we can say what a 'genuine' action is independently of our actual usage of verbs of action, breeds familiar but unwelcome paradoxes. If cases of accident must be analysed into a genuine action *plus* unintended effects, then, equally, normal action must be analysed into a genuine action *plus* intended effects. Firing the gun must be analysed on this view into pulling the trigger *plus . . .* and pulling the trigger into cocking the finger *plus . . .* So that in the end the only 'genuine actions' (if any) will be the minimal movements we can make with our body where nothing 'can' go wrong. These paradoxes are results of the insistence that 'action' is a descriptive concept definable through a set of necessary and sufficient conditions.

Sixthly. When we ascribe as private individuals rights or liabilities, we are not in the position of a judge whose decision is authoritative and final, but who is required only to deal with the claims and defences actually presented to him. In private life, decisions are not final, and the individual is not relieved, as the judge often is, from the effort of inquiring what defences might be pleaded. If, therefore, on the strength of merely the physical facts which we observe we judge 'Smith hit her' and do not qualify our judgement, it can be wrong or defective in a way in which the judge's decision cannot be. For if, on investigating the facts, it appears that we should have said 'Smith hit her accidentally', our first judgement has to be qualified. But it is important to notice that it is not withdrawn as a false statement of fact or as a false inference that some essential mental event necessary for the truth of the sentence 'He did it' had occurred. Our ascription of responsibility is no longer justified in the light of the new circumstances of which we have notice. So we must judge again: not *describe* again.

Finally, I wish to say, out of what lawyers call abundant caution, that there are two theses I have not maintained. I have maintained no form of behaviourism, for although it often is correct to say 'He did it' on the strength only of the observed physical movements of another, 'He did it' never, in my view, merely describes those movements. Secondly, I wish to distinguish from my own the thesis, often now maintained as a solution or dissolution of the problem of free will, that to say that an action is voluntary *means* merely that moral blame would tend to discourage the agent blamed from repeating it, and moral praise would encourage him to do so. This seems to me to confuse the question of what we mean by saying that a man has done an action with the question of why we bother to assign responsibility for actions to people in the way we do. Certainly, there is a connection between the two questions, that is between theories of punishment and reward and attempts to elucidate the criteria we do in fact employ in assigning responsibility for actions. No doubt we have come to employ the criteria we do employ because, among other things, in the long run, and on the whole not for the wretched individual in the dock but for 'society', assigning responsibility in the way we do assign it tends to check crime and encourage virtue; and the social historian may be able to show that our criteria slowly alter with experience of the reformative or deterrent results obtained by applying them. But this is only one of the things which applying these criteria does for us. And this is only one of the factors which lead us to retain or modify them. Habit, or conservatism, the need for certainty, and the need for some system of apportioning the loss arising from conduct, are other factors, and though, of course, it is open to us to regret

the intrusion of 'non-utilitarian' factors, it yet seems to me
vital to distinguish the question of the history and the pragmatic value and, in one sense, the morality of the distinctions
we draw, from the question what these distinctions are.

IX

The Language of Political Theory

MARGARET MACDONALD

To read the classical texts of political philosophy, in a critical
mood, is to be both fascinated and perplexed by the curious
notation in which they are written. One meets here a 'contract' which one is carefully warned was never contracted; an
'organism' unknown to biology; a superior 'person' or higher
'self' with whom one can never converse; an 'association' or
'corporation', whose objects are obscure and which is not
listed in any of the recognized directories. All these descriptions, analogies or pictures have been applied to the State.
One or other of them can be found in the works of the most
notable political philosophers from Plato and Hobbes to
Laski and MacIver. Here, too, will be found elaborate discussions and disputes about whether men are or are not 'naturally' social; whether they 'really' will what they don't will;
whether there is a Law of Nature or a 'natural law' not established by any known empirical methods; whether freedom
or 'objective' freedom is not properly judicious coercion in
the interests of order, etc.

There is a genuinely philosophic air about these strange
uses of ordinary words. They seem to resemble the replies
sometimes given to the haunting doubts which attack us
when we reflect on other subjects. On our sensible experience,
for example. Is it, perhaps, only a perpetual illusion? Or on
moral actions. Can an action ever be completely disinter-

ested? Or on other people. Do they have feelings as we do, or are they merely perfectly acting automata? How can we ever be sure? It seems, then, likely that the tales about the social contract and the unmeetable person will be related to similar puzzles. I do not, however, intend to expound in detail any of the answers in which the words I have given are key words. I shall avoid exegesis of Hobbes or of Hegel. I want rather to discuss how the uses of these words with the pictures or analogies they embody are related to the puzzles by which they were suggested and to the ordinary uses of language about social relationships and political affairs. What sort of propositions are they and how do they function? For, at first glance, they seem very peculiar. To be told you are party to a contract, of which you were unaware, and which is nothing like what anyone would ever call a contract, seems to have little to do with giving your vote at a general election, sending your child to a State school, or paying a fine for exceeding the speed limit. Nor is your depression at the Labour Exchange likely to be much relieved by being told that you 'really' willed your unemployment (you would never have thought so, unaided) or that the State is a very superior moral person, only even more anonymous and inaccessible than the Permanent Secretary to the Ministry of Labour.

One trouble in politics is to determine how far the questions are empirical and to what extent they are linguistic. Another is to discover what are the ordinary uses of the words involved. For many important words used in political discussion have a degree of vagueness which makes it even easier in political than in other branches of philosophy to disguise a linguistic elucidation or recommendation as an important factual discovery. A further problem is the causation of these puzzles. Is it merely philosophical discomfort about language that induces people to ask certain questions about their social life and accept these answers? If not, is this philosophically important?

It is sometimes said that no one can understand or criticize political theories without a thorough knowledge of history. Hobbes and Locke cannot be properly understood without knowing the history of the English Civil War, the Revolution of 1688 and their relation to these events. Rousseau cannot be detached from the conditions in France immediately before the French Revolution of 1789. Hegel is inexplicable apart from the luscious yet strenuous atmosphere of the Romantic Movement and the beginnings of German nationalism. All these theories arose in peculiar circumstances of crisis in the particular societies of which their writers formed part and cannot be discussed as though they were of general application like the propositions of mathematics. This, however, is not quite true. It is certainly true that the propositions of politics are not like those of mathematics and it does indicate that practical as well as purely philosophical dissatisfactions have frequently co-operated to move philosophers to write political philosophy. Indeed, they have usually done so with the avowed intention of influencing political affairs. Nevertheless, they never supposed themselves merely to be writing tracts for their times. Locke doubtless wished to justify the Revolution Settlement, but not merely by considering how a reasonable social life was possible in seventeenth-century England, but upon what relationship the life of the members of any community, divided into rulers and ruled, must be based if it is not to appear contemptible to rational human beings. What justifies us in forming political societies, in obeying laws, in being subjected to other persons? This is not a puzzle peculiar to any age. Moreover, so far from having died with the controversies of the seventeenth and eighteenth centuries, the 'contract theory' is now being revived.[1] But even this may be philosophically as well as historically important. For present political conditions may be somewhat similar to those in which contract theories formerly flourished. Historical circumstances, then, may be important in answering the question, 'Why have philosophers been induced to ask these questions and accept these answers?' It may be objected that this is to confuse causes and reasons. A philosopher may be moved to doubt the existence of matter because he has swallowed too much opium, but this would be completely irrelevant to any reason with which he supported his view. Why, then, should it be philosophically im-

[1] Cf. Gough, *The Social Contract*, 1936 (Introduction and last chapter), H. D. Lewis, 'Is there a Social Contract?', *Philosophy*, January and April, 1940.

portant that he asks certain philosophical questions because he feels oppressed by the government, or, alternatively, because, like Hobbes, he is worried by the lack of order in the country? It is because the circumstances in which they are asked and answered may work differently for different kinds of philosophical propositions in influencing their effects. And this may be connected with their philosophical 'point'. With some, e.g. those of 'pure epistemology', their importance may be negligible; with others, those of ethics, perhaps, and, even more, those of politics, they may be more important.

What must also be considered, then, are the practical and psychological effects of these problems and their answers. No one will deny that in political affairs philosophical nonsense may have serious effects. Is this philosophically relevant, or not? To deny that it is seems to reduce philosophizing to mere scholastic verbalism. Not for any moral reason. Not because philosophers ruin themselves and their subject by sitting in ivory towers and talking about the uses of words instead of considering how the people perish (or flourish) on nonsensical theories and slogans. But simply because, not to try to understand how this language has effects, even though it may give no information, is to miss half its philosophical point and so is bad philosophy. The philosophical 'point' of a remark (or the 'point' of a remark which is of philosophical interest) is, at least partly, connected with the cause or reason which induces people to go on making it, though it can neither be supported nor refuted by any empirical evidence. It may be false, it may, if taken literally, be meaningless, but they feel that it has some use. This does seem to be relevant to the understanding of some philosophical remarks, if not of all.

It is true that no solipsist refuses to converse with others, unless he is also suffering from incipient schizophrenia. Nor does the sceptic about the existence of material objects sit down very gingerly on every chair for fear it isn't really there. For these problems have not, usually, been suggested by any practical difficulties about communication or knowledge in ordinary life. Nor will any answer which the philosopher gives to them be likely to alter his subsequent behaviour. The problems of epistemology are mainly academic. Their practi-

cal causation and effects, therefore, are unimportant. That is,
perhaps, why it is easier to see from such examples the predominantly linguistic character of philosophical problems, so
emphasized recently by Wittgenstein, Wisdom and others.
They can be traced, roughly, to a certain discomfort which
the philosopher obscurely feels about what seem to be un-
justifiable inconsistencies in our uses of certain words, e.g.
those of 'know' and 'feel'. And once he can be made to realize
this and that no linguistic change which he may wish to suggest will give him that super-empirical information about the
world which he supposed possible, he will cease asking unanswerable questions. The whole drama might be played by
two solitary sages on a desert island. But I am not convinced
that Butler, e.g., was merely puzzled about the use or misuse
of the word 'interest' or that he supposed that such misuse
was the only mistake of his opponents. He was worried because their philosophical remark that 'All action is really selfish' was seducing many people to a disregard of their duties.
And though Burke, quite rightly, thought most of what Rousseau wrote was, strictly, nonsense, he did not underestimate
his influence on the French Revolution. For whereas a person would be thought slightly crazy who took seriously his
doubts about the uniformity of nature and refused to eat his
dinner for fear the laws of nature might have changed since
yesterday and it would now poison him, many people would
not think it at all *absurd* that anyone who said, 'An action is
right only if by doing it the agent will promote his own advantage' should so interpret this as to neglect most of the
actions that would ordinarily be called his duties. They
might think he would come to a bad end, but not necessarily
in Bethlem. Yet, in a sense, to ask whether all action isn't
really selfish is a senseless question. And to assert that all
action is 'really' selfish is to make not an empirical but a grammatical statement. It expresses either a misuse of or an intention to extend the use of 'selfish' to cover actions to which
it does not ordinarily apply. But the distinctions formerly
marked by the ordinary uses of 'selfish/unselfish' must reappear in the new notation if it is to fulfil all the tasks of the
old. Nor does this change give us any fresh information about
our duties to others. In this it resembles the epistemological

puzzle about 'know'. When clearly stated, it takes the form of a linguistic recommendation. Yet it has, or may have, or perhaps only seems to have, certain effects which have been considered important. Not that it predicts any such effects. A linguistic recommendation predicts nothing about behaviour. It is empty of factual content. How, then, does it work so as to seem to need taking seriously in practical life? How does anyone 'act' on a purely grammatical statement, except in speech and writing? Yet it does seem sometimes as if they do. The connection of utilitarianism with social reform is another instance. So that completely to understand ethical problems and theories, more than linguistic considerations are required. Or rather, perhaps, different sorts of elements may be involved in linguistic considerations.

If this is true of ethics, it is even more true of politics. Consider the statement, 'The authority of the State derives from the contract or agreement by which men consented to give up certain liberties, to form a society and submit to government in order to obtain greater benefits. The interests of a State, therefore, are subordinate to the interests of its members.' The attitude thus expressed may have importantly different results from the one expressed by 'The authority of the State is absolute for it embodies the "real" will and permanent interests of its members. It does, moreover, further certain historical and/or divine purposes incapable of fulfilment by any or all of its members. The State, therefore, is a moral person of a higher type than its members who must be subordinated to it.' There may be a sense in which neither of the theories epitomized in these statements is directly verifiable by the facts. For the 'contract' and the 'real will' may correspond to nothing directly discoverable. There may be another sense in which all the facts to which both theories appeal are the same for each. There is, then, no empirical means of deciding between them. But do not two statements or theories mean the same if all their empirical consequences are identical? Yet the 'contractual' and the 'organic' views of political relations would never be ordinarily said to mean the same and they have had very different effects. If the difference is not an empirical one of finding facts which will support the one and refute the other; if it is not a difference in

their truth or falsity, what sort of difference is it? How can
they differ in meaning without differing in verifiable consequences? But how *do* they differ? They differ, obviously, in
picturing political relationships with the help of two very different images. One represents them under the guise of a contract freely entered into between responsible agents who understand the provisions and are prepared to keep them unless
infringed by the other party. Joining society in general and
keeping its laws is rather like joining a Trade Union and
agreeing not to blackleg or work for less than the minimum
rates, so long as the Union, on its side, agrees to maintain
and improve the conditions of labour. Or it is like undertaking to provide goods or services in return for certain pay-
ment. Most people have had some experience of such agreements. They know what they imply and how they feel about
them. If they have accepted the terms, they do not resent
being bound by them, so long as they are observed by the
other contractees. And, if not, either the law will enforce the
terms or they will be released from their share of the obligation. They do not regard themselves, after entering such
agreements, as being any 'higher' or 'lower' than they were
before. Such contracts are convenient devices to secure desired social ends. They are useful, and their obligations
should be respected, but no sensible person would rhapsodize
about them. If, then, people picture the relation between
themselves, the State and the Government in these terms,
certain consequences will tend to follow. They will tend to
be affected, emotionally as well as intellectually, in some
ways rather than others. They will probably tend to stress
the fact of or the need for the *consent* of the governed to its
governors. For no one can enter a contract without consenting
to it. They will emphasize the importance of the *responsibility* of governors to the governed. No contract can be solely
one-sided. Because of the reciprocal nature of contract, their
attitude to rulers will be critical rather than reverential. Certainly nothing done by rulers to fulfil their part of the bargain
will be accepted because proceeding from a higher moral authority than that of mere individuals. The attitude induced
by the 'contract' picture might be expected to stress personal
freedom and the existence on sufferance of all governments;

to be, in general, liberal, democratic and unmystical. And it has, historically, tended to produce this result. It encourages the view that social arrangements of all kinds are made by men for their own ends and can be altered and even ended at their will and pleasure. This does not preclude acknowledging that some arrangements, e.g. those comprised by the State, are very important, even that they function as fundamental conditions for most others. Only that they are not sacrosanct. Nor does it follow that changes must or will be undertaken without due regard for the customs and traditions of the past and the welfare of the future as well as of the present. But only that if, in spite of all this, they are *consented* to by a majority of the present members of a society, no higher authority can be found with a *right* to prevent them. The 'contract' view can take account of every fact stressed by other views, but its own difference of emphasis alters their point or effects. In political theory, as, indeed, in philosophy generally, it is very often not what is said, but the spirit in which it is said, which makes the difference.

The other picture tells a very different story. My relation to an organism of which I form part or to my 'higher' self is not determined by free choice. 'The State', said Burke,[2] 'ought not to be considered as nothing better than a partnership agreement in a trade of pepper and coffee, calico or tobacco, or some other such low concern, to be taken up for a little temporary interest, and to be dissolved by the fancy of the parties. It is to be looked on with other reverence. . . . It is a partnership in all science, a partnership in all art, a partnership in every virtue and in all perfection . . . it is a partnership not only between those who are living, but between those who are living, those who are dead, and those who are to be born . . . linking the lower with the higher natures, connecting the visible and invisible world, according to a fixed compact sanctioned by the inviolable oath which holds all physical and all moral natures each in their appointed place.' Compared with this splendid spectacle we, who compose any society here and now, are very small fry indeed. Should we not accept with becoming gratitude the

[2] Burke, *Reflections on the Revolution in France.*

fortunate chance that permits us to abase ourselves before
this embodiment of 'all virtue and all perfection'? 'Consent',
'choice', can mean only acceptance of what seems good to it,
and not to our unimportant selves. This is the attitude of
submission to and reverence for what is done by Authority,
especially if the Authority is or represents what is old and
respectable—or, now-a-days, if it commands forces of great
physical power—which is induced by this language. Consent,
freedom, criticism, which the contract picture emphasized,
are not necessarily denied, but they are minimized or re-
interpreted. I am no foe to liberty, said Burke, but it must
be a liberty connected with *order*. If a man is misguided
enough to resist the General Will, say Rousseau and Bosanquet, he must be forced to be free. The individual is trivial;
the social organism or organization is almost sacred.

These two ways of picturing political relationships may,
then, have very different practical and psychological effects
which may induce people to want to go on using them, although they learn nothing much from them about political
affairs. Some people like to feel part of a vast and important
organization in which their chief function is to admire and
obey. The picture of themselves deliberating about contracts,
making decisions, criticizing representatives, is much too fa-
tiguing. For others, any picture in which they were wholly
subordinate would be intolerable. A similar situation sometimes occurs in science. It is true, I believe, that all the
planetary motions could, with suitable complications, be described as well by the Ptolemaic as by the Copernican system. In one sense, therefore, they mean the same. But that in
another they do not is shown by the fierce resistance met by
Copernicus and his followers. It had very little connection
with the scientific value of their theory. The Ptolemaic theory
included the picture of man and his world at the centre of
the universe with the heavens revolving round them in cosy
circles. The alternative Copernican picture terrified people.
They felt lost, insecure, unimportant. Something had gone
for ever. Yet nothing had gone, for the facts were precisely
the same for each. But the *point* of the two notations, with
their accompanying pictures, used to describe the facts was

very different. In their psychological effects they were very different theories.

It may be objected that this use of the words 'picture' and 'image' is itself a misuse, or, at least, an extension of the ordinary use of these words.[3] This is true. I cannot draw the social organism as I can a rat, nor paint a portrait of the 'higher' self. And though I can imagine the scene when King John signed Magna Carta, I cannot similarly imagine that when Hobbes' pre-social beings contracted to form society. I can have an image of signing a building contract but not of signing the social contract. But, it may be urged, when it is said that the State resembles an organism or is based on contract, no particular organism or contract is meant. What is thus asserted is a general resemblance between political relationships and those between the parts of *any* organism or *any* contractees. But this seems very peculiar. I cannot have an image or paint a picture of a general resemblance. The words 'image' and 'picture' appear to be used for something which cannot be imaged or pictured at all, in the ordinary senses of these words. But this peculiar usage can be recommended. It emphasizes the fact that philosophical remarks resemble poetic imagery rather than scientific analogy.[4] There is a pictorial or analogical element in most theories, scientific as well as philosophical. In poetry there are metaphors and images, but no theories. And philosophical theories have always seemed slightly odd, if not bogus. The use of 'analogy' suggests 'argument by analogy', i.e. the deduction of new verifiable facts from a suggested resemblance which increases our knowledge about the world. Philosophical theories have no such application. Nevertheless, in common with the scientific analogies they have other, psychological and semi-logical effects. Compare, e.g., the different effects of the planetary theories already mentioned or of the 'mechanistic' and 'purposive' hypotheses in biology. Philosophical remarks about social contracts and higher selves work chiefly in these ways. Perhaps to look for a contract or a new biological entity after reading Locke and Hegel on the State is only slightly

[3] I owe this point to Mr. G. Ryle.
[4] Cf. Wisdom, 'Other Minds', *Mind*, Vols. 49 and 50.

less absurd than to look for flaming tigers after reading Blake
or to ask how Wordsworth knew 'at a glance' that he saw ten
thousand daffodils. The theories of the scientist give new
information about empirical facts; they also induce certain
emotional and intellectual attitudes. The language of the
poet is predominantly emotive; that of the philosopher less
so, but both also have some relation to certain facts, though
not that involved in the application of a scientific analogy.
They do, however, partly by the use of certain images and
metaphors express or call attention in a very vivid way to
facts and experiences of whose existence we all know but
which, for some reason, it seems important to emphasize.[5]
I do not wish to say that philosophy *is* (inferior) poetry and
(not pseudo) science, for it is neither, but philosophy. But
it is sometimes useful when considering philosophical theories, and particularly political theories, to realize how unlike
scientific theories they are, in some respects, and how much,
in others, they resemble the works of the poets. Rousseau
is far more like Shelley than he is like Lavoisier. The use of
the words 'picture' and 'image' stresses this resemblance and
avoids the scientific associations of the word 'analogy'. This
gives some justification for the extended use of these words.

But, according to their authors, political theories profess
to explain certain puzzles about social life which must now
be examined.

The surprising fact about political life, according to Hume,
is the ease with which the many are governed by the few.
Why should people thus submit to the jurisdiction of others
of their own kind? Obviously, it is not solely because of the
constant exercise or threat of physical force to compel conformity. The ruled, as Hume said, are always more numerous
and therefore more powerful than the rulers. Not even Hitler
can literally turn the whole of Germany into a concentration
camp. For if he did, one result would be, presumably, that
production would cease, and power would soon be useless.
Nor is force any explanation. For it is conceivable that someone should prefer, and many people have preferred to die

[5] I think this is true of some poetry, at least, but I do not wish to
dogmatize about the function of poetry.

rather than obey rulers of whom they disapproved. Nevertheless, most people most of the time do obey laws and accept the control of governments. It must then be either because they want to, or because they believe they ought to do so. But they do not always want to, and sometimes when they do want to they think they ought not to. The fundamental puzzle of political philosophy, then, is to find a valid reason for political obligation. Why should men be obliged to obey laws and be penalized if they do not? This leads to consideration of the nature of that which appears to command and enforce laws, viz., the State. And there is, perhaps, an even more 'fundamental' puzzle. Why should man live with others of his own kind at all? The laws which political obligation acknowledges are the rules of societies. But is it necessary to form political societies? Is man 'naturally' social or only by convention? If the second, why was this convention adopted, and how? We all know how individuals join a trade union, a church, a club. These are particular societies. But how and why did we all join society in general? What sort of process was this?

These questions have the familiar tone. Philosophers do not ask whether Zulus or Dodos exist, but whether *any* material objects exist: not whether I can climb Mount Everest, if I choose, but whether I can do *any* action, however carefully I choose. So the political question is not 'Why should I pay income tax?' or 'Why should I support the present British Government?' but 'Why should I obey *any* law, support *any* Government, acknowledge the authority of *any* State?' Why, indeed, should I be a member of *any* civil society?

I cannot consider all the answers which have been suggested to all these questions. Two have already been mentioned. If I have contracted with others to form a society and obey certain rules then my justification for keeping the laws will be that I formerly promised to do so, at least as long as they were generally observed by the other parties to the contract. But this theory leads to no original in the facts. When did I sign this agreement and with whom? One answer is, you did not sign it, but your ancestors did, only so long ago that all trace of it has been lost. The original

Magna Carta of society has vanished. Can it really be on account of this undiscoverable transaction that we keep the laws of England in 1941? For suppose, after incredible labour, archaeologists found the lost document, should we feel happier about observing the Education Acts? Ah, that settles it. Now we know why we should send Johnny to school at five instead of into the fields to mind the sheep. Absurd, of course. And what are the provisions of the contract? Am I bound by it to observe laws yet to be made, of which I know nothing, just because they are laws of the contracted society and government? That would be a very peculiar contract to sign. No, the existence of a contract of the kind required cannot be verified. And no contract which could be discovered would answer our question. This is always admitted by political philosophers. 'The social contract theory is really an attempt at analysing the logical presuppositions rather than the historical antecedents of the State',[6] says Mr. Gough. The answer it gives to the question of political obligation is that our only justification for obeying laws and governments is that we have consented to do so and that political obligation is not an asymmetrical relationship between rulers and ruled. Hence the use of the contract picture in supporting the claims of individuals and groups against despotic governments.

The word 'contract', then, is admittedly not used in its ordinary legal sense of the State and the basis of political obligation. It is only 'as if' we had signed a contract. The contract theory points not to a contract but to the fact that what we mean by saying that we ought to obey a law is that we have consented to it. But, as Hume said, unless habit, indolence and indifference are to be taken as consent, very few laws would be obeyed at all on this criterion. To how many do we individually consent, and how do we do so? However important, this cannot be the whole story.

What, then, of the view that the laws of the State ought to be obeyed because they are the edicts of some higher being with which each of us is for the time being identified, or because they represent what we ourselves 'really' will in our

[6] *The Social Contract*, p. 4.

best moments? According to Rousseau, by the act of social union a moral and collective person, endowed with the general will, is thereby brought into existence and thereafter known as the State or Sovereign. Nor, he is careful to add, must this person be regarded as fictitious because not a man.[7] For Bosanquet, the State and its system of law and order represents my 'higher' self, and its actions, even those which I explicitly reject, ought to be accepted because they are willed by the General Will which is my 'real' will as opposed to my selfish and trivial actual will. The earlier quotation from Burke expresses a similar view. The essential point of this view is that the State or Society (no distinction is usually made between them) is something of far greater value than any or all of the individuals at any one time who compose it. What it ordains, therefore, and expresses as law must be good and must, therefore, be what I should also will if I were as wise as it is. In fact, it is what my higher self wills though I do not. Therefore, I 'really' will it and I ought to do what I 'really' want to do although I actually don't want to do it. I do not intend to examine all the linguistic shifts and ambiguities of this theory; the use of 'self' and 'will', e.g., and the tendentious use of 'higher' and 'lower' where difference of value should be proved and not merely asserted. In fact, the extremely perverse use of language by these philosophers often blinds one to the undoubted facts which they emphasize and which are neglected by alternative theories. The State is not identified with any one or with the whole collection of its members but is something over and above them. That is to say, propositions can be made about the State which would be nonsense if made about any or all of its members. E.g., 'The English State has been established for at least four hundred years'. The State is a moral person. That is to say, it is sensible to say of actions which we ascribe to the State that they are right—or wrong. The sense in which these words are used is different from that for individuals but it is not nonsense to say 'I think the State acts rightly in providing Old Age pensions', though the analysis of this statement would be very complicated. The State is greater

[7] *The Social Contract*, Chapters 6 and 7.

and more permanent than the individual. That is true. The generations pass, but English state power remains. It is, therefore, likely that laws made according to the Constitution will be such as may reasonably be accepted. There is a presumption in their favour. Nor will responsible citizens wish rashly to destroy an established power and order which has served the past and serves the present moderately well and may be valued by future generations. The State serves more important purposes than the individual. Without accepting a mystical march of history, this also may be admitted. The actions of few individuals, e.g., are likely to affect so many people for so long a time as do most State actions. The State has international functions, relations to colonies, to other States which may have lastingly bad or good effects. No individuals, in their private capacity, could perform such functions. None of these facts about the difference between the State and the individual need be denied. Indeed, they are important criteria for the use of 'political obligation'. But they are *differences* merely. It does not follow from them that the State is either morally better or worse than any individual. Nor are any or all of them a sufficient basis for political obligation. I do not mean by saying that 'I ought to obey this law', that I was born, without my choice, a member of English society from which I received education, culture, the means of livelihood and the general system of law and order without which these would be impossible. Even though it may be true that all that one is and can do, is due to the facilities provided by the State and the social order, it does not follow that all State action is right and that all laws should be obeyed. For it is not self-contradictory to say 'This is an English law but it is a bad law and ought not to be kept'. Moreover, this view leads to the absurd conclusion that the laws of any community are equally good. The Nuremberg laws, therefore, are good for the Germans though they are bad for everyone else. But if they are bad, they are bad also for the Germans, though they may not recognize this.

Then is it, perhaps, because of their social effects that laws ought to be obeyed? Do we mean by the State, the dispenser of social benefits on the largest possible scale? This is the Utilitarian or realist view of the State. The State, like any other institution, is justified by its works. It does not depend on mythical contracts or mystical organisms but on a pragmatic sanction. 'The State is an organization for enabling the mass of men to realize social good on the largest possible scale' and social good 'consists in the unity our nature attains when the working of our impulses results in a satisfied activity'.[8] I am justified in obeying the laws only if I am tolerably satisfied with my life in the community. And anyone's life will, or ought to be, tolerably satisfactory if his 'impulses' are being satisfied. But what is the criterion that they are? I can know whether I am satisfied with my life, but even if I am, what follows? Does it follow that I am justified in obeying the laws because the State does or will provide the conditions of such satisfaction? Or that I am entitled to rebel if my impulses are not satisfied? Could I not be satisfied as the result of a bad law and dissatisfied as the result of a good? But Laski would say, it will be urged, that the good must be social. State action should be approved only if it promotes this desirable unity for all or most people. But what exactly *is* this desirable state and how do we know whether it has been achieved for everyone? Without an adequate criterion of this, how do we know what laws to obey and what governments to approve? The conditions of personal satisfaction are numerous and many could not be provided by the most benevolent State. I do not wish to suggest that Laski, or any other philosopher, supposes that all the conditions of a happy life can be provided by the State. But it is not easy to see from his remarks on the social good why any should be excluded. The utilitarian criterion, which seems so practical, is not one of the easiest to apply, or even to state clearly. Bentham's criterion is at least clear, if impossible to accept. Once this is discarded what *is* the 'social good' or the 'general welfare' whose promotion is the purpose of the State and the criterion of the goodness or badness of its actions and laws? Only the vaguest statements ever seem to be offered. This may be condemned as pedantic. To say that the State is justified by its works is to say, and this is known by all but the perverse, that it should be judged by the way in which

---

[8] Laski, *Grammar of Politics*, pp. 24, 25. London, 1925.

it makes possible for all citizens the material and cultural conditions of good living. The laws of a State should be chiefly directed to securing for all its members, employment, a reasonable income, health, education, good houses, etc. Certainly not all the conditions can be provided communally, but a great many can and should, and the more a State provides the more it should be approved. In fact, only if it tends to maximize certain obvious benefits should any law be obeyed. No laws ought to be partial. That is, I think, the point of the theory, which is generally favoured by social reformers. Far be it from me to minimize its importance. But again, I think, it is not and cannot be the whole story. For is it not conceivable that all these desirable objects might be promoted by what everyone would call a bad, e.g. a completely tyrannous State? The government of such a State might be exceedingly efficient in promoting social welfare to obtain popular support and the majority of its citizens might be thoroughly satisfied that all their impulses were satisfactorily fulfilled. Ought one then to support such a government and respect its laws? The usual reply is, 'Ah, but there must always be some important impulses left unsatisfied by such a Government; no bad governments could possibly promote the general good'. But now, is this an empirical statement? Suppose people no longer feel these important impulses, why should they bother about their satisfaction? Does this remove the difficulty? If people no longer resent actions which would normally be called tyrannical, do they cease to be tyrannical? Is contented slavery not repulsive? Utilitarian philosophers would probably not agree. They would say, as most people would, that such actions *ought* to be resented, and that they are not does not make them good. But then the utilitarian view can surely be expressed in the tautology, 'Only the governments which we ought to support are those which we ought to support because they promote general social good'. This is not very enlightening.

The utilitarian view, then, which pictures the State as an institution or association for promoting the interests of its members is not adequate. The picture likens the State to any other association with a specific purpose, e.g. a trade union, a college, a commercial company or a church. But the difference is that the objects of these associations can all be fairly clearly stated and, indeed, must be before they are given legal status. The object of the State itself cannot be thus stated. High wages and good working conditions might conceivably be achieved by other means than combining in trade unions: a copper mine might be discovered and worked without floating a commercial company, but there is no describable purpose or object of social life as such any more than of human life as such, which could be obtained by some alternative means. This picture, then, remains as inapplicable as the others. But it, too, points to important criteria for our use of 'political obligation'. That some laws promote desirable social improvements in the general conditions of living for the majority of people, is a good reason for accepting them. But it is not the sole justification for accepting any and every law.

What, then, is the answer to the original puzzle, 'Why should I obey *any* law or acknowledge the authority of *any* State or Government?' to solve which these pictures were invented? The discussion of the three most prominent types of answer seems to show that even discounting nonsense or picturesque terminology, none of them alone is sufficient. May it not also suggest that no such general answer is either possible or necessary? This would not be surprising. A general proof of the existence of material objects seems impossible, and to ask for it, absurd. No general criterion of all right actions can be supplied. Similarly, the answer to 'Why should I obey *any* law, acknowledge the authority of *any* State or support *any* Government?' is that this is a senseless question. Therefore, any attempted reply to it is bound to be senseless, though it may perform certain other useful or harmful functions. It makes sense to ask 'Why should I obey the Conscription Act?' or 'Why should I oppose the present German Government?' because by considering the particular circumstances and the characteristics of all concerned, it is possible to decide for or against obedience and support. We all know the kind of criteria according to which we should decide these two issues. But although it looks harmless and even very philosophical to generalize from these instances to 'Why should I obey *any* law or support *any* government?'

the significance of the question then evaporates. For the general question suggests an equally general answer and this is what every political philosopher has tried to give. But no general criterion applies to every instance. To ask why I should obey *any* laws is to ask whether there might be a political society without political obligations, which is absurd. For we mean by political society, groups of people organized according to rules enforced by some of their number. A state of anarchy is just not a state of political society and to ask whether, since laws are not obeyed in the first state they ought to be obeyed in the second is to ask a nonsensical question. But neither does it follow, as some idealists seem to suppose, that all laws should be equally accepted because commanded by a political authority. For this is, in fact, only another attempt to find a general criterion for political obligation. But it is not that which we always apply when considering political action. The political theorists want an answer which is always and infallibly right, just as the epistemologists want a guarantee that there are material objects or that generalization to the unexamined must be valid. But these are all equally senseless requests, for they result from stretching language beyond the bounds of significance. I know how to determine on any particular occasion whether or not I am suffering from an optical illusion. Therefore, it is sensible to ask 'Is this line really crooked or does it only seem to be?' But to ask whether, after applying all the relevant tests unsuccessfully, I am still and always deluded, is senseless. For the word 'deluded' has now lost all significance since however hard and carefully I look I can never find a veridical perception with which to compare my delusions. The word 'delusion' no longer significantly opposed to 'veridical' becomes meaningless. Similarly, I can determine whether or not I ought to observe the Education Acts or the Income Tax law. Obviously, I think I ought partly because they were passed by a freely elected Parliament, according to all the usual procedure, so that in some complicated and indirect sense I have consented to them. Then, too, they promote useful social ends and there may be other criteria for rightly obeying them. One or two of these criteria might be absent and I should not think it right to resist, if too many of them were I might get restive but not yet rebellious. A trade unionist, e.g., might rightly think that the Trade Union Disputes Act passed after the general strike was harsh and unfair but not sufficient in itself to risk civil war about, especially since a new government which trade unionists could help to elect might repeal the Act. But if too many acts are passed in suspicious circumstances and with dubious objects, the duty to resist tyranny will over-rule the duty to obey law. When or how cannot be stated in advance. Nor can the criteria for accepting a law be precisely stated. Consent, tradition, objects promoted, all the criteria emphasized by the political theorists are important, but not all are equally important on every occasion, though if one or more were persistently absent over a long period we should, rightly, object. The manner in which they (and probably others) are blended is indefinitely various and no precise definition could describe our usage. Nevertheless, it does not in the least follow that we do not very often know that a law should be obeyed and a government supported and sometimes that both should be resisted. Just as we know very well that the pillar box is red and that Jane Austen was not vulgar, although both 'red' and 'vulgar' are used vaguely.

This may seem a disappointing conclusion and not likely to have the stirring effects of the homeric stories of the social contract and the 'higher' self or even of Burke's rhapsodies on the British Constitution. But I think it has some practical value. The general, metaphysical theories are really very simple. They seek to reduce all political obligation to the application of an almost magical formula. All laws which should be obeyed result from the social contract, or the general will, or promote the greatest happiness of the greatest number, so in order to know your political duties look for the trade mark and leave the rest to government. They do imply that we can know once and for all almost by learning a single sentence, how and when political obedience is justified. But if there is no general criterion, but an indefinite set of vaguely shifting criteria, differing for different times and circumstances, then it may often, if not nearly always, be necessary to scrutinize our political relations to see whether we are on this particular occasion justified in giving or withholding our support to a measure or a government. The value

of the political theorists, however, is not in the general information they give about the basis of political obligation
but in their skill in emphasizing at a critical moment a criterion which is tending to be overlooked or denied. The
common sense of Locke and the eloquence of Rousseau rein-
forced and guided the revolt against dogmatic authority by
vividly isolating and underlining with the contract metaphor
the fact that no one is obliged to obey laws concerning none
of which he has had a chance to express consent or dissent. It
does not follow that this is the sole criterion of political
obedience, still less that having derived all political obligations from a social contract or a general will we can accept
them all happily and go to sleep. As rational and responsible
citizens we can never hope to know once and for all what our
political duties are. And so we can never go to sleep.

X

Gods

JOHN WISDOM

1. *The existence of God is not an experimental issue in the
way it was.* An atheist or agnostic might say to a theist 'You
still think there are spirits in the trees, nymphs in the streams,
a God of the world.' He might say this because he noticed
the theist in time of drought pray for rain and make a sacrifice and in the morning look for rain. But disagreement about
whether there are gods is now less of this experimental or
betting sort than it used to be. This is due in part, if not
wholly, to our better knowledge of why things happen as they
do.

It is true that even in these days it is seldom that one who
believes in God has no hopes or fears which an atheist has
not. Few believers now expect prayer to still the waves, but

some think it makes a difference to people and not merely in ways the atheist would admit. Of course with people, as opposed to waves and machines, one never knows what they won't do next, so that expecting prayer to make a difference to them is not so definite a thing as believing in its mechanical efficacy. Still, just as primitive people pray in a businesslike way for rain so some people still pray for others with a real feeling of doing something to help. However, in spite of this persistence of an experimental element in some theistic belief, it remains true that Elijah's method on Mount Carmel of settling the matter of what god or gods exist would be far less appropriate to-day than it was then.

2. *Belief in gods is not merely a matter of expectation of a world to come.* Someone may say 'The fact that a theist no more than an atheist expects prayer to bring down fire from heaven or cure the sick does not mean that there is no difference between them as to the facts, it does not mean that the theist has no expectations different from the atheist's. For very often those who believe in God believe in another world and believe that God is there and that we shall go to that world when we die.'

This is true, but I do not want to consider here expectations as to what one will see and feel after death nor what sort of reasons these logically unique expectations could have. So I want to consider those theists who do not believe in a future life, or rather, I want to consider the differences between atheists and theists in so far as these differences are not a matter of belief in a future life.

3. *What are these differences? And is it that theists are superstitious or that atheists are blind?* A child may wish to sit a while with his father and he may, when he has done what his father dislikes, fear punishment and feel distress at causing vexation, and while his father is alive he may feel sure of help when danger threatens and feel that there is sympathy for him when disaster has come. When his father is dead he will no longer expect punishment or help. Maybe for a moment an old fear will come or a cry for help escape him, but he will at once remember that this is no good now. He may feel that his father is no more until perhaps someone says to him that his father is still alive though he lives

now in another world and one so far away that there is no
hope of seeing him or hearing his voice again. The child may
be told that nevertheless his father can see him and hear all
he says. When he has been told this the child will still fear
no punishment nor expect any sign of his father, but now,
even more than he did when his father was alive, he will feel
that his father sees him all the time and will dread distress-
ing him and when he has done something wrong he will feel
separated from his father until he has felt sorry for what he
has done. Maybe when he himself comes to die he will be
like a man who expects to find a friend in the strange country where he is going, but even when this is so, it is by no
means all of what makes the difference between a child who
believes that his father lives still in another world and one
who does not.

Likewise one who believes in God may face death differently from one who does not, but there is another difference
between them besides this. This other difference may still
be described as belief in another world, only this belief is
not a matter of expecting one thing rather than another here
or hereafter, it is not a matter of a world to come but of a
world that now is, though beyond our senses.

We are at once reminded of those other unseen worlds
which some philosophers 'believe in' and others 'deny',
while non-philosophers unconsciously 'accept' them by using
them as models with which to 'get the hang of' the patterns
in the flux of experience. We recall the timeless entities
whose changeless connections we seek to represent in symbols, and the values which stand firm[1] amidst our flickering
satisfaction and remorse, and the physical things which,
though not beyond the corruption of moth and rust, are yet
more permanent than the shadows they throw upon the
screen before our minds. We recall, too, our talk of souls and
of what lies in their depths and is manifested to us partially
and intermittently in our own feelings and the behaviour of
others. The hypothesis of mind, of other human minds and
of animal minds, is reasonable because it explains for each
of us why certain things behave so cunningly all by them-

[1] In another world, Dr. Joad says in the *New Statesman* recently.

selves unlike even the most ingenious machines. Is the hypothesis of minds in flowers and trees reasonable for like reasons? Is the hypothesis of a world mind reasonable for like reasons—someone who adjusts the blossom to the bees, someone whose presence may at times be felt—in a garden in high summer, in the hills when clouds are gathering, but not, perhaps, in a cholera epidemic?

4. *The question 'Is belief in gods reasonable?' has more than one source.* It is clear now that in order to grasp fully the logic of belief in divine minds we need to examine the logic of belief in animal and human minds. But we cannot do that here and so for the purposes of this discussion about divine minds let us acknowledge the reasonableness of our belief in human minds without troubling ourselves about its logic. The question of the reasonableness of belief in divine minds then becomes a matter of whether there are facts in nature which support claims about divine minds in the way facts in nature support our claims about human minds.

In this way we resolve the force behind the problem of the existence of gods into two components, one metaphysical and the same which prompts the question 'Is there *ever any* behaviour which gives reason to believe in *any* sort of mind?' and one which finds expression in 'Are there other mind-patterns in nature beside the human and animal patterns which we can all easily detect, and are these other mind-patterns super-human?'

Such over-determination of a question syndrome is common. Thus, the puzzling question 'Do dogs think?', 'Do animals feel?' are partly metaphysical puzzles and partly scientific questions. They are not purely metaphysical; for the reports of scientists about the poor performances of cats in cages and old ladies' stories about the remarkable performances of their pets are not irrelevant. But nor are these questions purely scientific; for the stories never settle them and therefore they have other sources. One other source is the metaphysical source we have already noticed, namely, the difficulty about getting behind an animal's behaviour to its mind, whether it is a non-human animal or a human one.

But there's a third component in the force behind these questions, these disputes have a third source, and it is one

which is important in the dispute which finds expression in
the words 'I believe in God', 'I do not'. This source comes out
well if we consider the question 'Do flowers feel?' Like the
questions about dogs and animals this question about flowers
comes partly from the difficulty we sometimes feel over inference from *any* behaviour to thought or feeling and partly
from ignorance as to what behaviour is to be found. But
these questions, as opposed to a like question about human
beings, come also from hesitation as to whether the behaviour
in question is *enough* mind-like, that is, is it enough similar to
or superior to human behaviour to be called 'mind-proving'?
Likewise, even when we are satisfied that human behaviour
shows mind and even when we have learned whatever mind-
suggesting things there are in nature which are not explained
by human and animal minds, we may still ask 'But are these
things sufficiently striking to be called a mind-pattern? Can
we fairly call them manifestations of a divine being?'

'The question', someone may say, 'has then become merely
a matter of the application of a name. And "What's in a
name?"'

5. *But the line between a question of fact and a question
or decision as to the application of a name is not so simple as
this way of putting things suggests.* The question 'What's
in a name?' is engaging because we are inclined to answer
both 'Nothing' and 'Very much'. And this 'Very much' has
more than one source. We might have tried to comfort
Heloise by saying 'It isn't that Abelard no longer loves you,
for this man isn't Abelard'; we might have said to poor Mr.
Tebrick in Mr. Garnet's *Lady into Fox* 'But this is no longer
Silvia'. But if Mr. Tebrick replied 'Ah, but it is!' this might
come not at all from observing facts about the fox which we
have not observed, but from noticing facts about the fox
which we had missed, although we had in a sense observed
all that Mr. Tebrick had observed. It is possible to have before one's eyes all the items of a pattern and still to miss the
pattern. Consider the following conversation:

'"And I think Kay and I are pretty happy. We've always
been happy."

'Bill lifted up his glass and put it down without drinking.

'"Would you mind saying that again?"' he asked.

' "I don't see what's so queer about it. Taken all in all, Kay and I have really been happy."

' "All right," Bill said gently, "just tell me how you and Kay have been happy."

'Bill had a way of being amused by things which I could not understand.

' "It's a little hard to explain," I said. "It's like taking a lot of numbers that don't look alike and that don't mean anything until you add them all together."

'I stopped, because I hadn't meant to talk to him about Kay and me.

' "Go ahead," Bill said. "What about the numbers." And he began to smile.

' "I don't know why you think it's so funny," I said. "All the things that two people do together, two people like Kay and me, add up to something. There are the kids and the house and the dog and all the people we have known and all the times we've been out to dinner. Of course, Kay and I do quarrel sometimes but when you add it all together, all of it isn't as bad as the parts of it seem. I mean, maybe that's all there is to anybody's life."

'Bill poured himself another drink. He seemed about to say something and checked himself. He kept looking at me.'[2]

Or again, suppose two people are speaking of two characters in a story which both have read[3] or of two friends which both have known, and one says 'Really she hated him', and the other says 'She didn't, she loved him'. Then the first may have noticed what the other has not although he knows no incident in the lives of the people they are talking about which the other doesn't know too, and the second speaker may say 'She didn't, she loved him' because he hasn't noticed what the first noticed, although he can remember every incident the first can remember. But then again he may say 'She didn't, she loved him' not because he hasn't noticed the patterns in time which the first has noticed but because though he has noticed them he doesn't feel he still needs to emphasize them with 'Really she hated him'. The line be-

[2] H. M. Pulham, Esq., p. 320, by John P. Marquand.
[3] E.g. Havelock Ellis's autobiography.

tween using a name because of how we feel and because of what we have noticed isn't sharp. 'A difference as to the facts', 'a discovery', 'a revelation', these phrases cover many things. Discoveries have been made not only by Christopher Columbus and Pasteur, but also by Tolstoy and Dostoievsky and Freud. Things are revealed to us not only by the scientists with microscopes, but also by the poets, the prophets, and the painters. What is so isn't merely a matter of 'the facts'. For sometimes when there is agreement as to the facts there is still argument as to whether defendant did or did not 'exercise reasonable care', was or was not 'negligent'.

And though we shall need to emphasize how much 'There is a God' evinces an attitude to the familiar[4] we shall find in the end that it also evinces some recognition of patterns in time easily missed and that, therefore, difference as to there being any gods is in part a difference as to what is so and therefore as to the facts, though not in the simple ways which first occurred to us.

6. *Let us now approach the same points by a different road.*

6.1. *How it is that an explanatory hypothesis, such as the existence of God, may start by being experimental and gradually become something quite different can be seen from the following story:*

Two people return to their long neglected garden and find among the weeds a few of the old plants surprisingly vigorous. One says to the other 'It must be that a gardener has been coming and doing something about these plants'. Upon inquiry they find that no neighbour has ever seen anyone at work in their garden. The first man says to the other 'He must have worked while people slept'. The other says 'No, someone would have heard him and besides, anybody who cared about the plants would have kept down these weeds'. The first man says 'Look at the way these are arranged. There is purpose and a feeling for beauty here. I believe that someone comes, someone invisible to mortal eyes. I believe that the more carefully we look the more we shall find confirmation of this.'

[4] 'Persuasive Definitions', *Mind*, July, 1938, by Charles Leslie Stevenson, should be read here. It is very good. [Also in his *Ethics and Language*, Yale, 1945.—EDITOR.]

They examine the garden ever so carefully and sometimes they come on new things suggesting that a gardener comes and sometimes they come on new things suggesting the contrary and even that a malicious person has been at work. Besides examining the garden carefully they also study what happens to gardens left without attention. Each learns all the other learns about this and about the garden. Consequently, when after all this, one says 'I still believe a gardener comes' while the other says 'I don't' their different words now reflect no difference as to what they have found in the garden, no difference as to what they would find in the garden if they looked further and no difference about how fast untended gardens fall into disorder. At this stage, in this context, the gardener hypothesis has ceased to be experimental, the difference between one who accepts and one who rejects it is now not a matter of the one expecting something the other does not expect. What is the difference between them? The one says 'A gardener comes unseen and unheard. He is manifested only in his works with which we are all familiar', the other says 'There is no gardener' and with this difference in what they say about the gardener goes a difference in how they feel towards the garden, in spite of the fact that neither expects anything of it which the other does not expect.

But is this the whole difference between them—that the one calls the garden by one name and feels one way towards it, while the other calls it by another name and feels in another way towards it? And if this is what the difference has become then is it any longer appropriate to ask 'Which is right?' or 'Which is reasonable?'

And yet surely such questions *are* appropriate when one person says to another 'You still think the world's a garden and not a wilderness, and that the gardener has not forsaken it' or 'You still think there are nymphs of the streams, a presence in the hills, a spirit of the world'. Perhaps when a man sings 'God's in His heaven' we need not take this as more than an expression of how he feels. But when Bishop Gore or Dr. Joad write about belief in God and young men read them in order to settle their religious doubts the impression is not simply that of persons choosing exclamations with which to face nature and the 'changes and chances of this mortal life'. The disputants speak as if they are concerned with a matter of scientific fact, or of trans-sensual, trans-scientific and metaphysical fact, but still of fact and still a matter about which reasons for and against may be offered, although no scientific reasons in the sense of field surveys for fossils or experiments on delinquents are to the point.

6.2. *Now can an interjection have a logic?* Can the manifestation of an attitude in the utterance of a word, in the application of a name, have a logic? When all the facts are known how can there still be a question of fact? How can there still be a question? Surely as Hume says '. . . after every circumstance, every relation is known, the understanding has no further room to operate'?[5]

6.3. When the madness of these questions leaves us for a moment *we can all easily recollect disputes which though they cannot be settled by experiment are yet disputes in which one party may be right and the other wrong* and in which both parties may offer reasons and the one better reasons than the other. *This may happen in pure and applied mathematics and logic.* Two accountants or two engineers provided with the same data may reach different results and this difference is resolved not by collecting further data but by going over the calculations again. Such differences indeed share with differences as to what will win a race, the honour of being among the most 'settlable' disputes in the language.

6.4. *But it won't do to describe the theistic issue as one settlable by such calculation*, or as one about what can be deduced in this *vertical* fashion from the facts we know. No doubt dispute about God has sometimes, perhaps especially in mediaeval times, been carried on in this fashion. But nowadays it is not and we must look for some other analogy, some other case in which a dispute is settled but not by experiment.

6.5. *In courts of law* it sometimes happens that opposing counsel are agreed as to the facts and are not trying to settle a question of further fact, are not trying to settle whether the man who admittedly had quarrelled with the deceased did or did not murder him, but are concerned with whether Mr.

[5] Hume, *An Enquiry concerning the Principles of Morals.* Appendix I.

A who admittedly handed his long-trusted clerk signed blank
cheques did or did not exercise reasonable care, whether a
ledger is or is not a document,[6] whether a certain body was
or was not a public authority.

In such cases we notice that the process of argument is not
a *chain* of demonstrative reasoning. It is a presenting and
representing of those features of the case which *severally co-
operate* in favour of the conclusion, in favour of saying what
the reasoner wishes said, in favour of calling the situation by
the name by which he wishes to call it. The reasons are like
the legs of a chair, not the links of a chain. Consequently
although the discussion is *a priori* and the steps are not a
matter of experience, the procedure resembles scientific argument in that the reasoning is not *vertically* extensive but
horizontally extensive—it is a matter of the cumulative effect
of several independent premises, not of the repeated transformation of one or two. And because the premises are severally inconclusive the process of deciding the issue becomes
a matter of weighing the cumulative effect of one group of
severally inconclusive items against the cumulative effect of
another group of severally inconclusive items, and thus lends
itself to description in terms of conflicting 'probabilities'.
This encourages the feeling that the issue is one of fact—that
it is a matter of guessing from the premises at a further fact,
at what is to come. But this is a muddle. *The dispute does
not cease to be* a priori *because it is a matter of the cumulative effect of severally inconclusive premises.* The logic of the
dispute is not that of a chain of deductive reasoning as in a
mathematic calculation. But nor is it a matter of collecting
from several inconclusive items of information an expectation
as to something further, as when a doctor from a patient's

---

[6] *The Times*, March 2nd, 1945. Also in *The Times* of June 13th,
1945, contrast the case of Hannah v. Peel with that of the cruiser cut
in two by a liner. In the latter case there is not agreement as to the
facts. See also the excellent articles by Dr. Glanville L. Williams in
the *Law Quarterly Review*, 'Language and the Law', January, and
April 1945, and 'The Doctrine of Repugnancy', October, 1943,
January, 1944, and April, 1944. The author, having set out how
arbitrary are many legal decisions, needs now to set out how far from
arbitrary they are—if his readers are ready for the next phase in the
dialectic process.

symptoms guesses at what is wrong, or a detective from many clues guesses the criminal. It has its own sort of logic and its own sort of end—the solution of the question at issue is a decision, a ruling by the judge. But it is not an arbitrary decision though the rational connections are neither quite like those in vertical deductions nor like those in inductions in which from many signs we guess at what is to come; and though the decision manifests itself in the application of a name it is no more merely the application of a name than is the pinning on of a medal merely the pinning on of a bit of metal. Whether a lion with stripes is a tiger or a lion is, if you like, merely a matter of the application of a name. Whether Mr. So-and-So of whose conduct we have so complete a record did or did not exercise reasonable care is not merely a matter of the application of a name or, if we choose to say it is, then we must remember that with this name a game is lost and won and a game with very heavy stakes. With the judges' choice of a name for the facts goes an attitude, and the declaration, the ruling, is an exclamation evincing that attitude. But *it is an exclamation which not only has a purpose but also has a logic*, a logic surprisingly like that of 'futile', 'deplorable', 'graceful', 'grand', 'divine'.

6.6. *Suppose two people are looking at a picture or natural scene.* One says 'Excellent' or 'Beautiful' or 'Divine'; the other says 'I don't see it'. He means he doesn't see the beauty. And this reminds us of how we felt the theist accuse the atheist of blindness and the atheist accuse the theist of seeing what isn't there. And yet surely each sees what the other sees. It isn't that one can see part of the picture which the other can't see. So the difference is in a sense not one as to the facts. And so it cannot be removed by the one disputant discovering to the other what so far he hasn't seen. It isn't that the one sees the picture in a different light and so, as we might say, sees a different picture. Consequently the difference between them cannot be resolved by putting the picture in a different light. And yet surely this is just what can be done in such a case—not by moving the picture but by talk perhaps. To settle a dispute as to whether a piece of music is good or better than another we listen again, with a picture we look again. Someone perhaps points to emphasize certain features and we see it in a different light. Shall we call this 'field work' and 'the last of observation' or shall we call it 'reviewing the premises' and 'the beginning of deduction (horizontal)'?

If in spite of all this we choose to say that a difference as to whether a thing is beautiful is not a factual difference we must be careful to remember that there is a procedure for settling these differences and that this consists not only in reasoning and redescription as in the legal case, but also in a more literal re-setting-before with re-looking or re-listening.

6.7. *And if we say as we did at the beginning that when a difference as to the existence of a God is not one as to future happenings then it is not experimental and therefore not as to the facts, we must not forthwith assume that there is no right and wrong about it,* no rationality or irrationality, no appropriateness or inappropriateness, no procedure which tends to settle it, *nor even that this procedure is in no sense a discovery of new facts.* After all even in science this is not so. Our two gardeners even when they had reached the stage when neither expected any experimental result which the other did not, might yet have continued the dispute, each presenting and representing the features of the garden favouring his hypothesis, that is, fitting his model for describing the accepted fact; each emphasizing the pattern he wishes to emphasize. True, in science, there is seldom or never a pure instance of this sort of dispute, for nearly always with difference of hypothesis goes some difference of expectation as to the facts. But scientists argue about rival hypotheses with a vigour which is not exactly proportioned to difference in expectations of experimental results.

The difference as to whether a God exists involves our feelings more than most scientific disputes and in this respect is more like a difference as to whether there is beauty in a thing.

7. *The Connecting Technique.* Let us consider again the technique used in revealing or proving beauty, in removing a blindness, in inducing an attitude which is lacking, in reducing a reaction that is inappropriate. Besides running over in a special way the features of the picture, tracing the rhythms, making sure that this and that are not only seen but noticed,

and their relation to each other—besides all this—there are other things we can do to justify our attitude and alter that of the man who cannot see. For features of the picture may be brought out by setting beside it other pictures; just as the merits of an argument may be brought out, proved, by setting beside it other arguments, in which striking but irrelevant features of the original are changed and relevant features emphasized; just as the merits and demerits of a line of action may be brought out by setting beside it other actions. To use Susan Stebbing's example: Nathan brought out for David certain features of what David had done in the matter of Uriah the Hittite by telling him a story about two sheep-owners. This is the kind of thing we very often do when someone is 'inconsistent' or 'unreasonable'. This is what we do in referring to other cases in law. The paths we need to trace from other cases to the case in question are often numerous and difficult to detect and the person with whom we are discussing the matter may well draw attention to connections which, while not incompatible with those we have tried to emphasize, are of an opposite inclination. A may have noticed in B subtle and hidden likenesses to an angel and reveal these to C, while C has noticed in B subtle and hidden likenesses to a devil which he reveals to A.

Imagine that a man picks up some flowers that lie half withered on a table and gently puts them in water. Another man says to him 'You believe flowers feel'. He says this although he knows that the man who helps the flowers doesn't expect anything of them which he himself doesn't expect; for he himself expects the flowers to be 'refreshed' and to be easily hurt, injured, I mean, by rough handling, while the man who puts them in water does not expect them to whisper 'Thank you'. The Sceptic says 'You believe flowers feel' because something about the way the other man lifts the flowers and puts them in water suggests an attitude to the flowers which he feels inappropriate although perhaps he would not feel it inappropriate to butterflies. He feels that this attitude to flowers is somewhat crazy *just as it is sometimes felt that a lover's attitude is somewhat crazy even when this is not a matter of his having false hopes about how the person he is in love with will act*. It is often said in such cases that reason-

ing is useless. But the very person who says this feels that
the lover's attitude is crazy, is inappropriate like some dreads
and hatreds, such as some horrors of enclosed places. And
often one who says 'It is useless to reason proceeds at once
to reason with the lover, nor is this reasoning always quite
without effect. We may draw the lover's attention to certain
things done by her he is in love with and trace for him a path
to these from things done by others at other times[7] which
have disgusted and infuriated him. And by this means we
may weaken his admiration and confidence, make him feel
it unjustified and arouse his suspicion and contempt and
make him feel our suspicion and contempt reasonable. It is
possible, of course, that he has already noticed the analogies,
the connections, we point out and that he has accepted them
—that is, he has not denied them nor passed them off. He has
recognized them and they have altered his attitude, altered
his love, but he still loves. We then feel that perhaps it is we
who are blind and cannot see what he can see.

8. *Connecting and Disconnecting*. But before we confess
ourselves thus inadequate there are other fires his admiration
must pass through. For when a man has an attitude which
it seems to us he should not have or lacks one which it seems
to us he should have then, not only do we suspect that he is
not influenced by connections which we feel should influence
him and draw his attention to these, but also we suspect he
is influenced by connections which should not influence him
and draw his attention to these. It may, for a moment, seem
strange that we should draw his attention to connections
which we feel should not influence him, and which, since
they do influence him, he has in a sense already noticed. But
we do—such is our confidence in 'the light of reason'.

Sometimes the power of these connections comes mainly
from a man's mismanagement of the language he is using.
This is what happens in the Monte Carlo fallacy, where by
mismanaging the laws of chance a man passes from noticing
that a certain colour or number has not turned up for a long
while to an improper confidence that now it soon will turn
up. In such cases our showing up of the false connections is

[7] Thus, like the scientist, the critic is concerned to show up the
irrelevance of time and space.

a process we call 'explaining a fallacy in reasoning'. To remove fallacies in reasoning we urge a man to call a spade a spade, ask him what he means by 'the State' and having pointed out ambiguities and vaguenesses ask him to reconsider the steps in his argument.

9. *Unspoken Connections. Usually, however, wrongheadedness or wrongheartedness in a situation, blindness to what is there or seeing what is not, does not arise merely from mismanagement of language but is more due to connections which are not mishandled in language, for the reason that they are not put into language at all.* And often these misconnections too, weaken in the light of reason, if only we can guess where they lie and turn it on them. In so far as these connections are not presented in language the process of removing their power is not a process of correcting the mismanagement of language. But it is still akin to such a process; for though it is not a process of setting out fairly what has been set out unfairly, it is a process of setting out fairly what has not been set out at all. And we must remember that the line between connections ill-presented or half-presented in language and connections operative but not presented in language, or only hinted at, is not a sharp one.

Whether or not we call the process of showing up these connections 'reasoning to remove bad unconscious reasoning' or not, it is certain that in order to settle in ourselves what weight we shall attach to someone's confidence or attitude we not only ask him for his reasons but also look for unconscious reasons both good and bad; that is, for reasons which he can't put into words, isn't explicitly aware of, is hardly aware of, isn't aware of at all—perhaps it's long experience which he *doesn't* recall which lets him know a squall is coming, perhaps it's old experience which he *can't* recall which makes the cake in the tea mean so much and makes Odette so fascinating.[8]

I am well aware of the distinction between the question 'What reasons are there for the belief that S is P?' and the question 'What are the sources of beliefs that S is P?' There are cases where investigation of the rationality of a claim

[8] Proust: *Swann's Way*, Vol. I, p. 58, Vol. II. Phoenix Edition.

which certain persons make is done with very little inquiry
into why they say what they do, into the causes of their beliefs. This is so when we have very definite ideas about what
is really logically relevant to their claim and what is not. Offered a mathematical theorem we ask for the proof; offered
the generalization that parental discord causes crime we ask
for the correlation co-efficients. But even in this last case,
if we fancy that only the figures are reasons we underestimate
the complexity of the logic of our conclusion; and yet it is
difficult to describe the other features of the evidence which
have weight and there is apt to be disagreement about the
weight they should have. In criticizing other conclusions and
especially conclusions which are largely the expression of an
attitude, we have not only to ascertain what reasons there are
for them but also to decide what things are reasons and how
much. This latter process of sifting reasons from causes is
part of the critical process for every belief, but in some
spheres it has been done pretty fully already. In these spheres
we don't need to examine the actual processes to belief and
distil from them a logic. But in other spheres this remains to
be done. Even in science or on the stock exchange or in ordinary life we sometimes hesitate to condemn a belief or a
hunch[9] merely because those who believe it cannot offer the
sort of reasons we had hoped for. And now suppose Miss
Gertrude Stein finds excellent the work of a new artist while
we see nothing in it. We nervously recall, perhaps, how pictures by Picasso, which Miss Stein admired and others rejected, later came to be admired by many who gave attention
to them, and we wonder whether the case is not a new instance of her perspicacity and our blindness. But if, upon
giving all our attention to the work in question, we still do not
respond to it, and we notice that the subject matter of the
new picture is perhaps birds in wild places and learn that
Miss Stein is a bird-watcher, then we begin to trouble ourselves less about her admiration.

It must not be forgotten that our attempt to show up misconnections in Miss Stein may have an opposite result and

[9] Here I think of Mr. Stace's interesting reflections in *Mind*,
January, 1945, 'The Problems of Unreasoned Beliefs'.

reveal to us connections we had missed. Thinking to remove
the spell exercised upon his patient by the old stories of the
Greeks, the psycho-analyst may himself fall under that spell
and find in them what his patient has found and, incidentally,
what made the Greeks tell those tales.

10. *Now what happens, what should happen, when we inquire in this way into the reasonableness, the propriety of
belief in gods?* The answer is: A double and opposite-phased
change. Wordsworth writes:

> '. . . And I have felt
> A presence that disturbs me with the joy
> Of elevated thoughts; a sense sublime
> Of something far more deeply interfused,
> Whose dwelling is the light of setting suns,
> And the round ocean and the living air,
> And the blue sky, and in the mind of man:
> A motion and a spirit, that impels
> All thinking things, all objects of all thought,
> And rolls through all things . . .'[10]

We most of us know this feeling. But is it well placed like
the feeling that here is first-rate work, which we sometimes
rightly have even before we have fully grasped the picture
we are looking at or the book we are reading? Or is it misplaced like the feeling in a house that has long been empty
that someone secretly lives there still. Wordsworth's feeling
is the feeling that the world is haunted, that something
watches in the hills and manages the stars. The child feels
that the stone tripped him when he stumbled, that the bough
struck him when it flew back in his face. He has to learn that
the wind isn't buffeting him, that there is not a devil in it,
that he was wrong, that his attitude was inappropriate. And
as he learns that the wind wasn't hindering him so he also
learns it wasn't helping him. But we know how, though he
learns, his attitude lingers. It is plain that Wordsworth's feeling is of this family.

Belief in gods, it is true, is often very different from belief
that stones are spiteful, the sun kindly. For the gods appear

[10] *Tintern Abbey.*

in human form and from the waves and control these things
and by so doing reward and punish us. But varied as are the
stories of the gods they have a family likeness and we have
only to recall them to feel sure of the other main sources
which co-operate with animism to produce them.

What are the stories of the gods? What are our feelings
when we believe in God? They are feelings of awe before
power, dread of the thunderbolts of Zeus, confidence in the
everlasting arms, unease beneath the all-seeing eye. They are
feelings of guilt and inescapable vengeance, of smothered
hate and of a security we can hardly do without. We have
only to remind ourselves of these feelings and the stories of
the gods and goddesses and heroes in which these feelings
find expression, to be reminded of how we felt as children
to our parents and the big people of our childhood. Writing
of a first telephone call from his grandmother, Proust says:
'. . . it was rather that this isolation of the voice was like a
symbol, a presentation, a direct consequence of another isolation, that of my grandmother, separated for the first time
in my life, from myself. The orders or prohibitions which
she addressed to me at every moment in the ordinary course
of my life, the tedium of obedience or the fire of rebellion
which neutralized the affection that I felt for her were at
this moment eliminated. . . . "Granny!" I cried to her . . .
but I had beside me only that voice, a phantom, as unpal-
pable as that which would come to revisit me when my grandmother was dead. "Speak to me!" but then it happened that,
left more solitary still, I ceased to catch the sound of her
voice. My grandmother could no longer hear me . . . I continued to call her, sounding the empty night, in which I felt
that her appeals also must be straying. I was shaken by the
same anguish which, in the distant past, I had felt once before, one day when, a little child, in a crowd, I had lost her.'

Giorgio de Chirico, writing of Courbet, says: 'The word
yesterday envelops us with its yearning echo, just as, on waking, when the sense of time and the logic of things remain
a while confused, the memory of a happy hour we spent the
day before may sometimes linger reverberating within us. At
times we think of Courbet and his work as we do of our own
father's youth.'

When a man's father fails him by death or weakness how much he needs another father, one in the heavens with whom is 'no variableness nor shadow of turning'.

We understood Mr. Kenneth Graham when he wrote of the Golden Age we feel we have lived in under the Olympians. Freud says: 'The ordinary man cannot imagine this Providence in any other form but that of a greatly exalted father, for only such a one could understand the needs of the sons of men, or be softened by their prayers and be placated by the signs of their remorse. The whole thing is so patently infantile, so incongruous with reality. . . .' 'So incongruous with reality'! It cannot be denied.

But here a new aspect of the matter may strike us.[11] For the very facts which make us feel that now we can recognize systems of superhuman, sub-human, elusive, beings for what they are—the persistent projections of infantile phantasies—include facts which make these systems less fantastic. What are these facts? They are patterns in human reactions which are well described by saying that we are as if there were hidden within us powers, persons, not ourselves and stronger than ourselves. That this is so may perhaps be said to have been common knowledge yielded by ordinary observation of people,[12] but we did not know the degree in which this is so until recent study of extraordinary cases in extraordinary conditions had revealed it. I refer, of course, to the study of multiple personalities and the wider studies of psychoanalysts. Even when the results of this work are reported to us that is not the same as tracing the patterns in the details of the cases on which the results are based; and even that is not the same as taking part in the studies oneself. One thing not sufficiently realized is that some of the things shut within us are not bad but good.

Now the gods, good and evil and mixed, have always been mysterious powers outside us rather than within. But they have also been within. It is not a modern theory but an old

[11] I owe to the late Dr. Susan Isaacs the thought of this different aspect of the matter, of this connection between the heavenly Father and 'the good father' spoken of in psychoanalysis.

[12] Consider Tolstoy and Dostoievsky—I do not mean, of course, that their observation was ordinary.

saying that in each of us a devil sleeps. Eve said: 'The serpent beguiled me.' Helen says to Menelaus:

> '. . . And yet how strange it is!
> I ask not thee; I ask my own sad thought,
> What was there in my heart, that I forgot
> My home and land and all I loved, to fly
> With a strange man? Surely it was not I,
> But Cypris there!'[13]

Elijah found that God was not in the wind, nor in the thunder, but in a still small voice. The kingdom of Heaven is within us, Christ insisted, though usually about the size of a grain of mustard seed, and he prayed that we should become one with the Father in Heaven.

New knowledge made it necessary either to give up saying 'The sun is sinking' or to give the words a new meaning. In many contexts we preferred to stick to the old words and give them a new meaning which was not entirely new but, on the contrary, *practically* the same as the old. The Greeks did not speak of the dangers of repressing instincts but they did speak of the dangers of thwarting Dionysos, of neglecting Cypris for Diana, of forgetting Poseidon for Athena. We have eaten of the fruit of a garden we can't forget though we were never there, a garden we still look for though we can never find it. Maybe we look for too simple a likeness to what we dreamed. Maybe we are not as free as we fancy from the old idea that Heaven is a happy hunting ground, or a city with streets of

[13] Euripides: *The Trojan Women*, Gilbert Murray's Translation. Roger Hinks in *Myth and Allegory in Ancient Art* writes (p. 108): 'Personifications made their appearance very early in Greek poetry. . . . It is out of the question to call these terrible beings "abstractions". . . . They are real daemons to be worshipped and propitiated. . . . These beings we observe correspond to states of mind. The experience of man teaches him that from time to time his composure is invaded and overturned by some power from outside, panic, intoxication, sexual desire.'

> 'What use to shoot off guns at unicorns?
> Where one horn's hit another fierce horn grows.
> These beasts are fabulous, and none were born
> Of woman who could lay a fable low.'—
> *The Glass Tower*, Nicholas Moore, p. 100.

gold. Lately Mr. Aldous Huxley has recommended our seeking not somewhere beyond the sky or late in time but a timeless state not made of the stuff of this world, which he rejects, picking it into worthless pieces. But this sounds to me still too much a looking for another place, not indeed one filled with sweets but instead so empty that some of us would rather remain in the Lamb or the Elephant, where, as we know, they stop whimpering with another bitter and so far from sneering at all things, hang pictures of winners at Kempton and stars of the 'nineties. Something good we have for each other is freed there, and in some degree and for a while the miasma of time is rolled back without obliging us to deny the present.

The artists who do most for us don't tell us only of fairylands. Proust, Manet, Breughel, even Botticelli and Vermeer show us reality. And yet they give us for a moment exhilaration without anxiety, peace without boredom. And those who, like Freud, work in a different way against that which too often comes over us and forces us into deadness or despair,[14] also deserve critical, patient and courageous attention. For they, too, work to release us from human bondage into human freedom.

Many have tried to find ways of salvation. The reports they bring back are always incomplete and apt to mislead even when they are not in words but in music or paint. But they are by no means useless; and not the worst of them are those which speak of oneness with God. But in so far as we become one with Him He becomes one with us. St. John says he is in us as we love one another.

This love, I suppose, is not benevolence but something that comes of the oneness with one another of which Christ spoke.[15] Sometimes it momentarily gains strength.[16] Hate and the Devil do too. And what is oneness without otherness?

[14] Matthew Arnold: *Summer Night.*
[15] St. John xvi. 21.
[16] 'The Harvesters' in *The Golden Age,* Kenneth Graham.

Second Series

And though a philosopher may live remote from business, the genius of philosophy, if carefully cultivated by several, must gradually diffuse itself throughout the whole society, and bestow a similar correctness on every art and calling.

DAVID HUME,
Enquiry concerning Human Understanding,
Sect. I, §5.

Introduction

A. G. N. FLEW

The success of *Logic and Language* (First Series) makes it possible to bring out this second and complementary volume. The aim of the former volume was a dual one—and different from that of similar collections which have appeared lately: both to provide, for the general interested and educated public, an introduction to the recent linguistic developments in philosophy; and to make available in book form, for students and specialists, some of the important articles which previously were only accessible in those libraries which take the philosophical journals. The aim of this second volume is similar: and therefore substantially the same criteria have been used for making the selection. There is no need to explain all these again; this was done in the previous Introduction. But there are four further points to be made now.

First: because this volume was designed to be complementary to the former one, extra weight has been given this time to the claims of those articles which deal with major themes which could not be touched there; and an effort has been made to avoid any overlapping between the two. Thus the papers on 'Universals' (chap. III) and on 'Categories' (chap. IV), as well as the contributions to the philosophy of history (chap. X), of mathematics (chap. XI) and of science (chap. XII), had an additional claim; because none of these subjects had been represented before. On the other hand, as always happens when multiple criteria are involved, other and conflicting claims were sometimes too strong to resist: though F. L. Will (chap. II) does deal with some of the problems of induction, others of which had already been attacked by Paul Edwards (vol. I, chap. IV); still these were for a very long time notoriously the great scandal of philosophy, and progress here deserves special prominence. And of course there are still gaps: for instance, aesthetics is entirely un-represented.[1]

Second: while all the papers in that volume had been previously published, this contains three which have not been: namely those by Dr. Waismann (chap. I) and G. J. Warnock (chap. VI), and the second one by D. F. Pears (chap. VII). There is no need to explain or to excuse this departure: but here it can be said relevantly that 'Language Strata' (chap. I) is in effect a continuation of the same author's 'Verifiability' (vol. I, chap. VII), which particularly appealed to many reviewers; and that the other two were originally part of a series of examinations of the logical peculiarities of members of that perplexing class of sentences—to which Kant was the first to draw attention—which seem to be both synthetic and *a priori*.

Third: fearing that by this second lap many of the less strenuous and less enthusiastic laymen would have dropped out, and hoping that the remainder would now be ready for some rather harder things, the balance has been tilted slightly —but still only slightly—more in favour of the specialist. Thus the bar raised against symbolism has been lowered a little, particularly in order to admit Professor J. J. C. Smart's 'Theory Construction' (chap. XII). This contains some mathematics: but the author agrees that his main line of argument will be perfectly intelligible even to those who choose to skip the calculations. Again, several of the contributions in this second series will need much more energetic attention than anything in the first: this is certainly true of both 'Universals' (chap. III) and 'Other Minds' (chap. VIII).[2] But any reader with a taste for philosophy—and not just the student (for whom both are essential)—will be rewarded for the pains he takes on these. There is perhaps only one paper included

---

[1] A volume, *Essays in Aesthetics and Language*, edited by William Elton, is now in course of preparation.

[2] This is the article enigmatically, and rather remotely, mentioned by Dr. Joad. 'More recently my attention has been drawn to the doctrines of an Oxford teacher whose contribution to a certain Symposium embodied a variation of logical positivist [*sic*] doctrine which put all the others out of court. This I was assured was the very latest thing.' (A *Critique of Logical Positivism*, p. 15).

—Professor G. E. Moore's 'Is Existence a Predicate?' (chap. v)—which can scarcely be expected to appeal to anyone but the specialist: but it would have been inexcusable not to include any work by the *doyen* of British philosophy; and this particular piece is constantly recommended to students.

Fourth: it should be put on record that the absence of any study of the logical peculiarities of any language other than English has been noted and regretted: but extraordinarily little seems to have been done on this, at least by professional philosophers. Some logicians have put a lot of work into specifying, and even constructing, artificial languages (usually so artificial that they are much more like mathematical calculi than like any natural language). Other philosophers have learnt from Wittgenstein the value of sometimes illustrating their arguments with references to imaginary truncated languages[3] (in much the same way as treatises on mechanics are illustrated by schematic diagrams). Others again have realized keenly how different the world may look to those whose languages are radically different; for instance, one of our contributors, Dr. Waismann (vol. I, chap. vii) has noticed how differently a person regards colour if his language expresses it by a verb—in Russian 'the sky blues'—rather than as English does by an adjective. But all this is very far from constituting a study of the logical peculiarities of exotic natural languages.[4] There seems to be a lot of room here for useful team work between anthropologists, sinologues, philologists and philosophers: to examine Nietzsche's neglected dictum that 'by the grammatical structure of a group of languages everything runs smoothly for one

[3] For Wittgenstein's methods it is now possible to refer to his *Philosophical Investigations* which is, since the author's death, at last to be publicly published (With an English translation: Blackwell, 1953).

[4] Some references might be useful: see, for example, I. A. Richards *Mencius on the Mind*; Arthur Waley, *Three Ways of Thought in Ancient China* and 'The Language Crisis in Ancient China' (which appeared in *Polemic* 4); (C. Kluckhorn and D. Leighton, *The Navaho* (Harvard U.P., 1947: the chapter on the Navaho language); and—a paper I wish I could have included in this collection—D. D. Lee, 'Conceptual Implications of an Indian language' (in *Philosophy of Science* for 1938).

kind of philosophical system, whereas the way is as it were barred for certain other possibilities'.

These four points—taken together with those made in the previous Introduction—should show the principles followed in making this second selection. This time it is unnecessary to compose a prefatory manifesto: for though manifestoes have their place—sometimes even in philosophy—to demand attention for the neglected or to proclaim a programme; these functions are finished when the attention has been granted and some of the performance, not merely the programme, is there to be judged. Reasoned discussion cannot be conducted at the top of one's voice: and an atmosphere of party conflict or of clique feud obstructs the progress of philosophy.

But one or two points, which it would be worth remarking on here, arise from comments on the former volume. *First*: people—especially those unsympathetic to recent developments—are inclined to give the name 'Logical Positivism' to any philosophizing in which the use of words, expressions and sentences is mentioned prominently. This is a very loose usage: and unfortunate because it generates heat and confusion. The term was originally coined to describe the views of the Vienna Circle, a group of scientists and philosophers which formed round Moritz Schlick in Vienna in the 'twenties.[5] The Vienna Circle were interested primarily in logic and scientific method: indeed many of them had been trained originally in natural science—usually physics—rather than in philosophy. At least in their published writings they often appeared narrow, dogmatic, philistine, uninterested in traditional philosophy, and militantly secular. In England they found a devastatingly iconoclastic spokesman in Professor A. J. Ayer. His brilliant and powerful statement of the Logical Positivist position (*Language Truth and Logic*: 1st edition 1936, 2nd edition with an important new Introduction 1946) deservedly became a classic, and the centre of passionate controversy: and it is mainly because for British readers the term 'Logical Positivism' suggests the position of

[5] For an account of the history of the Vienna Circle and associated groups see the Introduction to *Modern Science and its Philosophy* by Philipp Frank (Harvard U.P., 1949).

that book, that it is so confusing to use it loosely to cover the very different and very various views of our contributors. Though they may be wrong in this—guilty of a peculiarly vicious sort of parochialism—most of these do not think of themselves as members of any school or movement; but simply as philosophers.[6]

Second: it is felt that an inquiry, in so far as it is in any sense verbal, about words, must to that extent be trivial; and hence that philosophers who talk about the use of words must—as one reviewer vigorously phrased it—'be selling their truthright for a mess of verbiage'. Some verbal disputes are trivial and idle: it would indeed be trivial to criticize the same reviewer for using the word 'verbosopher', because it is a mongrel from mixed Latin and Greek parents. But other disputes about words are not trivial at all: sometimes even when all the facts are agreed much may depend on the decision as to which word to use: and much may reasonably be said for and against. Can it or can it not be called the action of a reasonable man? Are we to say he is sane or that he is insane? So not all disputes about words are '*mere* disputes about words'.

The idea that modern linguistic insights and interests must involve a trivialization, or even a betrayal, of philosophy has been crystallized in and encouraged by a favourite saying of the Logical Positivists: 'Philosophical questions are not problems to be solved but (pseudo-problems or) puzzles to be (dis)solved'. This saying had its value as a slogan against those who thought of philosophy as a sort of super-science (a usurper Queen of the sciences) or as a non-experimental para-science (science from an easy chair):[7] for it emphasized that philosophy is not science, nor yet super-science nor para-science. Yet philosophical problems are no more pseudo-problems because they are not scientific problems, than

---

[6] The refusal to coin, and reluctance to accept, a party name is deliberate: cf. G. Ryle, 'Taking Sides in Philosophy' in *Philosophy* for 1937. Most of his colleagues would, I think, agree with him in insisting that party banners and school loyalty have no place in philosophy.

[7] Compare Ezra Pound, 'After Leibniz's time a philosopher was just a guy who was too damn lazy to work in a laboratory'.

Americans are pseudo-Englishmen because they are not Englishmen. And the implicit suggestion that philosophy must
needs be trivial, just because it cannot be science, is grossly
philistine. It is a disreputable relic of the old Logical Positivist campaign to glorify natural science, especially physics,
at the expense of every other intellectual discipline.

But there are other sources of this anxiety about trivialization. One is, of course, that philosophers are no more exempt
than are other academics from the misconception that, because much research which is not obviously important has
various kinds of value, any or only research which is obviously
unimportant can be properly pursued in universities: and
hence work is often done which really is trivial. Another—
more fundamental and less avoidable—is the fact that once
anyone has seen how to dissolve a philosophic muddle or
has achieved a philosophic insight it becomes hard for him
any longer to understand how he or anyone else could ever
have failed to see what now to him seems so obvious. Philosophy has indeed been defined as 'the discovery of the
obvious'. Yet to deny the existence of a problem, to speak
of pseudo-problems, where considerable men may have been
perplexed, just because you believe that you know the way
out, is surely either excessively arrogant or excessively modest.
In so far as linguistic analysis has shown that, and also how
some classical philosophical problems consisted wholly or
partly in muddles and confusions, it has done something to
solve those problems.[8] To clear up an ancient confusion is not
a trivial achievement; not at least for 'those who have the
wish to understand, to escape from intellectual bewilderment':[9] and, as Russell was saying when he wrote this, it is in
any case only to them that philosophy has anything to offer.

Third: sometimes people coin or seize on epigrammatic
statements of what philosophy is; and proceed to rejoice or
deplore that this is all that it comes to. This must always be
mistaken: if only because 'philosophy' is one of those words

[8] Though in the advertisement 'the problem is not a problem at
all' to the advertiser who has the product which will solve it. We
do tend to speak of a solved problem as something which no longer
exists.

[9] Bertrand Russell, *Our Knowledge of the External World*, p. 28.

(like 'poetry', 'nation', or 'genius') the whole meaning of which cannot be given in a definition. When Professor Ryle writes of philosophy as 'the detection of the sources in linguistic idiom of recurrent misconstructions and absurd theories' (vol. I, chap. II *ad fin.*) or Professor Price claims that 'all the great philosophical discoveries are discoveries of the obvious',[10] they are to be taken as coining epigrams or slogans to draw attention to aspects of philosophical inquiry which had been neglected or overlooked. Compare the case of the man who says that he 'would define a tank as mechanized and armoured fire-power':[11] as a formal definition of 'tank' this will not do; but it is a very good epigram for the purpose for which it was coined—to draw attention to the fact that British tanks in World War II were chronically undergunned. Or compare the things people say about the nature of poetry, or nationality, or genius: poetry is emotion recollected in tranquillity; a nation is a society united by a common error as to its origins and a common aversion to its neighbours; genius is an infinite capacity for taking pains. As definitions of 'poetry', 'nation', or 'genius' none of these will do at all: they are obviously both in some ways far too narrow and in others far too comprehensive. But as epigrams about poetry, nations, and genius they all have value: there is a lot in each of them: they would all on occasion be good things to say.

But the whole idea that there is or should be some real essence of philosophy which has been or could be expressed in a single, final, comprehensive, 'true definition' is radically misguided. 'Philosophy' has not been in the past, and we should not now try to make it, that sort of word. It has been used to refer not to some wholly homogeneous investigation or series of investigations, but to a family of related but various inquiries and activities. If we introduced a standard definition we should have by it to exclude many activities which have a perfect right to the name 'philosophy'. Uni-

[10] 'The Permanent Significance of Hume's Philosophy' in *Philosophy*, 1940. This passage comes at p. 12 of this most relevant and excellent article.

[11] E. T. Williams in a broadcast review of the fourth volume of Mr. Churchill's war memoirs.

formity can be achieved—here as elsewhere—only at the cost of wholesale suppression and expulsion. If we were to insist that philosophy must be purely and exclusively a conceptual investigation—a study of the 'logic of our language'—we should find ourselves committed to excluding almost everything that had previously been called political philosophy: for only the most heroic and extreme measures of reinterpretation could fit Hobbes, Locke, Rousseau and Burke to this mould. We should also inevitably find that we had encouraged the narrow-minded, bureaucratic departmentalism which is already too common in what ought to be the loose association of the 'republic of letters'. A tight definition of 'philosophy' might perhaps inhibit possible future developments, and it would certainly encourage philosophers to neglect and despise worthy activities which could, on a broader usage of the term, be properly called philosophical; for unfortunately professional philosophers are not immune from the temptations which beset all specialists.[12] Whereas a loose definition would probably include far too much; and would certainly be so comprehensive as to be vacuously uninformative. So it is far better to attempt no definitions of 'philosophy': and if anyone asks what philosophy is, to answer him by pointing to various specimens; perhaps adding a few explanatory comments. The two volumes of *Logic and Language* contain a collection of characteristic specimens of the best work being done by English-speaking philosophers. But one necessary comment is to explain that they do not represent every sort of good work which could be or should be or is being done in philosophy; though no one who is concerned to do good philosophy can afford to remain unfamiliar with the new linguistic techniques and linguistic insights demonstrated by many of our contributors. (To say nothing here of their possible value and applications outside philosophy.)

Fourth: many are shocked to find philosophers so concerned about deviations from standard English (or whatever other language is being used or discussed) and the elucidation of the ordinary use of language. These conceptions have

---

[12] Even they need to beware the Specialist Fallacy: that of confusing 'I am only paid to know about X' with 'I am paid to know about X only' (and about nothing else).

recently been the subject of considerable—often fairly heated
—controversy among philosophers.[13] This is not the place to
try to go deeply into the problems: but two points might
usefully be added to those made in the Introduction to our
first volume. First: it has been suggested that there is no
such thing as ordinary or standard usage; because there is
no absolute, normative, unchanging and universal standard
of correctness. But this objection tries to prove too much,
giving reasons which are not enough. To prove that there is
never and nowhere any ordinary or standard usage of English
(or any other) words it is not enough to point out, truly,
that there is no universal, unchanging, normative and absolute standard of English (or any other) usage. And if it were
true—which it certainly and fortunately is not—that there is
no standard usage of words within any group at any time,
then it would not be merely a few perverse philosophers
whose position would be undermined. For though of course
much of our usage is constantly changing, and does vary considerably from district to district, and from social group to
social group; still it is only and precisely in so far as two
people use and understand words in some accepted, standard
way that verbal communication between them is possible.
Thus this objection tries to prove too much. (Philosophy is
not the first field in which conservatives have become the
unwitting allies of a revolution of destruction.) Second: it is
often thought that concern with the ordinary use of words
is no part of the business of a philosopher. But in so far as
philosophy is a conceptual inquiry, such concern is surely essential. For how else could one investigate the concept of
knowledge than by studying the various correct uses of the
word 'know'? (Which is of course one of the things which
Professor J. L. Austin is doing in vol. II, chap. VIII.) Though
this is not to say *either* that philosophy is only a conceptual
investigation *or* that philosophers should investigate only the
ordinary concepts of common sense *or* that they should never

[13] See for instance K. E. Baier in *P.A.S.* 1951/52; and papers
by Wisdom, Malcolm, etc., in *The Philosophy of G. E. Moore*
(Northwestern U.P., Evanston, 1942). Other useful references will
be found in footnotes to P. L. Heath's paper in *Philosophical Quarterly*, 1952.

try to improve any of the concepts they have investigated (which would necessarily involve changing the present use of the words concerned).[14]

King's College
Aberdeen

March 1952

I

Language Strata

FRIEDRICH WAISMANN

[This paper has not been published before; but was read in 1946 to the Jowett Society at Oxford. When Dr. Waismann came to revise it for publication here, he found that there was so much that he wished to alter, and so much else that he wished to develop at considerably greater length, that it was clear that the only practicable alternatives were either not to publish it at all or to publish it in its original form. In view of the facts, that it has already had considerable influence in that form, and that it had an important place in the plan of this volume, I tried—successfully—to persuade him to permit its publication here, substantially unchanged: but it is only fair to state these circumstances and to say that the eventual decision to publish was made rather against his better judgment. The morals are obvious.—EDITOR]

I. *Types of Ambiguity*

Both vagueness and 'open texture'[1] must be distinguished from, and likened to, another sort of lack of definition; ambiguity. Of the many types of ambiguity a few examples may be mentioned.

---

[14] Yet it is surely only prudent to elucidate the current nature of the concept (the current correct usage of the word and its synonyms —and any equivalents in any other language) before rushing forward with suggestions on how to reform it.

[1] See above, pp. 125 ff.

(i) A word may have two altogether different meanings, or better, there may be two words which have the sound in common; thus someone might say, 'How long it is since I have seen the Alps! How I long to see them'. This fact makes possible certain puns—as when a crying child is called the 'Prince of Wails'.

(ii) An extreme case of ambiguity is what is called the *antithetical sense of primal words*. There is evidence that in the oldest languages opposites such as: strong—weak, light—dark, large—small were expressed by the same root word. Thus, in ancient Egyptian *keu* stood for both strong and weak. In Latin *altus* means high and deep, *sacer* both sacred and accursed. Compare further *clamare*, to shout, and *clam*, quietly, secretly, or *siccus*, dry, and *succus*, juice. Nor is it only the ancient languages which have retained as relics words capable of meaning either of two opposites. The same applies to present-day languages. 'To cleave' means to split, but in the phrase 'cleave to' it means to adhere. The word 'without', originally carrying with it both a positive and a negative connotation, is used today in the negative sense only. That 'with' has not only the sense of 'adding to' but also that of 'depriving of' is clear from the compounds 'withdraw' and 'withhold'.

(iii) It is commonly impossible to distinguish between different senses of a word without considering how it is used in context. When used in different contexts, the same word may assume different senses. Take as an example the transitive and intransitive use of a verb: 'I smell the lilac', 'The lilac smells lovely'. But even when a verb is used transitively, it may take on different meanings when connected with words of different types: 'I caught him', 'I caught measles'. We use the word 'like' often in the sense of 'similar'; we say, for instance, 'That man is like his brother', and in this context we may also say 'very like', 'amazingly like', 'so like that one cannot tell them apart'. On the other hand, it would be amazing to learn of two triangles 'so alike that one cannot tell them apart'. In the one case the word admits of degrees of comparison, in the other it does not. Compare the phrase 'Find the key which—' with 'Find the number which—'. In spite of the sameness of the construction the difference in meaning is clearly felt. Thus I might have said 'Compute the number which—', but not 'Compute the key which—', a sign that the word is used according to different substitution rules. Again, compare 'I am trying to solve this equation', 'I am trying to remember a forgotten name', 'I am trying to fall asleep'.

(iv) A word which is used in a quite definite way and in quite definite contexts may be used in a new sort of context; with this change of use often goes a change in meaning. For instance: 'the fruit of a tree', 'the fruit of his labour', 'the fruit of his meditations'; 'to sow seed', 'to sow distrust'. What we use is a picture. If the image becomes a stereotyped figure of speech, we talk of 'figurative meaning'. (This is one of the means by which language grows. A speaker may, on the spur of the moment, place a word in a new collocation, thus giving rise to a new meaning—a process over which there is little control.) Now the point of this is that it is not always possible to say exactly where the metaphor ends and where the word starts having an independent meaning. The phrase 'to sow distrust' is felt to be a metaphor, perhaps also 'the fruit of his meditations', but not 'a fruitless attempt'. Here the pictorial element has faded. Glance through the following list and consider whether you would venture to draw a sharp line between a figure that is still a live image and one which has become a well-worn metaphor: 'The birth of tragedy', 'Drowned in sorrow', 'An abyss of grief', 'A radiant spirit', 'A flight of phantasy', 'A fiery temper'.

(v) A word may be used in a 'figurative sense'. Remember that almost all terms denoting the mental are derived from words whose primary connotation was sensuous. Thus we speak of an idea 'floating in the mind', we 'call it to mind', we say it is still 'hazy'; an idea is 'engraved upon my memory', it 'makes an impression upon me'; something 'moves us', 'touches us', so that we are 'carried away'; we feel 'stirred', 'beside ourselves'; we talk of a 'brilliant idea', a 'flash of wit'; and so on.

This rising of the meaning of a word from the sphere of the sensuous to that of the mental continues to the present

day. Think of expressions such as 'split personality', 'the layers of the subconscious', 'twilight of consciousness', etc. A
sensuous element gleams through most of the phrases which
denote emotions. We talk of 'shady' 'volcanic', 'unbridled',
'ebullient' characters; 'wooden', 'unpolished', 'crabbed' individuals; of an 'oily', 'smooth' manner, a 'stiff' attitude, a
'lukewarm', 'cool', 'icy' reception; of an 'arid', 'sparkling',
'will-o'-the-wisp' spirit.

The fact that language develops out of the sensuous into
the mental produces a peculiar phenomenon: we seem at
times to glimpse behind a word another sense, deeper and
half hidden, and to hear faintly the entry of another meaning, in and with which others begin to sound, and all accompany the original meaning of the word like the sympathetic
chimes of a bell. Hence that deep and sonorous ring in
words which is lacking in artificial and invented languages;
and hence also the multiplicity of meaning, the indefinite-
ness, the strange suggestiveness and evasiveness of so much
poetry. Hugo von Hofmannsthal once described this phenomenon.

It leads us into the innermost nature of Oriental poetry,
into the very mystery and being of language. For this mysteriousness is the deepest element in Eastern language and
poetry alike, in so far as everything in it is metaphorical,
everything remotely descended from ancient roots. The
original root is sensuous, primitive, concise and strong, but
the word moves away from it by subtle transitions to new,
related meanings, and then to meanings only remotely
related: yet in the remotest meaning there is still some
echo of the original sound of the word, still some darkly
mirrored image of the first sensuous impression . . . In
the limitless detail and particularity of description the
subject matter itself seems to oppress and overwhelm us:
but what would come so close to us as to hurt us, were we
limited to immediate meanings, resolves itself by virtue
of the multiplicity of meaning in the words into a magic
cloud, and so behind the immediate meaning we divine
another which is derived from it. Thus it is that we do not
lose sight of the proper and original sense: where, however,

this sense was commonplace and mean, it loses its implicit commonplaceness, and often, as we contemplate the word, we hesitate in our perceptive awareness between the particular reality which it symbolizes and a higher reality, and this in a flash leads up to the great and the sublime.

(vi) There are other cases in which the meanings cannot be as clearly separated out as, for instance, in the case of the word 'cold' (where I may say of a day or of a reception that it is cold). Consider a word like 'haughty'. That there is a difference in its use is shown in the fact that the word can be combined with words of very different logical types; thus we may speak of a haughty smile, a haughty tone of voice, a haughty face, a haughty look, a haughty bearing, a haughty speech, a haughty person. So there *is* a difference in meaning. Yet all these meanings are connected—in saying of somebody that he is haughty, at least part of what we mean is that he has a haughty face, or a haughty bearing, etc. So the meanings interpenetrate, and unite into a larger whole, a sort of cloud in which the several precise conceits are lost. We may say that they *dissolve into vagueness*. Such an example shows how ambiguity may gradually pass into vagueness.

'But shouldn't we still try to distinguish as clearly as possible all the different shades of meaning the word can assume?' Try, and you'll see how puzzling it is. Paul Valéry put this point very well when he said:

You must . . . at some time or another, have noticed this curious fact—that a given word, which may be perfectly obvious when used in the ordinary course of communication, which presents no difficulties whatever when caught up in the give and take of normal conversation, has a way of becoming almost magically embarrassing, strangely resistant and quite unmanageable in definition, as soon as you withdraw it from circulation with the object of examining it closely and apart from its neighbours, as soon, that is, as you try to establish its meaning in isolation from its momentary function. It is almost comic to note the difficulty with which we are confronted when we try to establish the *precise* meaning of a word which, in the ordinary routine of life, we use daily to our complete satisfaction . . . But isolate it, clip its wings and it turns and rends you. You soon become convinced that the number of its meanings is far in excess of its functions. Formerly it was only a *means*, but now it is an *end*, the object of a terrible philosophical desire. It is something entirely different from what it was, an enigma, an abyss, a source of mental torment.

(vii) Next, consider a number of statements made by psychologists: 'We perceive the surface of the metal, it is true, but its colour seems to lie *behind* this surface'. 'Lustre-light does not lie *in* the plane of the object to which it belongs, but appears rather either *before* the object or *superimposed on* it'. 'When a shadow moves it moves not *in* the surface of the object but *across* it'. 'When a person is speaking with someone in complete darkness, the voice of the one who answers usually sounds distinctly *behind* the darkness, not *in* the darkness'. 'If you look at a colour disk which turns round quickly, it is better to say that there is a flickering *across* the disk or *before* it in space than to say that the disk *itself* is flickering'. Notice that in all these cases the prepositions which symbolize spatial relations take on a somewhat new sense. In the last example, for instance, to say that there is a flickering *before* the disk in space is to use 'before' in a peculiar way, namely so as to make it *meaningless* to ask exactly what distance, precisely how many millimetres before the surface it lies. Here we have a sense of 'before' or 'in front of' which differs from the ordinary sense. The same holds of the 'behind' in our first example. There are intermediate ones: thus a glowing piece of iron is seen as luminous *throughout* its mass; a rainbow, though extended in space before the observer, does not possess a surface. One feels that one can penetrate more or less deeply *into* the spectral colours, whereas when one looks at the colour of a paper the surface presents a sort of barrier beyond which the gaze cannot pass. The words 'throughout' and 'into' come here closer to, though they have not exactly, the ordinary meaning. Many more examples could be collected, but these will do. 'The English prepositions', says Empson, 'from being used in so many ways and in combination with so many verbs, have acquired not so much a number of meanings as a body of meaning continuous in several directions'. Exactly, there are so many senses and they are so firmly interlocked that they seem to form one continuous body. Thus many words which we wouldn't suspect turn out to be ambiguous. One can hardly make too much of this ambiguity of language through which we often seem to see words like shapes in a mist.

(viii) Then there is such a thing as *systematic ambiguity*. This expression was first coined by Bertrand Russell in connection with his Theory of Types. Without entering into it here we can say that his idea, roughly speaking, is that we must distinguish between different *logical types of symbols*. Beginning with names which stand for 'individuals', we come next to predicates which possibly apply to those names, and then to second-order predicates which possibly apply to the first-order predicates, and so on. We are thus led to consider a hierarchy of symbols which, theoretically, goes on without end. This hierarchy corresponds to a similar hierarchy of *statements*. And statements are divided into different types according to whether they are statements about an individual, or statements about a class of individuals, or statements about a class of classes of individuals, and so on. A statement such as 'Socrates is mortal' is true when there is a corresponding fact, and false when there is no corresponding fact. But take now such a statement as 'All men are mortal'. The truth of it can no longer consist in its correspondence to a single fact, for there are indefinitely many facts such as 'Socrates is mortal', 'Plato is mortal', etc. Now Russell's point is that the meaning of 'truth' which is applicable to the latter sort of proposition is *not the same* as the meaning of 'truth' which is applicable to the proposition 'All men are mortal'; i.e. each type of statement has its own sort of truth.

The main ground for accepting that distinction is that it offers an escape from the paradoxes or antinomies which were a threat to logic.

The imaginary sceptic, who asserts that he knows nothing, and is refuted by being asked if he knows that he knows nothing, has asserted nonsense, and has been fallaciously refuted by an argument which involves a vicious-circle fallacy. In order that the sceptic's assertion may become significant, it is necessary to place some limitation upon the things of which he is asserting his ignorance, because the things of which it is possible to be ignorant form an illegitimate totality. *Principia Mathematica* (Vol. I, Introduction).

Take the case of the Liar, that is of a man who says 'I am lying'; if he is lying he is speaking the truth, and if he is speaking the truth he is lying. We may interpret his statement as saying, 'All propositions which I assert are false'. Is this proposition itself true or false? To clear up the paradox we must distinguish between elementary propositions which do not refer to a totality of propositions, first-order propositions which do refer to a totality of elementary propositions, second-order propositions which do refer to a totality of first-order propositions, and so on. Now if the liar asserts that all propositions which he asserts are false he is making a first-order statement which does not fall within its own scope, and therefore no contradiction emerges. The decisive point to realize is that the phrase 'all propositions' is an illegitimate totality. As soon as a suitable limitation has been put upon the collection of propositions we are considering, as soon as they are broken up into different orders, the contradiction disappears. We may put it like this: if somebody were to tell us that he is a liar, we could ask him, 'Well, a liar of what order?' If he says he is a liar of the first order he is making a statement of the second order, and this statement may be perfectly true. When he says 'I am a liar of the second order' (including the totality of first-order statements) this would be a statement of the third order; and so on. However far he may extend the scope of propositions to which he is referring, his statement about their falsehood will represent a proposition of higher order. Once we reach this stage, there is no contradiction.

Russell's solution is thus based on the ground that 'true' and 'false' are ambiguous, and that, in order to make them unambiguous, we must specify the order of truth or falsehood which we ascribe to a proposition. Similar considerations apply to negation and disjunction, and indeed to any logical particle. It might seem that they were symbols which had throughout the same meaning. But this is due to a systematic ambiguity in the meanings of 'not', 'or', etc., by which they adjust themselves to propositions of any order.

The ambiguity about which I want to speak is not connected with the Theory of Types but with what may be called the 'many-level structure' of language. I shall first of all explain what I understand by *a language stratum*.

II. Language Strata

Let me begin by introducing a distinction between two paths a logical inquiry may follow. It will perhaps be best to illustrate my point with a picture. In studying the geometry of a curve we may wish to find out its behaviour *at some particular point*—for instance, whether it has a tangent there, whether it is continuous there, what its measure of curvature is there, and the like. Then we are studying *local* properties of the curve. Or we may wish to study the behaviour of the curve *as a whole*—for instance, whether it is closed or not, and, if it is closed, whether it is convex, etc. Then we are studying its properties *at large*. This picture suggests two different types of investigation in logic. The one takes its orientation from the logical relations which hold between a number of given propositions; a question of this sort is to ask whether a given proposition follows from another one, or contradicts it, or is independent of it, etc. We are then concerned with the logical nexus *on a small scale*, so to speak with *local* relations between propositions. Suppose, on the other hand, considering a certain deductive theory based upon a number of suitable axioms, say Euclidean Geometry or the Theory of Deduction, we ask whether the system under consideration is *free from contradiction*, that is, whether it is ever possible to prove a certain theorem and its contradictory. This is a question of quite a different kind. Suppose we say, 'The theory in question contains no contradiction', then we are making an assertion, not about the relations between two or three or more single propositions, but about the theory *as a whole*. Again, we may inquire whether the deductive

theory we are considering is *complete*, i.e. whether any statements that can be constructed in accordance with the given
rules (of the theory) can always be decided (in one way or
the other) by the means of the theory and decided in a finite
number of steps; we may also be investigating whether two
given theories are isomorphic (i.e. of the same logical structure so that to each proposition of the one there corresponds
precisely one proposition of the other, and vice versa, and
that all the logical relations of the propositions in the one
are retained in the other). Now in pursuing such questions
we are concerned with what may be called the *macrological*
features of such theories, in contrast with questions concerning the *micrological* connections of single statements.

A technique has been worked out to deal with problems of
that macrological kind. Naturally, these methods—called
'metalogical' and 'metamathematical'—only apply to *deductive systems*. However, it does seem to me that there is also
good sense in talking of macro- and micrological features of a
language. Language, it is true, is not organized in the way
a deductive system is; compared with such a system it is of
a much more loosely knitted texture. And yet one feels a
marked difference when one compares such statements as:
a material object statement, a sense-datum[2] statement, a
law of nature, a geometrical proposition, a statement describing national characteristics, a statement describing a half-
faded memory picture, a statement describing a dream, a
proverb, and so forth. It is as if each of these statements was
constructed in a different *logical style*. (I will explain presently what I mean by this.) We may set ourselves the task
of grouping statements of our language according to the similarity of their usage in distinct domains, in *language-strata*
as I shall venture to call them. Thus laws will form one language stratum, material object statements another one, sense
datum statements yet another one, and so on. Now the question which I want to consider is this: Is it possible to develop
out of that vague feeling that 'each of them is built in a
different logical style' something more precise? Is it possible,

[2] For an explanation and discussion of this term see First Series,
Ch. VI.—EDITOR.

say, by characterizing each stratum on the basis of its intrinsic internal fabric or logical texture? To make this clearer let me return to the picture taken from geometry. It was a memorable achievement of mathematical thought when Gauss succeeded in characterizing a curved surface merely 'from within' without any reference to space outside, which amounted to this that he showed that if two-dimensional beings were living on the surface of a sphere, an egg or a wine-glass, etc., they could, merely through carrying out certain measuring operations within their abode, find out in what sort of surface they were living; in other words, they could learn the 'intrinsic geometry' of their habitation without any reference to three-dimensional space. Now the analogous problem in our case would be this: Can a given language stratum be characterized, not by reference to something outside the subject-matter by dubbing it 'material object', 'memory picture' or the like, but by purely formal motifs? Let us see what means we have at our disposal for such a programme.

We may first investigate the nature of the concepts which a given stratum contains: whether they are absolutely precise and definable with mathematical rigour, or vague, or of an open texture. We may next consider the statements themselves and ask what sort of logic is valid for them. By 'logic' I mean logic in the strict sense, the laws of inference. Aristotelian logic, including the modernized and refined form of its presentation in *Principia Mathematica*, has gone the same way as Euclidean geometry—a number of different 'logics' have grown up alongside it, more or less akin to it, just as Euclidean geometry is now surrounded by a number of similar and cognate systems. One effect of this development is the disappearance of that disturbing air of uniqueness that had puzzled philosophers for so long. Birkhoff and von Neumann, for instance, have indicated a system, different from classical logic, which seems to be in better harmony with the structure of quantum mechanics. On the suggestion of Brouwer a logic has been constructed different from classical logic in which is actually employed mathematical demonstration, a logic in which the law of excluded middle is no longer universally true. And, notice, when we pass from the one logic to the other, we get an altogether different mathematics;

which goes to show that the sort of logic we apply is an important characteristic ingrained in a certain field of propositions. Change the logic and then the propositions will take on new meanings. Take another example—the logic of half-faded memory pictures. Here the situation is such that we are often unable to call to mind one or the other point of detail, that is, that we are often unable to decide an alternative. What did that bathroom look like I saw the other day on a visit? Was it ivory, was it cream or pale biscuit or maize? Suppose a pattern-book were shown to me, and I was later asked whether *this* was the colour I had seen, perhaps I would not be able to decide. If I were pressed I might have to say, 'I can't remember so distinctly'; if another different shade of yellow were shown to me then I might give the same reply, finally adding, 'all I know is that it was some light yellowish colour'. Notice that, in this case, it is quite natural to use a *vague* term ('light colour') to express the indeterminacy of the impression. If language was such that each and every word was particular and each colour word had a definite, clearly defined meaning, we should find we could not use it. That is, we should come up against alternatives: 'Was it this colour or not?'—which we could not decide. I cannot get back to the impression I had then, it cannot be pinned down and preserved under glass for inspection like a dead beetle. To insist, in these circumstances, on the law of excluded middle, without any means of deciding the issue, is paying lip service to the laws of logic. There are only two alternatives open to us: We must either be prepared to drop the law of excluded middle when we wish to use a language with precisely defined terms; or we shall have to use a language whose words are in one way or another blurred. But we can't have it both ways. Another way of bringing out this point is to say that, if several colours are shown to me which differ only slightly, they do not necessarily exclude one another. This shows particularly clearly that our attitude towards a half-faded memory image is radically different from that towards a material object. No one would dream of ascribing two different lengths to the table in this room (a *real* table), and saying that both were right. One statement, if it proves true, excludes the other. Whereas it is perfectly correct to say of two slightly different colour statements, when applied to an indeterminate memory picture, that both are compatible; which just shows that the logic of colour words, when applied in this language stratum, is different from their usual logic.

Again, the logic of aphorisms seems to be very peculiar. A man who writes aphorisms may say a thing, and, on another occasion, the very opposite of it without being guilty of a contradiction. For each aphorism, as it stands, is quite complete in itself. Two different aphorisms are not parts of one and the same communication. Suppose you go to a museum where several paintings are hung on the wall. Would you complain that they are not correlated and do not fit into one and the same perspective? Well now, each painting has a pictorial space of its own; what is represented in two paintings, though the paintings may be adjacent, is not in the same pictorial space. It is the first aim of Art, it has been said, to set a frame around Nature. Sometimes the frame is large, sometimes small, but always it is there. An aphorism is Literature and done with ink instead of colours. Of two aphorisms each is in a frame of its own; hence no clash. It would be interesting to penetrate the logic of poems, or of mysticism. Here a contradiction may be a perfectly legitimate means to point to what cannot be said in language. No: seeming contradictions are not always absurd.

To return to our subject: I said that the examples given suggest looking upon a logic as a characteristic which sets its stamp upon a particular language stratum. But there are two further characteristics: truth and verifiability.

III. *Systematic Ambiguity of Truth and Verifiability*

Compare a variety of statements such as: a sense-datum statement, a material object statement, a law of nature, description of something half forgotten, a statement of my own motives, a conjecture as to the motives by which someone else was actuated, quotation of the exact words so-and-so was using, brief summary of the tenor of a political speech, characterization of the *Zeitgeist* of a certain historical period, a proverb, a poetic metaphor, a mathematical proposition, and so on. Now what I want to emphasize is that the idea of truth varies with the kind of statement; that it has a systematic ambiguity. Take, for instance, a mathematical proposition, say a theorem of geometry. To say that it is true simply means that it can be deduced from such-and-such axioms. As a consequence of this, it may be true in one system of geometry and false in another. And the axioms themselves? They are no concern of the pure mathematician: all he is concerned with is that *if* these and these axioms apply, *then* the theorems apply too. But whether the axioms actually do apply, is not for him to decide. He leaves that to applied mathematics. Hence Russell's definition of mathematics as 'the subject in which we never know what we are talking about, nor whether what we are saying is true'. Here, then, is a very good case for the 'coherence theory of truth'.

Again, a law of nature is never true in the same sense in which, say, 'There is a fire burning in this room' is, nor in the sense in which 'He is an amusing fellow' may be; and the two latter statements are not true in the same sense in which 'I've got a headache' is. Truth, when applied to a physical law, means roughly speaking that it is well established by experimental evidence or other observation, that it brings widely different things into a close connection and makes us 'understand' what seemed a mystery before; that it simplifies our theoretical system, and further, that it is fruitful in leading us to predictions and new discoveries. (That is, incidentally, why the pragmatist identifies truth with usefulness: he has really got hold of one facet, but of one facet only.) Truth, in this case, it may be said, is not *one* idea but a whole bundle of ideas. Nothing of this applies to truth in the case of a simple observation. Suppose you have to make sure that the light is on in your room. Now when you go and look and say 'All right, it's on', your statement is true, *not* because it brings widely different things into connection, *not* because it simplifies I don't know what, *not* because it is fruitful or suggestive —no, nothing of the sort; it is just true because it says so-and-so is as you say it is.

Again, in what sense is one to say of a proverb that it is true? Have you ever tried to put some rare and subtle experience, or some half-forgotten (but strong) impression into words? If you do, you will find that truth, in this case, is inseparably tied up with the literary quality of your writing: it needs no less than a poet to express fully and faithfully such fragile states of mind. How you say it matters even more than what you say.

Similar remarks apply to verification. A law of nature can be verified by experimental evidence, though not conclusively. Whether a material object statement is capable of conclusive verification is a moot point. Take next a case such as 'I've got a terrible toothache'. Suppose I go to the dentist, he examines my teeth and says, 'All right, there's nothing wrong with them'. Would I then reply, 'Oh, I beg your pardon, I *thought* that I've got a toothache, but now I see that I was mistaken'? My toothache cannot be argued away or refuted by examining my teeth, my nerves, etc. If I were asked how I know that I've got a toothache, I might be tempted to reply, 'Because I *feel* it'. What a queer sort of reply! Is there anything else I can do with a toothache but feel it? What my reply aimed at, however, was something different, namely to *shake off* the whole question as improper, beside the point. How do I know? I've simply got toothache, and that's the end of it. I do not grant that I may have fallen victim to a delusion, I do not recognize a medical examination, an observation of my teeth any psychological tests, a court of experts—no dentist in heaven or earth can refute me. In saying 'I just *feel it*' I am expressing the fact that the toothache is something *given in immediate experience*, not a thing *inferred from something else* on the strength of certain evidences. The first person singular has, amongst other uses, the function to indicate the character of *immediacy* of an experience.

Take the statement, 'There are sea serpents'. How would you verify it? Is it enough that some person has seen them? Perhaps for him; for you the situation is different: you have so far only a man who *says* that he has seen them. So you must check up what he says—you may test his eyesight, go into his past and examine his reliability, and so on. The result of this checking will be a number of statements each of which, in its turn, may again be checked: the expert who examined the man's eyesight may himself be examined, the witnesses who testified may in their turn be scrutinized, etc.

In following up the threads of verification we nowhere come to an absolute end, that is, we can never say, 'Now it is conclusively proved that the man was right'. What this particular example shows applies in general. At some point we do stop, it is true, for practical reasons, when the evidence seems to be sufficient. But theoretically we may go on checking and re-checking our statements as long as we please. So long as we move amongst statements concerning such evidences as illustrated above, verification has no natural end, but refers continually to ever new statements. In pursuing these fibres, however, we see how secondary lines branch off into other regions: the points where they come to a sudden end represent those immediate experiences which an observer has the moment he experiences them, and which, in this moment, cannot be checked against other evidences. These experiences, expressed in 'I'-sentences, are, so to speak, end points of verification—but of verification in a quite different sense. For if we try to use this verification later, it turns to dust. It lives in the moment, and is gone. Still these experiences are the moments of ultimate fulfilment. It is they from which all light of knowledge flows forth. Or, to change the metaphor, they are the points in which knowledge makes direct contact with reality. Without them all our sentences would float in the air cut off from actual facts. What establishes a connection between sentences and reality are these last points of verification, transitory though they may be. Thus a statement may be verified in two quite different senses: either by checking it against other statements, or by appealing to immediate experience. In the case of a material object statement, for instance, some lines refer to other material object statements, i.e. they lead from statement to statement within the same language stratum; some others branch off and penetrate into a different stratum, the 'I'-statements. Thus verification weaves a complicated net, a ramified pattern of lines.

It is easily seen that the term 'meaningful' displays the same ambiguity: its sense varies with the stratum. For instance, a sentence in a novel is meaningful, if (1) it is correct English, i.e. not a broth of words, and (2) it fits in with the other sentences. This meaningfulness has nothing whatever to do with verifiability. (That, by the way, is why Fiction is not false.) This criterion, however, does not apply to experiential statements where verifiability is of some relevance, although it would not be right to equate meaningfulness with verifiability. Again, in which sense is a rule, a definition, a request, a question meaningful? There may even be a sense in which metaphysical statements have a meaning. The trouble with the Logical Positivists was that they attached too rigid an import to 'meaningfulness' and lost sight of its ambiguity. By virtue of the multiplicity of meaning in this word they lost themselves in a magic cloud out of which they condemned everything that did not conform to their standards. In actual fact they had no machinery, such as they thought they had, by which the senselessness of metaphysics could be *proved*; though it must be admitted that metaphysicians made the greatest efforts to supply them with plausible arguments for such a view. I am afraid what has been said on this subject was of a profound shallowness.

To sum up this point: Statements may be *true* in different senses, *verifiable* in different senses, *meaningful* in different senses. Therefore the attempts at defining 'truth', or at drawing a sharp line between the meaningful and the meaningless, etc., are doomed to fail.

IV. *Completeness*

Up till now I have tried to sketch a few leit-motifs which might be used in characterizing a given language stratum. They were: the texture of the concepts together with the sort of logic which obtains and the appropriate senses of 'truth' and 'verifiability' (if the latter applies at all). To these must be added two more factors: the way in which a proposition is integrated into a larger whole; and the relations in which different strata stand to each other.

In order to approach the first point, it will be best to make use again of a geometrical illustration. Suppose you consider a number of statements which are about the same subject *a*. Each of these statements may be represented by a circular area, and the conjunction of two statements by that part of the areas which overlap. The more propositions we take, the smaller will the area become which is common to all the disks; at the same time, the more definite will become the description formed by all these statements. This gives rise to the following problem: Is there anything like a description of *maximum* definiteness, for instance, a description whose geometrical picture is a point? If there was such a thing, this would mean that the description is *complete* in the sense that nothing could be added to it which would make it more definite. Well now, are there language strata in which it is possible to construct something like a 'closed' description? And if so, will such a description contain a finite or an infinite number of single statements?

Geometry provides us with a model in which a complete (closed, perfect) description is attainable and with a finite number of statements. Thus a triangle is determined when its three sides are given: nothing can be added to these data that is not entailed by, or in contradiction with, them. Here, then, is an example of a description which, on logical grounds, cannot be extended.

A quite different situation seems to hold with regard to experiential statements. However many features I may assert of a thing, say of this chair, or however many relations I may state which hold between it and other things, or however many statements I may make about its life-history, I shall never reach a point where my description can be said to be *exhaustive*, that is, such that no further increment in knowledge is possible. Any real thing is inexhaustible. My knowledge of it is always extensible. There is no maximum description. To use the geometrical illustration: Such a description will always be represented by a whole *region*; a point will be a limit toward which the description tends without ever reaching it. Thus the picture which we make of an experiential statement on our map will never shrink to a point.

There are, however, cases where a complete description *is* attainable. Take, for instance, a game of chess played in a tournament: it can be described, completely, move by move, from the beginning to the end, say in the chess notation. Again, a melody is describable completely in the musical notation (disregarding, of course, questions of interpretation). The same is true of a carpet, viewed as a geometrical ornament of shape and colour.

How curious it is when I describe a dream: when I have narrated my dream, told everything that happened, in it, my description is finished. But it comes to an end in a very different way from that in which, e.g., the description of a game of chess comes to an end where there is a natural beginning and a natural end. A dream is fragmentary, enigmatic, and a dream cannot be integrated into a larger whole: you cannot ask, 'What happened before the dream began, or after it was over?' Or rather, *when* you ask such a question, you have already left the dream language and consider the sleeper from outside, from the point of view of a waking man. In this respect a dream has a unity and coherence which makes it nearly akin to a poem, or an aphorism.

The few examples given will suffice to show that statements may be *complete* in very different senses, and that the way they are complete or incomplete is a further important feature of a language stratum.

Finally, we have to investigate in what relations different strata stand to each other. I shall leave this for the moment and confine myself to mentioning one question only: whether the threads of verification, when we follow them up, remain within the given stratum, or lead outside it; in other words, whether a given stratum is *closed* with respect to verification.

V. *A New Picture of Language*

We are now in a position to sketch a new picture of language which, though still untried, seems to emerge from all these considerations; a picture of language naturally stratified into layers. This new conception contrasts with such a view as that held by Wittgenstein in his *Tractatus Logico-Philosophicus*: according to that view language consists of statements which can, one and all, be derived from atomic propositions by a uniform process. An atomic proposition is one asserting an atomic fact; an atomic fact is a fact which has no parts that are facts; and the uniform method by which any statement can be constructed is that of building up truth-functions of any selection of atomic propositions. This leads to an amazing simplication of the picture we can make for ourselves of the fabric of language. All statements are, so to speak, on a footing, and all are reducible to the same set of atomic propositions. Or better, the totality of propositions is defined by this method of generation. Too good to be true. Apart from the fact that no one has ever succeeded in producing a single atomic proposition, the whole thing is a myth. Moreover, we know for certain that there are many ways of building up statements which have nothing at all to do with truth-functions; such as unfulfilled conditional statements— 'If Hitler had won the war, then . . .' and many others. No: language does not fit this strait-jacket.

There are certain modern trends in Philosophy which seem to have some such background. Phenomenalism, for instance, seems to presuppose that there is one basic language, the sense-datum language, to which any other statement, or at least any material object statement, can be reduced. According to Phenomenalism a material object, say a cat, is a bundle of sense-data tied together and with the edges trimmed off; unless it is a bundle of *sensibilia*, that is the sort of thing which you *would* have seen, if you *had* ever looked, in short, a bundle of highly problematical entities. But no: we have simply to recognize that a statement about a cat is a statement about a cat: and not a truth-function of sense-datum statements, or an infinite class of perspectives, or an infinite group of *sensibilia*, or heaven knows what. A thing is, so to speak, a hard core that resists at any attempt at breaking it up and reducing it to the level of other data, whatever they may be. All this talk about material objects and sense-data is a talk about two language strata, about their relation, about the logic of this relationship. The problem arises along the plane where the two strata make contact, so to speak. The difficulty is to understand in precisely which way a material object statement is related to a sense-datum statement; that is, what sort of relations hold between members of different strata; and that is a problem of logic.

Similarly, Behaviourism is an attempt to reduce psychological statements, e.g., 'What a conceited fellow!' to a very, very long list of statements setting out in which way the person in question would behave under such-and-such circumstances; a very successful way of describing peculiarities of rats which has been transferred to men. The whole thing rests on a *naïveté*—that there is one basic language (suitable for describing the behaviour of rats) into which everything else must be translated. The motto 'Only rats, no men!' overlooks the fact that psychological statements belong to a stratum of their own, with a logic different from that of the language in which you say how a person looks, how he smiles, in short what he has in common with a rat.

We are now in a position to take a further step. It was hitherto the custom to refer to what I have called 'strata' by indicating their subject-matter, using terms such as: 'material object statements', 'descriptions of vague impressions', 'statements of laws of nature', and the like. What I now suggest we do—and this is a programme for the future—is to reverse the whole situation by saying: 'The formal motifs which we have been considering all combine to impress a certain stamp on a stratum; they give us the means to characterize each stratum "from within" that is with no reference to the subject'. If we carefully study the texture of the concepts which occur in a given stratum, the logic of its propositions, the meaning of truth, the web of verification, the senses in which a description may be complete or incomplete—if we consider all that, we may thereby characterize the subject-matter. We may say, for instance: a material object is something that is describable in a language of such-and-such structure; a sense impression is something which can be described in such-and-such a language; a dream is——, a memory picture is——, and so on. In this way we shall be able to *formalize* these concepts. The analogy with science is obvious. The questions, 'What is a point?' 'What is a straight line?' have been debated for more than 2000 years until the solution was found in a reversal of the problem situation. All the time it was thought that we must first define the meaning of the primitive symbols in geometry before we can see that the axioms are 'Self-evident truths' given in intuition. In modern times the terms 'point'. 'straight line', 'plane', 'between', 'congruent', etc., are defined as those things and relations which satisfy the axioms of geometry. That is, the axioms in their totality *determine* (within pure mathematics) the meaning of the primitive symbols. In like manner we may say that each stratum has a logic of its own and that this logic determines the meaning of certain basic terms. In some respects this is obvious. Whether a melody is a sequence of air-vibrations, or a succession of musical notes, or a message of the composer, depends entirely on the way you describe it. Similarly, you may look at a game of chess, or on the pattern of a carpet from very different aspects and you will then see in them very different things. Notice how all these words— 'melody', 'game of chess', etc.—take on a systematic ambiguity according to the language stratum in which you talk. The same applies to 'doing a sum', 'writing a letter', or to any action indeed. An action may be viewed as a series of movements caused by some physiological stimuli in the 'Only rats, no men' sense; or as something that has a purpose or a meaning irrespective of the way its single links are produced. An action in the first sense is determined by *causes*, an action in the second sense by *motives* or *reasons*. It is generally believed that an action is determined both by causes and by motives. But if the causes determine the action, no room is left for motives, and if the motives determine the action, no room is left for causes. Either the system of causes is complete, then it is not possible to squeeze in a motive; or the system of motives is complete, then it is not possible to squeeze in a cause. 'Well, now, do you believe that if you are writing a letter you are engaged in two different activities?' No; I mean that there are two different ways of looking at the thing; just as there are two different ways of looking at a sentence: as a series of noises produced by a human agent; or as a vehicle of thought. For a series of noises there may be causes but no reasons; for a series of words expressing thought there may be reasons but no causes. What we must understand is that the word 'action' has a systematic ambiguity. And yet we are continually invited to regard motives as a special sort of causes; perhaps because we have only the word 'Why?' to ask both for cause and motive. We do not see the ambiguity of the interrogative.

II

Will the Future be like the Past?

FREDERICK L. WILL

I

In the elaboration of arguments in the last two hundred years for and against scepticism concerning induction, one central point at issue has been that concerning the 'uniformity of nature' and the necessity of assumptions about that uniformity in all inductive reasoning. To this point the sceptics have again and again recurred, following the precedent of Hume, in their arguments to show the overall doubtfulness, the absolutely irremediable lack of cogency of inductive arguments in general; and to this point also have recurred their opponents in their endeavours to refute these same sceptical conclusions. The question which the sceptics have raised concerning the uniformity of nature is expressed partially and in non-technical language in the question of the above title, 'Will the future be like the past?'

There is an advantage of simplicity and clarity in expressing the question thus with reference to the future, as Hume himself did in the *Enquiry*, even though quite clearly the question of the validity of inductive procedures is by no means restricted to conclusions about future things or events. The question about induction which both the sceptics and their opponents have attempted, each in their own way, to answer is a question about all those procedures in which, in science and everyday life, we use the evidence of observed facts or states of affairs to conclude concerning unobserved ones. The unobserved matters about which the conclusion is drawn may be in the past or present as well as in the future. In each case the basic procedure is the same. On the basis of observations now being made or already made which reveal that certain things have a specified characteristic, or set of characteristics, it is concluded that other events or things of the same kind, though unobserved, in the past, present, or future, have these same characteristics. And the question raised about this procedure is likewise the same. By what right do we conclude from the observed to the unobserved? Granted that all the cases which have been tested have shown hydrogen to be inflammable, by what right do we conclude on this evidence that under similar conditions hydrogen has always been, is now, and will continue to be inflammable?

Abstracting from this more general question about induction it is permissible, in the interest of simplicity, to consider the question in but one of its temporal phases, namely that referring to the future. This phase may justly be viewed as a test case of the general question. To the extent that our inductive conclusions about the future can be justified, so can our inductive conclusions be justified generally. If inductive methods can be shown to be all completely without justification when their conclusions refer to the future, this conclusion can be easily generalized to apply to all inductive conclusions whatsoever; and if inductive procedures can be justified in so far as they refer to the future, by exactly the same procedure, and with exactly the same kind of evidence, they can be justified when their conclusions are drawn concerning the present and the past. It may be noted also that even with this restriction of reference solely to the future the question of inductive validity still bears directly upon the question of the validity of scientific laws, which is the aspect of induction which has always appeared to philosophers as most provocative as well as fundamental. For these laws are statements about the course of nature, the connections between things and events, not only as they are in the present, or have been in the past, but also as they will be in the future.

II

The standard argument for complete inductive scepticism, for the belief that inductive procedures have no rational and no empirical justification whatever, is the one stated in a small variety of ways in the writings of Hume. If one consults these writings in search of an answer to the question of inductive validity one finds the same clear answer argued first in technical detail in the *Treatise*, secondly compressed into a few non-technical paragraphs in the *Abstract of a Treatise of Human Nature*, and thirdly, presented again in a non-technical but somewhat fuller version in a chapter in the *Enquiry Concerning Human Understanding*. There is no basis whatever for any conclusion concerning future matters, according to this argument; there is no way whatever in which such conclusions can be established to be certainly true or even probable. For in the first place no such conclusion can be demonstrated by reasoning alone, since they are all conclusions about matters of fact, and since it is the case that the denial of any assertion of a matter of fact is not self-contradictory. But if one gives up the rationalistic aspiration to demonstrate propositions about matters of fact or existence *a priori*, and turns instead to experience, this road, though apparently more promising at first, likewise ends by leading one exactly nowhere. Clearly no statement about future matters of fact can be established by observation. Future things cannot be observed. Any event or state of affairs which can be observed is by definition not in the future. The only recourse which remains therefore is the inductive procedure of employing present or past observations and inferring therefrom the nature of the future. But this procedure to which we are all forced, or rather, to which we all should be forced if we did not, in company with the animals, use it naturally from birth, is in the light of close analysis completely indefensible. For such reasoning assumes, and is quite invalid without the assumption, that the future will be like the past.

> . . . all inferences from experience suppose, as their foundation, that the future will resemble the past, and that similar powers will be conjoined with similar sensible qualities. If there be any suspicion that the course of nature may change, and that the past may be no rule for the

future, all experience becomes useless, and can give rise to no inference or conclusion.[1]

Will the future 'resemble the past'? Or be 'conformable to the past'? These are the ways in which in the *Enquiry* Hume expresses the question concerning the uniformity of nature, restricting to its reference towards the future the question which already had been asked in broader terms in the *Treatise*. There, without the temporal restriction, it is argued that the principle of inductive conclusions, the principle upon which reason would proceed if reason determined us in these matters, is *'that instances, of which we have had no experience, must resemble those, of which we have had experience, and that the course of nature continues always uniformly the same'*. (Bk. I, Pt. III, Sect. VI).

However the principle is stated, the argument about it remains the same. It is indispensable, if inductive conclusions are to be justified; but just as it is absolutely indispensable, so, and this is the measure of our logical misfortune, it cannot be established as certain or as probable in any way. It cannot be established by any demonstrative argument. For it is clearly an assertion of a matter of fact, and therefore the kind of assertion whose denial is non-contradictory and conceivable.

That there are no demonstrative arguments in the case seems evident; since it implies no contradiction that the course of nature may change, and that an object, seemingly like those which we have experienced, may be attended with different or contrary effects. May I not clearly and distinctly conceive that a body, falling from the clouds, and which, in all other respects, resembles snow, has yet the taste of salt or the feeling of fire? Is there any more intelligible proposition than to affirm, that all the trees will flourish in December and January, and decay in May and June? Now whatever is intelligible, and can be distinctly conceived, implies no contradiction and can never be proved false by any demonstrative argument or abstract

[1] *Enquiry Concerning Human Understanding*, Sect. IV, § 32. The arabic numerals in references to this work indicate the marginal sections in the Selby-Bigge edition of 1902.

reasoning *à priori*. (*Enquiry*, Sect. IV, § 30. Cf. *Treatise*, loc. cit.)

Any further doubts about the doubtfulness of this principle which is the main-spring of inductive inference are quickly disposed of. No one who understands the principle with its reference to unobserved instances will suggest that it can be simply observed to be true. It is still true that one cannot observe the future, or the unobserved generally. And, finally, no one who has a sound logical conscience and appreciates the indispensability of the principle to induction generally will tolerate the suggestion that the principle may be established by inductions from experience. Such a process would be circular.

> It is impossible, therefore, that any arguments from experience can prove this resemblance of the past to the future; since all these arguments are founded on the supposition of that resemblance.

And again:

> . . . all our experimental conclusions proceed upon the supposition that the future will be conformable to the past. To endeavour, therefore, the proof of this last supposition by probable arguments, or arguments regarding existence, must be evidently going in a circle, and taking that for granted, which is the very point in question. (*Enquiry*, Sect. IV, §§ 32, 30.)

On this point the *Treatise* (loc. cit.) and the *Abstract* speak with one voice. One final quotation from the latter may serve to summarize the conclusion.

> 'Tis evident that *Adam* with all his science, would never have been able to *demonstrate*, that the course of nature must continue uniformly the same, and that the future must be conformable to the past. What is possible can never be demonstrated to be false; and 'tis possible the course of nature may change, since we can conceive such a change. Nay, I will go farther, and assert, that he could not so much as prove by any *probable* arguments, that

the future must be conformable to the past. All probable arguments are built on the supposition, that there is this conformity betwixt the future and the past, and therefore can never prove it. This conformity is a *matter of fact*, and if it must be proved, will admit of no proof but from experience. But our experience in the past can be a proof of nothing for the future, but upon a supposition, that there is a resemblance betwixt them. This therefore is a point, which can admit of no proof at all, and which we take for granted without any proof. (*Abstract*, 1938 ed., p. 15.)

All inductive inferences about the future depend for their validity upon a fundamental principle which, it now turns out, we have not the slightest reason for believing to be true but which nevertheless we simply take for granted. We have, accordingly, no reason for believing any of these inferences; they are all a matter of custom or habit, or, if one prefers more recent terminology, of 'animal faith'.

III

It would be more promising in respect to logical neatness and precision for one to consider the alleged circularity of all inductive procedure, which is the central point of the above argument, while using as a test case some specific scientific law or principle rather than some affirmation as vague and imprecise as that the future will resemble the past. But, for the purpose of analysing the sceptic's views and meeting the arguments by which these views have been defended, such a procedure would have this deficiency, that no matter what specific scientific generalization were chosen, one reply which would be sure to be made would consist of an appeal beyond this generalization to some general beliefs about uniformity, some general Principle of Uniformity which, it would be urged, is assumed somehow in the inductive establishment of this and other scientific generalizations. Since the sceptical argument has been presented in terms of general Principles of Uniformity, and it is in these terms that it is alleged to demonstrate the logical circularity of all inductive reasoning, it seems worth while to attempt to deal with this argument, if one can, in the same terms—in terms of some alleged Principle of Uniformity for which it has been claimed in recent philosophy that it does serve as a wide and basic inductive assumption.

In his *Treatise on Probability*, J. M. Keynes attempts to formulate a set of principles which, if assumed to be true of a given area of subject-matter, would justify, in accordance with the principles of probability, the employment of inductive methods in that area. One of the principles which he discusses, the simplest and at the same time the one for which it seems, at first view, most plausible to contend that it may serve as a broad inductive assumption, is the one to which he gave the name of the 'Principle of the Uniformity of Nature'. This Principle affirms that nature is uniform in a specific way; and that is in respect to position in space and time. 'It involves', writes Keynes, 'the assertion of a generalized judgment of irrelevance, namely, of the irrelevance of mere position in time and space to generalizations which have no reference to particular positions in time and space' (p. 226. Cf. also pp. 255–6, 263, 276). It is this principle, he argues, which

. . . supplies the answer, if it is correct, to the criticism that the instances, on which generalizations are based, are all alike in being past, and that any generalization, which is applicable to the future, must be based, for this reason, upon imperfect analogy. We judge directly that the resemblance between instances, which consists in their being past, is in itself irrelevant, and does not supply a valid ground for impugning a generalization (p. 256).

It is, however, difficult to interpret this so-called Principle in such a way that it makes a statement which is both definite and is not at the same time refuted in some areas of experience. Keynes observes that what this Principle affirms is 'that the same total cause always produces the same effect' (p. 248), and this is so; but the difficulty here is that of giving a definite meaning to the important adjective 'same' as it applies to causes and effects. Unless there is a specifiable meaning applicable to causes in all fields, the formula 'same cause—same effect' is not a univocal principle affirming the presence of a specific kind of uniformity in every area of natural phenomena. Yet, when one sets out to specify just what kind of sameness is meant when this formula is employed, one discovers that there is a great variety of interpretations of this word in different fields of inquiry, and that what determines whether a given set of circumstances is regarded as the same cause, for example, varies from field to field, depending upon the nature of the subject-matter as that is revealed in the various generalizations which are regarded as established for that subject-matter. These generalizations exhibit among themselves great differences in scope and precision, as well as in the degree of confidence with which they are accepted. They include, for example, the generalizations about the coherence and constancy of properties which are involved in our belief in and distinctions among various kinds of material objects. And they include the more precise generalizations, frequently expressed in the form of mathematical equations, which would normally be referred to as 'scientific laws', as well as the broader generalizations formulated in various accepted Principles and Theories. When this is understood, when one sees that in the employment of the Principle of Uniformity what determines the kind of sameness to which the Principle affirms that differences in mere position in space and time are irrelevant is the specific generalizations, the laws, principles, and so on, which have been established in that field, one is in a better position to understand this so-called Principle and its alleged employment as a general inductive assumption. In any given field the Principle of Uniformity states that mere differences in space and time are irrelevant in just this sense, that there are certain generalizations, true of this field, which describe the conditions under which certain objects exist and events occur, and in which differences in mere position in space and time make little or no detectable difference. That this is so, accordingly, is not an inductive assumption in that field in the sense that it is specified and made before all inductive inquiry in the field. It is an inductive assumption in the more usual sense that conclusions of previous experience and inquiries are available for employment in any field as bases for further investigation in that field.

The primary purpose here is not to elucidate and specify the variations of meaning which such a Principle or formula must undergo if it is to be understood as applying to the great variety of fields in which inductive inquiry is carried on, to the great variety in the kinds of uniformity which the generalizations in these fields describe. The primary purpose is to inquire whether the sceptics are right in insisting that it is impossible to provide genuine evidence for beliefs about uniformity, or whether, on the contrary, it is possible to furnish empirical evidence for these beliefs, which, in its employment, does not involve circular reasoning. It is granted that what the Principle of Uniformity affirms in any field, if 'Principle' it may be called, is that there is uniformity in that field in this sense and no other; that there are certain specific generalizations which apply to that field and in which mere differences of position in time and space are regarded as irrelevant. In the light of this interpretation of uniformity the question briefly is, how can such a broad affirmation be confirmed or verified by induction without circularity?

IV

For purposes of simplicity, in order to secure the clearest statement of the argument in the fewest words, it will be useful in what follows to abbreviate the statement of this Principle of Uniformity and also to consider it only in reference to time. If it can be shown that what the Principle affirms concerning the irrelevance of time in specific generalizations can be confirmed inductively, it can also be shown in exactly the same way that it is possible to confirm the Principle in its spatial reference also. So abbreviated and restricted, the Principle asserts that, in the specific way just defined, differences in time make no difference. Can this interpretation of the assertion that the future will resemble the past be confirmed? What, if any, is the evidence for it?

It follows directly from the interpretation which has just been given of this principle what the evidence for it must be. If the Principle affirms no more for any given area of fact than the validity in that area of certain generalizations which are uniform with respect to space and time, then the evidence for the Principle must be whatever evidence there is for these particular generalizations. This includes all the observations in the past and present which confirm the presence in that area of the uniformities of which these general statements speak. Belief in the uniformity in a given area is not something which is specifiable apart from the laws, principles, and other generalizations regarded as established in that area, but is itself belief in just the kind of uniformities which these generalizations describe and define. If it is correct, then, to say of any generalization, e.g. of any scientific law, that it is confirmed or verified by empirical evidence, is it not correct to say that, to that extent, there is evidence for belief in the uniformity of nature?

The sceptic's answer to this question repeats that final rejoinder of Hume. Granted that there is empirical evidence which has been used to establish various scientific laws, all that it is evidence for, he insists, is the assertion that *in the past* these laws were true, that in the past differences in time have made no difference. This evidence is absolutely worthless for inferences which speak about the future unless it is possible to assume that the future will be like the past. But stop! That is part of what one is trying to show, that is, that mere differences in temporal position, whether past or future, make no difference in these laws of nature. That the future will be like the past means, among other things, that in the future these laws will hold, that in this specific respect differences in time will make no difference. This cannot be inductively confirmed, the sceptic is saying, because any inductive argument for it assumes it and is therefore, as evidence, completely valueless.

One major source of the plausibility of the sceptic's reasoning lies in the analogies which knowing the future easily suggests and in terms of which one is apt to think and be misled. Is this not, one may ask, like any case of sampling? And must one not take care, when reasoning inductively from samples, that one's samples are fair? If a scientist reasons concerning the behaviour of oxygen, nitrogen or hydrogen on Mars, if such elements there be on Mars, on the basis of the known behaviour of these elements on the earth, he is assuming that in some respects the samples of the elements on the other planet are like those we have here. Similarly in reasoning about the future behaviour of these elements on the basis of present and past behaviour one must assume that future samples of these elements will be like present and past ones. Now if it is the case that past samples may be regarded as evidence about future ones only upon such an assumption, then no examination of past samples, however extensive, can be regarded as yielding evidence for the assumption itself. Any reasoning which did attempt to employ such samples as evidence for the assumption would be forced to use the assumption as a principle in the reasoning and would therefore beg the whole question at issue.

A physical representation of the kind of analogy presented here might be as follows: Suppose that there was somewhere in the world an enclosure beyond which it was impossible for anyone ever to go or to make any observations. Nothing could be seen, heard, or in any other way perceived beyond the border. The territory beyond the enclosure, for ever barred from human perception, is the land of Future. The territory within the enclosure is the land of Present and Past, but since it is overwhelmingly the latter, it all goes under the name of Past. Now suppose that someone within the enclosure is interested in some proposition about the way things behave beyond the enclosure, say, a simple and homely proposition about chickens, to the effect that beyond the enclosure roosters fight more than hens. And he wonders what evidence, if any, there is for this proposition. Of course he cannot observe this to be true. He must base it upon his observation in the land of Past; and if he does base it upon the observed fact that roosters in the land of Past fight more than hens, he must assume that in this respect chickens beyond the enclosure behave like chickens within it, so that, knowing that in the latter area roosters are the more pugnacious, he may employ this knowledge as evidence that things are this way also in the former area. This is an assumption which no empirical evidence, confined as it must be to evidence in Past, can be employed to support. Any attempt to support it with such evidence must itself assume that in respect to the phenomena involved differences between Past and Future are negligible; and since that is exactly what the reasoning is attempting to establish, the process is patently circular.

This is the kind of metaphor which makes friends, and influences people, in this case, to draw the wrong conclusions. There are several faults in the analogy. The chief one is that, as represented, the border between Past and Future is stationary, while in the temporal situation it is not. To duplicate the temporal situation in this respect the analogy should represent the border as constantly moving, revealing as it does constantly, in territory which has hitherto been Future, hens and roosters similar as regards difference in disposition to those already observed in Past. The matter of evidence for the proposition about hens and roosters is then also different. If this proposition is in a position analogous to the beliefs about uniformity which are represented in modern scientific laws, the situation is something like this. Previously inhabitants in Past had drawn more sweeping conclusions concerning the difference between the disposition to fight of male and female chickens. They have discovered recently that in respect to young chicks and pullets this generalization did not hold. They have therefore revised the proposition to exclude all the known negative instances and speak only and more surely of the behaviour of hens and roosters, meaning by these latter terms just fully grown and developed female and male chickens.

So far as there is any record, chickens in Past have verified this rule; so far as there is any record, every chicken revealed by the ever-receding border has likewise verified it; so far as there is any record there has not been one negative instance. Is it not the case that the inhabitants of Past do have evidence for the proposition that all chickens obey this rule, those already in Past, which they call 'Past-chickens', and those also which are not yet in Past but which will be subsequently revealed by the moving border, and which they call not unnaturally 'Future-chickens'? They have a vast number of positive instances of the rule, and no negative instances, except those in respect to which the rule has already been revised. In view of the present evidence that in all cases, year after year and century after century, the progressively revealed chickens have verified and do verify this rule, must one not conclude that the inhabitants of Past do have evidence for this proposition, and that anyone is wrong who says that they have actually no evidence one way or other?

The sceptic, however, is still prepared to argue his case, and his argument, in terms of the present analogy, has a now familiar ring. That the inhabitants of Past have no evidence whatsoever about the behaviour of Future-chickens, he will insist; and as grounds he will point out that although the border does progressively recede and reveal chickens like those previously observed in Past, these are really not Future-chickens. By the very fact that they have been revealed they are no longer Future-chickens, but are now Past-chickens. Observation of them is not observation of Future-chickens, and any attempt to reason from such observation to conclusions about Future-chickens must therefore assume that Future-chickens are like Past-chickens. For the inhabitants of Past, in these efforts to know the land beyond the border, this is both an inescapable and unknowable presumption.

What should one say of an argument of this kind? Only through some logical slip, one feels strongly, would it be possible to arrive at such a conclusion. One would have thought that the receding border was a matter upon which the inhabitants of Past may legitimately congratulate themselves in the light of their interest in learning what Future-chickens, when they become Past, are going to be like. If the border had not yet begun to recede they would indeed be in an unfortunate position for securing such knowledge. But happily this is not the case. The border is constantly receding. And granting that it will constantly recede, revealing always more of the land of Future, and even granting also that this means that there is an inexhaustible area to be revealed, the inhabitants of Past are in the fortunate position that with the progressive recession they may learn more and more about chickens, Past and Future. They may derive hypotheses from their experience of what has already been revealed and proceed further to test these by the progressive revelations of Future, in the light of which they may be confirmed, refuted, or revised. The sceptic's argument amounts to the assertion that all this apparent good fortune is really illusory and that the sorry Pastians are actually in no better position with respect to knowing about Future-chickens and Future-things generally than they would be if the border never moved at all. For the movement of the border does not reveal Future-chickens, since Future is by definition the land beyond the border. No matter how much or how little is revealed, by the very fact that it is revealed and on this side of the border it is not Future but Past, and therefore, since the land of Future always is beyond observation, no empirical method can produce any evidence that what is in that land is in any way similar to what is not. That this rendering of the sceptic's position, though in the language of the above metaphor, is undistorted and fair may be seen by consulting the words of an illustrious modern sceptic and follower of Hume, Bertrand Russell. In his chapter, 'On Induction', in *The Problems of Philosophy*, Russell expressed the matter in this fashion:

It has been argued that we have reason to know that the future will resemble the past, because what was the future has constantly become the past, and has always been found to resemble the past, so that we really have experience of the future, namely of times which were formerly future, which we may call past futures. But such an argument really begs the very question at issue. We have experience of past futures, but not of future futures, and the question is: Will future futures resemble past futures? This question is not to be answered by an argument which starts from past futures alone. We have therefore still to seek for some principle which shall enable us to know that the future will follow the same laws as the past (pp. 100–1).

This is the central difficulty urged by Hume, Russell and others in arguing that there can never be any empirical evidence that the future will be like the past. Empirically, in Russell's language, it is possible to have evidence only that this has been true of past and possibly present futures, not that it will be true of future futures. It is the situation in the land of Past all over again. There are generalizations which are constantly being confirmed by experience. But every time a confirming instance occurs it is nullified as evidence by the argument that it is not really a confirming instance at all. For by the fact that it has occurred it is an instance of a past future, and therefore it tells nothing whatever about future futures. In treating of the land of Past it was suggested that there is involved in arguing in this manner a logical slip or error. It remains to investigate how this is the case.

V

Suppose that in 1936, to take but a short span of time, a man says that in the above-defined sense the future will be like the past. In 1936, if he could somehow have shown that 1937 would be like 1936, this would have been evidence for his statement, as even a sceptic would admit. But in 1937, when he does establish that 1937 is like 1936, it has somehow ceased to be evidence. So long as he did not have it, it was evidence; as soon as he gets it it ceases to be. The constant neutralization of the evidence which is effected in this argument is effected by the same kind of verbal trick which children play upon one another in fun. Child A asks child B what he is going to do tomorrow. B replies that he is going to play ball, go swimming, or what not. Thereupon A says, 'You can't do that'.

B: Why not?

A: Because tomorrow never comes. When tomorrow comes it won't be tomorrow; it will be today. You can never play tomorrow; you can only play today.

Again, if a prophet announces that next year will bring a utopia, and if each succeeding year, when the predicted utopia does not come, he defends himself by pointing out that he said 'next year' and that obviously this is not next year, no reasonable person would pay much attention to him. Such a person would realize, on a moment's reflection, that the prophet is being deceptive with the word 'next'. In 1936, 'next year' means '1937'; in 1937 it means '1938'. Since every year 'next year' means a different year, a year yet to come, what the prophet says can never be verified or disproved. If in 1936 he meant by this phrase 1937, as he sensibly should, then this statement can be verified or refuted in 1937. But if, when 1937 comes, he insists that he did not mean 1937, but 'next year', and if in 1938 he again insists that he did not mean that year, and so on, then what he seems to be meaning by 'next year' is the $n + 1$th year where n is the ever progressing number of the present year. No one should alter his present activities or his plans for the future on the basis of such a prediction, for, of course, it really is not a prediction. While in the form of a statement about the future it does not say anything about the future, anything which could possibly be true or false in the infinity of time, if infinity it is, which yet remains to transpire. For what the prophet is saying is that utopia will come next year, and by his own interpretation of the words 'next year' he is affirming that next year will never come. In other words, at the time which never comes, and hence when nothing occurs, a utopia will occur. This is not even sensible speech; it is a contradiction.

In a similar though less simple way those who employ the sceptical argument about uniformity to show that there is no evidence whatever for any statement about the future are being themselves deceived and are deceiving others by their use of expressions like 'next', 'future', 'future future', and 'past future'. The man who said in 1936 that the future would be like the past, that mere differences in temporal position make no difference in the behaviour of nature which is described in scientific laws, meant, as he sensibly should, that this was true of the years 1937, 1938, and so on. He said something of the form 'all A's are B's' and it has been possible since 1936 to examine the A's of 1937 to 1952 and to see whether what he said is confirmed or disproved by the available evidence. If, however, now that it is 1952, and all this evidence is in, he should remark that since it is 1952 the years 1937–52 are no longer future and therefore have ceased to be evidence for the proposition, then he is guilty of using, or rather abusing, the word 'future' in the way in which the prophet in the previous example was abusing the word 'next'. For the only basis for his contention that the

observed A's are not confirming evidence, or what is the same
thing, that they are confirming instances only if one assumes
quite circularly that the future is like the past, is in his il-
lusive use of the word 'future'. Time does pass, and, because
it does, the present is a constantly changing one; and the
point of reference for the use of words like 'future' and
'past' is accordingly different. The correct conclusion to be
drawn from the fact that time passes is that the future is
constantly being revealed and that, in consequence, we have
had and shall have the opportunity to learn more and more
accurately what the laws of nature's behaviour are and how
therefore the future will be like the past. But this sceptical
man has his eyes fixed in fatal fascination upon the movement of time, the constantly changing present. And seeing
that, as the present changes, what was once future is not
now future, but present, and will shortly be past, he is led
to draw the conclusion that after all, for any present whatever, the future is forever hidden behind a veil.

Now in a sense this is true, and in a sense it is not. And
it is the confusion of the two senses which makes the trouble.
The one sense, the kind of future which is forever hidden
behind the veil of the ever-moving present, is not the kind of
future of which this man began to speak. The kind of future
of which he began to speak was the future of 1937, 1938
and so on; the kind of future years or futures which do become present and then past. This kind of future is constantly
being revealed; in this sense of 'future' the A's of 1937 to
1952 are positive instances confirming our beliefs about
scientific uniformity. But the sceptical man, although under
the impression that he is still talking about the future in
this sense, the sense of things which have not yet happened
but which may happen, is actually talking about the future
in the other sense; at least he is saying things which are true
only if the word is interpreted in this other way. That is why
he is deceived. He is unaware that the meaning of the word
has changed. He thinks when he asserts that there is no evidence that the future will be like the past, and that all one
has evidence for is that past futures have resembled their
pasts, that he is using this crucial word in the way in which
he began, in the way people are constantly using it to make

sensible observations about the next and future months, years, and so on. But he is not using it in this way, and the key to this particular puzzle about knowledge of the future lies finally in realizing that he is not. Like a prophet who says that a utopia lies around the next corner, a corner which, no matter how many corners we turn, and no matter how many utopias or hells on earth we find in turning, is still the next corner, like him the sceptical man is talking about a future which by definition will never come. In this sense of the word the statement that the future will be like the past no longer means, as it originally did, that the years, or rather events in the years 1937, 1938, and so on, have a certain characteristic. It means instead that in a future which is always future, in years which never come, events will have this characteristic. In short, he is now saying that at a time which never comes differences in time will make no difference, that at a time when no events occur (for if they did it would be present and not future) certain types of events will obey certain fairly uniform laws.

There are then, two senses of the word 'future' to be carefully discriminated. They may be designated future-1 and future-2. In the sense of future-1, when one speaks about the future he is speaking of events which have not occurred, of things which do not exist, but of events and things which, with the constant movement of the line of the present, may sometime occur or exist. In the sense of future-2, when one speaks about the future he is speaking of the time which is always beyond the line of the moving present, of a time which never comes, which by definition can never come, no matter how far the line of the present moves.

Interpreted in the sense of future-1 there are beliefs about the way the future will be like the past, which have been and are being confirmed constantly by the uniform experience of countless positive instances in everyday life and in vast areas of science. Because they have been thus confirmed they constitute a vast set of assumptions with which scientists and laymen approach their problems in the various areas to which the confirmation applies. It is when these beliefs are interpreted in the sense of future-2 that the sceptics are able to produce a plausible argument to show that these beliefs are not empirically confirmable and are hence unknowable. But, when these are so interpreted, the argument has no bearing whatever, favourable or unfavourable, upon the soundness or success of any inductive inquiry. It asserts that specific types of events occur in specific ways, not in 1945, 1955, or any other year which will ever come, but in a year and a time which will never come. That one cannot produce empirical evidence for the statement that at a time which never comes and when no events occur, events will occur in these rather than other ways, may be readily admitted. But this is no good reason for scepticism. No scepticism is entailed by this admission so long as it is made with the understanding that there is evidence about the other kind of future, the kind which will come and in which events do occur. And it is this latter kind of future only, of these two kinds, with which our inductions are concerned. It is this kind of future alone about which our inductions predict, and this kind alone which will ever confirm or refute our assertions. It is, therefore, not sensible for anyone to worry, in his inductive reasoning, about the character of a future which by definition can never come, about his incapacity to prove that if this future did come, which is itself a contradictory condition, it would have this or that character. And no one would worry about such a thing for an instant unless misled by fallacious reasoning such as that which has just been exposed. No one, for example, in the present international puzzlement or uncertainty, wastes a moment worrying about the kind of future wars, future-2 wars, which by definition cannot happen. The kind of future wars which one does worry about and is concerned to prevent is the kind which may come, which can occur in some present. And just as a future war which by definition cannot occur is not a future war in any sense which is pertinent to our present international deliberations, so generally a future event which by definition can occur in no present is not a future event in any sense which is pertinent to the validity of our inductive reasoning beyond the present and past, either in science or in everyday life.

III

Universals

D. F. PEARS

'Do universals exist?' This question was debated so long and
vehemently because it was mistaken for a factual question
about some airy realm of being. But why was this mistake
made? One diagnosis is that general words were tacitly assimi-
lated to proper names,[1] and that, when this practice is exposed, it becomes harmless but pointless.[2] But this is a description of what happened rather than an explanation; it
gives something more like a symptom than a cause. Could
so many philosophers have been so silly in such a simple
way? Even moderate scepticism on this point would lead to
an attempt to supplement this suggestion. This article is such
an attempt.

'Universals exist' has a deceptive logic. Realists offer it as
the conclusion of many arguments: but unlike the premises
of these arguments, it cannot be understood as a verifiable
statement of fact. On the other hand, if it is taken merely as
an esoteric way of stating those premises over again, the ve-
hemence of the controversy becomes inexplicable. Faced with
this difficulty of interpretation, some modern philosophers
suggest that it is no good puzzling about its literal meaning,
just as it is no good puzzling about the literal meaning of
dreams. For traditional philosophy provided a small set of
possible conclusions to arguments about the generality of
thought and language, and tradition was strong. If a tribe

[1] Cf. J. S. Mill, *Examination of Sir William Hamilton's Philosophy* (5th edn., London, 1878) chap. XVII, p. 381, and Berkeley,
Principles of Human Knowledge, Introduction § 18.
[2] Cf. M. Lazerowitz, 'The Existence of Universals' (*Mind*, 1946,
pp. 1 ff.).

educated its children to dream according to a tradition which restricted their manifest dream contents within narrow limits, it would be difficult to discover their much more varied latent dream contents.[3] Similarly, although realists are argumentative, it is difficult to answer the question why they maintain that universals exist. Any answer must be based on a selection from among the many reasons which they themselves proffer: and a good selection will be diagnostic; it will successfully explain the doctrine. There is no sharp boundary here between descriptions of the premises of philosophical arguments and diagnoses of their conclusions: because success in explaining, which is the criterion of a diagnosis, is a matter of degree, and because the reasons which philosophers themselves give for their doctrines sometimes completely explain why they held them. Quine's remark, that realists find a universal for every property which can be existentially generalized,[4] is an extremely brief description. The thesis of Berkeley and Mill was more than this: it was a diagnosis, but an inadequate one. I shall try to provide a less inadequate diagnosis.

'Because universals exist' is the answer to at least two general questions: 'Why are things what they are'?[5] and 'Why are we able to name things as we do'? Though Plato and Aristotle sometimes distinguished these two questions, it was characteristic of Greek thought to confuse them. Yet they can be clearly distinguished, the first requiring a dynamic answer from scientists, and the second a static answer from logicians. Now philosophy has often staked premature claims in the territory of science by giving quick comprehensive answers to questions which really required laborious detailed answers. And clearly this is what happened to the first of the two questions. When detailed causal answers were provided to it, the comprehensive answer 'Because universals exist' was no longer

[3] Cf. Freud, *The Interpretation of Dreams,* tr. A. A. Brill (London, 1913), p. 166.

[4] Cf. 'Designation and Existence' in Feigl and Sellars, *Readings in Philosophical Analysis* (New York, 1949), p. 48.

[5] Aristotle criticized Plato's theory largely as an inadequate answer to this question.

acceptable or necessary.[6] But what would detailed answers to
the second question be like? Presumably they would be explanations of the meanings of words. But philosophers are
easily led to neglect such detailed progressive answers to the
second question, and to seek instead a comprehensive and
ultimate explanation of naming. For, though comprehensive
answers to the first question are clearly futile, there are no
obvious penalties attached to answering the second question
in a comprehensive way. Yet, I shall argue—and this will be
my first thesis—that any comprehensive explanation of naming is necessarily circular: and that philosophers think that,
in spite of this disadvantage, such explanations have some
point largely because they wrongly assimilate naming to natural processes. Yet surely naming cannot be utterly artificial?
My second thesis will be that the desire to understand naming
leads to a hunt for a completely satisfactory analogy: but
that all other processes either already contain the very feature
of naming which was puzzling, or else are too natural or too
artificial to be really analogous; and that it was the inevitable
oscillation between these three points which prolonged the
controversy about universals.

It is unnecessary to produce evidence that philosophers
who proposed the existence of universals thought that they
were explaining the unity of classes and hence the possibility
of naming. What is debatable is whether this was an important motive, and this can be decided only in the sequel. My
first thesis, which I must now try to establish, is that realism
is necessarily a circular explanation of naming. Now the answer to the question 'Why are we able to name things as we
do?' is 'The reason varies'. For it is always possible with more
or less ingenuity, depending on the degree of atomicity of
the name, to give a detailed informative reason; and this reason will vary with the name. But ultimately there must be
some exit from the maze of words, and, wherever this exit is
made, it will be impossible to give an informative reason ex-

[6] Socrates in the *Phaedo* (100d) says that it is the only acceptable answer to the first question. But the advance of science has undermined this thesis more thoroughly than the advance of logic has
undermined the thesis that it is an acceptable answer to the second
question.

cept by pointing. For the only other way of giving an informative reason is to give a new word, and this would prevent the exit from the maze of words from being made at this place.[7] Still at the place where the exit is made it is always possible to give a detailed reason like 'We are able to call things red because they are red', which is too obviously circular even to look informative. Or alternatively it is possible to say 'We are able to call things Φ because they are Φ', and this is a general reason which is almost as obviously circular and uninformative. What philosophers who propose the existence of universals do is to propose a general reason which looks informative because it shifts to another level, but unfortunately is not. It merely marks time: but marking time can look very like marching if only the movements of the performers are watched, and not the ground which they profess to be covering. Yet this ground could not be covered. For the reason could not be informative even if it were detailed; since there could be a non-circular answer to the question 'What universal?' only if the exit from the maze of words were made at some different point, which would merely put off the moment of embarrassment from which in the end neither speech nor thought can be saved. Thus realism fails to escape the limitations of all explanations of naming; that they can be informative only if they are not general but detailed, and then only if they are not given at the point where an exit is made from the maze of words.

Uninformative answers have their point. They are silencing. What is wrong with realism is not this, but that it masquerades as an answer which advances knowledge one step further. The analytic machine acquires a momentum which carries it beyond the point where it ought to stop. And there is an inveterate philosophical habit which strengthens the tendency to go beyond this point, or rather to think that one has gone beyond it. 'A thing is called by a certain name because it instantiates a certain universal' is obviously circular

---

[7] Cf. the view sketched by Socrates in the *Theaetetus* 201e-202c, and Antisthenes' view given by Aristotle in *Met.* H, 1043 b 23–32; also L. Wittgenstein, *Tractatus* 5; M. Schlick, *Grundzüge der Naturphilosophie* (Vienna, 1948), p. 21; and A. J. Ayer, *Thinking and Meaning* (London, 1947), p. 28.

when particularized, but it looks imposing when it is left in
this general form. And it looks imposing in this general form
largely because of the inveterate philosophical habit of treating the shadows cast by words and sentences as if they were
separately identifiable. Universals, like facts and propositions,
are such shadows; and too often philosophers by appealing
to them in general terms have produced in their readers a
feeling of satisfaction which ought to have been produced
only by specifying them.[8] But universals are specifiable only
by reference to words. Similarly facts may be brute and propositions may be definite, but what exactly it is about them
which is brute or definite can be specified only by reference
to the sentences which were the unacknowledged starting-
points. In all these cases it is tacit re-duplication which makes
philosophers think that they can enjoy the benefits of specifying without actually specifying. Yet the explanation of naming is incomplete until a particular universal is specified, and,
when it is specified, the explanation immediately fails
through circularity. Naming is hazardous,[9] and any attempt
to make it foolproof by basing it on an independent foundation must fail in this way. It is impossible to cross the gap
between language and things without really crossing it.[10]

Since the failure of realism to perform this feat is inevitable, its rivals fail too. Nominalism, conceptualism and imagism,[11] in so far as they are rivals of realism, are attempts to
provide a unity which will explain naming. Nominalism says
that a name is merely connected with a multitude of things,

[8] The same trick is played by those who say that laws of nature
exhibit connections between universals. This gives the impression
that we could independently know the eternal framework in which
temporal things move and change, rather as we independently know
how a piston must move by looking at a cylinder: cf. what Köhler
says about Aristotle's astronomy and Descartes' neurology (*Gestalt
Psychology*, London, 1930, pp. 82–6).

[9] Cf. Bradley, *Appearance and Reality*, p. 22 and p. 533; and
C. S. Peirce, *Collected Papers* (vol. I, para. 145): 'Direct experience is neither certain nor uncertain, because it affirms nothing—it
just is.'

[10] Cf. Stuart Hampshire, 'Scepticism and Meaning' (*Philosophy*,
July 1950, p. 245).

[11] Cf. H. H. Price, *Thinking and Representation* (British Academy Lecture, 1946).

sometimes adding that these things are similar. Conceptualism says that the name is not directly connected with the
things but only via a concept, thus changing the nodal point.
Imagism says that the nodal point is an image. And realism
says that there is really no nodal point, since a name, though
it appears to be connected with a multitude of things is all
the time connected with only one thing, a universal. This is
an over-simplification of what these theories say about the
One and the Many; but it is enough for my next purpose,
which is to show that these rivals of realism cannot produce a
non-circular explanation of naming at those points where an
exit is made from the maze of words.

The two psychological theories say that one word can apply
to many things only because of the mediation of a concept
or of an image. Locke's abstract general idea is 'the workman-
ship of the understanding, but has its foundation in the
similitudes of things'.[12] And Berkeley replaces it by an idea
which 'considered in itself is particular but becomes general
by being made to represent or stand for all other particular
ideas of the same sort'.[13] But what similitudes, and what
representation? In the end both Locke's concept and Berkeley's image are completely identifiable only by their use.[14]
Of course we can partly identify images by describing their
features: and in this way we may even almost completely
identify them, since certain images most naturally stand for
certain things. And the same could be said of concepts, if
they were not merely philosophers' reifications of mental
processes. But this will not completely identify either of
them, since thought may not follow the most natural course;
nor is it always clear which is the most natural course. It is
not so much that thinking is speaking as that thinking is like
speaking in the only way that matters: it uses one thing as a
symbol to stand for many things. And the only tool which
could not be used differently is the use. Even something

[12] Locke, *Essay concerning Human Understanding*, Bk. III, Chap.
III, § xiii.

[13] Berkeley, *Principles of Human Knowledge*, Introduction, § 12.

[14] This is due to Wittgenstein: cf. e.g. *Tractatus*, 3.326, 'In order to recognize the symbol in the sign we must consider the significant use'.

which had its use written on it could be used differently.[15]
And, if the psychological tool, whether concept or image, can
be completely identified only by the things on which it is
used, it cannot explain naming without circularity. For, unless we point, the use can be specified only by backward reference to the name. Nor is this circularity surprising. For
psychological tools have no advantage over words: they are
like them in being symbols, and unlike them only in being
shadowy symbols.

The type of nominalism which says that a name is applied
to a number of things which are similar immediately falls
into the same circularity. For 'similar' is an incomplete predicate, anything being similar to anything in some way, perhaps
a negative way.[16] And in the end the kind of similarity which

[15] W. T. Stace in 'Russell's Neutral Monism' in *The Philosophy
of Bertrand Russell*, pp. 381–3, complains that neither Berkeley's
precise image nor Russell's vague image (in *An Inquiry into Meaning
and Truth*) succeeds in explaining the generality of thought. But
no description of any item of mental furniture which included only
its momentary properties and not its habitual use could possibly
explain the generality of thought.

[16] Hence the point of many riddles. Cf. Stuart Hampshire, 'Scepticism and Meaning' (*Philosophy*, July 1950, p. 238). Also Plato,
Protagoras 331 d. The Platonic theory avoids the 'similarity' difficulty, but not of course the general difficulty of which this is only
one form. Speusippus, who abandoned the Platonic theory, seems
to have held that, since every species is like every other species in
some way, it is impossible to define one species without defining
every other species. Cf. Aristotle, *Post. An.* 97 a 6–11. Cf. H. Cher-
niss, *Aristotle's criticism of Plato and the Academy* (I. 60), quoted
by W. D. Ross in his note on this passage. J. Stenzel, in Pauly-
Wissowa Real-Encyclopädie, *s.v.* Speusippus, pp. 1650 and 1655,
brings out the affinity between Speusippus' view and Post-Kantian
Idealism. Cf. Brand Blanshard on individuals (not species). 'One
never gets what is fully particular until one has specified its relations
of every kind with everything else in the universe', *The Nature of
Thought* (London, 1939), vol. I, p. 639. Curiously enough N. R.
Campbell arrives independently at a similar conclusion about species,
when he is discussing the definition of such substances as silver,
mercury or lead (*Physics. The Elements*, Cambridge, 1920, p. 50).
All attempts to explain the unity of a species by similarity—whether
by similarity of the individuals to one another, or by similarities and
differences between the species and other species—suffer from the
same incompleteness.

is meant can be specified only by a backward reference to the name. Equally the type of nominalism which merely says that a name is applied to a class of things cannot say which class without a backward reference to the name. Here the circularity is so obvious and there is so little to cushion the shock of the realization that naming is naming that this type of nominalism seems hardly tenable. For, however strongly nominalists react against realism, they can never quite escape its influence: once somebody had said that universals exist it could never be quite the same again. Surely, one wants to protest, there must be some way of giving the class besides reference to the name? Well there is, of course, enumeration. But this answer seems to fail to allow for the possibility of ever using the name correctly in any synthetic sentence. For, if the class is given by enumeration, surely every use of the name must be either incorrect or analytic? Since, if to call a thing 'Φ' is to include it in the class of things called 'Φ', then surely either it is incorrect to call it 'Φ' or else the class cannot be given without reference to it? It is the example of realism which encourages these protests. But it is a bad example. Such neatness is not to be had. For, first of all, these classes cannot be given by enumeration of all their members, since, except for words belonging to dead languages, they are never complete. Nor is it true even that each member must either contribute or not contribute towards giving a class; since a name may be applied to the same thing twice, once analytically and once synthetically, and even a single use of a name may be synthetic for the speaker and analytic for the hearer. In fact the disjunction 'Analytic or Synthetic' cannot be applied simply to the addition of a member to a class without further caveats. But this in itself is not enough to remove the difficulty; it only makes it reappear in a new form. For if the addition of a member to a class can be synthetic for the speaker and analytic for a subsequent lexicographer, then to what class was the member added? Surely we now have two classes on our hands instead of one? An analogy will help us to deal with this new form of the difficulty. Naming is like electing the sort of member who makes a difference to a club. Strictly we cannot say without qualification to what club he was elected, since it was one club before he was elected and another club after he was elected. The club building might be pointed out, and of course there is no parallel move in the case of naming, although realism pretends that there is. But, even if there were no building or anything else of that kind, the puzzle about the two clubs would not be very perplexing. Similarly, when we reject the simple application of the dichotomy 'Analytic or Synthetic' the resulting puzzle about two classes is not very perplexing. All that is necessary is to point out that a class is incompletely given by a changing quorum. This may be untidy, but why not? There is something radically wrong with a request to be given a class which is not satisfied either with a reference to the name or with progressive enumeration. It is a request to be given something without being given it; as if somewhere, if only philosophers searched long enough, there could be found something which possessed all the advantages of a word and none of its disadvantages, an epistemological vehicle which carried all its destinations.

I now turn to my second thesis, that nothing is sufficiently like naming without being too like naming. Defenders of realism, like defenders of the other theories of naming, might object that the criticism contained in my first thesis is obvious, superficial and directed against a man of straw. For realism does not offer a non-circular detailed explanation of naming—how could it?—but simply gives a general characterization of the sort of unity which makes naming possible. But notice how very like a dream realism is. Taken literally it seems to be of little importance. But, if it is taken as the expression of a doctrine which, if *per impossibile* it were true, would give it great importance, the suggestion is immediately repudiated. Yet it does express such a doctrine, even if its exponents intermittently deny that it does; and it is to the devious expression of this doctrine that it owes most of its attractiveness. Its manifest content is little more than a harmless caprice, but its latent content is a serious error.

But has realism no point when it is taken simply as a general characterization of the sort of unity which makes naming impossible? One might answer that it has no point, and that it succeeds in appearing to have some point only by the device of inventing a new comprehensive term: and that this

device is considered effective only in philosophy, since outside philosophy it is too obviously like making an impressive
gesture in the direction of the interesting object, opening
one's mouth and saying absolutely nothing. But such a denial
would be tantamount to a denial that any general characterization of the sort of unity which makes naming possible could
have a point. And surely such a denial would be wrong, since
something can be done towards explaining the general possibility of naming by finding analogous processes? For instance,
what makes naming possible is one thing which is in many
things as an ingredient.[17] But does this analogy throw much
light on naming? Any feature of logical mixing which is at all
interesting seems to distinguish it from all other sorts of mixing. The values of an unrestricted variable are strange recep-
tacles. What prevents contrary ingredients from being put in
together, or an implicant from appearing without its impli-
cate, is never the causal consequences. And anyway the whole
notion of mixing ingredients which were not there before the
mixing is peculiar. Could there be a logical conjuring trick?

Here defenders of realism might object that a new misunderstanding had replaced the old one. For, if realism is to be
understood, not only must a general characterization of naming be allowed, but also the verification principle must not
be applied too crudely. And anyway, if mixing is not a good
analogy, this only means that some better analogy must be
sought. This objection might lead to a tolerant examination
of other analogies.[18] But fortunately it also opens up a short
cut to the heart of the matter, which I shall soon take. Now
it would be taking too short a cut to repeat the platitude
that naming is *sui generis*. For it is natural to seek an analogy
even if the search can never be completely successful. And
anyway Butler's truism applies to everything. What is needed
in order to explain the peculiar persistence of the debate
about universals is something slightly longer, a demonstra-

[17] Cf. A. N. Whitehead, *Science and the Modern World* (Cambridge, 1928), pp. 197 ff. For a criticism of this analogy, cf. Bentham, *Works*, vol. VIII, p. 335.
[18] Metaphors must not be dismissed just because they are metaphors, as, e.g. 'copying' and 'participation' are by Aristotle, *Met.*
991 a 20.

tion that no analogy can be sufficiently close to satisfy philosophers without being too close.

It is most natural to seek a visible process as an analogy to
naming, particularly for the Greeks who began this controversy.[19] Now previously I insisted that it is impossible in the
end to give a detailed non-circular description of what makes
it possible to name anything. Here, however, it would be unfair to object that, if naming in general is compared to a
visible process, still that process itself must be named. For
this sort of circularity is the inevitable result of the philosopher's predicament. However, it is dangerous to begin speaking at all where so little can be said. For it is fatally easy to
think that one has separate access to what makes a name
applicable just because one has separate access to whatever
stands for this in the analogy. But, waiving this, let us now
take the short cut and ask what sort of visible process could
be analogous to naming. Let us try a rough analogy and say
that one word is connected with many objects in the same
way that the estuary of a river is connected with its many
sources. But this analogy fails because this connection just
happens naturally. We might then try to mend the analogy
by saying that water follows the easiest course. But this could
be called choice only anthropomorphically, in an extended
and weak sense of 'choice'. In order to introduce choice in a
restricted, strong sense, it is necessary to alter the analogy
and say that people by directing the streams choose which
sources shall feed the river. But, if the first process was too
natural to be like naming, the second is too artificial, since,
for the analogy to work, the sources ought to have something
in common besides the fact that the river is fed from them.
And it is difficult to find an analogy which is neither too
natural nor too artificial. The characteristic of naming which
is difficult to match is that the objects have something in
common besides being called by one name, but nothing in
common which counts except that in virtue of which they
are called by one name. And this characteristic can be
matched only by allowing that something makes it convenient

[19] Cf. J. Stenzel, *Plato's Method of Dialectic* (Oxford, 1940),
p. 37.

but not absolutely necessary for people to canalize streams into the river in the way they do, and that whatever it is which makes this choice convenient is the only thing common to the sources which counts. But this compromise between the two extremes introduces into the analogy the very feature which it was intended to explain. For just how something works in influencing usage was what was to be explained. Nor is there a fourth alternative. So after all even general analogical characterizations of naming do fall into a circularity which is closely related to the type of circularity which my first thesis exposed. Neither in detail nor in general is it possible to step outside language.

This short way with analogies looks too superficial. For suppose that it is granted that one of the things that metaphysicians do is to seek the unattainable: that they hunt for definitions which would in no way involve their definienda,[20] and for analogies which would in no way involve what they were intended to explain. Yet even so metaphysics is a natural and inevitable pursuit, since the easiest way to discover how far one can go is to try to go one stage farther. And anyway there is a difference between complete failure and partial success; since, so long as analogies do not reach the point of self-frustration they get better and better as they approach it. These two qualifications are just but they only serve to strengthen my thesis that it was oscillation between the three points which prolonged the controversy about universals. For unless the possible analogies are mapped out in this simple way, it seems always conceivable that some altogether better analogy might lurk in an unexplored corner.

And what more are the rival theories of naming doing than seeking a completely satisfactory analogy? It is only jargon which makes them appear to be doing something more. The type of nominalism which suggests that things which are called by one name have only their name in common represents the extreme of artificiality.[21] It suggests that there are never any ways of telling even approximately whether a word

[20] Cf. J. Wisdom, 'Metaphysics and Verification' (*Mind*, 1938, pp. 465 ff.)

[21] There are traces of such an extreme form of nominalism in Hobbes. Cf. *Leviathan*, Pt. I, chap. IV, p. 13 (Everyman edition).

is used in one sense or two senses. At the other extreme stands the type of realism which suggests that there is always one method of getting a precise answer to this question. In between are all the other theories of naming, which allow that it is neither impossible for the lexicographer to succeed in answering this question nor impossible for him to fail. None of these middle theories is really wrong, since of course we do bestow common names on certain chosen groups of things which exhibit certain similarities (else why should we do it?) or instantiate certain universals (why else were they invented?). But on the other hand none of them goes deep enough to satisfy the true metaphysician who is in all of us; since though they take us to the bottom of naming, we were in a simpler way already there, and they do not succeed in showing us how naming is founded on something else which lies even deeper. Hence each of these middle theories (except imagism, which says something empirical which seems to be false) develops its own thesis with embarrassing success up to a point, and can discredit its rivals only by accusing them of not going beyond that point. But, since naming cannot be explained by anything which really goes beyond a reasoned choice of usage, this is an unfair accusation. And its unfairness is concealed from those who make it only because each tacitly and wrongly assumes that his own theory alone does go beyond this point. Thus moderate nominalists maintain that similarity is a better explanation of the unity of a class than the presence of a universal. (But why should people not *just* recognize the presence of universals?) And moderate realists retort that this admits the existence of at least one universal, similarity. (But why should the presence of a universal explain the recognition of similarity if it cannot explain the recognition of anything else? Why should people not *just* recognize similarity?) Really these are not two arguments but two bare assertions of superiority. They are manœuvres which are carried out in a way which suggests that they are difficult and that they must be advances: but both these suggestions are false. Yet these theories do seem to be striving towards something. And they are. Their goal is the unattainable completely satisfactory explanation of naming. And, as so often happens in metaphysics, progress is

measured by distance from the starting-point and not by prox-
imity to the goal whose unattainability each uses against its
rivals without allowing it to deter itself.

Thus theories of naming, which seem to flout the verification principle without therefore saying nothing, can be interpreted as disguised analogies. And, though there is a common
limit beyond which they cannot go, the success with which
they stealthily approach this limit, camouflaged in the technical terms of epistemology, varies. But if this almost mechanical oscillation is avoided what else can be said about
naming? Certainly as the first part of this article showed,
detailed answers to the question why we name things as we
do will in the end be circular. Only the trick of giving a general answer as if it were a detailed one cloaks their failure.
If a word is explained ostensively, then however difficult this
process may be it really is explained ostensively. It is no good
trying to combine the concreteness of ostensive definition
with the clarity of verbal definition. Verbal definitions have
such an easy task just because ostensive definitions have such
a difficult task. Surveyors find it easier to fix the positions of
points which they can visit than to fix the positions of points
which they cannot visit. Similarly it is easy to fix the relative
positions of words: but the points in things to which words
are related are in the end inaccessible to logicians.

Then what else can be said about naming? How *does* the
lexicographer tell when a word is used in two senses rather
than in one sense? Surely there must be something in common to all well constructed series of things? Yes, just that
they *are* well constructed. For this question already contains
the equivalent of any possible comprehensive answer which
could be given to it. And, though in one way it is hard to see
what detailed answers could be given to it, in another way
it is only too easy to see. For we never reach a point where
an exit *must* be made from the maze of words. Admittedly,
if a verbal explanation is given at one point, it is only successful if at some other point a connection with things is
already understood; and at some points it is more natural
not to offer more words. But at no point is an exit obligatory.
So, if detailed reasons why we call a thing what we do are
required, it is easy to give them; but never ultimately or in

the end, since here *ex vi termini* it is impossible to give them.
But philosophers tend to ignore this kind of detailed answer
and press on. But where to? Perhaps to experimental psychology, in order to discover how changes in the sense organs,
in training and in interests alter the ways in which people
group things. But this sort of investigation only gives the
varying tests of the good construction of a series, and not its
essence. But what could its essence be? When general analogical characterizations of naming have been mentioned, and
detailed reasons why we call particular things by particular
names, and the psychological background of all this, what is
left? The desire to go on explaining naming is to some extent the result of the way these three fields have been confused, and to some extent the result of a natural feeling that
in such a vast territory there might be something which lies
outside these three fields. But above all it is the result of the
Protean metaphysical urge to transcend language.

IV

Categories

GILBERT RYLE

Doctrines of categories and theories of types are explorations
in the same field. And the field is still largely unexplored.
Moreover the exploration of it is at present handicapped by
certain vocabulary-differences between philosophers, which
hinder them from reading one another's maps. My object
in this paper is rather to remove certain obstacles to the
exploration than to proffer surveys of my own.

The matter is of some importance, for not only is it the
case that category-propositions (namely assertions that terms
belong to certain categories or types) are always philosopher's
propositions, but, I believe, the converse is also true. So we

are in the dark about the nature of philosophical problems
and methods if we are in the dark about types or categories.

I begin with some historical remarks, not in order to exhibit adeptness in philosophical palaeontology or even to
make upstart doctrines respectable by discerning Norman
blood in them, but as a convenient way of jointly opening
up the philosophical questions and explaining some traditional terminologies of the topic.

Aristotle's Categories

What did Aristotle think that his list of Categories was a
list of? The word 'category' meant what our word 'predicate'
means and shared all the vagueness and ambiguity of this
English substantive. But Aristotle's list of categories was not
a glossary of all the predicates that there are. On at least a
plausible interpretation of the doctrine, Aristotle's list is intended to be a list of the ultimate types of predicates. But
what does this mean?

There are simple propositions, namely those which do not
consist of more elementary propositions in conjunction with
each other, that is to say there are propositions into the expression of which there cannot enter such conjunctions as
'and', 'or', 'if', 'although', 'because', etc. Of these simple
propositions some are singular propositions, namely those
each of which is about at least one named or directly indicated particular.

Collect a range of simple, singular propositions, all similar
in being about the same particular or particulars, then the
respects in which these propositions differ from one another
will be their predicates. And these predicates are classified
into a finite number of families or types, the differences between which types can be indicated, though not defined, in
the following way.

Any simple proposition about Socrates, say, is an answer,
probably a false one, to some question about Socrates. Any
given question about Socrates will generate a range of possible answers, but not any proposition about Socrates will
be an answer to this question about him. There are as many

different types of predicates of Socrates as there are irreducibly different sorts of questions about him. Thus 'How big?' collects 'Six foot tall', 'five foot tall', 'ten stone', 'eleven stone', etc., and does not collect 'fair haired', 'in the garden', or 'a stonemason'. 'Where?' collects predicates of location, 'What sort?' collects predicates of kind, 'What like?' collects qualities, and so on.

Any two predicates which satisfy the same interrogative are of the same category, and any two which do not satisfy the same interrogative are of different categories. In the main Aristotle seems to content himself with taking ordinary language as his clue to the list of heads of questions, and so of types of predicates.

This programme of cataloguing types was then expanded, either by Aristotle or by his followers. We can not only ask about a particular a series of questions, each of which will yield in its answers a range of possible predicates of that particular; we can also ask with reference to any such predicate 'Who has it?' or 'What (in the sense of "which") has it?' The answers to these questions will name or indicate particulars, like 'Socrates', 'Fido', 'I' and 'the Queen'. Obviously these questions do not generate ranges of predicates, but ranges of subjects or possessors of predicates, that is, particular substances. So *Socrates* is in the category of Substance, whereas *snub-nosed* is in the category of Quality and *husband* in that of Relation. As a result of this expansion, 'category' no longer means 'type of predicate' merely, but 'type of term' where 'term' means 'abstractible factor in a range of simple, singular propositions'.

Aristotle's actual list of ten (or sometimes eight) types of terms is doubtless unsatisfactory. Certain of the alleged ultimate types are patently only subordinate branches of others, and the criteria used by Aristotle for determining whether a term is of this or that category are fairly loose, where they occur at all. But for his purposes this does not matter much. He chiefly required to be able to demarcate (*a*) qualities from relations, (*b*) both from substances, and (*c*) all three from sorts or kinds. And this he was now able in a rough and unprecise way to do. But we have other fish to fry, so we have to notice other defects in his scheme.

1. It is not an easy matter to decide when a sentence expresses a simple proposition. For the fact that a sentence contains only one verb and no conjunctions does not prove that the proposition expressed by it is simple, i.e. that the sentence *could* not be paraphrased by a sentence containing conjunctions and a plurality of verbs. And in fact any sentence containing a description, or any sentence containing a dispositional adjective like 'brittle', or, again, any sentence containing a kind-name is thus paraphrasable or 'exponible'. Most grammatically simple sentences express non-simple propositions and so are exponible. (Modern logic largely consists in taking exponibility seriously.) And this involves that the isolation of terms is no simple matter either. Grammatically simple nominative-expressions and predicative-expressions do not necessarily or often stand for logically simple constituents or components of propositions. The classification of types of abstractible factors in simple propositions must be postponed to the classification of the varieties of propositional forms. We require first a docketing of what are expressed by form-words, namely 'syncategorematic' words like *all, some, a, the, any, not, if, or, and, than,* etc., together with what are expressed by grammatical constructions, before we can hope to pin down for indexing any irreducible 'categorematic' words.

2. Moreover we need a method for exhibiting and, what is quite different, a method for establishing type-homogeneities and type-heterogeneities. Aristotle's method, so far as he had one, seems to have consisted in collecting the ordinary interrogatives of everyday speech. He then labels his more important types with nouns formed from these interrogative words. But no reason is given for supposing that the Greek stock of interrogative words is either as economical as possible or as rich as might be desired. However his clue, such as it was, was not a completely silly one. For after all 'propositional function' is only 'question' writ sophisticatedly. The propositional function 'x is snub-nosed' differs only in practical associations from 'Who is snub-nosed?'; and 'Socrates is Φ' exhibits no more or less than 'Where is Socrates?' or 'What-like (qualis) is Socrates?' or 'How big is Socrates?' according to the *genre* selected for Φ. (Cf. Lewis and Lang-

ford, *Symbolic Logic*, pp. 332–4; and Carnap on 'W . . . questions' in *Logical Syntax of Language*, p. 296.)

In order to state more precisely where Aristotle was on the right track and where his enterprise is unsuccessful, and also because I shall need them later on in the course of this paper, I want here to introduce some technical idioms. It is patent that in a certain sense, sentences contain parts; for two sentences can be partially similar and partially dissimilar. Let us call any partial expression which can enter into sentences otherwise dissimilar a 'sentence-factor'. Thus single words will be sentence-factors, but so will phrases of any degree of complexity as well as entire clauses. Thus in the sentence 'I am the man who wrote this paper', 'I', 'the man who', 'who wrote this paper', 'wrote this paper' are all sentence-factors.

I call them 'factors' rather than 'parts', since 'parts' would suggest, what is false, that the elements so abstracted can exist outside any such combinations as constitute sentences and, what is worse, that they can occur indifferently anywhere in any such combination, i.e. that they are both independent and freely shuffleable counters. The word 'factor' is intended to suggest, what is true, that they can only occur as factors in complexes of certain sorts, and can only occur in them in certain determinate ways.

Now though sentence-factors cannot be extracted from all combinations, they can be abstracted from any specified combination. If we take any sentence and substitute for any fragment of it a dotted line, or the phrase 'so and so', what is left is a sentence-factor with a signal (namely 'so and so' or the dotted line), to show that and how the sentence-factor requires completion. But the dotted line, though it requires some complement or other, would tolerate as its complements any out of an indefinite range of factors. Thus 'Socrates is . . .' or 'I am the man who so and so', or 'Such and such implies that tomorrow is Saturday', are not sentences but sentence-frames only, the gaps in which require to be completed by further sentence-factors. The required complements would, of course, have to be of different sorts in the three different frames. '. . . ugly' would complete one, '. . . visited Edinburgh yesterday' would complete the sec-

ond, and 'today's being Tuesday . . .' would complete the
third, and none would complete either of the others.

But though not any factor is fit to be the complement of
any gap, there is an indefinite range of possible factors of
the same pattern which would complete any given gap. So
we abstract a factor from the other factor or factors in any
concrete sentence by putting dotted lines or 'gap-signs' (like
'so and so' or 'x' or 'Φ' or 'p') in the place or places of the
other factor or factors. A gap-sign is not itself a word, or a
phrase or a clause, nor is it the name or description of one;
it is the name or index of a place for one or for any of a range
of appropriate sentence-factors.

Now sentences and sentence-factors are English or German, pencilled or whispered or shouted, slangy or pedantic,
and so on. What logic is concerned with is something which
is indifferent to these differences—namely (it is convenient
though often misleading to say), propositions and the parts
or factors of propositions. When two sentences of different
languages, idioms, authors or dates say the same thing, what
they say can be considered in abstraction from the several
sayings of it, which does not require us to suppose that it
stands to them as a town stands to the several signposts
which point to it. And, just as we distinguish propositions
from the sentences which propound them, so we must distinguish proposition-factors from the sentence-factors which
express them. But again we must not suppose that this means
that the world contains cows and earthquakes *and* proposition-factors, any more than we are entitled by the fact that
we can distinguish the two faces of a coin to infer that when
I have a coin in my hand I have three things in my hand,
the coin and its two faces.

Next, we have seen that the gap in a given sentence-frame
can be completed by *some* but not by *any* alternative complements. But there are two sorts of 'can' here. 'So and so
is in bed' grammatically requires for complements to the
gap indicated by 'so and so' nouns, pronouns or substantival
phrases such as descriptive phrases. So 'Saturday is in bed'
breaks no rule of grammar. Yet the sentence is absurd. Consequently the possible complements must be not only of
certain grammatical types, they must also express proposition-

factors of certain logical types. The several factors in a non-absurd sentence are typically suited to each other; those in an absurd sentence, or some of them, are typically unsuitable to each other. To say that a given proposition-factor is of a certain category or type, is to say that its expression could complete certain sentence-frames without absurdity.

If the interpretation that I have given of Aristotle's doctrine of categories is correct, we can say that in one important respect it was on the right track. For interrogative sentences, when considered in abstraction from their practical role as petitions or commands, are sentence-frames, and the interrogative words in them are gap-signs. And by distinguishing varieties of sorts of questions, Aristotle is using a general method for exhibiting varieties of type of the factors which would be answers to those questions or complements to those gap-signs.

On the other hand his procedure is defective in the following ways. He only attempts to classify the types of a small sub-class of proposition-factors, namely the constituents and components of simple, singular propositions. Let us call these by their traditional (and typically ambiguous) title of 'terms'. All terms are factors but most factors are not terms. He proffers no test of when a sentence-factor does and when it does not stand for a term, and seems to assume that a grammatically simple word always stands for a constituent or component of a simple proposition. He relies, apparently, solely upon common sense and common parlance for evidence that a given factor is suited to fill a given gap. But worse than this, he does not recognize that the types of factors control and are controlled by the logical form of the propositions into which they can enter, except in the solitary case of particular substances which, he recognizes, cannot occupy the berths of qualities, relations, magnitudes, positions, kinds, etc., in what he takes to be simple propositions.

He, with the logicians of later ages, seems to have thought that while terms are coupled in propositions and while there are various types of terms, yet there is only one sort of coupling. For the very same term which occurs in one proposition as 'subject' can occur in another as 'predicate'.

As any letter of the alphabet may be juxtaposed with any

other letter, without modifying the designs of those letters, so it seems to have been thought that there is no interaction between the form of a proposition and the types of the factors composing it. So no connection was established between the formal properties of propositions which render inferences embodying them possible or impossible, and the formal properties or types of the terms or other factors in them. The syllogistic rules which Aristotle discovered turn on the concepts expressed by such form-words as *all, some, this, not, and* and *implies*, but his treatment of them neither infects nor is infected by his classification of types of terms.

It is as though a grammarian were in his first chapter to give definitions of the types of parts of speech, such as nouns, prepositions, verbs, conjunctions, etc., and in a later chapter to give a quite independent discussion to the rules of syntax, when in truth just these rules must already be latent in the notions of noun, verb, conjunction, etc. It is to treat as freely shuffleable counters factors the determinate roles of which in the combination into which they can enter are just what constitute their types.

To know all about the logical form of a proposition and to know all about the logical types of its factors are to know one and the same thing. (I apologize, not very humbly, for terminology which, here and elsewhere in this paper I substitute for the terminology of 'propositional functions', 'variables', values and the rest. I do so for the simple reason that this terminology has led to many confusions. Especially it failed to make obvious whether in talking of functions, variables, values, etc., we were talking of certain sorts of expressions or talking *with* certain expressions *of* certain sorts of things. Should we say that Socrates or 'Socrates' is a value of the variable in 'x' is snub-nosed'? The terminology which I use is meant to be overtly semantic. Its items, too, are meant to be reasonable self-explanatory.)

Kant's Judgment-forms and Categories

Kant's doctrine of categories starts from quite a different quarter from that of Aristotle, and what he lists as categories are quite other than what Aristotle puts into his index. Kant quaintly avers that his purpose is the same as that of Aristotle, but in this he is, save in a very broad and vague sense, mistaken. Unfortunately Kant borrows for three out of his four heads of categories the same labels as Aristotle had used for three of his ten. As we shall see 'Quantity', 'Quality' and 'Relation' mean completely different sorts of things for the two philosophers.

Kant begins by giving a catalogue of judgment-forms, a catalogue, that is to say, of the several ways in which one proposition may resemble or differ from another not in topic but in form. He makes no attempt to define the notion of form, or even to justify his catalogue, save by declaring, what is false, that it derived from the findings of traditional logic, which he assumes to be a completed body of ascertained truth. (1) All propositions are determined in respect of 'Quantity', that is in respect of the extension of their subjects, and so must be either universal, particular or singular, i.e. of the 'all', 'some' or 'this' form; (2) all propositions are either affirmative, negative or infinite, which are the three 'Qualities' of propositions; (3) all propositions are of one of the three 'Relation' patterns, 's is P', 'if p then q', and 'p or q'; and (4) all propositions are of one of the three varieties of 'Modality', i.e. of the 'is' form, the 'may be' form or the 'must be' form. These judgment-forms are not yet Kant's categories, but they are the source from which he, somewhat mysteriously, proposes to derive or deduce them.

Kant's line of approach was, in principle, much more enlightened than Aristotle's had been. Unfortunately his execution was hopelessly misguided. His sub-variety of 'infinite' judgments is a fraud; there are several sorts of 'universal' judgment, but the sort which he was considering should come under the heading of hypothetical judgments; the division into assertoric, problematic and apodeictic is wrong-headed, the two last being special cases of hypotheticals; the division into categorical, hypothetical and disjunctive embodies a cross-division and contains one glaring omission, for (a) what he had in mind was the distinction between simple and compound propositions and (b) he omitted from this latter class conjunctive propositions of the 'p and q' form. Only of simple propositions is it true that they must be either affirmative or negative and either universal or particular or singular, since in a two-limbed conjunctive, disjunctive or hypothetical proposition, for instance, one of the conjoined propositions may be one while the second is one of the others. The distinction between the disjunctive and the hypothetical forms is false. No overt distinction is drawn between general and non-general propositions; no place is found for such propositions as 'seven cows are in the field', 'most men wear coats', 'John is probably dead'. And lastly, in simple singular propositions no distinction is drawn between attributive and relational propositions; Aristotle's category of relational predicates is completely ignored. Indeed Kant fails to follow Aristotle's doctrine of categories at all, for he notices no type-differences inside subject-predicate propositions, and purloins the titles 'Quality', 'Quantity' and 'Relation' for his own quite different purposes. Namely, in Aristotle's use 'green', 'sweet' and 'honest' signify qualities, but in Kant's use, 'Quality' signifies a proposition's being affirmative or negative. 'Quantity' is, for Aristotle, the name of the family of predicates of magnitude or size; for Kant it is the name of the respect in which propositions are of the 'all . . .' or the 'some . . .' or the 'this . . .' form. Relations, lastly, are in Aristotle's use such predicates as 'cousin of', 'above', 'bigger than', but in Kant's they are what are expressed by such conjunctions as 'if', 'or' and (he should have added) 'and'.

But when all this is said, it has to be acknowledged that Kant was recognizing as cardinal in the search for categories or types facts which Aristotle had not noticed at all in this connection. Kant saw that there is a variety of respects in which propositions may be formally similar and dissimilar. As we saw, in Aristotle's doctrine of categories, the roles of 'form-words' like *all, some, the, a, any, if, or, and, not* are unnoticed, and medieval followers relegated these words to limbo under the grudging appellation of 'syncategorematic'. Kant's doctrine (though he does not notice the point) restores them from the limbo of logic to its workshop.

Aristotle seems generally to suppose that while there is a moderate variety of types of factors, yet there is only one sort of coupling to which they are subject. (In his doctrine of Predicables he half sees that in general propositions there are different sorts of coupling, but this is not allowed to modify his theory of terms.) Kant sees that there is a galaxy of sorts of coupling and that these determine or are determined by the sorts of factors that can be coupled. Aristotle's is an 'alphabetic' theory of factors and a simple 'juxtaposition' theory of their combinations; Kant's is a 'syntactical' theory about the combinations of factors, and consequently a 'syntactical' theory about the types of those factors—or so I interpret his cryptic utterances about 'functions of unity'.

However, Kant's categories are not identical with his forms of judgment. They are, in some obscure way, the projections of these logical forms upon the fields of natural things and events. Natural facts, facts that is that are establishable by observation or by memory of or induction from or causal inference from observations, all embody certain principles of structure, which somehow derive from the items in the table of judgment-forms. Nature consists of things possessing extensive and intensive magnitudes, being in states at particular moments of time and undergoing mutations or perpetuations of state according to causal laws. Everything empirical must and nothing non-empirical can embody these categories. So metaphysical propositions trespass against category-rules.

The mysterious Metapsychology, by means of which Kant tries to prove both that Nature must be so constituted and that we can know that it must be so constituted, need not be considered here. What would be relevant would be an exposition of the differences that Kant professes to find between his logical types and his categories or natural types. It looks as though he confusedly believed that there exist two sorts of facts or propositions, logicians' facts or propositions and scientists' facts or propositions, and that the forms of the latter are step-children of those of the former. But this would be an absurd view, for in fact the logicians' forms are simply what they abstract from ranges of partially similar and partially dissimilar propositions which hail, very likely, directly from the text books of scientists, historians, explorers, mathematicians or theologians. So the alleged distinction is, I think, a bogus one.

Kant contributes nothing to the technical problem how to exhibit or symbolize type-homogeneities and heterogeneities in abstraction from the concrete factors which exemplify them. Nor does he explain how they are established, save by recommending us to read traditional logic.

Before leaving the history of the topic, we should notice one presupposition which Aristotle and Kant share, which is, I believe, unreflectively shared by a number of contemporary philosophers. Namely, it was supposed that there exists a finite catalogue of categories or types; for instance, that there exist just ten (or eight) types of terms, or that there exist just twelve judgment patterns, just as there exist just twenty-six letters in the English alphabet, just sixty-four squares on the chess-board and just six species of chessmen. This seems to be pure myth. There are various gambits at chess, but there is no finite roster of them; and there are various grammatical constructions of English sentences, but there can be no complete table of those varieties.

Scholasticism is the belief in some decalogue of categories, but I know of no grounds for this belief.

It follows that I do not think that we can ever say of a given code-symbolism in formal logic that its symbols are now adequate for the symbolization of all possible differences of type or form. It may, of course, be adequate for the exhibition of all the type-differences that concern us in the course of some particular inquiry.

Generalization of the Topic

When a sentence is (not true or false but) nonsensical or absurd, although its vocabulary is conventional and its grammatical construction is regular, we say that it is absurd because at least one ingredient expression in it is not of the right type to be coupled or to be coupled in that way with the other ingredient expression or expressions in it. Such sentences, we may say, commit type-trespasses or break type-rules. Latterly the attention of logicians has been focused on certain sorts of type-trespasses, like those which are committed by 'I am now lying' and ' "Heterological" is heterological'. These sorts are interesting, because their absurdities are not obvious but manifest themselves in the generation of contradictions or vicious circles, whereas 'Saturday is in bed' is obviously absurd before any contradictions are seen to result from the hypothesis that it is true.

Moreover we can be actually led by seemingly valid arguments to propounding propositions of the former sorts, whereas only the deliberate intention to produce balderdash would get us to formulate sentences of the latter sort. That is, some type-trespasses are insidious and others are not. It is the insidious ones which force us to consider type-rules; the others we only attend to because we are already considering type-rules. But it would be a mistake to restrict the theory of types to the theory of certain special type-rules.

To ask the question To what type or category does so and so belong? is to ask In what sorts of true or false propositions and in what positions in them can so and so enter? Or, to put it semantically, it is to ask In what sorts of non-absurd sentences and in what positions in them can the expression 'so and so' enter? and, conversely, What sorts of sentences would be rendered absurd by the substitution for one of their sentence-factors of the expression 'so and so'? I adopt the word 'absurd' in preference to 'nonsensical' or 'meaningless' for the reason that both the two last words are sometimes used for noises like 'brillig' and 'abracadabra', and sometimes for collocations of words having no regular grammatical construction. Moreover, both have recently been adopted for polemical purposes in aid of a special theory. 'Absurd' has helpful associations with the *reductio ad absurdum*, and even its nuance of ridiculousness is useful rather than the reverse, for so many jokes are in fact type-pranks.

What are Types Types of?

Only expressions can be affirmed or denied to be absurd. Nature provides no absurdities; nor can we even say that thoughts such as beliefs or supposals or conceptions are or are not absurd. For what is absurd is unthinkable.

So it is, on the whole, prudent to talk logic in the semantic idiom and to formulate our theories and inquiries in such a way as to advertise all the time that we are considering whether such and such expressions may or may not be coupled in such and such ways with other expressions.

The danger is, of course, that we shall be taken and shall unwittingly take ourselves to be talking grammar, as if it was all part of one topic to say 'Plural nouns cannot have singular verbs' and 'The dotted line in ". . . is false" can be completed with "What you are now saying . . ." and cannot be completed with "What I am now saying. . . ."'

We try, then, to say that absurdities result from the improper coupling not of expressions but of what the expressions signify, though the coupling and mis-coupling of them is effected by operating upon their expressions.

But there is not and cannot be any univocal title for all the *significata* of expressions, since if there was such a title, all these *significata* would be of one and the same type. And just this is what was at bottom wrong with the Lockean terminology of 'ideas' and the Meinongian terminology of 'objects', words which were employed to perform exactly this impossible task.

Other commonly used titles have extra nuisances as well. 'Terms' retains some of its traditional associations and should be used, if at all, for particulars-or-qualities-or-relations, etc. 'Concepts' does not cover either particulars or entire propositions or even complexes of concepts. So I use 'proposition-factor' (intending it to have all possible type-ambiguities), to collect whatever is signified by any expression, simple or complex, which can be a complement to a gap-sign in some sentence-frame or other (or which can be a value of a variable in some propositional function or other). And, if asked such questions as Do proposition-factors exist? How many of them are there? Are they mental? What are they like? my answer is 'All such questions are ridiculous, since "factor" is and is meant to be the meeting-place of all type-ambiguities'.

Of course we could dispense with any such word. Its functions are purely stenographic. Questions about the types of factors are, in a way, just questions about the possibilities of co-significance of certain classes of expressions. But just as the 'factor' idiom (like the 'idea' idiom) is liable to entrap us in myth, so the semantic idiom is liable to entrap us in a confusion between logical and grammatical questions.

Two proposition-factors are of different categories or types, if there are sentence-frames such that when the expressions for those factors are imported as alternative complements to the same gap-signs, the resultant sentences are significant in the one case and absurd in the other. It is tempting but not quite correct to say, as the converse of this, that two factors are of the same type if there is any case where both can fill the same gap. For 'I' and 'the writer of this paper' can be alternative nominatives to hosts of significant sentences but both cannot fill the gap in '. . . never wrote a paper'. It follows that though nearly, it is not quite true to say that every gap-sign in its context in a determinate sentence-frame indicates the category of all its possible complements. But wherever a particular gap-sign is thus tolerant of typically dissimilar complements, that gap-sign has typical ambiguity which a better symbolism would escape. For the fact that a given gap in a sentence-frame *can* be filled by complements between which there are certain differences of form is itself a fact about the types of those different complements.

The Genesis of Type-riddles

How do we come to be exercised about the forms of propositions or the types of proposition-factors? Or, to put it in a less new-fangled way, what makes it urgent for us to find definitions or analyses of concepts? For we do not gratuitously rummage in dictionaries or encyclopaedias after notions on which to perform elucidations. Type-problems seem to be forced upon us in two main ways.

(1) There are concepts with which we are perfectly familiar and which we are perfectly competent to employ—incessantly occurring, for instance, in questions which we know quite well how to solve. Yet whole classes of ordinary propositions embodying one or more of such concepts, some of which propositions we have perfectly good reasons for accepting as true, are ruled out as false by other propositions, no less well authenticated, embodying other equally familiar concepts. In a word, we are confronted by antinomies. We are sure that some out of one family of propositions are true and that some out of another family are true, yet the truth of any from the one family seems flatly to contradict all out

of the other. I see a bent stick and the stick is straight; I am to blame for an action, and the action issued from a character which my forebears bequeathed and my school moulded, and so on.

Now if the apparent contradiction or, rather, class of contradictions is resoluble, it can only be because the logical forms of the conflicting propositions are not what we had supposed, since it is only in virtue of the forms of propositions or the types of their factors that they do (or do not) imply (or imply the negatives of) one another.

(2) Then, when we have begun to explore the mechanics of some of our concepts and propositions, we find ourselves embarrassed by some purely technical perplexities. We are not quite sure how to use our own professional implements. But we only want to be sure of the designs of our trade-keys because we want to use them upon locks which were recalcitrant before we started our operations—unless we are carried away by virtuosity. Inquiries such as this one, into the nature of categories, or into the species of relations are in fact such technical questions. But *any* uncharted concept is liable to generate antinomies, for ignorance of its chart is ignorance of some of the implications and compatibilities of the propositions containing it. Concepts of common sense, of the sciences and of philosophy itself can and do all generate antinomies. The problem of the internality of relations arose out of antinomies resulting from the philosophers' technical concept of *relation*.

How are Types Determined?

It has long been known that what a proposition implies, it implies in virtue of its form. The same is true of what it is compatible and incompatible with. Let us give the label 'liaisons' to all the logical relations of a proposition, namely what it implies, what it is implied by, what it is compatible with, and what it is incompatible with. Now, any respect in which two propositions differ in form will be reflected in differences in their liaisons. So two propositions which are formally similar in all respects save that one factor in one is different in type from a partially corresponding factor in the other, will have liaisons which are correspondingly dissimilar. Indeed the liaisons of a proposition do not merely *reflect* the formal properties of the proposition and, what this involves, those of all its factors. In a certain sense, they are the same thing. To know all about its liaisons is to know all about the formal structure of the proposition, and vice versa. Though I can obviously entertain or believe a proposition without having yet noticed all its liaisons. Indeed I must grasp it before I can consider them, otherwise I could not be the victim of antinomies.

The operation of extracting the type of a factor cannot exclude the operation of revealing the liaisons of propositions embodying it. In essence they are one operation. Of course, with the familiar sorts of propositions upon which logicians have worked for centuries or decades, we short-circuit the inquiry, by subsuming them direct under the appropriate formulae. But to be told that a proposition is of the form 'S a P' or of the form 'Ex. Φx.∼ψχ' is to be told nothing unless we are able to work with the code-symbols according to the rules of their use, which means unless we know how to read off the liaisons, the patterns of which are what these symbols prescribe.

Now the operation of formulating the liaisons of a proposition just is the activity of ratiocination or argumentation (in which of course there need not be, though there may be, a polemical purpose). And this is why philosophizing is arguing, and it is just this element of ratiocination which, as a rule, is left out of the latter-day definitions of philosophy as 'analysis'. For these generally suggest that analysing is some sort of paraphrasing. But some sorts of paraphrase throw no philosophical light, for they fail to exhibit just those features of propositions and their factors, obscurity about which involves us in antinomies, namely their liaisons which flow from or constitute their logical types and forms. Mere increase of prolixity is not enough. When an argument is a philosophical one and when not, are further questions the discussion of which would not here be in place.

The Type of Category-propositions

I call a proposition a 'category-proposition' which asserts something about the logical type of a factor or set of factors. Some types have been officially recognized and endowed with trade-names, like 'quality', 'state', 'substance', 'number', 'logical construction', 'category', etc. We could call these 'category-words'. Carnap misleadingly calls them 'universal words'. But propositions asserting that factors are of named types differ only in brevity of expression from propositions asserting that factors are of described types.

All such propositions are philosophers' propositions (not necessarily, of course, of professional or paid philosophers), and the converse is also, I think, true.

Now assertions about the types of factors are, as we have seen, assertions about what sorts of combinations of them with other factors would and what would not produce absurdities. And as only collocations of symbols can be asserted to be absurd or, consequently, denied to be absurd, it follows that category-propositions are semantic propositions. This does not imply that they are of the same types as the propositions of philologists, grammarians or lexicographers. There are not English category-propositions as opposed to German ones, or Occidental as opposed to Oriental. Nor does it imply that they can say nothing about the 'nature of things'. If a child's perplexity why the Equator can be crossed but not seen, or why the Cheshire Cat could not leave its grin behind it is perplexity about the 'nature of things', then certain category-propositions will give the required information about the nature of things. And the same will hold good of less frivolous type-perplexities. But what are the tests of absurdity?

V

Is Existence a Predicate?

G. E. MOORE

(This paper was written as the second part of a Symposium the whole of which was originally printed in the *Proceedings of the Aristotelian Society*, Supplementary Volume XV, in 1936. It is reprinted here without alteration. The first part—by Mr. W. Kneale—has not been included: since it has already been reprinted in Feigl and Sellars, *Readings in Philosophical Analysis*; but the references to it in Professor Moore's paper are sufficiently self-explanatory. The same applies to his use of the technical term 'propositional function'. For an explanation and discussion of the term 'sense-datum' see above, Mr. G. A. Paul's article 'Is There a Problem about Sense-data?' —EDITOR.)

I am not at all clear as to the meaning of this question. Mr. Kneale says that existence is not a predicate. But what does he mean by the words 'Existence is not a predicate'?

In his second paragraph, he says that the word 'predicate' has two different senses, a logical sense and a grammatical one. If so, it would follow that the words 'Existence is not a predicate' may have two different meanings, according as the person who uses them is using 'predicate' in the logical or the grammatical sense. And I think it is clear that he means us to understand that when *he* says 'Existence is not a predicate', he is using 'predicate' in the logical sense, and not in the grammatical one. I think his view is that if anyone were to say 'Existence is a predicate', using 'predicate' in the grammatical sense, such a person would be perfectly right: I think he holds that existence really is a predicate in the grammatical sense. But, whether he holds this or not, I think it is clear that he does not wish to discuss the question whether it is or is not a predicate in the grammatical sense, but solely the question whether it is so in the logical one.

Now I think it is worth noticing that if we assert 'Existence is a predicate', using 'predicate' in the grammatical sense, our proposition is a proposition about certain *words*, to the effect that they are often used in a certain way; but not, curiously enough, about the word 'existence' itself. It is a proposition to the effect that the word 'exists' and other finite parts of the verb 'to exist', such as 'existed', 'will exist' or 'exist' (in the plural) are often the predicates (in some grammatical sense) of sentences in which they occur; but nobody means to say that the word 'existence' itself is often the predicate of sentences in which it occurs. And I think Mr. Kneale implies that, similarly, the proposition which anyone would express, if he asserted 'Existence is a predicate', using 'predicate' in the logical sense, is again equivalent to a proposition, *not* about the word 'existence' itself, but about the word 'exists', and other finite parts of the verb 'to exist'. He implies that 'Existence is a predicate', with this use of 'predicate', is equivalent to the proposition that the word 'exists', and other finite parts of the verb, often do '*stand for* a predicate in the logical sense'. It would appear, therefore, that one difference between the two different meanings of 'Existence is a predicate' is as follows: namely that, if a person who says these words is using 'predicate' in the grammatical sense, he is *not* saying that the words, 'exists', etc., ever '*stand for* a predicate in the logical sense'; whereas, if he is using 'predicate' in the logical sense, he is saying that they do (often, at least) '*stand for* a predicate in the logical sense'. What Mr. Kneale himself means by 'Existence is not a predicate' is apparently some proposition which he would express by saying: 'The words, "exists", etc., never *stand for* a predicate in the logical sense.'

What I am not clear about is as to what is meant by saying of a particular word (or particular phrase) in a particular sentence that it 'stands for a predicate in the logical sense'; nor, therefore, as to what is meant by saying of another particular word in another particular sentence that it does *not* 'stand for a predicate in the logical sense'. Mr. Kneale does, indeed, tell us that a 'predicate in the logical sense' is the same as 'an attribute'; but, though I think that the meaning of the word 'attribute' is perhaps a little clearer than that of the phrase 'predicate in the logical sense', it still seems to me far from clear: I do not clearly understand what he would mean by saying that 'exists', etc., do not 'stand for attributes'. But, from examples which he gives, it is, I think, clear that he would say that in the sentence 'This is red' the word 'red', or the phrase 'is red' (I am not clear which), does 'stand for an attribute'; and also that in the sentence 'Tame tigers growl', 'growl' so stands, and in the sentence 'Rajah growls', 'growls' does. It is, therefore, presumably some difference between the way in which 'exists', etc., are used in sentences in which they occur, and the way in which 'is red' (or 'red') and 'growl' and 'growls' are used in these sentences, that he wishes to express by saying that, whereas 'exists', etc., do *not* 'stand for attributes', these words in these sentences do. And if we can find what differences there are between the use of finite parts of the verb 'to exist', and the use of 'is red', 'growl' and 'growls', we may perhaps find what the difference is which he expresses in this way.

I

It will, I think, be best to begin with one particular use of 'exist'—the one, namely, which Mr. Kneale illustrates by the example 'Tame tigers exist'. He clearly thinks that there is some very important difference between the way in which 'exist' is used here, and the way in which 'growl' is used in 'Tame tigers growl'; and that it is a difference which does not hold, e.g. between the use of 'scratch' in 'Tame tigers scratch' and the use of 'growl' in 'Tame tigers growl'. He would say that 'scratch' and 'growl' both 'stand for attributes', whereas 'exist' does not; and he would also say that 'Tame tigers exist' is a proposition of a different *form* from 'Tame tigers growl', whereas I think he would say that 'Tame tigers growl' and 'Tame tigers scratch' are *of the same form*. What difference between 'Tame tigers exist' and 'Tame tigers growl' can be the one he has in mind?

1. That there is a difference between the way in which we use 'exist' in the former sentence and 'growl' in the latter, of a different kind from the difference between our usages of

'scratch' and 'growl' in the two sentences 'Tame tigers scratch' and 'Tame tigers growl', can, I think, be brought out in the following way.

The sentence 'Tame tigers growl' seems to me to be ambiguous. So far as I can see, it might mean 'All tame tigers growl', or it might mean merely 'Most tame tigers growl', or it might mean merely 'Some tame tigers growl'. Each of these three sentences has a clear meaning, and the meaning of each is clearly different from that of either of the two others. Of each of them, however, it is true that the proposition which it expresses is one which cannot possibly be true, unless some tame tigers do growl. And hence I think we can say of 'Tame tigers growl' that, whichever sense it is used in, it means something which cannot possibly be true unless some tame tigers do growl. Similarly I think it is clear that 'Tame tigers exist' means something which cannot possibly be true unless some tame tigers do exist. But I do not think that there is any ambiguity in 'Tame tigers exist' corresponding to that which I have pointed out in 'Tame tigers growl'. So far as I can see 'Tame tigers exist' and 'Some tame tigers exist' are merely two different ways of expressing exactly the same proposition. That is to say, it is not true that 'Tame tigers exist' might mean 'All tame tigers exist', or 'Most tame tigers exist', instead of merely 'Some tame tigers exist'. It always means just 'Some tame tigers exist', and nothing else whatever. I have said it is never used to mean 'All tame tigers exist', or 'Most tame tigers exist'; but I hope it will strike everyone that there is something queer about this proposition. It seems to imply that 'All tame tigers exist' and 'Most tame tigers exist' have a clear meaning, just as have 'All tame tigers growl' and 'Most tame tigers growl'; and that it is just an accident that we do not happen ever to use 'Tame tigers exist' to express either of those two meanings instead of the meaning 'Some tame tigers exist', whereas we do sometimes use 'Tame tigers growl' to mean 'All tame tigers growl' or 'Most tame tigers growl', instead of merely 'Some tame tigers growl'. But is this in fact the case? Have 'All tame tigers exist' and 'Most tame tigers exist' any meaning at all? Certainly they have not a clear meaning, as have 'All tame tigers growl' and 'Most tame tigers growl'. They are puzzling expressions, which certainly do not carry their meaning, if they have any, on the face of them. That this is so indicates, I think, that there is some important difference between the usage of 'exist' with which we are concerned, and the usage of such words as 'growl' or 'scratch', but it does not make clear just what the difference is.

I think this can be made clear by comparing the expressions 'Some tame tigers don't growl' and 'Some tame tigers don't exist'. The former, whether true or false, has a perfectly clear meaning—a meaning just as clear as that of 'Some tame tigers do growl'; and it is perfectly clear that both propositions might be true together. But with 'Some tame tigers don't exist' the case is different. 'Some tame tigers exist' has a perfectly clear meaning: it just means 'There are some tame tigers'. But the meaning of 'Some tame tigers don't exist', if any, is certainly not equally clear. It is another queer and puzzling expression. Has it any meaning at all? and, if so, what meaning? If it has any, it would appear that it must mean the same as: 'There are some tame tigers which don't exist'. But has *this* any meaning? And if so, what? Is it possible that there should be any tame tigers which don't exist? I think the answer is that, if in the sentence 'Some tame tigers don't exist' you are using 'exist' with the same meaning as in 'Some tame tigers exist', then the former sentence as a whole has no meaning at all—it is pure nonsense. A meaning can, of course, be given to 'Some tame tigers don't exist'; but this can only be done if 'exist' is used in a different way from that in which it is used in 'Some tame tigers exist'. And, if this is so, it will follow that 'All tame tigers exist' and 'Most tame tigers exist', also have no meaning at all, if you are using 'exist' in the sense with which we are concerned. For 'All tame tigers growl' is equivalent to the conjunction 'Some tame tigers growl, and there is no tame tiger which does not growl'; and this has a meaning, because 'There is at least one tame tiger which does not growl' has one. If, therefore, 'There is at least one tame tiger which does not exist' has no meaning, it will follow that 'All tame tigers exist' also has none; because 'There is no tame tiger which does not exist' will have none, if 'There is a tame tiger which does not exist' has none. Similarly 'Most tame tigers growl' is equivalent to the conjunction 'Some tame tigers growl, and the number of those (if any) which do not growl is smaller than that of those which do'—a statement which has a meaning only because 'There are tame tigers which do not growl' has one. If, therefore, 'There are tame tigers which don't exist' has no meaning, it will follow that 'Most tame tigers exist' will also have none. I think, therefore, we can say that one important difference between the use of 'growl' in 'Some tame tigers growl' and the use of 'exist' in 'Some tame tigers exist', is that if in the former case we insert 'do not' before 'growl', without changing the meaning of 'growl', we get a sentence which is significant, whereas if, in the latter, we insert 'do not' before 'exist' without changing the meaning of 'exist', we get a sentence which has no meaning whatever; and I think we can also say that this fact explains why, with the given meaning of 'growl', 'All tame tigers growl' and 'Most tame tigers growl' are both significant, whereas, with the given meaning of 'exist', 'All tame tigers exist' and 'Most tame tigers exist' are utterly meaningless. And if by the statement that 'growl', in this usage, 'stands for an attribute', whereas 'exist', in this usage, does not, part of what is meant is that there is this difference between them, then I should agree that 'exist', in this usage, does not 'stand for an attribute'.

But is it really true that if, in the sentence 'Some tame tigers exist', we insert 'do not' before 'exist', without changing the meaning of 'exist', we get a sentence which has no meaning whatever? I have admitted that a meaning *can* be given to 'Some tame tigers do not exist'; and it may, perhaps, be contended by some people that the meaning which 'exist' has in this sentence, where it is significant, *is* precisely the same as that which it has in 'Some tame tigers exist'. I cannot show the contrary as clearly as I should like to be able to do; but I will do my best.

The meaning which such an expression as 'Some tame tigers do not exist' sometimes does have, is that which it has when it is used to mean the same as 'Some tame tigers are imaginary' or 'Some tame tigers are not real tigers'. That 'Some tame tigers are imaginary' may really express a proposition, whether true or false, cannot I think be denied. If, for instance, two different stories have been written, each of which is about a different imaginary tame tiger, it will follow that there are at least two imaginary tame tigers; and it cannot be denied that the sentence 'Two different tame tigers occur in fiction' is significant, though I have not the least idea whether it is true or false. I know that at least one unicorn occurs in fiction, because one occurs in *Alice Through the Looking Glass*; and it follows that there is at least one imaginary unicorn, and therefore (in a sense) at least one unicorn which does not exist. Again, if it should happen that at the present moment two different people are each having an hallucination of a different tame tiger, it will follow that there are at the present moment two different imaginary tame tigers; and the statement that two such hallucinations are occurring now is certainly significant, though it may very likely be false. The sentence 'There are some tame tigers which do not exist' is, therefore, certainly significant, if it means only that there are some imaginary tigers, in either of the two senses which I have tried to point out. But what it means is that either some real people have written stories about imaginary tigers, or are having or have recently had hallucinations of tame tigers, or, perhaps, are dreaming or have dreamed of particular tame tigers. If nothing of this sort has happened or is happening to anybody, then there are no imaginary tame tigers. But if 'Some tame tigers do not exist' means all this, is it not clear that 'exist' has not, in this sentence, the same comparatively simple meaning as it has in 'Some tame tigers exist' or in 'No tame tigers exist'? Is it not clear that 'Some tame tigers do not exist', if it means all this, is not related to 'Some tame tigers exist', in the same simple way in which 'Some tame tigers do not growl' is related to 'Some tame tigers growl'?

2. There is, I think, also another important difference between this use of 'exist' and the use of 'growl', which may be brought out as follows.

Mr. Russell has said[1] 'When we say "some men are Greeks," that means that the propositional function "*x* is a man and a Greek" is sometimes true'; and has explained just

[1] *Introduction to Mathematical Philosophy*, p. 159.

previously that by 'sometimes true' he means 'true in at least one instance'. With this explanation of what he means by 'sometimes true', I do not think that his statement as to the meaning of 'Some men are Greeks' is strictly correct; since I think that the use of the plural implies that 'x is a man and a Greek' is true in *more* than one instance, that is to say, in at least two instances. Let us suppose that he would accept this correction and say that what 'Some men are Greeks' means is not, strictly, that 'x is a man and a Greek' is true in at least one instance, but that it is true in at least two. He has further implied[2] that to say of a propositional function that it is true in at least two instances is the same thing as to say that at least two 'values' of it are true; and he has told us[3] that the 'values' of propositional functions are propositions. With these explanations, his view would appear to be that what 'Some men are Greeks' means is that at least two propositions, related to the propositional function 'x is a man and a Greek' in some way which he expresses by saying that they are 'values' of that function, are true. Now I cannot imagine what sort of propositions would be 'values' of 'x is a man and a Greek', except propositions of the following sort. There are propositions which we express by pointing at (or indicating in some other way), an object which we are seeing (or perceiving in some other way) and uttering the words 'This is a so-and-so' (or equivalent words in some other language). Let us suppose that the kind of propositions which would be 'values' of 'x is a man and a Greek' would be propositions of this sort, where the words used were 'This is a man and a Greek'. Mr. Russell's doctrine would then be that 'Some men are Greeks' means that at least two different true propositions of this sort would be made: that there must have been at least two different objects at which a man might have pointed and said truly 'This is a man and a Greek'. And, if this is his doctrine, it seems to me to be true. Surely 'Some men are Greeks' cannot possibly be true, unless there are at least two different objects, in the case of each of which a man

[2] Ibid., p. 158.
[3] Ibid., p. 156.

might have seen it, pointed at it, and said with truth 'This is a man and a Greek'?

On this view 'Some tame tigers growl' means that at least two values of '*x* is a tame tiger and growls' are true; and this means that there are at least two objects, in the case of each of which a man might have seen it, pointed at it, and said with truth 'This is a tame tiger and growls'. Now in this sentence 'This is a tame tiger and growls' it is clear that, except for the difference consisting in the fact that 'growls' is in the singular and 'growl' in the plural, the word 'growls' has the same meaning as has the word 'growl' in 'Some tame tigers growl'. We can say, then, that one feature about our use of 'growl' is that, if we consider a 'value' of the propositional function which is such that 'Some tame tigers growl' means that at least two values of it are true, then the singular of 'growl' can be used, with the same meaning, in the expression of such a value. And perhaps this may be part of what is meant by saying that 'growl' 'stands for an attribute'. It may perhaps be meant that to point at an object which you are seeing, and utter the words 'This object growls', is significant—that the words and gesture together do really express a proposition, true or false.

But now consider 'Some tame tigers exist': is the same true of 'exist' in this sentence? Mr. Russell says:[4] 'We say that "men exist" or "a man exists" if the propositional function "*x* is human" is sometimes true'. And he goes on to protest that though the proposition 'Socrates is a man' is *'equivalent'* to 'Socrates is human', it 'is not the very same proposition'. For my part I doubt whether we ever do use 'is human' in such a way that 'Socrates is human' is equivalent to 'Socrates is a man'. I think Mr. Russell is using 'is human' in a very special sense, in which nobody but he has ever used it, and that the only way of explaining how he is using it is to say that he is using it to mean precisely that which we ordinarily express by 'is a human being'. If this is so, and if we are allowed to distinguish, as I think we ought, between 'men exist' and 'a man exists', and to say that 'men exist' means, *not* ' "*x* is a human being" is true in at least one instance', but ' "*x* is a

4 Ibid., pp. 171–2.

human being" is true in at least two instances', then I think
his doctrine is true; provided, again, that we are allowed to
regard the sort of propositions which we express, e.g. by pointing at an object which we are seeing and saying the words
'This is a human being', as being those which are values of
'*x* is a human being'. Surely 'Human beings exist' can be true
if, and only if, there are at least two objects, such that, if a
man were to see and point to one of them and utter the
words 'This is a human being', he would be expressing a true
proposition by what he did?

Now, if this is right, we see at once that the use of 'growl'
in 'Some tame tigers growl' differs from that of 'exist' in
'Some tame tigers exist', in the respect that, while the first
asserts that more than one value of '*x* is a tame tiger *and
growls*' is true, the second asserts, *not* that more than one
value of '*x* is a tame tiger *and exists*' is true, but merely that
more than one value of '*x* is a tame tiger' is true. Owing to
this view of his that 'Some tame tigers exist' means the same
as 'Some values of the propositional function "*x* is a tame
tiger" are true', Mr. Russell has been led to say[5] 'Existence is
essentially a property of a propositional function' and[6] ('It
is of propositional functions that you can assert or deny existence' and[7] that it is a fallacy to transfer 'to the individual
that satisfies a propositional function a predicate which only
applies to a propositional function'; so that, according to him,
existence is, after all, in this usage, a 'property' or 'predicate',
though not a property of individuals, but only of propositional functions! I think this is a mistake on his part. Even
if it is true that 'Some tame tigers exist' means the same as
'Some values of "*x* is a tame tiger" are true' it does not follow, I think, that we can say that 'exist' means the same as
'is sometimes true', and 'some tame tigers' the same as '*x* is a
tame tiger': indeed, I think it is clear that we can not say
this; for certainly ' "*x* is a tame tiger" exists' would not mean
the same as 'Some tame tigers exist'. But what I think does
follow from this interpretation of 'Some tame tigers exist' is

[5] *Monist*, April 1919, p. 195.
[6] Ibid., p. 196.
[7] Ibid., p. 197.

another thing which Mr. Russell himself holds, namely, that if a proposition which you express by pointing at something which you see and saying 'This is a tame tiger', is a 'value' of '*x* is a tame tiger', then if, pointing at the same thing, you were to say the words 'This exists', and, if you were using 'exists' merely as the singular of 'exist' in the sense in which it is used in 'Some tame tigers exist', what you did would not express a proposition at all, but would be absolutely meaningless. That is to say, there is between 'Some tame tigers growl' and 'Some tame tigers exist', not only the difference that, whereas the first asserts that some values of '*x* is a tame tiger *and growls*' are true, the second asserts only that some values of '*x* is a tame tiger' are true; there is also the further and more important difference that, why the second asserts only that some values of '*x* is a tame tiger' are true, is not because we happen to use 'This is a tame tiger' to mean the same as 'This is a tame tiger *and exists*', but because by pointing and saying 'This *exists*' we should express *no proposition at all*, so long as we were using 'exists' as the singular of the use of 'exist' with which we are concerned, whereas by pointing and saying 'This growls' we certainly should be expressing a proposition, even though we were using 'growls' merely as the singular of 'growl' with the meaning it has in 'Some tame tigers growl'. 'This is a tame tiger, *and exists*' would be not tautologous, but meaningless.

This, I think, gives us a second true thing, which may perhaps be sometimes part of what is meant by saying that 'exist', in this usage, 'does not stand for an attribute'.

II

So far I have been solely concerned with the use of 'exist' in such sentences as 'Some tame tigers exist', and have tried to point out two differences between its use here and the use of 'growl' in 'Some tame tigers growl', which may perhaps be part of what is meant by saying that 'exist', in this usage, does not 'stand for an attribute', whereas 'growl' does. But I cannot help thinking that there are other significant uses of 'exists'; and I want in particular, to try to point out two such, and to consider what, if anything, true can be meant by saying that in these usages also 'exists' does not 'stand for an attribute'.

1. I have just said that to point at a thing which you see and say 'This exists' seems to me to be meaningless, if 'exists' is the singular of 'exist' in the sense in which it is used in 'Tame tigers exist'; but I cannot help thinking that in the case of anything to point at which and say 'This is a tame tiger' is significant, it is also significant to point at it and say 'This exists', *in some sense or other*. My reason for thinking this is that it seems to me that you can clearly say *with truth* of any such object 'This *might* not have existed', 'It is *logically possible* that this should not have existed'; and I do not see how it is possible that 'This might have existed' should be true, unless 'This does in fact exist' is true, and therefore also significant. The statement 'It is logically possible that this should not have existed' seems to *mean* 'The sentence "This does not exist" is significant'; and if 'This does not exist' is significant, 'This does exist' must be significant too. Now I cannot help thinking that in every case in which I point at an object which I am perceiving and say significantly 'This is a tame tiger', 'This is a book', my proposition is in fact a proposition about some sense-datum, or some set of sense-data, which I am perceiving; and that part of what I am saying is that this sense-datum (or these sense-data) is 'of' a physical object. That is to say, I am saying of some sense-datum that it is 'of' a physical object in the sense in which it is true to say of an after-image which I see with my eyes shut that it is *not* 'of' a physical object. And I think that part, at least, of what we mean by 'This exists', where we are using 'this' in the same way as when we point and say 'This is a book', is 'This sense-datum is *of* a physical object', which seems to me to be certainly significant. If 'of' here stood for a relation, we might say that 'This is a book' was short for 'The thing which this sense-datum is "of" is a book', and therefore 'This exists' short for 'The thing which this sense-datum is "of" exists'; in which case the use of 'exists' in question would be that which in *Principia Mathematica* is symbolized by E!, and there would be the same sort of reason for saying that it

does not 'stand for an attribute' as in the case of the 'exist' which occurs in 'Some tame tigers exist'. I do not believe, however, that 'of' here does stand for a relation, nor therefore that 'This' in 'This is a book' can be said to be short for the sort of phrase which Russell has called 'a definite description'; and, this being so, I am not at all clear as to what that is true could be meant by saying that 'exists', in this usage, 'does not stand for an attribute'. The only suggestion I can make is this. It seems to me that 'This exists' (in this usage) always forms part of what is asserted by 'This is a book', 'This is red', etc. etc., where 'this' is used in the manner with which we are now concerned; and possibly part of what is meant by saying that 'is a book', 'is red', etc., 'stand for attributes', is that *part but not the whole* of what is asserted by any 'value' of '*x* is a book', '*x* is red', etc., is 'This exists'. In that case 'exists' in 'This exists' would not 'stand for an attribute', solely because the whole of what it asserts, and not merely a part, is 'This exists'.

2. Another reason why 'This exists', where 'this' is used as it is in 'This is a book' seems to me to be significant, is because it seems to me not only significant to say of a given sense-datum 'This *is* of a physical object' or 'This is *not* of a physical object', but also to say of the sense-datum itself 'This exists'. If this is so, we have to do with a new sense of 'exists', since certainly no part of the meaning of such an assertion with regard to a sense-datum is that it, or any other sense-datum, is 'of' a physical object. But my reason for holding that it is significant for me to say, for instance, of an after-image which I am seeing with my eyes shut, 'This exists', is similar to that which I gave in the last case: namely that it seems to me that in the case of every sense-datum which any-one ever perceives, the person in question could always say with truth of the sense-datum in question 'This might not have existed'; and I cannot see how this could be true, unless 'This does in fact exist' is also true, and therefore significant. That 'this exists' has any meaning in such cases, where, as Mr. Russell would say, we are using 'this' as a 'proper name' for something with which we are 'acquainted', is, I know, disputed; my view that it has, involves, I am bound to admit, the curious consequence that 'this exists', when used in this

way, is always true, and 'this does not exist' always false; and I have little to say in its favour except that it seems to me so plainly true that, in the case of every sense-datum I have, it is logically possible that the sense-datum in question should not have existed—that there should simply have been no such thing. If, for instance, I am seeing a bright after-image with my eyes shut, it seems to me quite plainly conceivable that I should have had instead, at that moment, a uniform black field, such as I often have with my eyes shut; and, if I had had such a field, then that particular bright after-image simply would not have existed.

But, supposing 'This exists', in this usage, has a meaning, why should we not say that 'exists' here 'stands for an attribute'? I can suggest no reason why we should not, except the same which I suggested in the last case.

VI

'Every Event Has a Cause'

G. J. WARNOCK

I

There is obviously something strange about the sentence 'Every event has a cause'. It is natural enough that there should sometimes be disagreement over the question whether some statement is true or false. Less commonly, but still understandably, there occur disputes about what some sentences mean, or whether they really mean anything. But in this case the situation is more complicated. Some in saying that every event has a cause (or in using more or less sophisticated variants of this) have believed without question that they were making a true statement. Others have adduced from widely diverse fields considerations which lead them to say that it is false. But views quite different from either of these have been put forward. It has been held that the statement that every event has a cause is not merely true in fact, but *necessarily* true; also that, though perhaps it is not in the ordinary way necessarily true, it is yet in some special way *unquestionable*; and also, perhaps most paradoxically, that despite appearances it is neither a true statement nor a false one, neither necessary nor unquestionable—indeed not a statement at all, but a kind of maxim, or precept, or exhortation. All this seems to show that the sentence 'Every event has a cause' is not understood as clearly as could be wished; for if it were understood it should surely be possible to decide whether what it says is contingent or necessary; or at least whether one who utters it is making a statement, adopting or commending a maxim, issuing an exhortation or expressing a resolution. Or perhaps it would be found that he is doing none of these things.

II

Those who have argued the question whether it is true or false to say that every event has a cause were often, certainly, at cross purposes. The motive for maintaining that it was true was usually the belief that every event is an instance of some scientific law, or law of nature, and could thus in principle at least be causally explained. And the motive for maintaining the contrary was not primarily the belief that this was not the case, but rather the conviction that at least some happenings can be explained by reference to the intentions, choices, and decisions of intelligent and responsible beings, or 'agents'. The contention that some events have no causes was sponsored on the assumption that only if this were so could it really be held that some events occur *because* responsible beings choose or decide to act in certain ways. However, it is by no means a clearly correct assumption that explanation of an event in terms of an agent's decision must exclude the possibility of giving a causal explanation of it as well. In order to maintain that the occupant of the next room *decided* to turn on the lights it is not necessary, nor indeed is it possible, to deny that their lighting up was an ordinary instance of the laws of electricity. And to say that the golf-ball finished short of the green because the player wanted to keep out of the bunkers does not make it either incorrect or impossible to explain its flight in terms of the elasticity of ball and club-face, the velocity of impact, and the state of atmosphere and ground.

III

This particular dispute might be continued into many further complications; but it has sometimes been swept aside as wholly misguided and inappropriate. It is, it has been argued, quite mistaken to ask whether it is true or false that every event has a cause, or what would be the consequences of affirming or denying its truth; for the alleged statement in dispute is not really a statement at all, so that questions of truth and falsity do not arise. Kant for example (in criticizing certain metaphysical arguments about a First Cause) found difficulties both in the claim that the alleged statement was true, and also in the assertion that it was false; and accordingly suggested that it must be regarded as an *injunction* to extend the search for causes as far as possible, and to seek always to make more coherent and comprehensive our formulations of natural laws.[1] Earlier, however, he had himself written as if the Law of Causation were a necessary truth; and indeed it does not seem at all to resemble what would ordinarily be thought of as maxims, injunctions, or rules. 'Do not rely on defective apparatus'; 'Do not draw general conclusions from a few observations made in unfavourable conditions'; or (cf. Darwin) 'Always pay special attention to instances apparently contradicting your hypotheses'—these for example would naturally be regarded as maxims for scientists, hints on how to succeed. To attempt to formulate coherent and comprehensive statements of law, on the other hand, seems to be rather what scientists actually do (almost, what scientists do *by definition*) than something which they should be enjoined or encouraged to do. To affirm the Law of Causa-

---

[1] *Critique of Pure Reason*, A498 (B526).

tion would be, on this view, to urge them to carry on with their activities, not to give them maxims or tips on how to succeed. And in any case, although one who says that every event has a cause would naturally be regarded as thereby *displaying* determination to carry on the search for laws, or perhaps as urging his audience not to give up, it is still the natural view to take that he is *stating* that, if he or they persist, success will be achieved. It at least looks as if he were urging the continued search for laws only by way of stating that there are in every field natural laws to be found. There is thus no case for adopting this Kantian view, unless the natural belief that we are dealing with some kind of statement turns out to be utterly untenable; and if it turns out to be untenable, the statement-like form 'Every event has a cause' must be abandoned as muddling.

IV

Some others who have held that it is out of place to argue about the truth or falsity of this alleged statement have, I think, had the idea that the Law of Causation is to the natural sciences what the laws of logic are to deductive disciplines. It is in this sense, I believe, that one must understand the contention that this Law is and must be 'presupposed' in all scientific investigation—that it must be accepted and cannot sensibly (or 'rationally') be questioned. It might be urged that, just as one cannot profitably engage in deductive argument without accepting rules specifying the difference between valid and invalid reasoning, so one cannot engage in scientific inquiry without accepting the Law of Causation. Put thus, however, this contention looks obviously wrong. The proper analogy would be that between the laws of logic and the canons of inductive argument. The pursuit of scientific inquiry certainly requires pretty general agreement on the difference between good evidence and bad, between well-established conclusions and rash hypotheses, between properly conducted tests and random gropings. But the Law of Causation has not much to do with this. For one who wishes to reject this Law need not, it would seem, deny that the grounds offered in support of most scientific conclusions are adequate; he need only maintain that there are or very well might be some cases in which no similar conclusions can be reached. This is certainly to reject the common assumption that the canons of inductive argument must be regarded as worthless unless one also accepts the Law of Causation; but this assumption is surely mistaken. It amounts to suggesting that the canons of inductive argument essentially require the guarantee, or at least the presupposition, that their observance will in principle always ensure success; but they do not in fact require so much as this. One might well recognize that to pay assiduous attention to inductive evidence is the best thing that one can do in attempting to formulate statements of law, and yet not assume that there are no cases at all in which the best attempts would be utterly baffled. It is probably true that most people who use inductive arguments do assume, or perhaps half-unconsciously take for granted, that if they try hard enough they will succeed in their quest; but it is not by any means *necessary* that they should assume this. One might well continue to do the best that one could, with failure accepted as a constant lurking possibility; and certainly one might accept without any disquiet the idea that inquirers in other fields might always fail. H. W. B. Joseph's assertion[2] that to accept this idea is to 'despair of reason and thought' is dramatic, but an exaggeration. Failure and despair in some cases are compatible with optimism and success in others.

So far, then, we have noted that the sentence 'Every event has a cause' has (often for extraneous and dubious reasons) given rise to debates about whether, as a statement, it is true or false; that it has been held to express a sort of precept or injunction—a paradoxical claim on which we suspended judgment; and that it has been held to be 'unquestionable' by rational persons who wish to use inductive arguments—a suggestion that we have rejected. I wish now to examine the suggestion with which I shall be mainly concerned—the suggestion, namely that the statement that every event has a cause is *synthetic a priori*, a *synthetic necessary truth*. I hope

[2] *Introduction to Logic*, p. 420.

that in the assessment of this suggestion the main source, or sources, of the difficulty will be discovered.

V

The question of synthetic necessary truth has been for some time a storm-centre in philosophy. That there should be disagreement here is understandable; but it seems that this question engages the emotions also. This is, I think, because upon this issue philosophers of sharply different casts of mind, however they may agree on this point or that, find themselves strongly inclined to take opposite sides. It appears to matter enormously which side is taken, and as if, here at least, the line between two opposing camps were clearly drawn out. This however is, most strikingly, not the case. Those who aver that there are synthetic necessary truths are apt to put forward the baffling contention that by some sort of insight, or intellectual gazing, we can see that some truths of fact are necessary truths; while those who contend that no synthetic truths are necessary maintain the hardly less cloudy doctrine that truths of fact can only be based on, and so might at any time be or might have been falsified by, Experience. These are large issues, and they excite strong feelings; but we must not at once range ourselves with one party or the other. Nothing but confusion can result (as it has often resulted) from considering this topic in wholly general terms, or from assuming that, whenever a claim to synthetic necessary truth is made or denied, some simple and single question is presented for decision.

To the sorts of statements which are most comfortably called synthetic it is natural also to apply such predicates as 'contingent', 'factual', 'empirical', or 'a posteriori'; and we expect the contradictories of these to be of exactly the same logical character. To expressions naturally regarded as analytic we are apt to attach also such predicates as 'logically necessary', 'true by definition', and 'a priori'; and here we expect the contradictories to be logically impossible, self-contradictory. We would hesitate to say that a statement was quite ordinarily synthetic unless it appeared also to rank as con-

tingent, factual, and empirical; we feel uneasy in labelling
an expression 'analytic' unless we can show that it is somehow
necessary, true by definition; and we expect the normal behaviour of contradictories. Thus, if one refuses to submit to
this dichotomy and seeks to bridge it by the phrase 'synthetic
a priori', one's refusal may be due to a variety of discomforts.
Perhaps the statement that it is proposed to call synthetic
a priori is, though not analytic, not contingent either; perhaps it appears to be empirical but not *a posteriori*; it may
seem to be necessary but not true by definition, or logically
necessary and factual at the same time. The notions involved
in all this are numerous, related no doubt, but nevertheless
diverse. There is accordingly scope for a good many difficulties
in the customary attempt to divide all significant indicative
sentences into two classes; there is no good reason to suppose
that in all cases we can effect a single, orderly, exhaustive,
and satisfying classification; and so there are correspondingly
numerous and various reasons for clutching at some such
straw as 'synthetic *a priori*'. Or perhaps it resembles a smoke-
screen rather than a straw; the phrase is nobody's salvation,
but it serves to cloak many a tangle behind the lines.

In this case we shall consider the claim made for the sentence 'Every event has a cause', without insisting that what
is said of this case has necessarily any application to other
cases, and allowing that other sentences for which this claim
is made may well require a very different treatment.

VI

First we must try to make clear what is or might be involved in the claim that the Law of Causation is a synthetic
a priori truth. For saying that it is synthetic there seem to
be two (related) reasons. First, the sentence 'Every event has
a cause' cannot plausibly be represented as analytic; it is not
like 'Every bicycle has two wheels'. For whereas, in giving the
meaning of the word 'bicycle' it would be necessary to make
it clear that a bicycle has two wheels, it does not seem that,
in defining the word 'event', it would be correct or necessary
to stipulate that every event has a cause. There is no defini-

tion of 'event' by the help of which 'Every event has a cause' can be transformed into a manifest tautology. Conversely, the sentence 'Some events have no causes' is not self-contradictory. H. A. Pritchard, indeed, claimed that to realize the truth of the Law of Causation we need only consider what we mean by 'a physical event';[3] but this is for several reasons peculiar. His claim was intended, but even if correct would fail, to support the idea that this Law is synthetic *a priori*; it does not in any case seem to be true that 'having a cause' is part of what is *meant* by 'a physical event'; and there seems to be no good reason why the events of which the Law says that every one has a cause should be only *physical* events. However, the point at present is only this—that it seems impossible to hold that 'Every event has a cause' is analytic, tautologous, true by definition; and this inclines us to conclude that it must be synthetic. For if it is not analytic what else could it be?

A second reason for inclining to this conclusion is that the Law of Causation appears to make a statement, and indeed a fundamentally important statement, about the course of nature—about what actually occurs in the universe we inhabit. It does not appear merely to illustrate, or to analyse, what we mean by the word 'event', but rather to say something of enormous importance about the way things actually are. Is it not a fundamental fact about the universe that we find in it the Rule of Law?

Such, then, are the main considerations that may lead us to say that the Law of Causation is a synthetic statement. Some would say that, if we allow these considerations to have weight, we thereby make it impossible to hold that the Law is also *a priori*; for it is sometimes argued that the expression '*a priori*' can only mean the very same as 'analytic', and hence that the expression 'synthetic *a priori*' is self-contradictory. This contention, however, is not acceptable. There may be reasons, even if not good reasons, for saying that some statements are synthetic *a priori*, and it is unhelpful, whatever suspicions we may have, to dismiss this suggestion at the outset as logically absurd; but also it is by no means obvious

[3] *Kant's Theory of Knowledge*, p. 300.

that 'analytic' and '*a priori*' do mean the same. Neither term is in fact quite unambiguous, but the first seems to be somewhat narrower than the second. Certainly, if we define the term 'analytic' so that only those sentences are rightly so called which can, with the help of definitions, be transformed into formal tautologies, it will be an error to hold that only analytic sentences are *a priori*. For there are sentences (e.g. 'Nothing can be red and green all over') which it would be natural and proper to regard as *a priori*—anyone who knows English knows that they are necessarily true—but which cannot be shown to be tautologous by the use of *definitions*. In a sense, certainly, they owe their necessary truth to linguistic rules; but the rules governing the use of 'red' and 'green' cannot be expressed as definitions. But quite apart from such cases as these, there are reasons for holding that 'analytic' and '*a priori*' do not mean the same. For to say of a statement that it is true *a priori* is to say that it can be seen or shown to be true without appeal to empirical evidence or tests; and though it might be that this could rightly be said only of expressions that are in fact analytic, still to say this would not be to say the very same thing as is said when we say that those expressions are analytic. I suggest, then, that those who say that the Law of Causation is, as well as a synthetic, an *a priori* truth, may be taken to mean that what it states about the course of nature can be seen to be true without appeal to empirical evidence; or perhaps (though this as will be seen is a very different matter) that we can see that no empirical evidence against it could be found. There is no denying that this is a curious claim. If the Law really tells us something about the course of nature, surely we must find out whether or not it is true by discovering what the course of nature actually is; and surely there must be something that could count against it—namely nature's not pursuing the course that the Law says that nature does in fact pursue. Certainly the claim is strange; but it is worth examining.

In what follows I shall try to show that, although there are considerations that might incline us to say that the Law of Causation is true *a priori*, these considerations in fact cancel completely the reasons that there seemed to be for saying that the Law was a synthetic statement. This is not to say that the expression 'synthetic *a priori*' is in general and in every case self-contradictory (though I think it is always unhelpful); it is only to say that, in the present instance, the case for applying the predicate 'synthetic' is destroyed by the case for applying the predicate '*a priori*'; there may be a case for each, but not for both at once.

VII

As a preliminary move it will be desirable to re-phrase the sentence 'Every event has a cause'. For this sentence has many rather misleading features, some of which (by no means all) it will be helpful here to eliminate. It is in particular, as has often been pointed out, misleading to suggest that for any event there is some *one* other event to be described, and alone described, as its cause. Suppose, for example, that I cause my house to collapse by improvidently removing an oak beam from the cellar. Although we should no doubt ordinarily say that it collapsed *because* I thus interfered with its structure, it is obvious enough that it would not have collapsed unless the whole house was actually so constructed as to depend for its stability upon this beam. It was thus not merely my removal of the beam which occasioned its collapse, but this removal combined with the other structural features of the house. A full account of the disaster would have to include an account of these other features, as well as the statement that the beam was removed—just as a full report on an outbreak of fire would have to include an account of the inflammable materials in the area and perhaps of the conditions of atmosphere, as well as the statement that a cigarette was dropped into a waste-paper basket. The event in question (the collapse, the outbreak of fire) occurred because certain quite complex conditions were present; from these we might, as we often do, pick out as *the* cause that which was brought about immediately before the event occurred, or (sometimes) that which was unusual. (It might be said that my house collapsed *when* I removed the beam *because* I had taken to storing several tons of books in the attic.) But not uncommonly it is pointless or impossible to

pick out any one occurrence as *the* cause of an event—not
because the event is random or inexplicable or mysterious,
but because there is no case for stressing any one in particular
of the numerous conditions sufficient for its occurrence. What
is important is that there should *be* conditions sufficient for
its occurrence, not that it should be always possible to select
some one of these as the single cause; and the statement that
every event has a cause does not, presumably, claim that this
is always possible. (If it did so it would be clearly synthetic,
and false.)

Suppose, then, that we re-write the sentence 'Every event
has a cause' in some such way as this: 'For any event E, there
is some set of antecedent conditions such that, whenever
these conditions obtain, an event of the kind E occurs.' (I
refer to this hereafter as S.)

This is still a comparatively unsophisticated formula, and
it might be criticized on various grounds which, however, are
here of no great importance. Some might say that it fails to
distinguish between causal and co-incidental connections—
might it not happen, by sheer coincidence, that whenever
certain conditions obtain a certain kind of event occurs? This
version allows also the possibility that more than one set of
conditions may be sufficient for the occurrence of some kinds
of events, and it might be held that ideally this should be
ruled out. It might also be said that, at least in some of the
sciences, there is no reason for being specially interested in
antecedent conditions; what we require are statements of
law permitting inference from any state of a given system at
any time to its state at any other time, with no special bias
towards prediction or interest in the future. It might be held,
too, that the vague word 'event' should be eliminated as ill-
suited to scientific exactitude. All these are reasonable points
in their way; but I think there is at present no reason why we
should seek to translate 'Every event has a cause' into a form
and vocabulary acceptable to scientists; for in the present
argument nothing turns on this. The version adopted above
will serve well enough, though I certainly would not deny
that it might be improved upon.

VIII

Suppose one were to ask how the alleged statement S is to be verified; this at once brings out one curious feature of it. First, it is in a comparatively ordinary way of unrestricted generality. It appears to make a statement about any and every event that ever occurred, occurs, or will occur. It might thus be thought that, while we have no doubt some reason for inclining to the view that S is true, we could not possibly have good reason for affirming positively that it is true. How could we rightly venture to make positive assertions about absolutely every event? But then there is worse still to come. For it will be seen that S also makes a statement of unrestricted generality about each of an unrestricted number of events—namely that for each event there are conditions such that, whenever they obtain, an event of that kind occurs. It would thus seem that causal statements really are, as all empirical statements were once supposed to be, indefinitely vulnerable to time. If we say that conditions ABC are sufficient for the occurrence of an event E (or that A, or B, or C, is the cause of E), what we say now will have to be retracted if at any time these conditions obtain and E does not occur. We can say 'There really was a telephone here, but now it's vanished'; we cannot say 'This was the cause of E, but now it isn't'. For to say that conditions ABC may now obtain and event E not occur is to admit that we were wrong in saying earlier that ABC were its sufficient conditions. It would thus appear that even particular causal statements are indefinitely exposed to falsification; far more so then the doubly general assertion that of every event some such statement could be truly made. By this line of argument we might be led to the view that it would be unpardonably rash, almost a mere act of faith, to affirm S with confidence; one can understand why this affirmation is made, but one cannot feel much confidence in its truth.

IX

But now there is quite another side to the case. Suppose that there are indefinitely many cats, and that someone says (of all cats there ever were, are, or will be) that every cat has a tail. Here we might say that there could hardly be good reason for accepting this statement with confidence as true—after all we can only actually inspect a finite and rather small number of cats. Furthermore, we have no difficulty in saying what would show this universal statement to be false—namely the discovery of a cat without a tail—and such a discovery might be made at any time. Now it was suggested in the previous paragraph that S, being of doubly unrestricted generality, is doubly and indefinitely exposed to the risk of falsification. Suppose then that we now raise the question what would have to occur in order to establish that S is false?

A verbal answer—'an uncaused event'—of course springs to mind. But this answer raises obvious difficulties. It is easy enough to imagine an event E, conditions sufficient for the occurrence of which have always been supposed to be ABC; and that some day these conditions may obtain and yet the event E does not occur. But clearly this has no tendency to falsify S. For it was said in S only that there are *some* conditions sufficient for the occurrence of any event; it was not specified what these conditions actually are in any instance, nor was it implied that anyone necessarily knows in any instance what conditions are sufficient. To say that there are some laws of nature does not imply that anyone knows, or indeed ever will know, what exactly they are. And thus the affirmation of S is compatible with the rejection of every particular statement of law, and every causal statement, that is or ever has been or will be asserted. If I say 'Someone now in this house has green hair', it can be shown that what I say is untrue; for everyone now in this house can be paraded and none observed to have green hair. But if I say 'There once was or is or will be, somewhere in the universe, a person who has green hair', I need never admit that I am wrong. For it could never be said that every part of the universe at every possible date had been inspected and found to contain no green-haired person. Similarly, if I were to say 'Some set of the conditions ABCDF is sufficient for the occurrence of E', it could be shown that I am mistaken. For all of the finite number of combinations could be tried and none found to be sufficient for the occurrence of E. But if I merely affirm that there are *some* conditions, and do not delimit the area of search for them at all, I need never admit that I am mistaken. For it could never be said that every conceivable factor and set of factors that might be conditions of E had been tried and rejected; and so it could always be said that the right combination of conditions had not yet been found.

Thus, there could never occur any event which it would be necessary, or even natural, to describe as an uncaused event. (There are of course events whose causes are not known.) It could never be said that among its complex and indefinitely numerous antecedents *none* could be said to be sufficient for its occurrence. And this is to say that nothing could occur which would require us to hold that S is false. Whatever occurred we might still affirm that S.

It is in this way that S resembles a tautology, an *a priori* truth. It is completely independent of the actual course of events, compatible with anything and everything that does or might happen. It calls indeed for no supporting empirical evidence, for none could count against it. It cannot be empirically tested, for no test could fail—or rather nothing could be made to count as a test. But, clearly enough, if these points were brought to support the contention that S is *a priori*, they would tell conclusively against the claim that it is synthetic. For if S can be affirmed whatever may be the course of events, it says nothing of what the course of events in fact is. It does not tell us what we shall find in our experience, for whatever we find we may assert it without fear of mistake. This is not to say, what I think is plainly untrue, that S is tautologous or analytic. It resembles a tautology in being compatible with any and every state of affairs; but it escapes the possibility of falsification not because it is necessary, but rather because it is vacuous. It is more like the assertion that there are invisible, intangible, odourless, soundless, and otherwise indetectable tigers in the garden—though

it is less conspicuously vacuous than this, the reasons for its
unfalsifiability being different and much less obvious.

X

All this, I think, shows that there must be something
wrong with, for example, the sort of argument that Kant
brings in favour of the view that S (or something like S) is
a synthetic *a priori* truth.[4] Very roughly, the argument is
that S lays down what is almost a defining property of human experience—unless it were the case that every event has
a cause, our experience would be so unimaginably different
that we could not think or speak about it in any way, there
would merely be chaos and confusion. Thus, it might be
contended, the fact that we can *say* that every event has a
cause, and be understood, itself shows that what we say is
actually the case; for if it were not, neither this nor anything
else could intelligibly be said. This sort of argument is, I
believe, an exaggeration of something interesting and important. It is true that if there were *too many* random, inexplicable, quite unforeseeable happenings, we should find ourselves
not merely in practical but also in linguistic difficulties. If,
for example, it were the case that objects frequently changed
colour in a seemingly quite random manner, we could no
longer say what colour things really were, but only what
colour they looked at some particular time; and this would be
a nuisance, particularly in cases where colour is a criterion
of identity. (There would then be no Cabbage Whites or
Scarlet Ramblers.) And we could not say with confidence
'This is an apple' unless we could be sure that the object of
which we spoke would behave and respond to treatment as
apples do. What this shows, however, is that we could not
speak and act as we do if there were *too much* disorder and
chaos in our environment; it does not show that we could
not tolerate any at all. Nor, of course, does it show that it
must be *true* that every event has a cause; for, as we have
seen, to affirm that S is compatible with any sort of happenings whatever. We would presumably be unable to speak and

[4] *Critique of Pure Reason*, Second Analogy.

act as we now do if, though there were in fact conditions sufficient for the occurrence of any event, these conditions were too complex or too numerous for us to discover them. A world whose behaviour could only be rightly described in statements of law too complicated for us to formulate or comprehend would be, for our purposes, every bit as intractable as a world whose behaviour was merely random and chaotic—it would in fact be indistinguishable from such a world. There are, no doubt, some statements of fact about the world which would only be falsified by some radical change in the whole character of our experience; and it may be that some of these statements state conditions essential to the use of language (or at least to the use of any languages now used). If so, there will indeed be certain statements which, if they can be uttered at all, are thereby verified; for if their contradictories were true they could not be said. But the supposed statement that every event has a cause cannot rightly be regarded as a statement of this kind. It lays down no essential conditions; for it lays down nothing.

XI

The suggestion that the expression 'Every event has a cause' is—owing to the impossibility of describing any circumstance that could show it to be false—vacuous and utterly uninformative, may well cause some dissatisfaction. There is a natural feeling that it does say something, and furthermore something of the greatest importance. However, this feeling arises, I believe, from confusion. There are indeed certain matters of importance that abut, so to speak, on the territory of the Law of Causation; but these important matters are its neighbours, not identical with it, nor yet are they its dependants. And thus they need neither be ignored nor rejected when the Law itself is accused of vacuousness.

It is, first of all, a patently important fact that there are many people nowadays who do seek for statements of law, who do not attempt to understand, control, or alter the course of events entirely by prayers or spells or ritual performances, and who do not merely wait indifferently for what may occur. This is an important, synthetic and true state-

ment about what many people actually do. If they did not do
this or did not do it with conviction, we might properly (not
by saying 'Every event has a cause') urge or encourage them
to persist in their inquiries. It is a different but equally important synthetic true statement that those who seek to
formulate statements of law meet with considerable, and on
the whole with constantly increasing, success. (Human beings
might have been much less intelligent, and the course of
events might have been much more complicated.) But to say
that for every event there are some conditions sufficient for
its occurrence is clearly not to say that people often succeed
in discovering them, nor is it to say that none will constantly
elude discovery; to say that every crime is committed by
somebody is not to say that no criminals go undetected nor
to say that the record of the police force is good. Again, to
say that correct statements of law are 'simple' is clearly to
say something synthetic; and as the physicists multiply 'fundamental particles' it may well cease to be regarded as true.
(A single sort of 'corpuscle' or 'atom' is not, of course, nowadays thought to be enough for all purposes). It is also synthetic to say of natural laws that they are spatially and
temporally invariant; and this also, I believe, is no longer universally taken to be the case. And that the sufficient conditions
for any event are to be found within a certain limited area
of space and among some quite small number of possibilities,
though usually and no doubt reasonably assumed, is also
clearly not necessarily true.

These, then, are some of the important matters which
belong in the same area as the Law of Causation; and there
are no doubt others. I believe that those who attach fundamental importance to the so-called Rule of Law often have
in mind some of these, and do not mean merely to utter the
vacuous phrase that 'every event has a cause'. Or rather they
do not think of this phrase as vacuous. It suggests that the
universe is like a well-ordered house where everything runs
exactly to plan and up to time; there is nothing just random
and therefore unintelligible; what seems inexplicable will one
day be explained. Certainly there is, as a rule, an important
disagreement between one who says, and one who denies, that
every event has a cause; they *intend* at any rate, to state dif-

ferent things. But what they actually *say* cannot be plausibly represented as stating any of the important facts mentioned in the last paragraph; and confusion is apt to result from not noticing this. For whereas these facts are indeed important and interesting, they are not necessary facts; and if we confuse them with the vacuous Law of Causation, we may come to attach to them, with resulting bewilderment, the property of being invulnerable to falsification which properly attaches alone to that vacuous Law.

XII

In conclusion, and with some trepidation, I must say something of the 'indeterminacy principle'; for it has often been said that, here at any rate, we find something that counts against the Law of Causation. It is extremely difficult for those who are not physicists to come to grips with this perplexing affair; and physicists often seem to feel a similar difficulty. The suggestion that I would offer is merely this—that although certain features of quantum physics might make it even more than usually *pointless* to insist that every event has a cause, they could not establish that this is actually a false statement. To support this I submit the following considerations. It may be that, given certain conditions, it is sometimes impossible for us actually to predict what will occur; and this may be a theoretical and not a merely practical difficulty. It may be (and this is really the same point again) that the determination of a certain quantity theoretically precludes us from determining another; and perhaps in this case we should even refuse to speak of both quantities as being determinate—what point is there in this if we cannot discover both? However, this is not to say that, given certain conditions, sometimes one thing and sometimes another occurs; it is only to say that we cannot discover whether or not this is so nor what will occur; and hence perhaps we refuse to regard the question as a proper one. But one who says that for any event at all there are some conditions sufficient for its occurrence, need not assert, as we have already seen, that anyone does or could know what these conditions are; and he need not hold that every event is in fact, or even in theory, predictable. Perhaps then he is, though doubtless rightly ignored, not flatly refuted by the contemporary physicist. If he is prepared to speak of what admittedly cannot be experimentally tested, he may remain invulnerable. I need hardly say that no great value attaches to this type of invulnerability; but I would suggest that the Law of Causation is vacuous enough to elude the attack even of this unusual and well-armed opponent. It escapes, indeed, by way of saying something that cannot in any way be tested; but it says no more than this in any case, and thus only exhibits in this unfamiliar field the same peculiarity on which it trades elsewhere. To say that the Law can be refuted *here* is to imply that elsewhere it might have been but is not; I have tried to show, however, that nowhere at all does it run the risk of refutation.

VII

Incompatibilities of Colours

D. F. PEARS

The sentence 'Nothing can be red and green all over' expresses a very striking incompatibility. Few would deny that it is necessarily true or *a priori*. For if it were contingent or *a posteriori* one could look for exceptions. But anyone who began to look for exceptions would betray that he did not really understand the sentence. But why is it necessarily true? Some say that the reason is that it is analytic, claiming that all necessary truths are analytic. And since an analytic sentence is either a truth of logic or else reducible to a truth of logic by means of a definition, this is a fairly clear explanation. Others say that the reason is that it is a synthetic necessary truth, refusing to allow that all necessary truths are analytic. The positive meaning of this is sometimes taken to be that the sentence states a principle of natural necessity; which is obscure. Negatively it is always taken to mean at least that the sentence is necessarily true and yet not analytic; which, being the denial of a fairly clear thesis, is less obscure.

But perhaps the sentence is neither analytic nor synthetic. This suggestion has much to recommend it. It is diplomatic, and it avoids both the obscurity of principles of natural necessity and the implausibility of alleged definitions of 'red' or 'green'.[1] Another of its advantages is that it commends itself to common sense. For there is something very academic about the fierce debate whether the sentence owes its necessary truth to the way things behave or to the way words behave, to nature or to convention. It would seem more sensible to say that neither of these two answers is quite adequate; rather that the sentence is necessarily true because the words 'red' and 'green' pick out two classes which just do not overlap. One could say that this lack of overlap is the result of the way in which the two words are used: but since the two words pick out two classes of things, one could say equally well that it is the result of the nature of the things. Each of these two answers emphasizes one aspect of the truth. But perhaps emphasis on either side is a mistake; perhaps the culprit is neither convention alone nor nature alone.

This suggestion, however correct, is not adequate as it stands. It would not satisfy everyone who was puzzled by the problem. Some, after considering it, would re-open the question by protesting: 'But if it is neither analytic nor synthetic what is it? If nature and convention conspire to produce this necessary truth, then it ought to be both synthetic and analytic. But that is nonsense.' To answer this, more is needed.

What is needed as a supplement might be an account of the way we use, and learn to use, colour words. But there are grounds for thinking that a more technical approach to the problem is advisable. After all, the problem emerged because a useful technique was over-worked. Accordingly this

[1] Few words are given full definitions in dictionaries, but 'red' and 'green' could not be, since they are words which are necessarily taught almost entirely by examples.

discussion may well begin almost historically, taking over the technique, and making it its first task to explain the necessary truth of the sentence, if possible, within the traditional framework, without falling back on the obscure thesis that a principle of natural necessity is involved.

Since no definition of 'red' exists the first thing to do is to try to invent one; or rather to invent a fragment of one, to the effect that 'red' means among other things 'not green'. Next the situation can be exhibited schematically. One might say that the word 'red' is connected with red things by a designatory rule; and that the word 'green' is connected with green things by another, parallel designatory rule. This can be illustrated by a simple diagram of four dots arranged in a square, the two top corners being occupied by the two words, and the two lower corners being occupied by the two groups of things. Then the two vertical sides can be sketched in immediately to represent the two designatory rules. And the problem becomes: which of the two horizontal sides should be sketched in? Those who say that the sentence is analytic would sketch in the top side with a verbal rule to the effect that 'red' means among other things 'not green': while those who say that it is a synthetic necessary truth usually wish to sketch in the lower side with a principle of natural necessity.

Now there is a well-known, simple treatment which is sometimes successful with such recalcitrant sentences. For instance an entomologist who said that all Large White butterflies have two black patches on each forewing might be asked whether his statement was analytic or synthetic. Perhaps he would be unable to answer until he was told that any given use of the sentence could not be both, and which it was would depend on how the species was defined. Then he might be unwilling to answer, on the ground that he did not need to decide whether this was a defining characteristic of the species or not. If specimens with three black patches began to occur, he might say at first that they were a variety or aberration. Only if they bred true would he be likely to claim the discovery of a new species. But even about this he would prefer not to commit himself in advance. Meanwhile his answer would be that the sentence was certainly not both analytic and synthetic at once, and which it was did not matter for the moment. And this would be a perfectly satisfactory answer. One would understand the two alternatives, and also the reason for leaving the choice between them open.

But unfortunately this simple treatment will not work here. For it is not merely that 'not green' is not part of an existing definition of 'red'. Nor is it merely that one does not want to decide in advance whether or not to accept it as part of a newly invented definition. The trouble is that one does not understand what difference its acceptance would make. And since one does not understand this, one is not confronted with a genuine choice. And this is a serious difficulty. For those who say that the sentence is analytic claim that it owes its necessary truth to a verbal rule. But the suggested verbal rule seems to make no difference since, without it, the sentence already seems to be necessarily true. And it seems that this can only be because the lower side of the square is already occupied by a principle of natural necessity.

It is worth emphasizing that the failure of the simple treatment is not the result of a wildly implausible appeal to conventions. Those who say that the sentence is analytic do not suggest that it owes its necessary truth to a verbal rule which is conventional in the trivial sense in which 'yellow' might mean what 'red' now means if we adopted this different convention. For it could not matter what word was written in at the top left-hand corner, since one word at the top left-hand corner would have the same meaning as another substituted for it there, and the point at issue is how any word at the top left-hand corner gets its meaning. What they suggest is, at most, that if the sentence rested merely on the two designatory rules it would be contingent: but that in that case it would be such an excellent contingent sentence, never in fact falsified, that we might as well make it analytic by adding the verbal rule; and that this verbal rule, though conventional, would be well chosen, not all conventions being capricious.

The reason for the failure of the simple treatment is that the convention is so well chosen that it seems to make no difference at all. And the explanation of this seems to be that the lower side of the square is already occupied by a principle of natural necessity.

However, there is a possible alternative explanation. Perhaps the two designatory rules are alone sufficient to ensure the necessary truth of the sentence, so that there is no need to sketch in either the top or the lower side of the square. This solution is a fuller development of the one suggested at the beginning. If it is correct, it is a mistake to suggest that the sentence would be contingent unless either a verbal rule or a principle of natural necessity were added. The sentence will owe its necessary truth simply to the two designatory rules.

The way in which this comes about is hard to describe. Certainly it would be a mistake to describe it by saying that the sentence is analytic, since no non-ostensive definition is involved. So, if all other sentences were synthetic, it would follow that this one is synthetic: and, since it is necessary, it would be a synthetic necessary truth. But it is unwise to say this: partly because many have meant something more by it, namely that there is here a principle of natural necessity; and partly because synthetic sentences are usually taken not to include any which are true solely because of the meanings of their words. And this sentence is true solely because of the meanings of its words, and so necessarily true. For anyone who contradicted it would betray, without any possibility of an alternative plea, that he did not know the meanings of its words. But this does not imply that an alteration in language would bring about an alteration in things or that the total extinction of all speakers of all languages would effect the abolition of the differences between things. That would be an absurd error.

With equal correctness one might say that it is necessarily true because the two classes of things necessarily differ. For this description of the situation is precisely equivalent to the other. But those who adopt it must beware of a danger. It is fatally easy to talk carelessly about things in a way which suggests that they stand out there already labelled in a way which indicates their properties. And this illusion may be a source of the probably mistaken view that there is here a principle of natural necessity.[2] Of course things are what they are, and differ from one another because they possess the properties which they do possess. But to say that two classes of things necessarily differ is not only to SAY something, but also to DO something. The two classes of things can be said to differ necessarily only because they have been picked out, in the saying, by two words according to designatory rules which ensure just that. One refers airily to THE two classes, as if one could say WHICH two classes without using the words.

This crucial point is the tautology that we cannot name a class without naming it. But it is none the worse for being a tautology. It needs stating because its importance is so easily forgotten. Both geologists and philosophers can describe the world with no people in it. But geologists, who are interested only in the things in such a world, need not ask themselves how their describing was done: whereas philosophers do ask themselves just this question, and so cannot keep themselves out of their inquiry. This difference is easily overlooked, and the tautology keeps it in view.

The tautology can be generalized so as to apply not only to naming but also to thinking. One cannot think about a class without thinking about it. And if, for instance, such thinking needs a concept, then the concept will pick out the class in much the same way that the name picked it out. And the same can be said of images, and of any other suggested instrument of thought. The point is not restricted to language, but quite general.

It is particularly important here, because one cannot say anything very informative about the meanings of 'red' and 'green', but can only offer examples. But when a man shows the meaning of such a word by examples, what are the examples examples of? All one can answer is that they are ex-

---

[2] It would not be a mistaken view if it merely saw as real the same necessity which can be seen as verbal at least equally well, and if even such analytic sentences as 'A flower cannot be a butterfly' were included among the principles of natural necessity. And why not? It is things that we sort, even when we can explain how we sort them. But this extended use of the phrase would rob it of whatever point it is intended to convey.

amples of that feature in them in virtue of which the word is applied to them. This may sound as if it said something further; but it does not, since it is circular. Now the two words 'red' and 'green' pick out two classes of things which necessarily differ. How do they necessarily differ? One can only offer pairs of examples. But what are the pairs of examples examples of? All one can say is that they are examples of that difference between them in virtue of which the two words are applied to them. This is circular in the same way. But those who do not clearly realize that it is circular slip easily into thinking that they have found an additional necessary difference over and above the necessary difference which is the result of the way in which the two words pick out the pairs of things. And this would be an illusion, the illusion of taking the same necessary difference twice over, once in the words and once in the things, and thinking that there were really two necessary differences. And perhaps this illusion is a source of the claim to have found a principle of natural necessity.

So long as all these errors are avoided by both sides, it does not matter which description of the situation is adopted, that which talks about words or that which talks about things. Then is the suggested solution, these errors having been removed, acceptable as it now stands?

One thing which recommends it is that it explains the emergence of the problem and its protracted discussion (which may stand in need of explanation in the future). For initial success in showing that many necessary truths are analytic naturally encouraged the hope that this might be done for all necessary truths. Consequently, when recalcitrant necessary truths like this one were encountered, it was felt that further analysis would discover some elusive verbal rule more convincing than the one already produced, which would show that the sentence was after all analytic. But since 'red' and 'green' are not further analysable, the discovery was not likely to be made. Yet such was the prestige of the technique that some persisted in the hopeless quest, while others announced their refusal to accept anything which might be found. And all the time it was the technique which was at fault. Either it ought to have been admitted that some neces-

sary truths, resting on unexpandible designatory rules, are
not analytic. Or else the use of ostensive definitions ought
to have been allowed in the reduction of analytic sentences
to truths of logic, so that these outlying cases could be taken
in. (But, though the spirit of this second alternative can be
understood, literally it is unintelligible, since qualities cannot appear in logic books instead of adjectives, any more
than railway journeys can be stacked in automatic machines
instead of tickets.)

However, the suggested solution is not acceptable as it
stands. For it is inadequate in ways which there is not space
to correct fully.

First of all there is something specially mysterious about
this necessary truth which rests on designatory rules which
cannot be expanded verbally. This can be illustrated by a
series of examples arranged progressively.

About designatory rules which can be expanded verbally
there is no mystery. The entomologist can name Large White
butterflies, and in doing so follows a designatory rule. But he
can also expand this designatory rule by stating their defining
characteristics in verbal rules. And, as in the case already considered, by adopting new verbal rules he can alter the original
designatory rule.

Nor is there much mystery about designatory rules which
can be expanded only in a language of signs. For imagine
some primitive hunter who slew mammoths of two closely
resembling species and correctly sorted them into two heaps.
Suppose that he had names for the two species, but not for
their *differentiae*. Then he could teach an apprentice the
difference between the two species only by producing pairs
of examples. Would what the hunter acquired and handed
on to his apprentice be for them a synthetic necessary truth?
There is a slight inducement to give an affirmative answer,
because, unlike the entomologist, they could not expand their
designatory rules verbally. But the inducement is very slight,
since if they noticed the *differentiae* they could do something almost as good. The teacher could point to the *dif-
ferentia* in a specimen of one kind, then name the other
species, and then shake his head and grind his teeth. And

this would be almost as effective as stating the incompatibility of the possession of a certain property with membership of a certain class. The problem under discussion is not narrowly linguistic: it concerns any symbol or instrument of thought which can be made to stand for any class of things.

But now take a case where there is some mystery. A man sips two kinds of port and notices a difference between the two flavours. He may learn names for them, and assent to the proposition that they cannot both be present in the same sip, and yet he may be unable to expand his two designatory rules verbally. And this might not be the result merely of a deficient vocabulary. For there might not be anything separately noticeable in each flavour which made it the flavour that it was. Would the proposition to which he assented be for him a synthetic necessary truth? An affirmative answer is more likely here, since these two designatory rules are quite unexpandible.

Finally the necessary truth about the two colours, red and green, is even more mysterious. The colours, like the flavours, contain no separately noticeable marks. But this simplicity is more unexpected in the case of the colours, and so more baffling. It is more unexpected because sight is a successful, organizing sense, and most words for seen qualities find their places in elaborate logical networks. Also colours, unlike flavours, can be pointed to, and one is surprised by the discovery that there is a limit beyond which pointing cannot select from within a quality further separate marks of that quality. Also sight is so sharp that colours are as finely apprehended as objects, almost as if they too were independent objects:[3] and one feels that objects ought to carry separately noticeable marks. But, whatever explanations of this mysteriousness are produced, will they not all serve only to remove a strong prejudice against the view that this necessary truth rests squarely on two unexpandible designatory rules, and so leave

[3] Not physically independent as flavours and smells are physically independent of the objects that emit them: the independence meant is of a different kind, the kind which won for colours names of their own, while many flavours and smells have to borrow the names of the objects that emit them.

us free to say that the two classes are different because that
is how we pick them?[4]

A second inadequacy of the suggested solution is that it
was not quite correct to say that there is no need for the
verbal rule that 'red' means among other things 'not green'.
Admittedly, if someone who had learnt the meanings of the
two words by examples were asked whether the rule was valid,
he would answer IMMEDIATELY that it was, and add that the
question was a silly one. And it would be a silly question to
ask him, since nobody who had learnt the meanings of the
two words by examples would be in any danger of contravening the rule. Such a person would feel that it need not be
included in his lesson. For it is usually a waste of time to
indicate what a thing is not AFTER indicating what it is, unless
a confusion is likely. He would not feel this so strongly if
the two colours were red and orange: since the same person
might well call the same thing in the same light at one time
red and at another time orange (provided that he did not
know that it was the same thing in the same light, and so
that he was being inconsistent). But with complementary
colours, like red and green, this possibility is remote. Nevertheless, it remains true that someone who contravened the
verbal rule would betray that he had not really learnt his lesson. So perhaps it is unnecessary to enunciate it only because
it is so necessary to have obeyed it already.

But there is a difficulty here. Possibly someone who called
a thing red and green all over would not be contravening
THAT verbal rule. He might be making a mistake not about
the meanings of the two colour words, but about the meaning
of 'all over' or of 'uniform surface colour'. A few examples
will show that, if anyone with a normal experience of the
full range of colours said this extraordinary thing, it would
be more natural to assume that his mistake was of this other
kind. Only a perverse inference would lead such a person to
say it about roses seen through green glasses, or about a mix-
ture of red and green paints. But he might say it more reasonably about green buses shining in the reflected light of

---

[4] OBJECTION: 'Absurd! Suppose they were not picked by anybody?' REJOINDER: 'Then which would THEY be?'

red buses, or about the green glint of red ink, or about the sheen on shot silk or on a dove's throat. And if he did, it would be natural to correct him by explaining depths of colour, or by explaining the fragmentation of some fields of colour and showing him a butterfly's wing under a microscope.

However, someone who had experienced only a restricted range of colours might really be in danger of contravening such verbal rules about colour words. A child might be taught by examples the meaning of 'red' without ever seeing anything green. Would it really know what red was before it was confronted with green which it was not? The best way to decide this would seem to be to see whether it called its first green thing red. If it did, then it could not have known what 'red' meant in spite of its previous success. But if it refused to call it red, it would not FOLLOW that it did know previously what 'red' meant. It might be said to have known previously that red was not any other colour; but this knowledge would be very thin until it was filled out by actual experience of several other colours. But when the only main experience lacking was that of green, one would be very reluctant to say that, even if tomorrow it will say that a green thing is not red, still today it does not yet really know the meaning of 'red'. The totality of colours, when learnt, form a system, and so it seems impossible fully to learn one colour without learning at least some of the others (the extreme case is the complete impossibility of learning one in a monochrome world). But it does not seem necessary to learn all the others: partly because, when a child has learnt two or three colours, it can learn the meaning of 'colour', and so perhaps of 'other colour';[5] and partly because lessons in individual colours do not impart isolated and fully developed blocks of knowledge, and, if a child does not call its first green thing red, this may

[5] Nobody would be surprised if a child achieved this. It is describing the achievement by stages which is difficult. For colour has no abstractible GENERIC mark: it is a concrete universal smoothly built into either red or green or one of its other species. Hence one can make oneself unable to understand the question 'Could a completely new colour be discovered?'

be because its lessons enable it to make later discoveries about what in a way it knew before.

This partial reinstatement of the verbal rule seems to re-open the whole case. But the correction of the third inadequacy of the suggested solution may help to keep it closed.

Its third inadequacy is that it is too schematic in what it says about rules. For the way children learn is enough to show that verbal rules are not as numerous as it seems to assume. But this is not a very important point: philosophers often have to state precisely what is seldom stated, even vaguely. Also, what is more important, there are no designatory rules which cannot be expanded verbally; since something which cannot be expanded verbally cannot be a rule (for instance ' "Shrill" means shrill'). And this is not just a terminological point. Calling them rules suggests wrongly that they do take analysis one stage further, in the way in which only genuine rules can, and this false suggestion may be a source of the claim that a principle of natural necessity is involved. Finally the most important fault of the schematism is that it implied that the two designatory rules are independent of the verbal rule. The falsity of this has emerged in the subsequent discussion. One does not first study examples, and then QUITE SEPARATELY learn the incompatibility. This point is worth emphasizing, since in a way it is the schema that generates the problem. If the two designatory rules were independent of the verbal rule, and if one could adopt the verbal rule without fear of having to alter either of the designatory rules, surely this could only be because there is here a principle of natural necessity?

The adoption of a misleading schematism needs some defence. Two excuses may be given for it. Without it, the emergence of the problem and its protracted discussion would go unexplained. Also, without it, both the problem and its solution might be lost from view in an apparently aimless discussion of colour words. The schema secures historical continuity, and, like scaffolding which in the end will be dismantled, it enables the case to be built up visibly in the traditional way which made its satisfactory completion seem impossible.

VIII

Other Minds

J. L. AUSTIN

[This paper was written as the second part of a Symposium, the whole of which was originally printed in the *Proceedings of the Aristotelian Society*, Supplementary Volume XX, in 1946. It is reprinted here without significant alteration. The first part, by Mr.—now Professor—John Wisdom, was a distillation of his very long and never concluded series of articles on 'Other Minds', which appeared in *Mind* from 1940 onwards. As this series, including the first part of the symposium, is now available separately (Wisdom, J., *Other Minds*, Basil Blackwell, 1952), Professor Wisdom's paper is not included here. I hope that—with the help of the footnotes I have added—Professor Austin's paper will be entirely intelligible even though torn out of context. If it is not the fault is wholly mine—EDITOR.]

I feel that I agree with much, and especially with the more important parts, of what Mr. Wisdom has written, both in his present paper and in his beneficial series of articles on 'Other Minds' and other matters. I feel ruefully sure, also, that one must be at least one sort of fool to rush in over ground so well trodden by the angels. At best I can hope only to make a contribution to one part of the problem, where it seems that a little more industry still might be of service. I could only wish it was a more central part. In fact, however, I did find myself unable to approach the centre while still bogged down on the periphery. And Mr. Wisdom himself may perhaps be sympathetic towards a policy of splitting hairs to save starting them.

Mr. Wisdom, no doubt correctly, takes the 'Predicament' to be brought on by such questions as 'How do we know that another man is angry?' He also cites other forms of the question—'Do we (ever) know?', 'Can we know?', 'How can we know?' the thoughts, feelings, sensations, mind, etc., of another creature, and so forth. But it seems likely that each of these further questions is rather different from the first, which alone has been enough to keep me preoccupied, and to which I shall stick.

Mr. Wisdom's method is to go on to ask: *Is it like the way in which we know* that a kettle is boiling, or that there's a tea-party next door, or the weight of thistledown? But it seemed to me that perhaps, as he went on, he was not giving an altogether accurate account (perhaps only because too cursory a one) of what we should say if asked 'How do you know?' these things. For example, in the case of the tea-party, to say we knew of it 'by analogy' would at best be a very sophisticated answer (and one to which some sophisticates might prefer the phrase 'by induction'), while in addition it seems incorrect because we don't, I think, claim to *know* by analogy, but only to *argue* by analogy. Hence I was led on to consider what sort of thing does actually happen when ordinary people are asked 'How do you know?'

Much depends, obviously, on the sort of item it is about which we are being asked 'How do you know?' and there are bound to be many kinds of case that I shall not cover at all, or not in detail. The sort of statement which seems simplest, and at the same time not, on the face of it, unlike 'He is angry', is such a statement as 'That is a goldfinch' ('The kettle is boiling')—a statement of particular, current, empirical fact. This is the sort of statement on making which we are liable to be asked 'How do you know?' and the sort that, at least sometimes, we say we don't know, but only believe. It may serve for a stalking horse as well as another.

When we make an assertion such as 'There is a goldfinch in the garden' or 'He is angry', there is a sense in which we imply that we are sure of it or know it ('But I took it you *knew*', said reproachfully), though what we imply, in a similar sense and more strictly, is only that we *believe* it. On making such an assertion, therefore, we are directly exposed to the questions (1) 'Do you *know* there is?' 'Do you *know* he is?' and (2) 'How do you know?' If in answer to the first question we reply 'Yes', we may then be asked the second ques-

tion, and even the first question alone is commonly taken as
an invitation to state not merely *whether* but also *how* we
know. But on the other hand, we may well reply 'No' in
answer to the first question: we may say, 'No, but I think
there is', 'No, but I believe he is'. For the implication that
I know or am sure is not strict: we are not all (terribly or
sufficiently) strictly brought up. If we do this, then we are
exposed to the question, which might also have been put to
us without preliminaries, 'Why do you believe that?' (or
'What makes you think so?' 'What induces you to suppose
so?', etc.).

There is a singular difference between the two forms of
challenge: '*How* do you know?' and '*Why* do you believe?'
We seem never to ask '*Why* do you know?' or '*How* do you
believe?' And in this, as well as in other respects to be noticed later, not merely such other words as 'suppose', 'assume',
etc., but also the expressions 'be sure' and 'be certain', follow
the example of 'believe', not that of 'know'.

Either question, 'How do you know?' or 'Why do you believe?', may well be asked only out of respectful curiosity,
from a genuine desire to learn. But again, they may both be
asked as *pointed* questions, and, when they are so, a further
difference comes out. 'How do you know?' suggests that perhaps you *don't* know it at all, whereas 'Why do you believe?'
suggests that perhaps you *oughtn't* to believe it. There is no
suggestion[1] that you *ought* not to know or that you *don't*
believe it. If the answer to 'How do you know?' or to 'Why
do you believe?' is considered unsatisfactory by the chal-
lenger, he proceeds rather differently in the two cases. His
next riposte will be, on the one hand, something such as
'Then you *don't* know any such thing', or 'But that doesn't
prove it: in that case you don't really know it at all', and on
the other hand, something such as 'That's very poor evidence
to go on: you oughtn't to believe it on the strength of that
alone'.[2]

---

[1] But in special senses and cases, there is—e.g., if someone has
announced some top secret information, we can ask 'How do *you*
know?', nastily.

[2] An interesting variant in the case of knowing would be 'You
oughtn't to say (you've no business to say) you know it at all'. But

The 'existence' of your alleged belief is not challenged, but the 'existence' of your alleged knowledge *is* challenged. If we like to say that 'I believe', and likewise 'I am sure' and 'I am certain', are descriptions of subjective mental or cognitive states or attitudes, or what not, then 'I know' is not that, or at least not merely that: it functions differently in talking.

'But of course', it will be said, ' "I know" is obviously more than that, more than a description of my own state. If I *know*, I *can't be wrong*. You can always show I don't know by showing I am wrong, or may be wrong, or that I didn't know by showing that I might have been wrong. *That's* the way in which knowing differs even from being as certain as can be.' This must be considered in due course, but first we should consider the types of answer that may be given in answer to the question 'How do you know?'

Suppose I have said 'There's a bittern at the bottom of the garden', and you ask 'How do you know?' my reply may take very different forms:

(*a*)   I was brought up in the Fens
(*b*)   I heard it
(*c*)   The keeper reported it
(*d*)   By its booming
(*e*)   From the booming noise
(*f*)   Because it's booming.

We may say, roughly, that the first three are answers to the questions 'How do you come to know?' 'How are you in a position to know?' or 'How do *you* know?' understood in different ways: while the other three are answers to 'How can you tell?' understood in different ways. That is, I may take you to have been asking:

(1)   How do I come to be in a position to know about bitterns?
(2)   How do I come to be in a position to say there's a bittern here and now?

---

of course this is only superficially similar to 'You oughtn't to believe it': you ought *to say* you believe it, if you do believe it, however poor the evidence.

(3)   How do (can) I tell bitterns?

(4)   How do (can) I tell the thing here and now as a
        bittern?

The implication is that in order to know this is a bittern, I
must have

(1)   been trained in an environment where I could be-
        come familiar with bitterns

(2)   had a certain opportunity in the current case

(3)   learned to recognize or tell bitterns

(4)   succeeded in recognizing or telling this as a bittern.

(1) and (2) mean that my experiences must have been of
certain kinds, that I must have had certain opportunities:
(3) and (4) mean that I must have exerted a certain kind
and amount of acumen.[3]

The questions raised in (1) and (3) concern our *past* experiences, our opportunities and our activities in learning to
discriminate or discern, and, bound up with both, the correctness or otherwise of the linguistic usages, we have acquired. Upon these earlier experiences depends how *well* we
know things, just as, in different but cognate cases of 'knowing', it is upon earlier experience that it depends how *thoroughly* or how *intimately* we know: we know a person by sight
or intimately, a town inside out, a proof backwards, a job in
every detail, a poem word for word, a Frenchman when we
see one. 'He doesn't know what love (real hunger) is' means
he hasn't had enough experience to be able to recognize it
and to distinguish it from other things slightly like it. According to how well I know an item, and according to the kind
of item it is, I can recognize it, describe it, reproduce it,
draw it, recite it, apply it, and so forth. Statements like 'I
know *very well* he isn't angry' or 'You know *very well* that
isn't calico', though of course about the current case, ascribe

---

[3] 'I know, I *know*, I've seen it a hundred times, don't keep on
telling me' complains of a superabundance of opportunity: 'knowing
a hawk from a handsaw' lays down a minimum of acumen in recognition or classification. 'As well as I know my own name' is said to
typify something I *must* have experienced and *must* have learned
to discriminate.

the excellence of the knowledge to past experience, as does
the general expression 'You are old enough to know better'.[4]

By contrast, the questions raised in (2) and (4) concern
the circumstances of the current case. Here we can ask 'How
definitely do you know?' You may know it for certain, quite
positively, officially, on his own authority, from unimpeacha-
ble sources, only indirectly, and so forth.

Some of the answers to the question 'How do you know?'
are, oddly enough, described as 'reasons for knowing' or 'reasons to know', or even sometimes as 'reasons why I know',
despite the fact that we do not ask 'Why do you know?'
But now surely, according to the Dictionary, 'reasons' should
be given in answer to the question 'Why?' just as we do in
fact give reasons for believing in answer to the question 'Why
do you believe?' However, there is a distinction to be drawn
here. 'How do you know that IG Farben worked for war?' 'I
have every reason to know: I served on the investigating
commission': here, giving my reasons for knowing is stating
how I come to be in a position to know. In the same way we
use the expressions 'I know *because* I saw him do it' or 'I
know *because* I looked it up only ten minutes ago': these
are similar to 'So it is: it *is* plutonium. How did you know?'
'I did quite a bit of physics at school before I took up philology', or to 'I ought to know: I was standing only a couple
of yards away'. Reasons for *believing* on the other hand are
normally quite a different affair (a recital of symptoms, arguments in support, and so forth), though there are cases
where we do give as reasons for believing our having been in
a position in which we could get good evidence: 'Why do
you believe he was lying?' 'I was watching him very closely.'

Among the cases where we give our reasons for knowing
things, a special and important class is formed by those where
we cite authorities. If asked 'How do you know the election
is today?', I am apt to reply 'I read it in *The Times*', and
if asked 'How do you know the Persians were defeated at

<hr>

[4] The adverbs that can be inserted in 'How . . . do you know?'
are few in number and fall into still fewer classes. There is practically
no overlap with those that can be inserted in 'How . . . do you
believe?' (firmly, sincerely, genuinely, etc.).

Marathon?', I am apt to reply 'Herodotus expressly states that they were'. In these cases 'know' is correctly used: we know 'at second hand' when we can cite an authority who was in a position to know (possibly himself also only at second hand).[5] The statement of an authority makes me aware of something, enables me to know something, which I shouldn't otherwise have known. It is a source of knowledge. In many cases, we contrast such reasons for knowing with other reasons for believing the very same thing: 'Even if we didn't know it, even if he hadn't confessed, the evidence against him would be enough to hang him.'

It is evident, of course, that this sort of 'knowledge' is 'liable to be wrong', owing to the unreliability of human testimony (bias, mistake, lying, exaggeration, etc.). Nevertheless, the occurrence of a piece of human testimony radically alters the situation. We say 'We shall never know what Caesar's feelings were on the field of the battle of Philippi', because he did not pen an account of them: *if* he *had*, then to say 'We shall never know' won't do in the same way, even though we may still perhaps find reason to say 'It doesn't read very plausibly: we shall never *really* know the *truth*' and so on. Naturally, we are judicious: we don't say we know (at second hand) if there is any special reason to doubt the testimony: but there has to be *some* reason. It is fundamental in talking (as in other matters) that we are entitled to trust others, except in so far as there is some concrete reason to distrust them. Believing persons, accepting testimony, is the, or one main, point of talking. We don't play (competitive) games except in the faith that our opponent is trying to win: if he isn't, it isn't a game, but something

[5] Knowing at second hand, or on authority, is not the same as 'knowing indirectly', whatever precisely that difficult and perhaps artificial expression may mean. If a murderer 'confesses', then, whatever our opinion of the worth of the 'confession', we cannot say that 'we (only) know indirectly that he did it', nor can we so speak when a witness, reliable or unreliable, has stated that he saw the man do it. Consequently, it is not correct, either, to say that the murderer himself knows 'directly' that he did it, whatever precisely 'knowing directly' may mean.

different. So we don't talk with people (descriptively) except in the faith that they are trying to convey information.[6]

It is now time to turn to the question 'How can you tell?' i.e. to senses (2) and (4) of the question 'How do you know?' If you have asked 'How do you know it's a goldfinch?' then I may reply 'From its behaviour', 'By its markings', or, in more detail, 'By its red head', 'From its eating thistles'. That is, I indicate, or to some extent set out with some degree of precision, those features of the situation which enable me to recognize it as one to be described in the way I did describe it. Thereupon, you may still object in several ways to my saying it's a goldfinch, without in the least 'disputing my facts', which is a further stage to be dealt with later. You may object:

(1)   But goldfinches *don't* have red heads

(1*a*) —But that's not a *goldfinch*. From your own description I can recognize it as a gold*crest*

(2)   But that's not enough: plenty of other birds have red heads. What you say doesn't prove it. For all you know, it may be a woodpecker.

Objections (1) and (1*a*) claim that, in one way or another, I am evidently unable to recognize goldfinches. It may be (1*a*)—that I have not learned the right (customary, popular, official) name to apply to the creature ('Who taught you to use the word "goldfinch"?'):[7] or it may be that my powers of discernment, and consequently of classification, have never been brought sharply to bear in these matters, so that I remain confused as to how to tell the various species of small British bird. Or, of course, it may be a bit of both. In making

[6] Reliance on the authority of others is fundamental, too, in various special matters, e.g. for corroboration and for the correctness of our own use of words, which we learn from others.

[7] Misnaming is not a trivial or laughing matter. If I misname I shall mislead others, and I shall also misunderstand information given by others to me. 'Of course I knew all about his condition perfectly, but I never realized that was *diabetes*: I thought it was cancer, and all the books agree that's incurable: if I'd only known it was diabetes, I should have thought of insulin at once.' Knowing *what a thing is*, to an important extent, knowing what the name for it, and the right name for it, is.

this sort of accusation, you would perhaps tend not so much to use the expression 'You don't know' or 'You oughtn't to say you know' as, rather, 'But that *isn't* a goldfinch (*goldfinch*)', or 'Then you're wrong to call it a goldfinch'. But still, if asked, you would of course deny the statement that I do know it's a goldfinch.

It is in the case of objection (2) that you would be more inclined to say right out 'Then you don't know'. Because it doesn't prove it, it's not enough to prove it. Several important points come out here:

(*a*) If you say 'That's not enough', then you must have in mind some more or less definite lack. 'To be a goldfinch, besides having a red head it must also have the characteristic eye-markings': or 'How do you know it isn't a woodpecker? Woodpeckers have red heads too'. If there is no definite lack, which you are at least prepared to specify on being pressed, then it's silly (outrageous) just to go on saying 'That's not enough'.

(*b*) Enough is enough: it doesn't mean everything. Enough means enough to show that (within reason, and for present intents and purposes) it 'can't' be anything else, there is no room for an alternative, competing, description of it. It does *not* mean, e.g. enough to show it isn't a *stuffed* goldfinch.

(*c*) '*From* its red head', given as an answer to 'How do you know?' requires careful consideration: in particular it differs very materially from '*Because* it has a red head', which is also sometimes given as an answer to 'How do you know?', and is commonly given as an answer to 'Why do you believe?' It is much more akin to such obviously 'vague' replies as 'From its markings' or 'From its behaviour' than at first appears. Our claim, in saying we know (i.e. that we can tell) is to *recognize*: and recognizing, at least in this sort of case, consists in seeing, or otherwise sensing, a feature or features which we are sure are similar to something noted (and usually named) before, on some earlier occasion in our experience. But, this that we see, or otherwise sense, is not necessarily *describable in words*, still less describable in detail, and in non-committal words, and by anybody you please. Nearly everybody can recognize a surly look or the smell of tar, but few can describe them non-committally, i.e. otherwise than as 'surly' or 'of tar': many can recognize, and 'with certainty', ports of different vintages, models by different fashion houses, shades of green, motor car makes from behind, and so forth, without being able to say 'how they recognize them', i.e. without being able to 'be more specific about it'—they can only say they can tell 'by the taste', 'from the cut' and so on. So, when I say I can tell the bird 'from its red head', or that I know a friend 'by his nose', I imply that there is something *peculiar* about the red head or the nose, something peculiar to goldfinches or to him, by which you can (always) tell them or him. In view of the fewness and crudeness of the classificatory words in any language compared with the infinite number of features which are recognized, or which could be picked out and recognized, in our experience, it is small wonder that we often and often fall back on the phrases beginning with 'from' and 'by', and that we are not able to *say*, further and precisely, *how* we can tell. Often we know things quite well, while scarcely able at all to say 'from' what we know them, let alone what there is so very special about them. Any answer beginning 'From' or 'By' has, intentionally, this saving 'vagueness'. But on the contrary, an answer beginning 'Because' is dangerously definite. When I say I know it's a goldfinch 'Because it has a red head', that implies that all I have noted, or needed to note, about it is that its head is red (nothing special or peculiar about the shade, shape, etc., of the patch): so that I imply that there is no other small British bird that has any sort of red head except the goldfinch.

(*d*) Whenever I say I know, I am always liable to be taken to claim that, in a certain sense appropriate to the kind of statement (and to present intents and purposes), I am able to *prove* it. In the present, very common, type of case, 'proving' seems to mean stating what are the features of the current case which are enough to constitute it one which is correctly describable in the way we have described it, and not in any other way relevantly variant. Generally speaking, cases where I can 'prove' are cases where we use the 'because' formula: cases where we 'know but can't prove' are cases where we take refuge in the 'from' or 'by' formula.

I believe that the points so far raised are those most genu-

inely and normally raised by the question 'How do you know?'
But there are other, further, questions sometimes raised under the same rubric, and especially by philosophers, which
may be thought more important. These are the worries about
'reality' and about being 'sure and certain'.

Up to now, in challenging me with the question 'How do
you know?', you are not taken to have *queried my credentials
as stated*, though you have asked what they were: nor have
you *disputed my facts* (the facts on which I am relying to
prove it's a goldfinch), though you have asked me to detail
them. It is this further sort of challenge that may now be
made, a challenge as to the *reliability* of our alleged 'credentials' and our alleged 'facts'. You may ask

(1) But do you know it's a *real* goldfinch? How do you
know you're not dreaming? Or after all, mightn't it be a
stuffed one? And is the head really red? Couldn't it have
been dyed, or isn't there perhaps an odd light reflected on it?

(2) But are you certain it's the *right* red for a goldfinch?
Are you quite sure it isn't too orange? Isn't it perhaps rather
too strident a note for a bittern?

These two sorts of worry are distinct, though very probably
they can be combined or confused, or may run into one another: e.g. 'Are you sure it's really red?' may mean 'Are you
sure it isn't orange?' or again 'Are you sure it isn't just the
peculiar light?'

I. Reality

If you ask me 'How do you know it's a real stick?' 'How
do you know it's really bent?' ('Are you sure he's really angry?'), then you are querying my credentials or my facts (it's
often uncertain which) in a certain special way. In various
special, recognized ways, depending essentially upon the nature of the matter which I have announced myself to know,
either my current experiencing or the item currently under
consideration (or uncertain which) may be abnormal, *phoney*.
Either I myself may be dreaming, or in delirium, or under
the influence of mescal, etc.: or else the item may be stuffed,
painted, dummy, artificial, trick, freak, toy, assumed, feigned,
etc.: or else again there's an uncertainty (it's left open)

whether *I* am to blame or *it* is—mirages, mirror images, odd lighting effects, etc.

These doubts are all to be allayed by means of recognized procedures (more or less roughly recognized, of course), appropriate to the particular type of case. There are recognized ways of distinguishing between dreaming and waking (how otherwise should we know how to use and to contrast the words?), and of deciding whether a thing is stuffed or live, and so forth. The doubt or question 'But is it a *real* one?' has always (*must* have) a special basis, there must be some 'reason for suggesting' that it isn't real, in the sense of some specific way, or limited number of specific ways, in which it is suggested that this experience or item may be phoney. Sometimes (usually) the context makes it clear what the suggestion is: the goldfinch might be stuffed but there's no suggestion that it's a mirage, the oasis might be a mirage but there's no suggestion it might be stuffed. If the context doesn't make it clear, then I am entitled to ask 'How do you mean? Do you mean it may be stuffed or what? *What are you suggesting*?' The wile of the metaphysician consists in asking 'Is it a real table?' (a kind of object which has no obvious way of being phoney) and not specifying or limiting what may be wrong with it, so that I feel at a loss 'how to prove' it *is* a real one.[8] It is the use of the word 'real' in this manner that leads us on to the supposition that 'real' has a single meaning ('the real world' 'material objects'), and that a highly profound and puzzling one. Instead, we should insist always on specifying with what 'real' is being contrasted—not what I shall have to show it is, in order to show it is 'real': and then usually we shall find some specific, less fatal, word, appropriate to the particular case, to substitute for 'real'.

Knowing it's a 'real' goldfinch isn't in question in the ordinary case when I say I know it's a goldfinch: reasonable precautions only are taken. But when it *is* called in question, in *special* cases, then I make sure it's a real goldfinch in ways essentially similar to those in which I made sure it was a gold-

---

[8] Conjurers, too, trade on this. 'Will some gentleman kindly satisfy himself that this is a perfectly ordinary hat?' This leaves us baffled and uneasy: sheepishly we agree that it seems all right, while conscious that we haven't the least idea what to guard against.

finch, though corroboration by other witnesses plays a specially important part in some cases. Once again the precautions cannot be more than reasonable, relative to current intents and purposes. And once again, in the special cases just as in the ordinary cases, two further conditions hold good:

(*a*) I don't by any means *always* know whether it's one or not. It may fly away before I have a chance of testing it, or of inspecting it thoroughly enough. This is simple enough: yet some are prone to argue that because I *sometimes* don't know or can't discover, I *never* can.

(*b*) 'Being sure it's real' is no more proof against miracles or outrages of nature than anything else is or, *sub specie humanitatis*, can be. If we have made sure it's a goldfinch, and a real goldfinch, and then in the future it does something outrageous (explodes, quotes Mrs. Woolf, or what not), we don't say we were wrong to say it was a goldfinch, *we don't know what to say*. Words literally fail us: 'What would you have said?' 'What are we to say now?' 'What would *you* say?' When I have made sure it's a real goldfinch (not stuffed, corroborated by the disinterested, etc.) then I am *not* 'predicting' in saying it's a real goldfinch, and in a very good sense I can't be proved wrong whatever happens. It seems a serious mistake to suppose that language (or most language, language about real things) is 'predictive' in such a way that the future can always prove it wrong. What the future *can* always do, is to make us *revise our ideas* about goldfinches or real goldfinches or anything else.

Perhaps the normal procedure of language could be schematized as follows. First, it is arranged that, on experiencing a complex of features C, then we are to say 'This is C' or 'This is a C'. Then subsequently, the occurrence either of the whole of C or of a significant and characteristic part of it is, on one or many occasions, accompanied or followed in definite circumstances by another special and distinctive feature or complex of features, which makes it seem desirable to revise our ideas: so that we draw a distinction between 'This looks like a C, but in fact is only a dummy, etc.' and 'This is a real C (live, genuine, etc.)'. *Henceforward*, we can only ascertain that it's a *real* C by ascertaining that the special feature or complex of features is present in the appropri-

ate circumstances. The old expression 'This is a C' will tend
as heretofore, to fail to draw any distinction between 'real,
live, etc.', and 'dummy, stuffed, etc.' If the special distinctive
feature is one which does not have to manifest itself in *any*
definite circumstances (on application of some specific test,
after some limited lapse of time, etc.), then it is not a suitable feature on which to base a distinction between 'real' and
'dummy, imaginary, etc.' All we can then do is to say 'Some
Cs are and some aren't, some do and some don't: and it may
be very interesting or important whether they are or aren't,
whether they do or don't, but they're all Cs, real Cs, just the
same'.[9] Now if the special feature is one which must appear
in (more or less) definite circumstances, then 'This is a real
C' is not necessarily predictive: we can, in favourable cases,
make sure of it.[10]

II. Sureness and Certainty

The other way of querying my credentials and proofs ('Are
you sure it's the *right* red?') is quite different. Here we come
up against Mr. Wisdom's views on 'the peculiarity of a man's
knowledge of his own sensations', for which he refers us to
'Other Minds VII' (*Mind*, vol. LII, N.S., No. 207), a passage with which I find I disagree.

Mr. Wisdom there says that, excluding from consideration
cases like 'being in love' and other cases which 'involve prediction', and considering statements like 'I am in pain' which,
in the requisite sense, do *not* involve prediction, then a man
cannot 'be wrong' in making them, in the most favoured sense
of being wrong: that is, though it is of course possible for
him to *lie* (so that 'I am in pain' may be false), and though
it is also possible for him to *misname*, i.e. to use the word

[9] The awkwardness about some snarks being boojums.

[10] Sometimes, on the basis of the new special feature, we distinguish, not between 'Cs' and 'real Cs', but rather between Cs and
Ds. There is a reason for choosing the one procedure rather than the
other: all cases where we use the 'real' formula exhibit (complicated
and serpentine) likenesses, as do all cases where we use 'proper', a
word which behaves in many ways like 'real', and is no less nor
more profound.

'pawn', say, instead of 'pain', which would be liable to mislead others but would not mislead himself, either because he regularly uses 'pawn' for 'pain' or because the use was a momentary aberration, as when I call John 'Albert' while knowing him quite well to be John—though it is possible for him to be 'wrong' in these two senses, it is not possible for him to be wrong in the most favoured sense. He says again that, with this class of statement (elsewhere called 'sense-statements'), to know directly that one is in pain is 'to say that one is, and to say it on the basis of being in pain': and again, that the peculiarity of sense-statements lies in the fact that 'when they are correct and made by X, then X knows they are correct'.

This seems to me mistaken, though it is a view that, in more or less subtle forms, has been the basis of a very great deal of philosophy. It is perhaps the original sin (Berkeley's apple, the tree in the quad) by which the philosopher cast himself out from the garden of the world we live in.

Very clearly detailed, this is the view that, at least and only in a certain favoured type of case, I can 'say what I see (or otherwise sense)' almost quite literally. On this view, if I were to say 'Here is something red', then I might be held to imply or to state that it is really a red thing, a thing which would appear red in a standard light, or to other people, or tomorrow too, and perhaps even more besides: all of which 'involves prediction' (if not also a metaphysical substratum). Even if I were to say 'Here is something which looks red', I might still be held to imply or to state that it looks red to others also, and so forth. If, however, I confine myself to stating 'Here is something that looks red to me now', then at least I can't be wrong (in the most favoured sense).

However, there is an ambiguity in 'something that looks red to me now'. Perhaps this can be brought out by italics, though it is not really so much a matter of emphasis as of tone and expression, of confidence and hesitancy. Contrast 'Here is something that (definitely) *looks to me* (anyhow) red' with 'Here is something that looks to me (something like) *red* (I should say)'. In the former case I am quite confident that, however it may look to others, whatever it may 'really be', etc., it certainly does look red to me at the mo-

ment. In the other case I am not confident at all: it looks
reddish, but I've never seen anything quite like it before, I
can't quite describe it—or, I'm not very good at recognizing
colours, I never feel quite happy about them, I've constantly
been caught out about them. Of course, this sounds silly in
the case of 'red': red is so *very* obvious, we all know red when
we see it, it's *unmistakable*.[11] Cases where we should not
feel happy about red are not easy (though not impossible) to
find. But take 'magenta': 'It looks rather like magenta to
me—but then I wouldn't be too sure about distinguishing
magenta from mauve or from heliotrope. Of course I know
in a way it's purplish, but I don't really know whether to say
it's magenta or not: I just can't be sure.' Here, I am not interested in ruling out consideration of how it looks to others
(looks *to me*) or considerations about what its *real* colour
is (*looks*): what I am ruling out is *my being sure or certain*
what it looks to me. Take tastes, or take sounds: these are so
much better as examples than colours, because we never feel
so happy with our other senses as with our eyesight. Any
description of a taste or sound or smell (or colour) or of a
feeling, involves (is) saying that it is like one or some that
we have experienced before: any descriptive word is classificatory, involves recognition and in that sense memory, and
only when we use such words (or names or descriptions,
which come down to the same) are we knowing anything, or
believing anything. But memory and recognition are often
uncertain and unreliable.

Two rather different ways of being hesitant may be distinguished.

(*a*) Let us take the case where we are tasting a certain
taste. We may say 'I simply don't know what it is: I've never
tasted anything remotely like it before . . . No, it's no use:
the more I think about it the more confused I get: it's perfectly distinct and perfectly distinctive, quite unique in my
experience'. This illustrates the case where I can find nothing in my past experience with which to compare the current
case: I'm certain it's not appreciably like anything I ever

[11] And yet she always *thought* his shirt was white until she saw
it against Tommy's Persil-washed one.

tasted before, not sufficiently like anything I know to merit
the same description. This case, though distinguishable
enough, shades off into the more common type of case where
I'm not quite certain, or only fairly certain, or practically
certain, that it's the taste of, say, laurel. In all such cases,
I am endeavouring to recognize the current item by searching in my past experience for something like it, some likeness
in virtue of which it deserves, more or less positively, to be
described by the same descriptive word:[12] and I am meeting
with varying degrees of success.

(b) The other case is different, though it very naturally
combines itself with the first. Here, what I try to do is to
savour the current experience, to *peer* at it, to sense it vividly.
I'm not sure it *is* the taste of pineapple: isn't there perhaps
just *something* about it, a tang, a bite, a lack of bite, a cloying
sensation, which isn't *quite* right for pineapple? Isn't there
perhaps just a peculiar hint of green, which would rule out
mauve and would hardly do for heliotrope? Or perhaps it is
faintly odd: I must look more intently, scan it over and over:
maybe just possibly there is a suggestion of an unnatural
shimmer, so that it doesn't look quite like ordinary water.
There is a lack of sharpness in what we actually sense, which
is to be cured not, or not merely, by thinking, but by acuter
discernment, by sensory discrimination (though it is of course
true that thinking of other, and more pronounced, cases in
our past experience can and does assist our powers of discrimination).[13]

Cases (a) and (b) alike, and perhaps usually together, lead
to our being not quite sure or certain what it is, what to say,
how to describe it: what our feelings really are, whether the
tickling is painful exactly, whether I'm really what you'd call
angry with him or only something rather like it. The hesitation is of course, in a sense, over misnaming: but I am not
so much or merely worried about possibly misleading others
as about misleading myself (the most favoured sense of be-

---

[12] Or, of course, related to it in some other way than by 'similarity' (in any ordinary sense of 'similarity'), which is yet sufficient
reason for describing it by the same word.

[13] This appears to cover cases of dull or careless or uninstructed
perception, as opposed to cases of diseased or drugged perception.

ing wrong). I should suggest that the two expressions 'being certain' and 'being sure', though from the nature of the case they are often used indiscriminately, have a tendency to refer to cases (a) and (b) respectively. 'Being certain' tends to indicate confidence in our memories and our past discernment, 'being sure' to indicate confidence in the current perception. Perhaps this comes out in our use of the concessives 'to be sure' and 'certainly', and in our use of such phrases as 'certainly not' and 'surely not'. But it may be unwise to chivvy language beyond the coarser nuances.

It may be said that, even when I don't know exactly how to describe it, I nevertheless *know* that I *think* (and roughly how confidently I think) it's mauve. So I do know *something*. But this is irrelevant: I *don't* know it's mauve, that it definitely looks to me now mauve. Besides, there are cases where I really don't know what I think: I'm completely baffled by it.

Of course, there are any number of 'sense-statements' about which I can be, and am, completely sure. In ordinary cases ordinary men are nearly always certain when a thing looks red (or reddish, or anyhow reddish rather than greenish), or when they're in pain (except when that's rather difficult to say, as when they're being tickled): in ordinary cases an expert, a dyer or a dress designer, will be quite sure when something looks (to him in the present light) reseda green or nigger brown, though those who are not experts will not be so sure. Nearly always, if not quite always, we can be quite, or pretty, sure if we take refuge in a sufficiently *rough* description of the sensation: roughness and sureness tend to vary inversely. But the less rough descriptions, just as much as the rough, are all 'sense-statements'.

It is, I think, the problems of sureness and certainty, which philosophers tend (if I am not mistaken) to neglect, that have considerably exercised scientists, while the problem of 'reality', which philosophers have cultivated, does not exercise them. The whole apparatus of measures and standards seems designed to combat unsureness and uncertainty, and concomitantly to increase the possible precision of language, which, in science, pays. But for the words 'real' and 'unreal' the scientist tends to substitute, wisely, their cash-value substitutes, of which he invents and defines an increasing num-

ber, to cover an increasing variety of cases: he doesn't ask
'Is it real?' but rather 'Is it denatured?' or 'Is it an allotropic
form?' and so on.

It is not clear to me what the class of sense-statements is,
nor what its 'peculiarity' is. Some who talk of sense-statements (or sense data) appear to draw a distinction between
talking about simple things like red or pain, and talking
about complicated things like love or tables. But apparently
Mr. Wisdom does not, because he treats 'This looks to me
now like a man eating poppies' as in the same case with 'This
looks to me now red'. In this he is surely right: a man eating
poppies may be more 'complex' to recognize, but it is often
not appreciably more difficult, than the other. But if, again,
we say that non-sense-statements are those which involve
'prediction', why so? True, if I say 'This is a (real) oasis'
without first ascertaining that it's not a mirage, then I do
chance my hand: but if I *have* ascertained that it's not, and
can recognize for sure that it isn't (as when I am drinking
its waters), then surely I'm not chancing my hand any longer.
I believe, of course, that it will continue to perform as (real)
oases normally do: but if there's a *lusus naturae*, a miracle,
and it doesn't, that won't mean I was wrong, previously, to
call it a real oasis.

With regard to Mr. Wisdom's own chosen formulae, we
have seen already that it can't be right to say that the peculiarity of sense-statements is that 'when they are correct,
and made by X, then X knows they are correct': for X may
think, without much confidence, that it tastes to him like
Lapsang, and yet be far from certain, and then subsequently
become certain, or more certain, that it did or didn't. The
other two formulae were: 'To know that one is in pain is to
say that one is and to say it on the basis of being in pain' and
that the only mistake possible with sense-statements is typi-
fied by the case where 'knowing him to be Jack I call him
"Alfred", thinking his name is Alfred, or not caring a damn
what his name is'. The snag in both these lies in the phrases
'on the basis of being in pain' and 'knowing him to be Jack'.
'Knowing him to be Jack' means that I have recognized him
as Jack, a matter over which I may well be hesitant and/or
mistaken: it is true that I needn't recognize him *by name*

as 'Jack', and hence I may call him 'Alfred'), but at least I must be recognizing him correctly as, for instance, the man I last saw in Jerusalem, or else I *shall* be misleading *myself*. Similarly, if 'on the basis of being in pain' only means 'when I am (what would be correctly described as) in pain', then something more than merely *saying* 'I'm in pain' is necessary for knowing I'm in pain: and this something more, as it involves recognition, may be hesitant and/or mistaken, though it is of course unlikely to be so in a case so comparatively obvious as that of pain.

Possibly the tendency to overlook the problems of recognition is fostered by the tendency to use a direct object after the word *know*. Mr. Wisdom, for example, confidently uses such expressions as 'knowing the feelings of another (his mind, his sensations, his anger, his pain) in the way that *he* knows them'. But, although we do correctly use the expressions 'I know your feelings on the matter' or 'He knows his own mind' or (archaically) 'May I know your mind?', these are rather special expressions, which do not justify any general usage. 'Feelings' here has the sense it has in 'very strong feelings' in favour of or against something: perhaps it means 'views' or 'opinions' ('very decided opinions'), just as 'mind' in this usage is given by the Dictionary as equivalent to 'intention' or 'wish'. To extend the usage uncritically is somewhat as though, on the strength of the legitimate phrase 'knowing someone's tastes', we were to proceed to talk of 'knowing someone's sounds' or 'knowing someone's taste of pineapple'. If, for example, it is a case of *physical* feelings such as fatigue, we do not use the expression 'I know your feelings'.

When, therefore, Mr. Wisdom speaks generally of 'knowing his sensations', he presumably means this to be equivalent to 'knowing *what* he is seeing, smelling, etc.', just as 'knowing the winner of the Derby' means 'knowing *what won* the Derby'. But here again, the expression 'know what' seems sometimes to be taken, unconsciously and erroneously, to lend support to the practice of putting a direct object after *know*: for 'what' is liable to be understood as a relative, = 'that which'. This is a grammatical mistake: 'what' *can* of course be a relative, but in 'know what you feel' and 'know what won' it is an interrogative (Latin *quid*, not *quod*). In this respect, 'I can smell what he is smelling' differs from 'I can know what he is smelling'. 'I know what he is feeling' is not 'There is an *x* which both I know and he is feeling', but 'I know the answer to the question "What is he feeling?"'. And similarly with 'I know what I am feeling': this does *not* mean that there is something which I am *both knowing and feeling*.

Expressions such as 'We don't know another man's anger in the way he knows it' or 'He knows his pain in a way we can't' seem barbarous. The man doesn't 'know his pain': he feels (not knows) what he recognizes as, or what he knows to be, anger (not his anger), and he knows that he is feeling angry. Always assuming that he does recognize the feeling, which in fact, though feeling it acutely, he may not: 'Now I know what it was, it was jealousy (or gooseflesh or angina). At the time I didn't know at all what it was, I had never felt anything quite like it before: but since then I've got to know it quite well'.[14]

Uncritical use of the direct object after *know* seems to be one thing that leads to the view that (or to talking as though) sensa, that is things, colours, noises and the rest, speak or are labelled by nature, so that I can literally *say* what (that which) I *see*: it pipes up, or I read it off. It is as if sensa were *literally* to 'announce themselves' or to 'identify themselves', in the way we indicate when we say 'It presently identified itself as a particularly fine white rhinoceros'. But surely this is only a manner of speaking, a reflexive idiom in which the French, for example, indulge more freely than the English: sensa are dumb, and only previous experience enables *us* to identify them. If we choose to say that they 'identify themselves' (and certainly 'recognizing' is not a highly voluntary activity of ours), then it must be admitted that they share

[14] There are, of course, legitimate uses of the direct object after *know*, and of the possessive pronoun before words for feelings. 'He knows the town well', 'He has known much suffering', 'My old vanity, how well I know it!'—even the pleonastic 'Where does he feel his (= the) pain?' and the educative tautology '*He* feels *his* pain'. But none of these really lends support to the metaphysical 'He knows his pain (in a way we can't)'.

the birthright of all speakers, that of speaking unclearly and untruly.

If I Know I can't be Wrong

One final point about 'How do you know?', the challenge to the user of the expression 'I know', requires still to be brought out by consideration of the saying that 'If you know you can't be wrong'. Surely, if what has so far been said is correct, then we are often right to say we *know* even in cases where we turn out subsequently to have been mistaken—and indeed we seem always, or practically always, liable to be mistaken.

Now, we are perfectly, and should be candidly, aware of this liability, which does not, however, transpire to be so very onerous in practice. The human intellect and senses are, indeed, *inherently* fallible and delusive, but not by any means *inveterately* so. Machines are inherently liable to break down, but good machines don't (often). It is futile to embark on a 'theory of knowledge' which denies this liability: such theories constantly end up by admitting the liability after all, and denying the existence of 'knowledge'.

'When you know you can't be wrong' is perfectly good sense. You are prohibited from saying 'I know it is so, but I may be wrong', just as you are prohibited from saying 'I promise I will, but I may fail'. If you are aware you may be mistaken, you oughtn't to say you know, just as, if you are aware you may break your word, you have no business to promise. But of course, being aware that you may be mistaken doesn't mean merely being aware that you are a fallible human being: it means that you have some concrete reason to suppose that you may be mistaken in this case. Just as 'but I may fail' doesn't mean merely 'but I am a weak human being' (in which case it would be no more exciting than adding 'D.V.'): it means that there is some concrete reason for me to suppose that I shall break my word. It is naturally *always* possible ('humanly' possible) that I may be mistaken or may break my word, but that by itself is no bar against using the expressions 'I know' and 'I promise' as we do in fact use them.

At the risk (long since incurred) of being tedious, the parallel between saying 'I know' and saying 'I promise' may be elaborated.[15]

When I say 'S is P', I imply at least that I believe it, and, if I have been strictly brought up, that I am (quite) sure of it: when I say 'I shall do A', I imply at least that I hope to do it, and, if I have been strictly brought up that I (fully) intend to. If I only believe that S is P, I can add 'But of course I may (very well) be wrong': if I only hope to do A, I can add 'But of course I may (very well) not'. When I only believe or only hope, it is recognized that further evidence or further circumstances are liable to make me change my mind. If I say 'S is P' when I don't even believe it, I am lying: if I say it when I believe it but am not sure of it, I may be misleading but I am not exactly lying. If I say 'I shall do A' when I have not even any hope, not the slightest intention, of doing it, then I am deliberately deceiving: if I say it when I do not fully intend to, I am misleading but I am not deliberately deceiving in the same way.

But now, when I say 'I promise', a new plunge is taken: I have not merely announced my intention, but, by using this formula (performing this ritual), I have bound myself to others, and staked my reputation, in a new way. Similarly, saying 'I know' is taking a new plunge. But it is *not* saying 'I have performed a specially striking feat of cognition, superior, in the same scale as believing and being sure, even to being merely quite sure': for there *is* nothing in that scale superior to being quite sure. Just as promising is not something superior, in the same scale as hoping and intending,

[15] It is the use of the expressions 'I know' and 'I promise' (first person singular, present indicative tense) alone that is being considered. 'If I knew, I can't have been wrong' or 'If she knows she can't be wrong' are not worrying in the way that 'If I ("you") know I ("you") can't be wrong' is worrying. Or again, 'I promise' is quite different from 'he promises': if I say 'I promise', I don't say I *say* I promise, I *promise*, just as if he says he promises, he doesn't say he says he promises, he promises: whereas if I say 'he promises', I do (only) say he *says* he promises—in the other 'sense' of 'promise', the 'sense' in which *I* say *I* promise, only *he* can say he promises. I *describe* his promising, but I *do* my own promising and he must do *his* own.

even to merely fully intending: for there *is* nothing in that scale superior to fully intending. When I say 'I know', I *give others my word: I give others my authority for saying* that 'S is P'.

When I have said only that I am sure, and prove to have been mistaken, I am not liable to be rounded on by others in the same way as when I have said 'I know'. I am sure *for my part*, you can take it or leave it: accept it if you think I'm an acute and careful person, that's your responsibility. But I don't know 'for my part', and when I say 'I know' I don't mean you can take it or leave it (though of course you *can* take it or leave it). In the same way, when I say I fully intend to, I do so for my part, and, according as you think highly or poorly of my resolution and chances, you will elect to act on it or not to act on it: but if I say I promise, you are *entitled* to act on it, whether or not you choose to do so. If I have said I know or I promise, you insult me in a special way by refusing to accept it. We all *feel* the very great difference between saying even 'I'm *absolutely* sure' and saying 'I know': it is like the difference between saying even 'I firmly and irrevocably intend' and 'I promise'. If someone has promised me to do A, then I am entitled to rely on it, and can myself make promises on the strength of it: and so, where someone has said to me 'I know', I am entitled to say I know too, at second hand. The right to say 'I know' is transmissible, in the sort of way that other authority is transmissible. Hence, if I say it lightly, I may be *responsible* for getting *you* into trouble.

If you say you *know* something, the most immediate challenge takes the form of asking 'Are you in a position to know?': that is, you must undertake to show, not merely that you are sure of it, but that it is within your cognizance. There is a similar form of challenge in the case of promising: fully intending is not enough—you must also undertake to show that 'you are in a position to promise', that is that it is within your power. Over these points in the two cases parallel series of doubts are apt to infect philosophers, on the ground that I cannot foresee the future. Some begin to hold that I should never, or practically never, say I know anything—perhaps only what I am sensing at this moment: others, that I should never, or practically never, say I promise—perhaps only what is actually within my power at this moment. In both cases there is an obsession: if I know I *can't be wrong*, so I can't have the right to say I know, and if I promise I *can't fail*, so I can't have the right to say I promise. And in both cases this obsession fastens on my inability to make *predictions* as the root of the matter, meaning by predictions claims to know the future. But this is doubly mistaken in both cases. As has been seen, we may be perfectly justified in saying we know or we promise, in spite of the fact that things 'may' turn out badly, and it's a more or less serious matter for us if they do. And further, it is overlooked that the conditions which must be satisfied if I am to show that a thing is within my cognizance or within my power are conditions, not about the future, but about *the present and the past*: it is not demanded that I do more than *believe* about the future.[16]

We feel, however, an objection to saying that 'I know' performs the same sort of function in talking as 'I promise'. It is this. Supposing that things turn out badly, then we say, on the one hand 'You're proved wrong, so you *didn't* know', but on the other hand 'You've failed to perform, although you *did* promise'. I believe that this contrast is more apparent than real. The sense in which you 'did promise' is that you did *say* you promised (did say 'I promise'): and you did *say* you knew. That is the gravamen of the charge against you when you let us down, after we have taken your word. But it may well transpire that you never fully intended to do it, or that you had concrete reason to suppose that you wouldn't be able to do it (it might even be manifestly impossible), and in another 'sense' of promise you *can't* then have promised to do it, so that you *didn't* promise.

Consider the use of other phrases analogous to 'I know' and 'I promise'. Suppose, instead of 'I know', I had said 'I swear': in that case, upon the opposite appearing, we should say, exactly as in the promising case, 'You *did* swear, but you were wrong'. Suppose again that, instead of 'I promise', I had said 'I guarantee' (e.g. to protect you from attack): in that case, upon my letting you down, you can say, exactly as in

---

[16] If 'Figs never grow on thistles' is taken to mean 'None ever have and none ever will', then it is implied that I *know* that none ever have, but only that I *believe* that none ever will.

the knowing case 'You *said* you guaranteed it, but you *didn't*
guarantee it'.[17] Can the situation perhaps be summed up as
follows? In these 'ritual' cases, the approved case is one where
in the appropriate circumstances, I say a certain formula: e.g.
'I do' when standing, unmarried or a widower, beside a
woman, unmarried or a widow and not within the prohibited
degrees of relationship, before a clergyman, registrar, etc.,
or 'I give' when it is mine to give, etc., or 'I order' when I
have the authority to, etc. But now, if the situation tran-
spires to have been in some way not orthodox (I was already
married: it wasn't mine to give: I had no authority to order),
then we tend to be rather hesitant about how to put it, as
heaven was when the saint blessed the penguins. We call the
man a bigamist, but his second marriage was not a marriage,
is null and void (a useful formula in many cases for avoiding
saying either 'he did' or 'he didn't'): he did 'order' me to do
it, but, having no authority over me, he *couldn't* 'order' me:
he did warn me it was going to charge, but it wasn't or anyway I knew much more about it than he did, so in a way he
couldn't warn me, didn't warn me.[18] We hesitate between
'He didn't order me', 'He had no right to order me', 'He
oughtn't to have said he ordered me', just as we do between
'You didn't know', 'You can't have known', 'You had no right
to say you knew' (these perhaps having slightly different
nuances, according to what precisely it is that has gone
wrong). But the essential factors are (*a*) You said you knew:
you said you promised (*b*) You were mistaken: you didn't
perform. The hesitancy concerns only the precise way in
which we are to round on the original 'I know' or 'I promise'.

To suppose that 'I know' is a descriptive phrase, is only

[17] 'Swear' 'guarantee' 'give my word' 'promise', all these and similar words cover cases both of 'knowing' and of 'promising', thus
suggesting the two are analogous. Of course they differ subtly from
each other: for example, *know* and *promise* are in a certain sense
'unlimited' expressions, while when I swear I swear *upon* something,
and when I guarantee I guarantee that, upon some adverse and more
or less to be expected circumstance arising, I will take *some more or
less definite action* to nullify it.

[18] 'You can't warn someone of something that isn't going to
happen' parallels 'You can't know what isn't true'.

one example of the *descriptive fallacy*, so common in philosophy. Even if some language is now purely descriptive, language was not in origin so, and much of it is still not so. Utterance of obvious ritual phrases, in the appropriate circumstances, is not *describing* the action we are doing, but *doing* it ('I do'): in other cases it functions, like tone and expression, or again like punctuation and mood, as an intimation that we are employing language in some special way ('I warn', 'I ask', 'I define'). Such phrases cannot, strictly, *be* lies, though they can 'imply' lies, as 'I promise' implies that I fully intend, which may be untrue.

If these are the main and multifarious points that arise in familiar cases where we ask 'How do you know that this is a case of so-and-so?', they may be expected to arise likewise in cases where we say 'I know he is angry'. And if there are, as no doubt there are, special difficulties in this case, at least we can clear the ground a little of things which are not special difficulties, and get the matter in better perspective.

As a preliminary, it must be said that I shall only discuss the question of feelings and emotions, with special reference to anger. It seems likely that cases where we know that another man thinks that 2 and 2 make 4, or that he is seeing a rat, and so on, are different in important respects from, though no doubt also similar to, the case of knowing that he is angry or hungry.

In the first place, we certainly do say sometimes that we know another man is angry, and we also distinguish these occasions from others on which we say only that we *believe* he is angry. For of course, we do not for a moment suppose that we *always* know, of *all* men, whether they are angry or not, or that we could discover it. There are many occasions when I realize that I can't possibly tell what he's feeling: and there are many *types* of people, and many individuals too, with whom I (they being what they are, and I being what I am) never can tell. The feelings of royalty, for example, or fakirs or bushmen or Wykehamists or simple eccentrics—these may be very hard to divine: unless you have had a prolonged acquaintance with such persons, and some intimacy with them, you are not in any sort of position to know what their feelings are, especially if, for one reason or another, they can't or don't tell you. Or again, the feelings of some individual whom you have never met before—they might be almost anything: you don't know his character at all or his tastes, you have had no experience of his mannerisms, and so on. His feelings are elusive and personal: people differ so much. It is this sort of thing that leads to the situation where we say 'You never know' or 'You never can tell'.

In short, here even more than in the case of the goldfinch, a great deal depends on how familiar we have been in our past experience with this type of person, and indeed with this individual, in this type of situation. If we have no great familiarity, then we hesitate to say we know: indeed, we can't be expected to say (tell). On the other hand, if we *have* had the necessary experience, then we can, in favourable current circumstances, say we know: we certainly can recognize when some near relative of ours is angrier than we have ever seen him.

Further, we must have had experience also of the emotion or feeling concerned, in this case anger. In order to know what you're feeling, I must also apparently be able to imagine (guess, understand, appreciate) what you're feeling. It seems that more is demanded than that I shall have learned to discriminate displays of anger in others: I must also have been angry myself.[19] Or at any rate, if I have never felt a certain emotion, say ambition, then I certainly feel an *extra* hesitation in saying that his motive is ambition. And this seems to be due to the very special nature (grammar, logic) of feelings, to the special way in which they are related to their occasions and manifestations, which requires further elucidation.

[19] We say we don't know what it must feel like to be a king, whereas we do know what one of our friends must have felt when mortified. In this ordinary (imprecise and evidently not whole-hog) sense of 'knowing what it would be like' we do often know what it would be like to be our neighbour drawing his sword, whereas we don't know (can't even guess or imagine), really, what it would feel like to be a cat or a cockroach. But of course we don't ever 'know' what in our neighbour accompanies the drawing of his sword in Mr. Wisdom's peculiar sense of 'know what' as equivalent to 'directly experience that which'.

At first sight it may be tempting to follow Mr. Wisdom, and to draw a distinction between (1) the physical symptoms and (2) the feeling. So that when, in the current case, I am asked 'How can you tell he's angry?' I should answer 'From the physical symptoms', while if *he* is asked how *he* can tell he's angry, he should answer 'From the feeling'. But this seems to be a dangerous over-simplification.

In the first place, 'symptoms' (and also 'physical') is being used in a way different from ordinary usage, and one which proves to be misleading.

'Symptoms', a term transferred from medical usage,[20] tends to be used only, or primarily, in cases where that of which there are symptoms is something undesirable (of incipient disease rather than of returning health, of despair rather than of hope, of grief rather than of joy): and hence it is more colourful than 'signs' or 'indications'. This, however, is comparatively trivial. What is important is the fact that we never talk of 'symptoms' or 'signs' except *by way of implied contrast with inspection of the item itself*. No doubt it would often be awkward to have to say exactly where the signs or symptoms end and the item itself begins to appear: but such a division is always implied to exist. And hence the words 'symptom' and 'sign' have no use except in cases where the item, as in the case of disease, is liable to be *hidden*, whether it be in the future, in the past, under the skin, or in some other more or less notorious casket: and when the item is itself before us, we no longer talk of signs and symptoms. When we talk of 'signs of a storm', we mean signs of an impending storm, or of a past storm, or of a storm beyond the horizon: we do *not* mean a storm on top of us.[21]

[20] Doctors nowadays draw a distinction of their own between 'symptoms' and '(physical) signs': but the distinction is not here relevant, and perhaps not very clear.

[21] There are some, more complicated, cases like that of inflation, where the signs of incipient inflation are of the same nature as inflation itself, but of a less intensity or at a slower tempo. Here, especially, it is a matter for decision where the signs or 'tendencies' end and where the state itself sets in: moreover, with inflation as with some diseases, we can in some contexts go on talking of signs or symptoms even when the item itself is quite fairly decidedly present, because it is such as not to be patent to simple observation.

The words function like such words as 'traces' or 'clues'. Once you know the murderer, you don't get any more clues, only what were or would have been clues: nor is a confession, or an eyewitness' view of the crime, a particularly good clue —these are something different altogether. When the cheese is not to be found or seen, then there may be traces of it: but not when it's there in front of us (though of course, there aren't, then, 'no traces' of it either).

For this reason, it seems misleading to lump together, as a general practice, all the characteristic features of any casual item as 'signs' or 'symptoms' of it: though it is of course sometimes the case that some things which could in appropriate circumstances be called characteristics or effects or manifestations or parts or sequelae or what not of certain items may *also* be called signs or symptoms of those items in the appropriate circumstances. It seems to be this which is really wrong with Mr. Wisdom's paradox[22] about looking in the larder and finding 'all the signs' of bread, when we see the loaf, touch it, taste it and so on. Doing these things is not finding (some) signs of bread at all: the taste or feel of bread is not a sign or symptom of bread at all. What I might be taken to mean if I announced that I had found signs of bread in the larder seems rather doubtful, since bread is not normally casketed (or if in the bin, leaves no traces), and not being a transient event (impending bread, etc.), does not have any normally accepted 'signs': and signs, peculiar to the item, have to be more or less normally accepted. I might be taken to mean that I had found traces of bread, such as crumbs, or signs that bread had at one time been stored there, or something of the kind: but what I could *not* be taken to mean is that I had seen, tasted, or touched (something like) bread.

The sort of thing we do actually say, if the look is all right but we haven't yet tasted it, is 'Here is something that looks like bread'. If it turns out not to be bread after all, we might

22 [In 'Other Minds III' he had discussed the logic of a possible complaint, from a man who was actually looking at, touching, smelling, tasting, bread, that nevertheless, though admittedly all the *signs* of bread were present still it might not be quite safe to say that there actually *was* bread there.—EDITOR.]

say 'It tasted like bread, but actually it was only bread-substitute', or 'It exhibited many of the characteristic features of bread, but differed in important respects: it was only a synthetic imitation'. That is, we don't use the words sign or symptom at all.

Now, if 'signs' and 'symptoms' have this restricted usage, it is evident that to say that we only get at the 'signs' or 'symptoms' of anything is to imply that we never get at *it* (and this goes for '*all* the signs' too). So that, if we say that I only get at the *symptoms* of his anger, that carries an important implication. But *is* this the way we do talk? Surely we do not consider that we are never aware of more than *symptoms* of anger in another man?

'Symptoms' or 'signs' of anger tend to mean signs of *rising* or of *suppressed* anger. Once the man has exploded, we talk of something different—of an expression or manifestation or display of anger, of an exhibition of temper, and so forth. A twitch of the eyebrow, pallor, a tremor in the voice, all these may be symptoms of anger: but a violent tirade or a blow in the face are not, they are the acts in which the anger is vented. 'Symptoms' of anger are not, at least normally, contrasted with the man's own inner personal feeling of anger, but rather with the actual display of anger. Normally at least, where we have only symptoms to go upon, we should say only that we *believe* that the man is angry or getting angry: whereas when he has given himself away we say that we *know*.[23]

The word 'physical' also, as used by Mr. Wisdom in contrast to 'mental', seems to me abused, though I am not con-

[23] Sometimes, it is said, we use 'I know' where we should be prepared to substitute 'I believe', as when we say 'I know he's in, because his hat is in the hall': thus 'know' is used loosely for 'believe', so why should we suppose there is a fundamental difference between them? But the question is, what exactly do we mean by 'prepared to substitute' and 'loosely'? We are 'prepared to substitute' *believe* for *know* not as an *equivalent* expression but as a weaker and therefore preferable expression, in view of the seriousness with which, as has become apparent, the matter is to be treated: the presence of the hat, which would serve as a proof of its owner's presence in many circumstances, could only through laxity be adduced as a proof in a court of law.

fident as to whether this abuse is misleading in the current case. He evidently does not wish to call a man's feelings, which he cites as a typical example of a 'mental' event, *physical*. Yet this is what we ordinarily often do. There are many physical feelings, such as giddiness, hunger or fatigue: and these are included by some doctors among the physical signs of various complaints. Most feelings we do not speak of as either mental or physical, especially emotions, such as jealousy or anger itself: we do not assign them to the *mind* but to the *heart*. Where we do describe a feeling as mental, it is because we are using a word normally used to describe a physical feeling in a special transferred sense, as when we talk about 'mental' discomfort or fatigue.

It is then, clear, that more is involved in being e.g., angry than simply showing the symptoms and feeling the feeling. For there is also the display or manifestation. And it is to be noted that the feeling is related in a unique sort of way to the display. When we are angry, we have an impulse, felt and/or acted on, to do actions of particular kinds, and, unless we suppress the anger, we do actually proceed to do them. There is a peculiar and intimate relationship between the emotion and the natural manner of venting it, with which, having been angry ourselves, we are acquainted. The ways in which anger is normally manifested are *natural* to anger just as there are tones *naturally* expressive of various emotions (indignation, etc.). There is not normally taken to be[24] such a thing as 'being angry' apart from any impulse, however vague, to vent the anger in the natural way.

Moreover, besides the natural expressions of anger, there are also the natural *occasions* of anger, of which we have also had experience, which are similarly connected in an intimate way with the 'being angry'. It would be as nonsensical to class these as 'causes' in some supposedly obvious and 'external' sense, as it would be to class the venting of anger as the 'effect' of the emotion in a supposedly obvious and 'external' sense. Equally it would be nonsensical to say that there are three wholly distinct phenomena, (1) cause or occasion (2)

---

[24] A new language is naturally necessary if we are to admit unconscious feelings, and feelings which express themselves in paradoxical manners, such as the psycho-analysts describe.

feeling or emotion and (3) effect or manifestation, which are related together 'by definition' as all necessary to anger, though this would perhaps be less misleading than the other.

It seems fair to say that 'being angry' is in many respects like 'having mumps'. It is a description of a whole pattern of events, including occasion, symptoms, feeling and manifestation, and possibly other factors besides. It is as silly to ask 'What, really, *is* the anger *itself*?' as to attempt to fine down 'the disease' to some one chosen item ('the functional disorder'). That the man himself feels something which we don't (in the sense that he feels angry and we don't) is[25] evident enough, and incidentally nothing to complain about as a 'predicament': but there is no call to say that 'that' ('the feeling')[26] *is* the *anger*. The pattern of events whatever its precise form, is, fairly clearly, peculiar to the case of 'feelings' (emotions)—it is not by any means exactly like the case of diseases: and it seems to be this peculiarity which makes us prone to say that, unless we have had experience of a feeling ourselves, we cannot know when someone else is experiencing it. Moreover, it is our confidence in the general pattern that makes us apt to say we 'know' another man is angry when we

[25] In the absence of Mr. Wisdom's variety of telepathy. [Professor Wisdom wrote: 'Likewise we can imagine a man doing what we now can seldom do, something which people have called "looking into the mind of another". This man doesn't examine present symptoms and predict how the patient will go on. He sees scenes in a glass or in his mind's eye and knows they are what another sees, he feels distress and knows that another is in distress. If this is to be called seeing what another sees or feeling what he feels, if this would be real knowledge of the thoughts and feelings of another, then when someone says "We cannot know the feelings of others" what he refers to is the familiar fact that few of us can do this'—EDITOR.] There is, it seems to me, something which does actually happen, rather different from Mr. Wisdom's telepathy, which does sometimes contribute towards our knowledge of other people's feelings. We do talk, e.g. of 'feeling another person's displeasure', and say, e.g. 'his anger could be felt', and there seems to be something genuine about this. But the feeling we feel, though genuine 'feeling', is *not*, in these cases, displeasure or anger, but a special *counterpart* feeling.

[26] The 'feelings', i.e. sensations, we can observe in ourselves when angry are such things as a pounding of the heart or tensing of the muscles, which cannot in themselves be justifiably called 'the feeling of anger'.

have only observed parts of the pattern: for the parts of the pattern are related to each other very much more intimately than, e.g. newspapermen scurrying in Brighton are related to a fire in Fleet Street.[27]

The man himself, such is the overriding power of the pattern, will sometimes accept corrections from outsiders about his own emotions, i.e. about the correct description of them. He may be got to agree that he was not really angry so much as, rather, indignant or jealous, and even that he was not in pain, but only fancied he was. And this is not surprising, especially in view of the fact that he, like all of us, has primarily learnt to use the expression 'I am angry' of himself by (a) noting the occasion, symptoms, manifestation, etc., in cases where other persons say 'I am angry' of *themselves* (b) being told by others, who have noted all that can be observed about *him* on certain occasions, that 'You are angry', i.e. that he should say 'I am angry'. On the whole, 'mere' feelings or emotions, if there are such things genuinely detectable, are certainly very hard to be sure about, even harder than, say, tastes, which we already choose to describe, normally, only by their occasions (the taste 'of tar', 'of pineapple', etc.).

All words for emotions are, besides, on the vague side, in two ways, leading to further hesitations about whether we 'know' when he's angry. They tend to cover a rather wide and ill-defined variety of situations: and the patterns they cover tend to be, each of them, rather complex (though common and so not difficult to recognize, very often), so that it is easy for one of the more or less necessary features to be omitted, and thus to give rise to hesitation about what exactly we should say in such an unorthodox case. We realize, well enough, that the challenge to which we are exposed if we say we *know* is to *prove* it, and in this respect vagueness of terminology is a crippling handicap.

So far, enough has perhaps been said to show that most of the difficulties which stand in the way of our saying we know a thing is a goldfinch arise in rather greater strength in the case where we want to say we know another man is angry.

[27] It is therefore misleading to ask 'How do I get from the scowl to the anger?'

But there is still a feeling, and I think a justified feeling, that there is a further and quite *special* difficulty in the latter case.

This difficulty seems to be of the sort that Mr. Wisdom raises at the very outset of his series of articles on 'Other Minds'. It is asked, might the man not exhibit all the symptoms (and display and everything else) of anger, even *ad infinitum*, and yet still *not* (really) *be* angry? It will be remembered that he there treats it, no doubt provisionally, as a difficulty similar to that which can arise concerning the reality of any 'material object'. But in fact, it has special features of its own.

There seem to be three distinguishable doubts which may arise:

(1) When to all appearances angry, might he not really be labouring under some other emotion, in that, though he normally feels the same emotion as we should on occasions when we, in his position, should feel anger and in making displays such as we make when angry, in this particular case he is acting abnormally?

(2) When to all appearances angry, might he not really be labouring under some other emotion; in that he normally feels, on occasions when we in his position should feel anger, and when acting as we should act if we felt anger, some feeling which we, if we experienced it, should distinguish from anger?

(3) When to all appearances angry, might he not really be feeling no emotion at all?

In everyday life, all these problems arise in special cases, and occasion genuine worry. We may worry (1) as to whether someone is *deceiving* us, by suppressing his emotions, or by feigning emotions which he does not feel: we may worry (2) as to whether we are *misunderstanding* someone (or he us), in wrongly supposing that he does 'feel like us', that he does share emotions like ours: or we may worry (3) as to whether some action of another person is really deliberate, or perhaps only involuntary or inadvertent in some manner or other. All three varieties of worry may arise, and often do, in connection with the actions of persons whom we know very well.[28] All work together in the feeling of loneliness which affects everybody at times. Any or all of them may be at the bottom of the passage from Mrs. Woolf.[29]

None of these three special difficulties about 'reality' arises in connection with goldfinches or bread, any more than the special difficulties about, e.g. the oasis arise in connection with the reality of another person's emotions. The goldfinch cannot be assumed, nor the bread suppressed: we may be deceived by the appearance of an oasis, or misinterpret the signs of the weather, but the oasis cannot lie to us and we cannot misunderstand the storm in the way we misunderstand the man.

Though the difficulties are special, the ways of dealing with them are, initially, similar to those employed in the case of the goldfinch. There are (more or less roughly) established procedures for dealing with suspected cases of deception or of misunderstanding or of inadvertence. By these means we do very often establish (though we do not expect *always* to establish) that someone is acting, or that we were misunderstanding him, or that he is simply impervious to a certain emotion, or that he was not acting voluntarily. These special cases where doubts arise and require resolving, are contrasted with the normal cases which hold the field[30] *unless* there is some special suggestion that deceit, etc., is involved, and deceit, moreover, of an intelligible kind in the circumstances, that is, of a kind that can be looked into because motive, etc., is specially suggested. There is no suggestion that I *never* know what other people's emotions are, nor yet that in particular cases I might be wrong for no special reason or in no special way.

Extraordinary cases of deceit, misunderstanding, etc. (which are themselves not the normal), do not, *ex vi termini*,

[28] There is, too, a special way in which we can doubt the 'reality' of our own emotions, can doubt whether we are not 'acting to ourselves'. Professional actors may reach a state where they never really know what their genuine feelings are.

[29] [Professor Wisdom had quoted a paragraph from *Jacob's Room*.—EDITOR.]

[30] 'You cannot fool all the people all of the time' is 'analytic'.

ordinarily occur: we have a working knowledge of the occasions for, the temptations to, the practical limits of, and the
normal types of deceit and misunderstanding. Nevertheless,
they *may* occur, and there may be varieties which are common without our yet having become aware of the fact. If
this happens, we are in a certain sense wrong, because our
terminology is inadequate to the facts, and we shall have
thenceforward to be more wary about saying we know, or shall
have to revise our ideas and terminology. This we are constantly ready to do in a field so complex and baffling as that
of the emotions.

There remains, however, one further special feature of the
case, which also differentiates it radically from the goldfinch
case. The goldfinch, the material object, is, as we insisted
above, uninscribed and *mute*: but the man *speaks*. In the
complex of occurrences which induces us to say we know
another man is angry, the complex of symptoms, occasion,
display and the rest, a peculiar place is occupied by the man's
own statement as to what his feelings are. In the usual case,
we accept this statement without question, and we then say
that we know (as it were 'at second-hand') what his feelings
are: though of course 'at second-hand' here could not be used
to imply that anybody but he could know 'at first-hand', and
hence perhaps it is not in fact used. In unusual cases, where
his statement conflicts with the description we should otherwise have been inclined to give of the case, we do not feel
bound to accept it, though we always feel some uneasiness
in rejecting it. If the man is a habitual liar or self-deceiver,
or if there are patent reasons why he should be lying or deceiving himself on this occasion, then we feel reasonably
happy: but if such a case occurred as the imagined one[31]
where a man, having given throughout life every appearance
of holding a certain pointless belief, leaves behind a remark
in his private diary to the effect that he never did believe it,
then we probably should not know what to say.

I should like to make in conclusion some further remarks
about this crucial matter of our believing what the man says

[31] [Professor Wisdom had considered the case of a man who
persistently claimed that he believed that flowers feel.—EDITOR.]

about his own feelings. Although I know very well that I do not see my way clearly in this, I cannot help feeling sure that it is fundamental to the whole Predicament, and that it has not been given the attention it deserves, possibly just because it is so obvious.

The man's own statement is not (is not treated primarily as) a sign or symptom, although it can, secondarily and artificially, be treated as such. A unique place is reserved for it in the summary of the facts of the case. The question then is: 'Why believe him?'

There are answers that we can give to this question, which is here to be taken in the general sense of 'Why believe him ever?' not simply as 'Why believe him this time?' We may say that the man's statements on matters other than his own feelings have constantly been before us in the past, and have been regularly verified by our own observations of the facts he reported: so that we have in fact some basis for an induction about his general reliability. Or we may say that his behaviour is most simply 'explained' on the view that he does feel emotions like ours, just as psycho-analysts 'explain' erratic behaviour by analogy with normal behaviour when they use the terminology of 'unconscious desires'.

These answers are, however, dangerous and unhelpful. They are so obvious that they please nobody: while on the other hand they encourage the questioner to push his question to 'profounder' depths, encouraging us, in turn, to exaggerate these answers until they become distortions.

The question, pushed further, becomes a challenge to the very possibility of 'believing another man', in its ordinarily accepted sense, at all. What 'justification' is there for supposing that there is another mind communicating with you at all? How can you know what it would be like for another mind to feel anything, and so how can you understand it? It is then that we are tempted to say that we only mean by 'believing him' that we take certain vocal noises as signs of certain impending behaviour, and that 'other minds' are no more really real than unconscious desires.

This, however, is distortion. It seems, rather, that believing in other persons, in authority and testimony, is an essential part of the act of communicating, an act which we all constantly perform. It is as much an irreducible part of our experience as, say, giving promises, or playing competitive games, or even sensing coloured patches. We can state certain advantages of such performances, and we can elaborate rules of a kind for their 'rational' conduct (as the Law Courts and historians and psychologists work out the rules for accepting testimony). But there is no 'justification' for our doing them as such.

Final Note

One speaker at Manchester[32] said roundly that the real crux of the matter remains still that 'I ought not to say that I know Tom is angry, because I don't introspect his feelings': and this no doubt is just what many people do boggle at. The gist of what I have been trying to bring out is simply:

(1) *Of course* I *don't* introspect Tom's feelings (we should be in a pretty predicament if I did).

(2) *Of course* I *do* sometimes know Tom is angry.

Hence

(3) to suppose that the question 'How do I know that Tom is angry?' is meant to mean 'How do I introspect Tom's feelings?' (because, as we know, that's the sort of thing that knowing is or ought to be), is simply barking our way up the wrong gum tree.

[32] [Where the Symposium was held.—EDITOR.]

IX

On Grading[1]

J. O. URMSON

A. An Outline of Some Typical Grading Situations

If you have an apple tree you know very well that all the apples will not be worth eating and that in a normal season there will be more apples on the tree which are fit for eating than you can eat immediately on ripening. Therefore, when you gather your crop, you will probably divide it into three lots—the really good apples, the not-so-good but edible, and the throw-outs. The good ones you will store (or perhaps sell some at a high price), the not-so-good you will use at once (and perhaps sell some at a lower price), the throw-outs you will throw out, or give to your pigs, or sell at a very low price for someone else's pigs. Let us call this process by the name which, in more complicated forms, it bears in the packing sheds of commercial growers—*grading*. Let us call *grading labels* the adjectives which we apply to the different grades as names of those grades—good, bad, indifferent; first-rate, second-rate, third-rate; high quality, medium quality, low quality; and so on.

In the sequel I intend to extend the expressions 'grading' and 'grading labels' beyond their normal employment to cover operations and words which, from the viewpoint from which I shall discuss them, seem to me to be essentially similar to grading in its narrower sense. There will be no harm in this if we realize that we are doing it and if we make sure that

[1] Many of my Oxford colleagues will notice unauthorized borrowings, sometimes involving distortions, from their theories. Mr. Hare suffers worst; I have had the benefit of many discussions on this subject with him. Professor Austin suffers next worst, but many others will notice minor peculations.

the other operations and words are really essentially similar to the more obvious cases of grading.

First I will make a series of fairly non-controversial remarks about the more obvious and unmysterious cases of grading.

(1) Often, instead of carrying out the physical process of grading, which may be futile or impossible, we do something which I shall call mental grading (on the analogy of 'mental' arithmetic). For example, a permanent-way inspector examining railway sleepers will presumably grade them mentally in such grades as 'in good condition', 'in fair condition' and 'unserviceable'. But though he does not rip the sleepers from the track and put them in piles he is clearly not doing something importantly different from physical grading. Mental grading is obviously more common than physical grading. We shall not often need to distinguish them.

(2) Grading and the application of grading labels are common activities. Inspectors of goods, tea-tasters and the like (and examiners) do it professionally; we all need to do it for the ordinary purposes of life.

(3) In the case of physical grading one can learn to carry out the physical processes correctly, in some cases at least, without any previous knowledge of the objects being graded and with absolutely no knowledge of the opinions about and attitude towards the objects being graded of the person from whom one learns to carry out the processes, or, for that matter, of anybody else. Thus, for example, a person who had never seen an apple before, nor tasted one, and who knew nothing of your, or anybody else's, opinions about and attitude towards apples, would, with reasonable intelligence, and after a period of observation, learn to help you to put the apples into the correct piles merely by watching you do it. The greater his intelligence and the longer his apprenticeship, the more nearly infallible he would become; of course, there would be marginal cases in which he would differ from you, but in these you might as easily have differed from yourself. An instructive point should, however, be noticed here. Without further information our intelligent apprentice, although he would have learnt to grade the apples, or sleepers, in the sense in which a parrot can learn to speak English,

might realize no more than the parrot that he was grading. He might not guess but that he was playing some rather tedious game, or tidying up, just as if he were sorting out white and black draughts pieces, or assisting in some scientific classification; he need not speculate on what he is doing at all. As we might say that the parrot was not really speaking English, knowing just what we meant to convey by this, so we might say that the apprentice, unlike you, was not really grading. This state of affairs would be particularly likely to occur if you either did not tell him what grading labels you were employing, or else used such words as are not usually used for grading purposes.

Clearly the same possibilities and limitations would occur in the case of mental grading providing that the apprentice heard the grading labels used with reference to the various objects without recognizing them as grading labels.

One moral of this is quite obvious; grading, like speaking English in the sense in which parrots cannot speak English, or lying, or committing murder, is something which you cannot in a full sense do without understanding what you are doing. The other moral, equally obvious, is that grading is quite different from tidying up or scientific classification, but the difference lies in the purpose of the grader, not in its external form.

(4) It is perhaps instructive to notice a possible half-way house between your situation as a fully conscious grader and that of your ignorant and inexperienced, but intelligent and observant, apprentice. Suppose that you use the grading labels 'good', 'indifferent' and 'bad' of your piles of apples; then (more on this topic later), since they are adjectives, which are consecrated to use as grading labels, your apprentice, in addition to his former capacity of going through the right motions, will presumably also realize that he is grading. What he will lack which you have will be firstly an understanding of why you grade one pile more highly than another, though he will be able to distinguish the sets and know which you grade more highly, and secondly any conviction whether he would himself choose to grade on your principles if left to himself. Here too, for these reasons, there would be some

point, though not as much as in the case imagined in (3) above, in saying that the apprentice is not really grading. Compare with this our tendency to say that the person who merely echoes conventional moral judgments correctly is not really making moral judgments, remembering especially what Plato has to say of those who have only opinion and not knowledge in moral matters.

(5) In our examples we have considered cases of grading, mental and physical, where we have dealt with a large number of objects of a certain type, such as apples or railway sleepers. These are perhaps the only cases which can properly be called grading. But we do sometimes apply the same grading labels to single objects without explicit reference to any others, but using the same criteria. I cannot see any important difference in the two situations, and I shall refer to this type of situation as grading as well as the other. This is one of the ways in which, as I admitted, I intend to stretch the word.

(6) Finally, it should be clear that, whatever else there may be that is puzzling about grading, in ordinary typical cases, at least, there is no puzzle about or doubt that it is a business done in accordance with principles and which one can learn to do in the way other people do it. There is no doubt that even the most ignorant apprentice can learn how to go through the right motions by watching other people do it. As a spokesman of the Ministry of Agriculture has wisely said, 'proficiency in grading to the most rigid standards is easily acquired in practice, although a precise, and at the same time simple, definition of those standards in words or pictures is a matter of difficulty'.

B. *Types of Grading Labels*

Before trying to throw any further light on the nature of grading and its difference from other language-using procedures such as scientific classification it would be advisable to examine a little more closely the grading labels which we use in grading.

(1) It is clearly possible, and often done, to employ *ad*

hoc, without abuse of one's language, a very wide range of words (marks, etc.) as grading labels, including made-up words and words which sometimes are used for purposes other than grading. For example, I might use 'red', 'white', 'blue' in this way, or 'class X', 'class Y', 'class Z', where it would be necessary explicitly to say what order of merit they convey; I could equally well use 'red' for the best and 'green' for the worst, or vice versa. Still avoiding controversial issues, it might none the less be worth pointing out here one of the advantages of the use of *ad hoc* labels. More professional grading labels naturally tend to become emotionally charged for good or ill, especially extreme ones; using *ad hoc* grading labels in their place is a way of ensuring objective unbiased calm. It is easier to hand back a paper to a pupil marked 'δ' than marked 'stupid and worthless'.

(2) But there is also a large class of words, called 'professional' in the preceding paragraph, which are used almost exclusively, or quite exclusively, as grading labels. Some obvious examples are 'first class', 'third rate', 'good', 'indifferent', 'bad', 'medium quality'. These can be used as grading labels without explicit warning; they themselves give warning, if it is not otherwise evident, that the object of the exercise *is* grading. Furthermore, it is easy and natural to choose sets whose order is clearly defined. It would be an abuse of language to use 'indifferent' of a higher grade than 'good'. It is indeed almost a necessary professional qualification of grading words to show their order; not so invariably (nor would we wish it), some show also their absolute position in the hierarchy of grades immediately. Thus 'first rate', 'second rate', 'third rate' show both order and absolute position— therefore they require careful handling as more precise tools do. But, whereas 'good', 'bad', and 'indifferent' show their order, they do not show their absolute position. This has to be determined from time to time, if precision is required. 'Good' for example can be at the top of a hierarchy or quite low down. Many parents have received school reports in which their children's work has been graded in different subjects as

V.G., or G., or F., and, at the bottom will appear some such list as

$$E. = \text{Excellent}$$
$$V.G. = \text{Very Good}$$
$$G. = \text{Good}$$
$$F. = \text{Fair}$$

etc.

One obvious trick of sellers of graded wares is to use 'good' very nearly at the bottom and a number of superlatives above it.

(3) Some words which are professionally used mainly or exclusively as grading labels can be used in grading many different kinds of objects, persons, activities, etc. This applies, for example to 'good', 'bad' and 'indifferent'. Other professional grading words, which, for this and other reasons to be given below, may be called 'specialized', are restricted to one or a few types of objects. For example, the terms 'Super', 'Extra Fancy', and 'Domestic' are, so far as I know, used as an ordered series with absolute position only of commercial consignments of apples. No doubt they could be used in a slightly less specialized way of other merchandise. Some, at least, of them could only be used very abnormally and metaphorically for people or activities.

An especially interesting and important set of specialized grading labels must be mentioned here. In calling them grading labels at all I acknowledge my second stretch of the word 'grading' and I must defend it. 'Rash', 'brave', 'cowardly', 'extravagant', 'liberal', 'mean', 'boorish', 'eligible (bachelor)', 'arrogant' are examples. Aristotle, in Books III and IV of the N.E. and Theophrastus in his *Characters* give numerous examples of such grading labels and seek to set out the criteria for their employment. As Aristotle noticed, we tend to have explicit grading labels only for some positions in some of the implied scales. Similarly 'indifferent' is a more sophisticated word than 'good' and 'bad'; it tends not to be used in popular discourse. They can be recognized as grading labels in that they show order of merit.[2]

---

[2] ἔνια γὰρ εὐθὺς ὠνόμασται συνειλημμένα μετὰ τῆς φαυλότητος.

If an Army Company Commander were, as a preliminary to choosing a band of men for an important operation, to go through his Company roll marking each man as 'rash', 'brave' or 'cowardly' we would surely not find it abnormal to say he was grading them (from a specialized point of view). If one were merely to say 'He is a brave man' one would not normally call it grading; but I cannot see that the stretch of the word so to call it is harmful. One resistance to calling 'brave' a grading label arises from the fact that being more specialized than 'good' it enables one to predict more accurately, though in a narrower field, the behaviour of a man so graded. This inclines people to think that it is a descriptive word in the way that 'ferocious' normally is. But this is just a mistake; the resistance must be overcome. It would be better to regard 'brave' as a grading label restricted to human behaviour in tight places, whereas 'good' grades in all places, including tight ones.

(4) As would be expected, specialized grading labels show absolute position as well as order more explicitly and more frequently than more general ones.

(5) In addition to professional and *ad hoc* grading words there are a number of what we might call enthusiastic amateurs—words of which it is difficult to say whether they function as grading labels or in ordinary classification. Sometimes they are obviously being used for the one purpose, sometimes for the other; often we seem to be killing two birds with one stone and grading and classifying at the same time. Examples of such words would be (*a*) *valuable*; contrast 'Her jewels were in bad taste but valuable' with 'That was valuable information'; (*b*) *nonsensical,* especially as it occurs in the works of some Logical Positivists—it is often hard to say whether a Logical Positivist who states that ethical statements are nonsensical wishes thereby to rate them lower than scientific statements, or merely to note a difference of logical type; one often suspects he is doing both. *Normal* is another example.

Aristotle, N.E., 1107 a 9. Aristotle unfortunately says this of a few words and does not see that it applies to nearly everything which he discusses in this work.

Conversely, even the most professional grading labels can be used sometimes practically descriptively—almost entirely so in the case of 'I walked a good four miles'; and often 'He gave him a good hiding' is used more to indicate severity than propriety.

There is nothing surprising or disconcerting in this. It will be convenient in the main, however, to examine typical, un-equivocal examples of grading situations. One should be aware of marginal cases, but one should not harp on them.

(6) Apart from these marginal cases a further qualification must be made. Sometimes I merely describe an object and do not grade it explicitly when clearly my prime object is to grade. Thus two of the criteria for being a boor which The-ophrastus gives us in his *Characters* are singing in one's bath and wearing hobnailed boots. Now I might mention that a man sings in his bath and wears hobnailed boots and not say that he is a boor although my prime object was to grade him as a boor. The reverse, too, can no doubt happen. In the packing sheds an employee might mention that a certain pro-portion of a batch of apples was Extra Fancy when his prime object was to give the implied descriptive information. Or I might tell you that a man has a good complexion primarily to enable you to recognize him. It seems worth while explicitly to make this point because when made it is clearly not a dam-aging admission. If I distinguish commands from descriptions it would not be damaging to admit that I might say 'The door is open' with the prime intention of getting you to shut it.

(7) A further reason for distinguishing specialized from more general grading labels in that the specialized ones tend to have more clear cut and explicit criteria for their employ-ment. This can best be illustrated by an actual example, so I will now quote from a Government publication the directions for the use of the grading labels *Super* and *Extra Fancy*, which were mentioned in (3) and which have been estab-lished by regulations made under the Agricultural Produce (Grading and Marketing) Acts of 1928 and 1931.[3] For brevity's sake the criteria for the grades *Fancy* and below are

[3] *Apple Packing*, Bulletin number 84 of the Ministry of Agri-culture and Fisheries, Appendix I. Published by H.M. Stationery Office.

not quoted here. They are similar in principle and are given in full in the original document.

DEFINITIONS OF QUALITY

SUPER GRADE (DESSERT APPLES ONLY)

Size.—Each apple not less than 2½ in. in diameter. The apples in any tray to be closely uniform in size and not to vary by more than ⅛ in. in diameter.

Ripeness.—Each apple to have reached that stage of maturity which allows the subsequent completion of the ripening process.

Shape.—Each apple to be of good shape.

Blemish (other than russet).—Each apple to be entirely free from all blemishes including mechanical injuries, bruises and apple-scab.

Russeting.—Russeting in which the apple is cracked, and corky russeting, are not permitted on any apple. Solid russeting in the stem cavity and lightly dispersed russeting sprinkled over an aggregate of one-eight of the surface are permitted.

Colour.—Closely uniform in any tray.

Condition.—The apples in any tray to be closely uniform in stage of maturity.

EXTRA FANCY GRADE

Size.—Dessert.—Each apple not less than 2¼ in. in diameter.
 Cooking.—Each apple not less than 2½ in. in diameter. } The apples in any container to be reasonably uniform in size and not to vary more than ¼ in. in diameter.

Ripeness.—Each apple to have reached that stage of maturity which allows the subsequent completion of the ripening process.

Shape.—No apple to be mis-shapen or malformed.

Blemish (other than russet).—Each apple to be free from such blemishes, bruises and other mechanical injuries as may affect keeping quality during the period which normally elapses between the time of packing and retail sale.

Uncracked apple-scab on any one dessert apple not to exceed ⅛ in. square in the aggregate, and no one scab to be larger than 1/16 in. square (a pin head).

Uncracked apple-scab on any one cooking apple not to exceed ⅛ in. square in the aggregate and no one scab to be more than ⅛ in. in diameter.

Other superficial, non-progressive blemishes on any one apple not to exceed 4 in. square in the aggregate on dessert apples and ⅜ in. square in the aggregate on cooking apples.

Russeting.—Russeting in which the apple is cracked is not permitted. Solid or corky russeting in the stem cavity and eye basin is permitted. Dispersed russeting, together with solid russet spots not exceeding ½ in. in diameter sprinkled over an aggregate of one-third of the surface, is permitted.

Colour.—Dessert apples in any container to be reasonably uniform in colour.

Condition.—Dessert apples in any container to be reasonably uniform in stage of maturity.

(8) Many grading labels which have a specialized meaning can also in isolation be used more generally. 'Super', in slang usage, is an example. This constitutes a further reason for the use in technical contexts of *ad hoc* grading labels.

Since these have no conventional criteria for employment there is no danger of confusing a general with a specialized employment as would be possible in the case of such a statement as 'That was a super consignment of apples'.

(9) In addition to the general philosophical problem of the nature of grading, the more general (less specialized) grading labels raise special problems of their own. It is perhaps partly for this reason that philosophers, who relish difficulties, have concentrated their attention on such general grading labels as 'good' and 'bad'. (There seems to be no good reason why they have neglected 'indifferent'.) One unfortunate result of concentrating on examples which raise special problems in contexts (ethical ones) which are especially complicated has been that the *general* problem of the nature of grading has been made to appear vastly more difficult than it is.

As a matter of fact 'first class' raises practically all the special problems which 'good' does, but for convenience I will now mention some of these special problems using 'good' as my example.

(*a*) Granted that 'good' is a grading label, is it used so generally because the criteria for its employment (corresponding to the technical criteria for the use of Extra Fancy) are very general, or because a different set of criteria is used in each different type of context (one set for apples, one for cabbages, one for guns, one for moral agents, and so on)?

(*b*) Granted that there are criteria for the use of some specialized grading labels which it would be linguistic eccentricity not to accept, is it so obvious that in every situation there are accepted criteria for the use of the label 'good', whether general or specially adapted to the context? Certainly if there are any criteria for the employment of the label 'good' they will be vague; but are there any, however vague, which are generally accepted? (This will be recognized as the familiar ethical difficulty about moral relativity.)

(*c*) Do there not appear to be many meanings of 'good'? Even if it turns out to be a grading label with accepted, though vague, criteria in some contexts (e.g. apple grading) may there not be others where, though not used as a natural description (as in 'good hiding'), it is not used as a grading label either?

(10) These special difficulties about such very general labels as 'good' must be admitted to infect more specialized grading labels in some cases, since many of them conceal a reference to good amongst their criteria. For example, in the show ring some of the criteria for judging animals are such pedestrian questions as whether this bit of the body is in line with that. But nearly always, I suspect, certainly in some cases, points are given for something like 'good general appearance' or 'good bearing in the ring'. See also the example of grading standards given in B(4) above.

C. *The General Nature of Grading*

In B we outlined some of the special problems about 'good'. Some of the most famous conundrums were missing, but this was partly because they apply to all grading labels. The basic problem *why* I grade higher a truthful man than a liar, or regard a whole apple as better than a pest-infested one, applies equally to the question why the criteria for Super should not be exchanged for the criteria of Extra Fancy. I shall start, therefore, by dealing with some of the general questions about grading, avoiding the special problems raised by 'good' and kindred words as long as I conveniently can.

Let us take a symbolic instance where X is a specialized label and A, B and C are the acknowledged natural criteria for its application. Let us further concentrate just on elucidating the question of how logically the use of a sentence 'This is X' differs from other uses of sentences, and how much and in what way it resembles some other uses. Thus for the present such questions as *why* A B C are the criteria for X will be disregarded.

The first thing which seems clear is that the question whether this is X is, granted the acknowledged criteria, as definitely decidable as are the empirical questions whether this is A, or B, or C. Of course, if A = 'not less than 2 inches in diameter', then the question whether this is X might be disputed in a marginal case because it might be disputed whether it *is* not less than 2 inches in diameter. But this kind of uncertainty obviously need not detain us now. The point is that if this has the empirical characters A, B, C, then it merits the grading label X, and if not, not; and this, in the required sense, is a decidable issue.

The facts noticed in the last paragraph tempt us to say that 'This is X' is just an ordinary empirical statement, that X is just an abbreviation for A B C; the relation of 'Super' to its criteria will be the same as 'Bramleys' to *its* criteria. But this doctrine, which will be recognized as a close relation of the doctrine of ethical naturalism, surely does not survive much reflection. At this stage we may merely note that the puzzle of how our intelligent apprentice was to distinguish apple grading from sorting out black and white draughts pieces is in effect repudiated by this naturalistic doctrine with the answer that there is no real distinction. And this is obviously false.

A second possible theory of the relation of X to A B C is a close relation of the doctrine of ethical intuitionism. Having rejected naturalism, but recognizing the close connection between X and A B C, we shall say, on this view, that X-ness (say, Extra Fanciness) is a non-natural, intuitable, toti-resultant character supervening on situations in which A B C are present, necessarily, but synthetically, connected with A B C. (If X-ness had been goodness and A knowledge this would not have been too much of a parody of intuitionism.) One negative argument for the view is that we have seen that naturalism fails, and that since the question whether this is X is decidable (objective) subjectivism will not do; nor, clearly, is it plausible to regard 'This is an Extra Fancy consignment of apples' as a squeal of delight. So in default of other theories Intuitionism stands. More positively we may say that 'Extra Fancy' is an adjective used in true or false statements; it must stand for some character; but it is not possible to see, hear, smell, Extra Fanciness, so it must be a non-natural character. Though I clearly do not accept this theory, I shall not attack it; probably even those who support it in the case of 'goodness' would not wish to support it in the case of Extra Fanciness or Full Fruit Standardness.

The reason for mentioning it as a theoretical possibility is that all the arguments of Moore and Ross can be converted to apply in all cases of grading labels. It is hard to see why it should be true of 'goodness' but not of 'Extra Fanciness'.

I suppose that a case can be made for a Stevensonian[4] analysis in all grading situations. In stressing the close relation between X and A B C, it will be said, we have been concentrating on the second pattern of analysis too closely. Why the equivalence between X and A B C does not hold will become clear if we consider the neglected first pattern of analysis. To call an apple Extra Fancy would perhaps be to express a special type and degree of approval and call for it from others. Grading words will differ from others by the possession of a special emotive charge.

Certainly it cannot be denied that amongst words which are or become highly charged emotively are the more extreme of the more general grading labels ('good' and 'bad', but not so much 'indifferent', for obvious reasons). But we have already noticed that one extremely valuable use of *ad hoc* grading words is that by using them it is possible to grade without emotional repercussions.[5] It is perfectly intelligible that professional grading words should normally be emotively significant; it is true that we often exploit this emotive significance;[6] but to the true nature of grading these facts appear to be quite peripheral.

But all these three views, naturalism, intuitionism and the emotive theory have seized on some points of importance (so, we shall see later, have ordinary subjectivism and utilitarianism). Naturalism rightly emphasizes the close connection between the grading label and the set of natural characters which justify its use; intuitionism rightly emphasizes that this close connection is not identity of meaning and insists on the different logical character of grading labels and natural descriptions. Both rightly stress the objective character of grading. The emotive theory, agreeing with intuitionism about the fault of naturalism, rightly stresses that

---

[4] C. L. Stevenson, *Ethics and Language*. (Yale University Press, 1944).
[5] See B (1).
[6] See B (2).

the intuitionist cure of suggesting that grading labels are a special kind of non-natural descriptive adjective will not do.

At some stage we must say firmly (why not now?) that to describe is to describe, to grade is to grade, and to express one's feelings is to express one's feelings, and that none of these is reducible to either of the others; nor can any of them be reduced to, defined in terms of, anything else. We can merely bring out similarities and differences by examples and comparisons. That, too, in the end, would presumably be the only way of bringing out the difference between asking questions and giving orders (here, again, the marginal case such as 'Won't you go now?' must not be overstressed).

We can, for example, tell stories of people sorting out mixed piles of fruit into apples, plums and pears, and of people sorting mixed piles of apples into Blenheims, Bramleys, etc., and notice the difference between this activity and that of people who sort piles of mixed fruit into good, bad and indifferent piles, or Super, Extra Fancy, etc., piles. We can tell stories comparing also the distinction between mental classification and grading. Also, since philosophers are wedded to the expectation that indicative sentences will all be used for describing things, it will be as well to remind them of other non-descriptive (and non-emotive) uses of indicative sentences—Austin's performatory sentences, for example.[7]

Or let us go back to the problem of the relation between the natural criteria A B C and the grading label X which they justify. Is the sentence 'Anything which is A B C is X' analytic or synthetic? We have already noticed the naturalistic difficulties involved in answering 'analytic'; but yet the pointlessness, the impossibility, of maintaining that a thing is X if it is not A B C or denying that it is X if it is A B C makes the answer 'synthetic' equally unplausible.[8] But if we see that grading is different from ordinary description we can understand why this dilemma is insoluble; for the question

---

[7] [See above, pp. 363 ff.—EDITOR.]

[8] This will have to be modified later. See pp. 404–6. But this modification does not detract from the force of the argument in this context, where the acceptance of A B C as criteria is not being questioned.

whether the connection between two sets of characteristics is analytic or synthetic is a question which is designed to be asked where the related characters are descriptive. If not pressed too hard, the analogy of the relation between possession of the legal qualifications for a right or privilege and the possession of that right or privilege illuminates better the relation between natural criteria and grade far better than the analogy of expanded descriptive phrases and defined abbreviations. For to assert the possession of the legal qualifications for a certain right (say the vote), e.g. that one is a British subject twenty-one or more years old, not a peer, not mad, etc., is not to assert analytically the possession of the legal right; but to assert the legal right is not to assert the possession of any additional characteristics of a descriptive kind beyond these qualifications.[9] There are, of course, differences too; otherwise, being graded and possessing rights would be indistinguishable.

It may also be helpful to compare and contrast grading and choosing:

(a) There is an analogy between examining various objects and then saying 'I'll have that one'—which is a choice not a prediction—and mental grading.

(b) There is an analogy between examining various objects, and then picking one out to have, and physical grading.

There is a difference also in these cases which can be put by saying that between examining and choosing one grades, and chooses on the basis of one's grading.

Therefore (c) we may make up a more artificial example. Two captains picking sides will normally pick them on their estimate of the grade of the candidates for selection. But suppose there were certain rules for picking sides (say, that you have to pick the person who is first in alphabetical order) so that there would be a right and wrong way of picking your side. This example brings out the logical disparity which there can be between a non-descriptive activity like taking as a member of your side and the descriptive criteria for picking, and to that extent should make the relation between a grading label and its criteria less mysterious. It is not sur-

[9] [See above, First Series, Ch. VIII.—EDITOR.]

prising that there should be a close connection between
such an activity as picking something and the rules in accordance with which it is done and yet it be impossible to
ask whether this connection is analytic or synthetic; the same
thing should not be mysterious in regard to the natural criteria and physical grading. And if we see the unimportance
of the difference between choosing something and saying 'I
will have this' (we cannot ask whether the rule for choosing
entails 'I will have this one'), we might also see how unimportant is the difference between grading and applying a
grading label. Of course, choosing in accordance with a rule is
very different in many ways from grading; the analogy which
I want to stress is between the relation of rule to choice and
criteria to grade label.

As a final attempt to bring out the general nature of grading it might be worth considering the word 'approve' for a
while. It has been used frequently in recent philosophy to
elucidate some specific grading situations.

Many philosophers recently[10] have been examining the
distinction in English between the present perfect tense (I
sit, I run, I play) and the present continuous tense (I am
sitting, running, playing). It is obvious that they have very
different uses. Some verbs appear to have no present continuous, nor does their use in the present perfect appear similar to the use of other verbs in either the present perfect or
present continuous tense (I know, I believe, I regret). 'I
approve' seems also to be such an anomalous verb. It is, indeed, possible to use its present continuous tense but an
example will show how anomalous such a usage is: suppose
Smith has to obtain your approval if he wishes to do a certain
thing. Then you will signify your approval by writing 'I approve' (not 'I am approving'). Now supposing someone were
to dash into your room and say 'What are you doing?' just
while you are writing these words, you might possibly answer
'Oh, I'm just approving Smith's application'. Here 'I am approving' describes what I am doing, but the doing which I
describe is not asserting, expressing, evincing or having any

---

[10] I have learnt something about this from Professors Ryle and
Austin. I do not know who owns the patent.

feeling or emotion or state of mind. I am writing 'I approve'
and it is this action which I describe when I say 'I am approving'. To say, or write, 'I approve', however, is not to describe
anything at all—it can be described but is not itself a case of
describing. In the case above it is something like giving your
authority for an action.

Our other uses of 'approve' differ from this in many ways,
but at least resemble it in that they are not descriptive
uses.[11] Suppose, for example, someone says 'On the whole,
I approve of the licensing laws'. Clearly this is not so absurd
a thing to say as to give his authority for something which
does not need his authority. A better suggestion is that he
is grading the licensing laws as being on the whole at least
satisfactory. He might change his mind and henceforth disap-
prove, but this kind of change of mind is not the correction
of a factual error.

I do not wish to examine further the logic of approval
for its own sake. I agree, however, with the subjectivists and
emotivists in considering that the analogy between approving and grading is illuminating—but not in the way they
think, in that I deny that 'I approve' is a description of the
subjective events or that 'Please approve' is a request to have
certain feelings.

That is all I can do in the way of a logical description of
grading. Before going on to consider such other general problems as how we get the criteria in order to start grading we
may first consider some of the special problems about 'good'
and other very general grading labels.

D. Some Special Problems about 'Good'

We shall start with the assumption (to be argued later)
that 'good' is a grading label applicable in many different
types of contexts, but with different criteria for employment
in each. Now first it must be pointed out that such general
grading labels have a character equivalent to the vagueness
and open texture to which Dr. Waismann has drawn atten-

[11] If I say 'I approve—do so as well' there is no descriptive element in my statement.

tion[12] in the case of ordinary descriptive words. Take the example of an apple again; what are the criteria for its being good? First no doubt it must have a pleasant taste and straightway we have a case of a vague and open textured criterion. A pleasant taste for whom? it will be asked; and there is no definitely right answer. But we must not exaggerate this vagueness. For if we answer 'to a majority of apple eaters' there is nothing seriously wrong with the answer as there would be if we answered 'to the Archbishop of Canterbury' or 'to squirrels'. But can we guarantee that it will be a stable majority? Clearly not; but this should not be philosophically worrying; the simple fact is that but for the contingent fact that there is such a stable majority we should have to give up grading apples altogether or else give up using pleasant taste as one of the criteria for grading apples.[13]

The writings of some philosophers seem to suggest that pleasant taste is the only criterion of goodness in apples,[14] but this is surely false. Other criteria are size, shape, keeping quality, nutritive value, pleasing appearance and, perhaps, feel. Now we have already noticed vagueness and open texture within one criterion. But the list itself has the same properties. No one can give the precise list; some will omit a criterion I have given, add another, vary the emphasis, and none of them need be wrong (though we could produce a list which would be certainly wrong). And it is always possible to think of something else which might be taken as a criterion or which has been implicitly used as such and not been noted. But surely as long as we recognize this it need not worry us any more than the vagueness of the criteria for the use of descriptive adjectives. 'Good' is *very* vague—so is

[12] *Proceedings of the Aristotelian Society*, Supplementary Volume for 1945. [Reprinted above, First Series, Ch. VII.—EDITOR.]

[13] As a matter of fact in the technical grading of apples taste is not used as a criterion. This, no doubt, is partly because you cannot both taste and sell whole, partly because the taste of varieties is constant and it is assumed that only varieties will be further graded which have already survived the test of taste.

[14] ' "This is good", may mean "This is pleasant" as when we say "This is good cheese" ' Paton, *Proceedings of the Aristotelian Society*, Supp. Vol. XXII, p. 110.

'bald', or 'middle-aged'. So long as there is a general consensus in the employment of criteria all is well. If, as sometimes happens in the case both of vague descriptions and
of vague grading labels, this consensus is missing, communication becomes uncertain (democratic, body-line bowling).

In contrast with the apple consider a cabbage (the contrast could be made much greater). Many of the criteria will
be quite different from those in the case of apples—firm
heart, a bright green or bluish-green colour, few spreading
outer leaves, long-standing, etc.

Now, if the grading label 'good' were, in each of these and
all other cases, merely shorthand for the sum of the criteria
(naturalism) we should have the absurd situation that 'good'
was a homonym with as many punning meanings as the situations it applied to; it could not significantly be used of a
theatrical performance in the sense in which it is used of an
apple. This, granted our present assumptions, constitutes a
most graphic refutation of naturalism. On the other hand,
to regard the relation between 'good' and the criteria for a
good apple as synthetic is equally absurd. If someone were
to admit that an apple was of 2 inches diameter, regularly
shaped, of pleasing taste, high vitamin content and pest-free,
nor claimed that it lacked some other essential characteristic
but none the less denied that it was a good apple it would
not merely be empirically surprising; it would involve a break-
down in communication.

The obvious naturalistic reaction to this, which, though
for different reasons, might be shared by other schools of
thought, would be to deny any assumption that the criteria
are different in each different type of situation. 'The real
criteria', they might say, 'for the employment of "good" are
much more general than you have made it appear. The criteria which a show judge might mention for a good Short-
horn cow or a cutler for a good knife are not the real criteria
of goodness. The real criterion is easy production of a desired
end, approximate or ultimate, in each case. 'The so-called
criteria', they might say, 'of the judge and the cutler are
really no more than signs or symptoms that the object in
question will satisfy this general criterion.' 'We must distinguish', they might add, 'the various senses of "good," pro-

visionally limiting ourselves to the modest distinction of good
as a means and good as an end. Then there will be one general criterion of good as a means—already given, and one for
good as an end which is perhaps something like "worth choosing for its own sake". Perhaps, on reflection', they conclude,
'we might wish to distinguish other senses, but we do not
require the myriad of punning senses you suggested but only
a few which in any case will be paronyms, not homonyms.'

No doubt this presentation of their argument could be
bettered in many details, but it is not in detail that I wish
to attack it, so perhaps it will suffice. Let me first admit that
if one examines the kinds of thing which one employs as
criteria, then, though this may not be the best way of putting
it, one possible division of the criteria employed is into criteria which we choose for themselves and others which we
choose for their consequences. Some criteria, too, as Plato
pointed out in the *Republic*, we choose both for themselves and their consequences. Let me also admit that some
criteria are less central than others, that some *are* used mainly
as signs of the presence of criteria more difficult to detect in
themselves. But these admissions in no way justify a distinction of two senses of 'good'—good as a means and good as
an end. Firstly, the criteria which we employ for the grading
label 'good' in any given case will usually include criteria of
both types, and of Plato's dual type; if there are indeed
any things for the goodness of which all criteria fall into
either class these are limiting cases and not normal types. It
would be a great mistake to imagine that farmers, cutlers
and fruit growers value their products only as means to ends;
and the consumer pays less for an unsightly vegetable because
it *is* unsightly and not because of any detrimental effects of
unsightliness. If I am asked whether a good apple is good as
a means or as an end I should not know how to answer; it is
not a real question. But the division of *criteria* which we
have admitted would only justify a distinction of two senses
of 'good' if it were logically impossible to mix the two sets
of criteria, if at all.

It might perhaps be replied to this, though even before
argument it is not very plausible, that all we have shown is
that normally anything which we grade as good we call good

in both senses of the word at once—*that* was why I could not answer in which sense of 'good' the apple was good. Still I have not established that there really are different sets of criteria for different types of situation. Let us answer that, even if an apple, *per impossibile*, satisfied all the criteria which we require for good as an end and good as a means in the case of cabbages, it would not be a good apple. Though we have agreed that some criteria are less central than others, there still remains a hard core of criteria which have to be satisfied in each different case, which cannot be generalized into any one or two formulae. Why an apple which tasted like a good cabbage would certainly be a very bad apple we have not yet ventured to discuss; but a very bad apple it certainly would be; I cannot see how my imaginary opponents would be able to explain this fact, which seems to require different criteria for goodness in apples and cabbages (and *a fortiori* in men and guns). Omitting consideration of certain cant or slang phrases I see no reason for thinking that there is more than one sense of the word 'good'. On the other hand, since I deny an analytic identity of meaning between criteria and grading labels I still hold that the criteria are, as the facts seem to require, different in each situation.

I add at this stage two small points which perhaps illuminate and are illuminated by the above discussion.

1. Suppose that I, ignorant of horses, point to a horse in a field and say 'That's a good horse'. In a way we want to say that I know what I mean—after all I know how to use the various words and understand their syntax. But in a way we might want to say that I do not really know what I mean. For suppose that an expert had said 'That's a good horse'. Now, looking at it once, and at a distance, he may be mistaken; he needs more facts than he has in order to be confident of the truth of his statement. But the kind of lack of confidence which I ought to feel is quite different; for, unlike the expert, I will not be enabled by further examination of the horse to decide at all whether it is a good horse. And because I have made a statement which I just do not know how to verify or falsify (in the way grading statements are verified and falsified) we tend, as I suggested, to say that I did not really know what I meant.

2. Grading statements being, as I maintain, objectively decidable, they are, for many reasons, more important and impressive than mere indications of personal likes and dislikes. We therefore tend to use them when all we are really entitled to do is to state our likes and dislikes. Thus I might easily say 'That's a good horse' being ignorant of the criteria for a good horse and therefore really only entitled to say that I like the look of it. We really know this, as becomes clear when we reflect that only a very conceited person would chance his arm by saying 'That's a good horse' unless he knew or believed that his companion was as ignorant of horses as he was. We might say it to a city clerk—but not to a Newmarket trainer. These considerations help, I think, both to bring out the difference between grading and expressing one's likes, and to explain why some people, observing that we naughtily interchange them, tend to confuse them.

So much for the way we use such general grading labels as 'good' and how their use differs from that of more specialized grading labels, though the distinction is not a hard and fast one.

E. *The Establishment of Grading Criteria*

So far we have confined our study of grading to cases where it is fairly clear that there are criteria for grading, and without asking whether there must always be accepted criteria, or why the accepted criteria are accepted. We have certainly said nothing whatsoever to deal with such special problems as that raised by the moral reformer, who is often clearly intelligible and yet may almost be defined as the man who does not accept the accepted criteria. I cannot pretend to offer a complete answer to these problems, but there are a few things which are perhaps worth saying about them.

The first point to be made is that the question whether there are any objective and accepted criteria for grading and how they function, which we have just left, is a quite different problem from the problem why we employ and accept these criteria. This, I think, has not always been fully realized; but certain theories could be much more powerfully stated if they took it into account.

Subjectivism, in its traditional varieties as an account of how we use the word 'good' in general, for example, is usually stated in a manner which makes it an utterly absurd view. To say that there are no objective criteria, that there is no right or wrong opinion about whether this is good cheese or (to take a case of something which is clearly not good as a means) a good lap-dog, seems quite preposterous. Anyone who knew about cheese or dogs would laugh at you. It is equally preposterous, as Broad points out,[15] to hold that a statement that some cheese is good is a statistical statement about peoples' likes and dislikes, passions and emotions. But if we remodel this latter subjectivist theory and treat it not as a theory about the way we use the word 'good' but as a theory about how the criteria for grading cheese or lap-dogs come to be accepted and established, it becomes a much more plausible theory. The theory will now admit our account of how we use the word 'good'; its contribution will be as follows: it is a fact that there is a stable majority (we need not now settle among which people the majority will be) who prefer, like, choose, cheese with the characteristics A B C. Then A B C become the characteristics which are accepted even by the minority, for grading cheese. Thus even if one happens to hate all cheese, one will still be able sensibly to distinguish good from bad cheese; *mutatis mutandis* the same applies to lap-dogs or anything else. Before the acceptance of such conventional criteria for good cheese the question whether some sample of cheese is good will have no answer.[16] After their acceptance the question will have a definite answer. This seems to me, thus recast as an answer to a different question, a very formidable theory. In the case of cheese it is just about right.

But few philosophical theories have the monopoly of all truth; any rival which survives long does so because it has got hold of some important point. But most of the prevalent philosophical theories about the meaning of 'good' can be recast as theories of how we arrive at criteria of goodness.

Now, *a priori* there is no reason why there should be any

---

[15] See his essay on Hume in *Five Types of Ethical Theory*. I do not necessarily agree that Hume held this preposterous view.

[16] See pp. 405–7 below on this point.

one answer to the question why we accept the criteria which
we do accept. We might adopt some criteria for certain reasons and some for others. Consider a utilitarian theory of
goodness, for example, recast as a theory that we choose the
criteria we do choose because things satisfying these criteria
in a high degree subserve more easily the ends for which we
employ them. As a general theory this is no doubt lamenta-
bly inadequate, but as an account of why we employ *some*
criteria (e.g. sharpness in the case of a knife) it seems very
plausible, and I have no doubt that if it makes this limited
claim it is correct.

Or consider social theories of goodness (especially moral
goodness) which hold that a man or form of behaviour is
good in so far as he or it contributes to social life and well-
being. Once again, considered as an account of why we accept *some* of the criteria of goodness, I have no doubt that it
is of value. No doubt truthfulness as a criterion of a good
man is at least in part accepted for this kind of reason. And
if anyone wishes to maintain that this is a *rational* ground
for accepting the criterion, why not?

I have no doubt that there are other reasons for accepting
criteria for grading, but we cannot aim at a complete catalogue; in no circumstance could we have a right to regard
any catalogue as complete. No doubt some criteria for some
things are retained for all kinds of odd reasons. Perhaps few
people nowadays could imagine why a family is better if the
names of more of its former members and their interrela-
tionships are recorded.

But what of matters where there is not complete agreement on the criteria for grading something? This is a situation which surely does sometimes arise. If the disagreement
is minor it matters no more than minor disagreements about
the requirements for baldness. But disagreement is admittedly not always minor; the slayer and eater of aged parents
and the moral reformer now rear their (respectively) ugly
and reverend heads.

Schematically, the main patterns of moral and other grading disagreements seem to be as follows:

(1) We accept roughly or exactly the same criteria of
goodness (or of being first class, etc.) but haven't yet exam-

ined them all. When one says of some object under discussion
that it is good and the other says that it is bad, we will be
speculating on partial evidence. We can settle the question
by examining the other agreed criteria. This raises no problems, and its frequent occurrence is therefore insufficiently
noticed by philosophers.

(2) We accept the same criteria but it is a marginal case.
Here perhaps we shall never settle our agreement. But this
raises no more problems than the unsettlable dispute as to
who won a close race. Such disputes quite often occur and
naturally last longer and attract more attention than the first
type.

(3) We have no agreement, or very little, on criteria. Here
we just cannot settle our problems for the overwhelmingly
good reason that we cannot discuss them. We shall normally
assume that we have the same criteria and talk at cross
purposes until we find that we cannot settle our dispute. We
shall then either recognize what has happened and try to
reach some agreed criteria failing which further discussion
will be worthless, i.e. we shall stop discussing the undiscus-
sable question whether this O is good and discuss the question how to grade Os. The reasons we shall offer for accepting the criteria we propose will be such as were mentioned
in our last discussion. Or if we do not recognize our predicament we shall think each other stupid and/or dishonest and
fall back on rhetoric and abuse.

(4) We may have important disagreements on criteria
and Jones, the reformer, may know it. He may then openly
reveal himself as not asking the question whether a thing is
good or not by accepted standards, but as advocating new
standards, new criteria. In this case it will be clear that we
are not arguing whether a thing is good or bad in the ordinary
way as in (1) and (2) above but arguing what criteria to use
in order to argue that kind of question. More likely, and perhaps not so clear-headedly, he will use the rhetorical device
of talking as though his proposed new criteria were the accepted criteria; this is one of the most effective methods of
getting new criteria accepted.[17] This trick is commonly em-

---

[17] Stevenson, *Ethics and Language*, Ch. IX 'Persuasive Definitions' is very relevant here.

ployed not merely by moral reformers but also by advertisers
—they try to make you accept the characteristics of their
wares as criteria of goodness in that class of merchandise by
pretending that everyone (or all the best people) knows that
these *are* the accepted criteria. If people do not recognize this
device for what it is, it may either be successful with enough
people to get the standards actually changed or else we shall
go through all the trying manœuvres of type (3) above.

It should be added that criteria of grade can change without the impetus of a militant reformer. No doubt 'eligible'
was a grading word as applied to bachelors in the eighteenth
and nineteenth centuries. No doubt also the criteria of
eligibility gradually shifted, under the pressure of social evolu-
tion, from such things as a baronetcy and land to a good job
and railway shares.

If this rough schema of disagreements be accepted (in
practice of course the types will be complicated and mixed
up with each other) the answer to the problem of disagreement about grading criteria seems to be this: grading words
can only be *used* successfully for communication where criteria are accepted. Where they are not there can only be confusion and cross purposes until it is seen that the only discussion possible between such people is what criteria for grading
to adopt—grading words must then be discussed, not used.

The need for agreed criteria can perhaps be further illustrated in the following way. There are situations in which we
do not naturally use grading words at all and where, therefore, there are no accepted criteria for grading. Consider for
example the prime numbers. So far as I know, no one has
yet graded the prime numbers as good and bad, or first and
second class, and so far as I know there are no criteria for doing
so. Unless my inadequate mathematical training misleads me,
I suggest that if anyone were to say '17 is an exceptionally
bad prime number' there would be a complete failure to
communicate—a failure not due to anybody's ignorance or
incapacity. Only after criteria were adopted (I cannot imagine what in this case they would possibly be unless superstitious astrological ones) would such a statement be of any
use in communication. (Whether it would therefore be previously meaningless may be left to the reader to decide.)

But the extreme vagueness of the criteria in some grading situations undoubtedly makes it appear that there are no criteria to philosophers who like and expect things to be clear cut. Pre-eminently people might think this to be the case with the moral goodness of a person. We cannot hope to deal adequately with this point now but a few observations might be permitted and must suffice.

A good man, without further qualification, obviously must fulfil different criteria in different contexts (for club and church membership, for example). This appears to be so even if we qualify our grading label and write 'morally good'. In some contexts, one might almost say, the criteria of moral goodness in earlier twentieth-century England can be roughly specified as being conformity to Ross's list of *prima facie* duties. In other contexts what a man does will be less important and why he does what he does more important ('Motive not action makes a man good or bad'). Roughly the way to find out what criteria are being employed is to ask why the man has been graded thus. But however the criteria may vary from context to context they must and can be recognized for effective communication; without it we tend all too often merely to 'recite Empedoclean verses'.

A further resistance to recognizing the ordinary grading mechanism as operating in morals is set up by the undoubted fact that moral grading is so much more important; we feel so much more strongly about the attainment of high moral grades than others. Being a good cricketer is excellent in its way, but not vital; being a good citizen, a good father, a good man, is very different. This creates the impression that to call someone a good man is logically different from calling him a good cricketer. The one point I shall make about this is that in grading people in non-moral matters and in grading things we are dealing with dispensable qualifications in people and dispensable things. But moral grade affects the whole of one's life and social intercourse—a low grade in this makes other high gradings unimportant. The nearest approach to morals in indispensability is made by manners; and surely it is significant that we feel next most strongly after morals about manners—indeed there is a borderline where it is hard to distinguish which we are dealing with. But when we acknowledge these facts we surely give no reason for expecting a logical difference as well.

F. The Relation between Alternative Sets of Grading Criteria

Now for the final problem; when there are differences of opinion about what grading criteria to adopt in a given situation is there not a right and wrong about it; can we not say that these are the right, these are the wrong criteria; or are we to say that the distinction, for example, between higher and lower, enlightened and unenlightened, moral codes is chimerical? In some cases we would perhaps be content to admit that there was no right or wrong about it; the differences in criteria arise from different interests, different environments, different needs; each set is adequate to its own sphere. But in others we certainly do not want to say this; the distinction, for example, between higher and lower moral codes cannot be lightly brushed aside. Roughly the question of whether we wish to decide this issue appears to depend largely on whether the simultaneous use of different sets of grading criteria by juxtaposed groups is in departmental, dispensable matters, or in all-embracing matters such as moral codes (more or less enlightened) and manners (more or less polished or cultivated).

This problem is clearly a large one which for adequate treatment would require a book in itself. We can here only sketch a method of dealing with it.

Clearly when we debate which of two moral codes is more enlightened there is no ultimate court of appeal, no umpire, unless some agreed revealed religious code is treated as a *deus ex machina*. Nor will it do to say that 'more enlightened' means the same as 'the one I advocate'. This is shown by the fact that though I cannot admit that the code I advocate is less enlightened than yours, I can admit that it may be; just as I cannot admit that my present belief about anything is mistaken, but can admit that it may be.

The important clue for dealing with this problem is to notice that *enlightened, unenlightened, higher, lower* are grading labels. Of course, we cannot, when debating what criteria to use for moral grading, grade the criteria morally. But we can grade them by enlightenment provided, of course, that the disputants have an agreed set of criteria of enlightenment. We cannot hope now to give a complete and clear list of these criteria; no doubt they are vague; and it is easier to employ criteria than to recognize them. But surely one criterion would be that the reasons for adopting the criteria are not superstitious or magical; that some reasons can be given would seem to be another. Again, the contrast between the health, wealth and happiness of people living under different moral codes cannot prove the superiority of one code over another, but it does seem to be a criterion of enlightenment. The misery of slaves, for example, is surely a potent cause for the rejection of a moral code as unenlightened in which a slave owner or trader is a good man.

If people have not agreed criteria for enlightenment, I do not know what one can do about it. All co-operative activities, all uses of language, must start from some agreed point. One needs a fixed point to move the world with one's lever.

Finally two postscripts.

(1) I am not wedded to the words 'grade' and 'criterion'. I use 'grade' rather than 'evaluate', for example, largely because 'evaluate' tends to be associated with a special kind of theory. Again, in the Government directions for grading apples the word 'standard' is used as a synonym for my word 'criterion'. Possibly it is better in some ways but has the dangerous overtone for philosophers of 'moral standard'.

(2) Nothing has been said in this paper about 'right', 'wrong' and cognate words. The discussion has ranged widely enough without that. But it might be as well to make it quite clear that I do not regard them as grading labels. They function quite differently, and what I have said does not apply to them.

X

Historical Explanation

A. M. MACIVER

The ultimate stuff of history is the countless individual doings of individual human beings through the ages, together
with such natural events and facts as have conditioned those
human doings—events such as the normal alternation of fair
and foul weather or the cycle of the seasons, as well as earthquakes, inundations and droughts, and facts such as the fact
that here is sea and there is dry land, this land is fertile and
that is barren, this has coal and iron and that has none. But
these natural facts and events are important to the historian
only in so far as they condition human doings. The actual
individual doings, on the other hand, collectively make up his
subject-matter.

This is a plain fact which Idealist philosophers of history,
with their slogan that 'all history is contemporary history',
completely overlook. Oakeshott or Collingwood calls the history (let us say) of the Peloponnesian War a 'mode of experience', meaning by this his own experience in his twentieth-
century Oxford or Cambridge college room, forgetting that
what made the history was experience all right, but the experience of thousands of poor devils two dozen centuries ago.
The Idealist philosophers have unthinkingly transferred to
history an argument that was plausible enough when applied
to physical science. It is easy to argue that atoms and electrons are mere postulates of theory; nobody has ever met one
in the flesh; to say that they have such and such characters,
or behave in such and such ways, is only to say that this is
what physicists at present find it convenient to suppose. But,
whatever may be the case with atoms and electrons, human
beings are not mere creatures of theory. To say that we are

now doing whatever we are actually doing, and for the reasons for which we are actually doing it, is not to say merely that this is what some future historian is going to find it convenient for his purposes then to suppose. And, by parity of reasoning, whatever men were doing a thousand years ago does not depend upon what historians find it convenient to suppose now.

Individual human doings collectively make up the stuff of history. What each one of us is doing here and now is part of the subject-matter of the history that will be written in the future. If what we were all doing now were different, the history of this period would be different. But history is not itself the record of all these doings. The historian selects and (what is more important) generalizes. It is thanks to this that the proposition that 'all history is contemporary history' is not patently absurd, because it is true that each historian selects and generalizes with reference to his own contemporary interests. But his generalizations are true or false in proportion as they represent or misrepresent all the individual doings and happenings. (This is the foundation-stone upon which I am going to build the whole of my argument in this paper—a stone which the builders of philosophies of history hitherto have, so far as I can understand them, almost universally rejected.) To show up by contrast the character of all actual written history, we may perhaps find it convenient to suppose an ideal written history, which would tell the whole story of everything that ever happened to every human being, which we might call 'the Book of the Recording Angel'. The function of the historian (we might then say) is not, indeed, to copy out extracts from the Book of the Recording Angel, but it is to make an intelligent précis of some part of it. This is not to depreciate the work of the historian. The function of the Recording Angel could, after all, in a fully mechanized Heaven, be performed by an electrical device, whereas the making of the historian's précis requires intelligence. But, though the précis may be made for some particular purpose and omit what is not relevant to that purpose, it must not misrepresent the contents of the original.

But, although all history rests upon this same foundation and all actual history generalizes, there are many different levels of historical generality. What I have called 'the Book of the Recording Angel' may be regarded as the ideal limit to which history approximates as generalization tends to zero. At the lowest level of generality of all kinds of historical writing is biography—particularly that kind of biography which hardly professes to be more than a collection of anecdotes about its subject arranged in chronological order. This hardly generalizes at all: it differs from the Book of the Recording Angel itself only in that it selects, and that according to no fixed principle other than the accidental limitations of the writer's sources of information. Almost at the other extreme stands the sort of general world history which knows no epochs except the great technological revolutions which completely transformed the whole background of human life, for which hardly anything worth mentioning happened between the discovery of the smelting of metals at the close of the Neolithic Age and the perfection of the steam engine by James Watt. Slightly (but only slightly) less general than this is Marxian history, which considers events only in so far as they have affected or followed from changes in the large-scale organization of society for the production, distribution and consumption of economic goods. History at all these different levels is (that is to say, can be) equally good history. We do not get a better or a worse view of a field according as we take a bird's eye, or a man's eye, or a worm's eye view of it, though we get a different view; and yet they are all views of the same field.

Serious trouble only begins when levels are not distinguished. From this many futile disputes arise. Take for example the question, still often eagerly disputed, whether the acts of individuals determine the course of history. Obviously they do. The only proper question is: How much? History is nothing but the resultant of all the acts of millions of individuals, but the consequences of some individual acts are still distinguishable after a considerable lapse of time, while the consequences of others blend together almost immediately. The fact that John Smith at a particular time on a particular morning hurried to the local branch of his own bank and withdrew a much larger sum than he would normally have withdrawn, because he had heard that another bank had failed or was about to fail, goes down to history only as part of the fact that there was a run on the banks in that week, which precipitated a world financial crisis; John Smith's contribution can no longer be distinguished. On the other hand, the fact that General Brown, overcome by a fit of pessimism, surrendered the strategically vital fortress of which he was in command, when a more resolute general could have held it until relief arrived, perhaps led immediately to the loss of the war and a whole string of consequences, all of which can be traced back to that single act. Certainly the loss of the war will have other contributory causes. General Brown's surrender would perhaps not have had this result if the relieving force had been in a position immediately to retrieve the situation, but in fact it was not, because it was inadequately armed, because there had been financial corruption in the quartermaster-general's department, the causes of which corruption ramify back into the whole political and social history of the country. Still the fact remains that General Brown need not have capitulated, and that, if he had not, the war could have been won, so that the loss of the war and all that followed from it was the direct consequence of this individual act of capitulation. (The case might equally have been that of an unknown private soldier, who might have prevented the enemy from gaining what proved to be a vital point, though in that case it would probably escape mention in the history-books, for the question is only whether a chain of consequences could be traced back to an individual act, if it were known.) It is possible that, if General Brown had not capitulated unnecessarily, some other commander on the same side would have done so, but this is not certain and anyhow he might not have surrendered such a vitally important position. As, however, we take a broader and a broader view, such possibilities may begin to accumulate into probabilities. If General Brown was constitutionally liable to fits of pessimism, he should never have been appointed to command a strategically vital fortress in time of war. A country whose administration made such unwise appointments might by good luck come successfully through one war, but would hardly survive a series of wars if it persisted in the habit. Where such appointments are favoured by persistent conditions, such as the general decay of a social class from which military officers continue to be drawn, resulting in turn from a cause such as the ruin of a country's agriculture by the appearance of a more powerful competitor on the world market, it may be possible to predict that such a country will ultimately either be conquered in war or else succumb without fighting; though not precisely how or when.

We can see how this bears upon that favourite example in arguments about the influence of 'great men' in history—the part played by Julius Caesar in the history of the Roman Empire. It is almost certain that, if Julius Caesar had died in infancy, someone else would have unified the Mediterranean world under a single autocratic monarchy. The situation was ripe for it. Both Sulla and Pompey had already very nearly achieved it. As seen by the universal historian who thinks in no time-unit less than a century and no social unit smaller than a whole civilization, the picture would be just the same even if Julius Caesar had never lived. For those who take a closer view, however, the picture would have been very different. If Caesar had not lived, Rome might have had to wait another generation or even longer for a man who combined the necessary ambition with the necessary abilities, and the resulting prolongation of senatorial anarchy might have had effects which would have been felt for centuries. For his actual contemporaries the difference would have been all-important.

History at different levels has different periods and different turning-points. For his own subjects the death of an individual autocrat may mark an epoch, but for later historians it may be some event in the middle of his reign, perhaps hardly noticed by contemporaries, which marks the end of one period, which began long before he was born, and the beginning of another, which continued long after he was dead, the death of the ruler himself being something quite insignificant. Marx, though he introduced the conception of the Industrial Revolution, attached no particular importance to the introduction of power-driven machinery. His historical researches were mainly concerned with the transition from feudalism to capitalism, with the ultimate object of applying the lesson to predict the course of the expected subsequent transition from capitalism to socialism. Most interesting to him was the change in the distribution of social force which came when production for profit took the place of production for use. The introduction of power-driven machinery appears in his account as a mere incident in the subsequent development —just one of the devices by which capitalists, in a competitive economy, sought to turn the labour-power of the workers to more and more profit. Marx duly considers its multifarious social repercussions, but, from his point of view, none of them is so important as the introduction, centuries earlier, of the new economic motive of profit. If, however, we try to look at the history of the last few hundred years through the eyes of historians living thousands of years hence, we can see at once that the difference made by the transition from feudalism to capitalism will then have become almost imperceptible, but differences made by the introduction of power-driven machinery will be impossible to overlook. Yet this does not mean either that Marx was mistaken or that the historians of the future will be mistaken, but only that history divides into different periods at different levels of historical generality.

Now we can introduce the subject of 'historical explanation'. By this we must understand, I think, only such explanation as is part of the historian's business as such, and not include any further explanations in which use happens to be made of the historian's results. In this sense, whatever 'historical explanation' may be, it is not the scientific sort of 'explanation' described in Mill's *System of Logic*, Book III, chapter XII—the discovery of hitherto unknown universal laws of which particular phenomena are instances, and the resolution of universal laws into mere special cases of other universal laws even more general. When we say that history 'generalizes', we do not mean that it seeks to establish universal laws. We contrast the 'generality' of historical statements with the individuality of the facts on which they are based, meaning that they are related to those facts as the general proposition 'I possess some philosophical books' is related to the individual facts (my possession of this copy of Plato's *Republic*, and that copy of Kant's *Critique*, and so forth) which make it true. In logical terminology, the his-

torical proposition is 'general', but 'particular', not 'universal'.
A typically historical statement is 'The Normans defeated the
English at Hastings in 1066'. The battle itself was a vast med-
ley of individual actions and experiences—this man shooting
this arrow, that man avoiding it or being hit by it, horses
stumbling, men feeling pain or fear or exultation—but the
historical statement takes it as a whole and selects for mention just that aspect of it which bears upon the historian's
purpose—in this case, the fact that as a result the Duke of
Normandy was able to make himself King of England. It is
not the business of the historian to 'generalize' in any other
sense than this.

To say this is not to give orders to historians. It is only to
put a limitation on the use of the word 'history' in this discussion, which is, I think, supported by ordinary usage. I
think that most people would agree, for example, that in
Toynbee's *Study of History*, while many of the 'annexes' and
incidental digressions are real 'history', the body of the work
is not—it is a new sort of 'science'. Its object is 'explanation'
in Mill's sense—to discover the hitherto unknown laws governing the establishment and disintegration of civilizations. This
is something which only a trained historian can attempt, since
it demands an immense equipment of historical knowledge,
but, when he attempts it, he is going beyond history. It is
possible—we may grant this hypothetically, without committing ourselves—that historical research is wasted if its results
are not afterwards applied in this way; but, even so, the application is not historical research itself, any more than the
collection of social statistics is by itself the formulation of a
social policy, even if it is true that statistics are wasted unless
made the basis of a policy. It would be 'historical explanation' to account for the rise of the Sumerian, or the fall of
the Minoan, civilization, but it is 'scientific explanation' to
account for the rise and fall of civilizations as such. Even if
'historical explanation' is (as it may be) explanation by reference to universal laws, it differs from 'scientific explanation' in taking the laws as known and concentrating upon
the analysis of the particular event, asking which of the known
laws actually account for it, and how, and in connection
with what other particular events. This is what a historian

ordinarily does whenever he professes to 'explain' an event, or the origin of an institution, or any of the other things which it is thought to be his business to explain, and I take it that the question which we are intended to answer here is, what sort of an explanation this is (or can be).

Half of the correct answer to this question is, I submit, that there is a different historical explanation appropriate to every different level of historical generality. Even in the Book of the Recording Angel there will be explanation as well as simple narrative. It will say, not merely 'Napoleon was annoyed', but 'Napoleon was annoyed because his breakfast coffee had been weaker than he liked it'. This 'because' raises familiar philosophical problems. It suggests some such major premiss as 'All human beings are annoyed whenever they do not get exactly what they like', but we know that this is not in fact universally true. It is in a more recondite manner than this that the lukewarmness of the coffee 'explains' Napoleon's irritation. But I will assume that the nature of this sort of 'explanation' is a question for another symposium. It is not these problems, concerning the kind of 'explanation' appropriate to individual human actions, which are troubling us when we are puzzled about specifically 'historical explanation'. We are thinking of explanation at higher levels of historical generality. But the second half of my answer to this, the question which concerns us here and now, is that correct explanation at these higher levels can be nothing but the reflection of correct explanation at the individual level. Individual acts have individual causes. This I take as acknowledged, whatever the philosophical difficulties concerning the precise kind of causation involved. Just as the historical *statement* summarizes a large number of individual acts, representing a character which runs through them all—perhaps the way in which they all contributed to a particular result—neglecting all their multitudinous features which were irrelevant to this, so in the historical *explanation* some of the individual causes of the individual acts disappear as unimportant, but others add up to something which can be stated generally. Its validity consists in representing fairly the balance of the underlying causes. The difference between a correct explanation and an incorrect one, at any particular level of historical generality, corresponds to the difference, in optics, between an undistorted and a distorted picture, at any particular degree of reduction of scale, at which some details inevitably disappear.

Historical explanation becomes confused whenever there is confusion of levels. Perhaps for brevity's sake we must sometimes say such things as that Mr. Jones votes Conservative because he is a business man; but it is always dangerous. Mr. Jones votes Conservative for his own personal reasons, which can be indicated (though not without already generalizing) by saying that he was brought up as a Conservative, that all his friends are Conservatives, that his business experience has drawn his attention to the considerations in favour of the Conservative policy and against the Socialist, that nothing has ever happened to induce him to pay equal attention to the considerations on the other side, and that he is more biased than he himself realizes in favour of a political policy which would tend to his personal advantage. Other business men like Mr. Jones also vote Conservative, each for his own reasons, but all for similar reasons, because their situations are similar. This is the basis for the legitimate historical generalization that 'business men vote Conservative because the Conservative Party represents their class interests'. But it is confusion of levels to use this generalization to explain individual behaviour. Marxist historians are frequently guilty of this confusion, which results in absurd notions of 'economic determinism', implying that it is impossible for an individual to have any political opinions which are not those of his economic class. Idealist historians may commit the same confusion, implying that no individual can make his own judgments but that they are forced upon him by the Spirit of the Age. For events at the individual level explanations must be found at the same level. But the generalization that the Conservative Party is the party of the business men can legitimately be used (say) to explain the decline of the Conservative Party as a natural consequence of the decreasing importance of private, as compared with public, enterprise in the national economy. This is (that is to say may be, provided that the facts support it) a valid historical explanation at what we may call the 'Marxist' level of historical generality.

In historical explanation at all levels above the purely individual, whatever is unimportant is disregarded. This sounds subjective, but in fact there is no subjectivity in it, apart from the subjectivity of the motive dictating choice of a particular level. The test of importance, at any particular level, is a purely quantitative one. Factors are important in proportion as their influence is felt all over the field under examination. This is forgotten by those who object against the Marxian conception of history that it neglects all the spiritual achievements of mankind. So it does; but only because they are actually negligible at the level of generality with which it is concerned. In the case of every individual there are respects in which he resembles all or very many of his contemporaries and differs noticeably from any man of another period, and other respects in which he differs from all his contemporaries and may perhaps most nearly resemble some individuals of other periods. What are called the great spiritual achievements of mankind represent that individual distinction which sets the great man apart as much from his contemporaries as from any predecessors or successors. But this individual distinction has comparatively little influence on the course of history. What influence it does have may be called 'vertical' rather than 'horizontal'; that is to say, the great mind influences only comparatively few individuals in any particular generation, but continues to exert that influence (generally through the survival of writings, though it might be by an oral tradition) through many centuries. The influence of Plato or Aristotle in philosophy would be an obvious example. This sort of influence is imperceptible at the level of generality of Marxian history.

This is concerned with the general state of a whole society at a particular date, and its relation to the general state of the same society at an earlier or later date, and cannot be expected to attend to the achievements of individuals, however 'great', except in so far as they were immediately responsible for large-scale social changes which would not have occurred without them. And this happens even less often than it appears to do, for a movement may bear the name of a great individual, yet the part which it played in history may have comparatively little to do with him. Thus it would be absurd to deny that there is a Christian tradition which has done more to form our present ways of thinking and feeling than any other intellectual influence from the past, and equally absurd to deny that a great deal in Christianity derives from Christ, but it may well be doubted whether it is this part of Christianity which has ever had most general influence. What has determined the course of history, viewed on any large scale, at any particular period, has not been Christianity as such, but, if anything, the Christian Church as it was at that period, focusing a mass of beliefs of very varied origins, some of them old, some comparatively new (though perhaps expressed in old terms), traditions, moral intuitions, prejudices, considerations of sectional interest, and personal ambitions, in which the immediate contemporary interests of the clergy and the faithful bulk much larger than the general Christian heritage. Marxist historians can fairly be criticized for claiming (as they often seem to do) that history cannot legitimately be studied except at their own chosen level, but not for insisting that, at that level, it is only 'materialist' explanations which really explain. This is a simple consequence of the fact that men are more often bad than good, and more often stupid than intelligent, so that the acts of the exceptional individuals disappear from view as soon as the human scene is contemplated from any distance.

But there is also a level at which ideas have a history of their own, which is the level at which Idealist historians prefer to work. This is quite as legitimate as working at any other level, so long as it is remembered that 'absolute mind' is only a logical construction—that this sort of history is only another set of historical generalizations from the same mass of individual acts and thoughts of which we suppose the whole story written in the Book of the Recording Angel. New conceptions and methods of approach to intellectual questions are introduced by individuals, become fashionable and are very widely applied, until finally they are found for one reason or another unsatisfactory and gradually abandoned. Changes in material conditions can exert an influence here, because they may raise new problems which the old conceptions and methods cannot solve, thus hastening their abandonment; but the importance of this is probably much exaggerated by Marxists, and the Idealist historians may often be justified in disregarding it. In any case it is very naive to think that methods and conceptions will ever be abandoned merely because problems have arisen which they cannot solve. The fact that the old methods cannot solve the new problems will not be recognized. It will be alleged that they have in fact been solved already, or else that, though not solved yet, they will be solved soon, still by the old methods, or perhaps that they are completely insoluble. What forces the abandonment of old methods and conceptions is always the invention of new methods and conceptions which prove their superiority in competition, and this requires a certain lapse of time and may have to wait for the appearance of some individual of genius. In such a case it is not misrepresentation of the facts, provided that it is recognized as being representation at a very high level of generality, to tell the whole story in terms of problems, criticisms and suggested solutions—a doctrine failing to stand up to criticism, thus producing a problem, to which various tentative solutions are offered until finally the solution is found which is associated with a great name.

But it must be owned that Idealist philosophers of history show a disposition to suppose that the history of ideas must itself be 'ideal', in the sense of describing what they think ought to have happened rather than what actually did. When the individual of genius appears, he may not be immediately recognized, and will certainly not be recognized universally. Every educated person now knows something about the greatest thinkers of the past, but the minor writers are read only by historical specialists, and the great mass of the public, which wrote nothing, tends to become quite forgotten, and in consequence we are apt to remember those who were immediately influenced by a great mind and forget that there were many at the time who never tried to think for themselves hard enough to become aware that there was anything unsatisfactory about the conceptions and methods to which they had been brought up—to whom the views of the great man were nothing but unintelligible newfangled nonsense. I may be unfair to Collingwood, but it has sometimes seemed to me that, in his account of the 'presuppositions' of different historical periods, he considered only those outstanding philosophers whose achievement was so permanent that their works are still compulsory reading for 'Greats' at Oxford. But this is to confuse what the men of a period actually presupposed with what they *would* have presupposed if they had realized that Descartes (or whoever it might be) had solved their problems, when in fact most of them did not. And this seems to have tempted Idealist philosophers of history into an account of 'historical explanation' which is inadequate even to the history of ideas, to which the Idealist conception of history properly applies. They think that they have 'explained' the acceptance of a doctrine when they have shown that it solved a certain problem. But to show that the doctrine actually solved the problem is logic, not history. The historical question is, how it came to be accepted, which is not accounted for by the mere fact that it solved the problem, for a problem may be solved and the solution never be generally acknowledged, while conversely doctrines may be generally accepted which conspicuously fail to solve very urgent problems.

Practising historians may be expected to dislike an account of 'historical explanation' which reminds them that history rests on facts in the shape of actual human doings. This is the skeleton in their cupboard, and they prefer Idealist or Marxist theories of history, which enable them to keep the door shut on it. We may expect criticism on lines familiar to philosophers, being that used against all representative theories of perception and correspondence theories of truth. It will be said that our test of historical truth is a test which can never be made. We can never check a historical generalization against the individual facts on which it is based, because we are never presented with both together. For immediate contemporary history or at least that small section of it which we are ourselves actually living through—we have the individual facts, but it is notorious that we always find them so complex and confusing that we cannot at the time summarize them in any general historical statement. Historical generalization becomes possible as the events recede into the past, but then the individual facts are no longer there for comparison with the generalization. From some arguments in this vein it is difficult to see what is meant to follow, if not that a historian is a purely imaginative writer like a novelist, though this is not, I think, a conclusion which any practising historian would welcome. But all that is in fact shown is that the historian's conclusions rest wholly on circumstantial evidence and are peculiarly fallible. What is asked of him is nothing resembling the absurdity demanded by crude representative theories of perception—that it should be decided by mere inspection of 'representative ideas' whether or not they are good copies of 'things in themselves' which nobody has ever had knowledge of. The historian cannot pretend that he has no knowledge of any individual human action, since he is acquainted at least with his own actions and those of his friends, and we only ask him never to forget that the justification for all his statements (if they have any) is nothing but the similar actions of similar human beings, even if they lived a long time ago and in very different circumstances. Owing to lack of imagination, or simple ignorance, he may make what would have seemed to those about whom he is talking absurd mistakes concerning what they did or the reasons why they did it, and the mistakes may be inevitable in the sense that he has no evidence which should have enabled him to avoid them, but in the case of each particular mistake he might always have had such evidence that he would not have made it. He cannot claim that any of his statements is wholly true to the facts, but he also cannot pretend that there is any impassable barrier making it impossible for him to have known more of the facts than he actually does. It is true that he cannot check his statements by the facts, but only by the evidence, which is a different thing. The facts are individual, but historical evidence is often already at a high degree of generality—for example, memoirs and dispatches, not to speak of the writings of previous historians (what are called 'authorities'). Practising historians, therefore, naturally prefer what we may call 'coherence theories', according to which historical truth consists in agreement with the evidence, which they have before them, rather than with the facts, which they have not. This makes things much easier for them, just as it would be easier for the members of a jury if they could only feel that it was their duty merely to give a true verdict according to the evidence. But in fact every juryman feels that he would be giving an unjust verdict if he condemned a man who was actually innocent, whatever the evidence. If the verdict is according to the evidence, that makes its injustice excusable, but does not make the defendant justly condemned, if he has not in fact committed the crime. Similarly the historical statement which is the most probable on the evidence available may be the best that can reasonably be expected of the historian, but, if it misrepresents the facts, it is not true. As for Idealist talk of 'so-called historical facts' being nothing but what historians have said, that is only a device to increase the self-satisfaction of historians by enabling them to forget that, however near they may come to the real facts, they might always have come nearer.

These are topical questions now, not only in philosophy (owing to the publication of the posthumous works of Collingwood) but also in politics. The doctrine that 'all history is contemporary history' might seem nothing more than a stimulating paradox when enunciated by Croce or Collingwood, but we may well feel doubtful about it when we see how it is officially adopted and acted upon in the Soviet Union. In 1917, according to all contemporary accounts, from whatever source they emanated, without distinction of politics, Lenin's principal lieutenant in the Russian Revolution was Trotsky; but, according to the history of the Revolution as now taught in Russia and to Communists throughout the world, the second part was played by Stalin, of whom hardly any mention will be found in documents of the time. This is perfectly in accordance with the principles of the Idealist philosophers of history, according to whom what happened in the past is nothing but whatever it suits our purposes now to suppose to have happened then. Being themselves quiet Bourgeois Liberals, they thought only of quiet Bourgeois Liberal purposes and their conception of history remained mild and inoffensive. But now it has suddenly grown teeth, when it is found to have the consequence that the

Battle of Hastings might come to have been fought, not in 1066, but in 1067, or perhaps even in this present year 1947, and to have been won, not by the Normans, but by the English, or perhaps even by the Russians, if that happened to be demanded by the 'Party Line' in the twentieth, or the twenty-first, or the twenty-second century. I do not mean to imply that a doctrine ought to be rejected merely because it has received its final polish in Russia; but Russian ruthlessness in drawing logical conclusions does seem to me to have put it beyond doubt that this conception of history is radically false, although, as half-heartedly presented by Croce and Collingwood, it could still seem plausible.

At the root of this false conception lie, I think, two closely connected false assumptions. We are concerned with them here only as affecting history, but their influence is actually much more extensive. One is the assumption that, because we can never hope to free our opinions from all trace of error, therefore there is no truth, or the word 'truth' must be re-defined and re-applied to lend dignity to favoured errors. People like to think of the truth as something which they can hope some day actually to attain—not as something which will always be beyond them, even if they can always come nearer and nearer to it—and they are ready to re-define the term 'truth' to gratify this inclination. Historians do not like to think that their ideal is undistorted representation of actual past human doings, since this is something which one can do better than another, but none can do perfectly. They prefer to make their criterion of 'historical truth' agreement with the available evidence and the needs of their own time, success in this being in principle attainable. Yet it is surely obvious that a judgment may be the best that could possibly be made in certain particular circumstances, and yet false. We find it quite natural to say that the judgments of a particular historian are sound within certain limits, but in certain respects distorted by his nineteenth-century prejudices. In these respects we consider his judgments mistaken, without thinking that, living in the nineteenth century, he could have been expected to judge differently. Most of us are ready to allow that our own judgments are probably similarly distorted by twentieth-century prejudices, although we cannot say in what respects, since otherwise we should already have corrected them. When we say that they are distorted, we mean that they misrepresent the facts. If we did not recognize the ideal of correspondence with the facts, we could only say that the judgment would have been false if it had been made in the present century, but it was not, and in its own century it was true. Collingwood does say things like this when he remembers his own philosophical position, but sooner or later his natural good sense asserts itself and then we find him stating roundly that we can now see that on some points past historians were mistaken, though owing to causes which they could not help, such as lack of evidence.

The other false assumption is that, because no judgment can ever be wholly free from bias, therefore a less biased judgment is no better than a more biased one. In fact it is possible, even if difficult, to reduce one's own bias, though certainly not to eliminate it completely, and, other things being equal, the judgment is the more likely to be true, the less the amount of bias. (We may reflect that the world has come to a pretty pass when anything so obvious need be said, but every philosopher knows that this does not now go without saying.) But modern philosophies of history encourage historians to glory in their own bias and exaggerate it, and to approve or condemn other historians purely according as they do or do not share the same bias. There is Communist history, Fascist history and Liberal history, and it is approved or condemned as Communist or Fascist or Liberal according to the allegiance of the critic. Thought on this subject is almost always confused by considerations of the desirability of passionate convictions for resolute action, in which it is generally forgotten that, the more fervent the heart, the greater the need of a cool head. Marx himself (though not some modern Marxists) was well aware of this; just because he was devoted heart and soul to the Socialist cause, he insisted that an investigation of the means by which Socialism could be attained must be true to the facts and undistorted by wishful thinking; hence his life-long war against 'Utopian Socialists'. A historian may be none the worse for studying the past with an eye to applications in the present, but we must distinguish two very different kinds of application. There is narration

of past events in such a way as to encourage present support-
ers and discourage opponents, distorting wherever necessary
for this purpose; this is 'history' according to the prescription
of the Idealist philosophers, whose criterion is contemporary
needs, and in fact it is not history at all, but propaganda.
(Idealist philosophers will indignantly deny that this is what
they mean, and I know quite well that it is not what they intend, but in that case they ought to be more careful about
what they say.) The other kind of application is the discovery
that something happened in the past which may serve as a
guide to action in the present—indicating, for example, the
likely consequences of a particular course of action. This sort
of application I have already described as going beyond the
business of the historian as such, since it implies the detection of universal laws in the historical process, but it does
make use of the historian's results. What is important for our
purposes here is that it is a sort of application which would
be impossible with purely Idealist 'history'. The contemporary application depends upon the historical representation
being true to the facts, in the sense of what really happened
in the past; otherwise it would be merely misleading. In history we may say that pure Idealism meets its Waterloo, because in history we cannot do without 'things in themselves',
and the problem has to be faced, how they are 'represented'.

XI

Mathematics and the World

DOUGLAS GASKING

My object is to try to elucidate the nature of mathematical
propositions, and to explain their relation to the everyday
world of counting and measurement—of clocks, and yards of
material, and income-tax forms. I should like to be able to

summarize my views in a few short phrases, and then go on
to defend them. Unfortunately I cannot do this, for, as I
shall try to demonstrate, I do not think any short statement
will do to express the truth of the matter with any precision.
So I shall proceed by approximations—I shall discuss several
different views in the hope that in showing what is right and
what is wrong with them, clarification will come about.

The opinions of philosophers about the nature of mathematical propositions can be divided, as can their opinions
about so many things, into two main classes. There are those
who try to analyse mathematical propositions away—who say
that they are *really* something else (like those writers on
ethics who say that goodness is really only pleasure, or those
metaphysicians who say that chairs and tables are really groups
of sensations, or colonies of souls). I shall call such 'analysing-
away' theories 'radical' theories. On the other hand there are
those who insist that mathematical propositions are *sui
generis*, that they cannot be analysed into anything else, that
they give information about an aspect of reality totally different from any other (compare those philosophers who maintain, e.g. that goodness is a simple unanalysable quality, or
those realists who maintain that a chair is a chair, an external
material substance, known, perhaps, by means of sensations,
but not to be confused with those sensations). For convenience, I shall call these types of theory which oppose any
analysing-away, 'conservative'. I should maintain that in general what I call 'conservative' opinions in philosophy are
perfectly correct, but rather unsatisfactory and unilluminat-
ing, whereas opinions of the 'radical' type are untrue, but
interesting and illuminating.

I shall start by considering the 'radical' theories about the
nature of mathematics. Those I know of fall into two main
types. (1) Some people maintain that a proposition of mathematics is *really* a particularly well-founded empirical generalization of a certain type, or that it is logically on the
same footing as a very well-established scientific law. Mill's
theory was of this type, and many scientists I have talked to
have tended to have similar opinions. Let us call these 'empirical' theories about mathematics. (2) Then, on the other
hand, there is a great variety of theories usually called 'con-

ventionalist', which analyse away mathematical propositions into propositions about the use of symbols. Examples: 'By a mathematical proposition the speaker or writer merely expresses his intention of manipulating symbols in a certain way, and recommends or commands that others should do likewise'. 'A mathematical proposition is really an empirical proposition describing how educated people commonly use certain symbols.' 'A mathematical proposition is really a rule for the manipulation of symbols.' (Ayer, for example, and C. I. Lewis have expressed opinions of this general type.)

First for the 'empirical' theories. According to these a mathematical proposition just expresses a particularly well-founded empirical generalization or law about the properties and behaviour of objects, obtained by examining a large number of instances and seeing that they conform without exception to a single general pattern. The proposition '7 + 5 = 12', for instance, just expresses (on one version of this theory) the fact of experience that if we count up seven objects of any sort, and then five more objects, and then count up the whole lot, we always get the number twelve. Or again, it might be maintained that the geometrical proposition 'Equilateral triangles are equiangular' just expresses the fact that wherever, by measurement, we find the sides of a triangle to be equal, we will find, on measuring the angles with the same degree of accuracy, that the angles are equal too. It is contended that such propositions are essentially like, for example, Boyle's Law of gases, only much better founded.

But '7 + 5 = 12' does not mean the same as the proposition about what you get on counting groups. For it is true that 7 + 5 does equal 12, but it is not true that on counting seven objects and then five others, and then counting the whole, you will always get twelve. People sometimes miscount, and sometimes the objects counted melt away (if they are wax) or coalesce (if they are globules of mercury). Similarly the geometrical proposition that equilateral triangles are equiangular does not mean the same as the proposition that any triangle which is equilateral by measurement will be found to be equiangular when measured. The former is true; the latter false. We sometimes make mistakes with our rulers and protractors.

To this it might be objected that this shows that the empirical proposition offered as a translation of the mathematical one is not a correct translation, but that it has not been demonstrated that it is impossible to find an empirical proposition about counting and measurement, which is a correct translation. Let us try some alternatives, then. It might be suggested that '7 + 5 = 12' means 'If you count *carefully and with attention*, you will get such and such a result'. But, even with the greatest care in counting, mistakes sometimes happen at any rate with large numbers. Shall we then say: '7 + 5 = 12' means 'If you count *correctly* you will get such and such results'? But, in the first place, even if you count objects correctly, you do not always get a group of seven objects and a group of five adding up to twelve. It sometimes happens that a person correctly counts seven objects, then correctly counts five, and then correctly counts the total and gets eleven. Sometimes one of the objects does disappear in the course of counting, or coalesces with another. And even if this were not so, the suggested translation would not give you a simple empirical proposition about what happened when people counted, as a translation of 7 + 5 = 12, but would give you a mere tautology. For what is the criterion of correctness in counting? Surely that when you add seven and five you should get twelve. 'Correctness' has no meaning, in this context, independent of the mathematical proposition. So our suggested analysis of the meaning of '7 + 5 = 12' runs, when suitably expanded: '7 + 5 = 12' means 'If you count objects *correctly* (i.e. in such a way as to get 12 on adding 7 and 5) you will, on adding 7 to 5, get 12'.

No doubt there *are* important connections between mathematical propositions, and propositions about what results people will usually get on counting and measuring. But it will not do to say that a mathematical proposition means the same as, or is equivalent to, any such empirical proposition, for this reason: A mathematical proposition is 'incorrigible', whereas an empirical proposition is 'corrigible'.

The difference between 'corrigible' and 'incorrigible' propositions can best be explained by examples. Most everyday assertions that we make, such as that 'Mr. Smith has gone away for the day', are corrigible. By this I mean simply that, whenever we make such an assertion, however strong our grounds for making it, we should always freely withdraw it and admit it to have been false, *if* certain things were to happen. Thus my assertion, that Smith is away for the day, is corrigible, because (although I may have the excellent grounds for making it that when I met him in the street this morning he said he was on his way to the railway-station) if, for example, I were to go to his room now and find him sitting there, I should withdraw my assertion that he was away and admit it to have been false. I should take certain events as proving, if they happened, that my assertion was untrue.

A mathematical proposition such as '$7 + 5 = 12$', on the other hand, is incorrigible, because no future happenings whatsoever would ever prove the proposition false, or cause anyone to withdraw it. You can imagine any sort of fantastic chain of events you like, but nothing you can think of would ever, if it happened, disprove '$7 + 5 = 12$'. Thus, if I counted out 7 matches, and then 5 more, and then on counting the whole lot, got 11, this would not have the slightest tendency to make anyone withdraw the proposition that $7 + 5 = 12$ and say it was untrue. And even if this constantly happened, both to me and to everyone else, and not only with matches, but with books, umbrellas and every sort of object—surely even this would not make us withdraw the proposition. Surely in such a case we should not say: 'the proposition "$7 + 5 = 12$" has been empirically disproved; it has been found that $7 + 5$ really equals 11'. There are plenty of alternative explanations to choose from. We might try a psychological hypothesis, such as this: we might say that it had been discovered by experiment that everyone had a curious psychological kink, which led him, whenever he performed counting operations of a certain sort, always to miss out one of the objects in his final count (like the subject in some experiments on hypnosis who, under suggestion, fails to see any 't's on a printed page). Or we might prefer a physical hypothesis and say: a curious physical law of the universe has been experimentally established, namely, that whenever 5 objects are added to 7 objects, this process of addition causes one of them to disappear, or to coalesce with another object. The one thing we should *never* say, whatever happened, would be that the proposition that $7 + 5 = 12$ had been experimentally disproved. If curious things happened, we should alter our physics, but not our mathematics.

This rather sweeping assertion that mathematical propositions are completely incorrigible is, I think, an over-simplification, and needs qualifying. I shall mention the qualifications later, rather than now, for simplicity of exposition. So if you will accept it for the moment as very nearly true, I should like to draw your attention to certain of its consequences. A *corrigible* proposition gives you some information about the world—a completely *incorrigible* proposition tells you nothing. A corrigible proposition is one that you would withdraw and admit to be false if certain things happened in the world. It therefore gives you the information that *those* things (i.e. those things which would make you withdraw your proposition *if* they happened) will *not* happen. An incorrigible proposition is one which you would never admit to be false *whatever* happens: it therefore does not tell you *what* happens. The truth, for example, of the corrigible proposition that Smith is away for the day, is compatible with certain things happening (e.g. your going to his room and finding it empty) and is not compatible with certain other happenings (e.g. your going to his room and finding him there). It therefore tells you what sort of thing will happen (you will find his room empty) and what sort of thing will not happen (you will not find him in). The truth of an incorrigible proposition, on the other hand, is compatible with any and every conceivable state of affairs. (For example: whatever is your experience on counting, it is still true that $7 + 5 = 12$). It therefore does not tell you which events will take place and which will not. That is: the proposition '$7 + 5 = 12$' tells you nothing about the world.

If such a proposition tells you nothing about the world, what, then, is the point of it—what does it do? I think that in a sense it is true to say that it prescribes what you are to *say*— it tells you *how to describe* certain happenings. Thus the proposition '$7 + 5 = 12$' does not tell you that on counting $7 + 5$ you will not get 11. (This, as we have seen, is false, for you sometimes do get 11.) But it does *lay it down*, so to speak, that *if* on counting 7 + 5 you do get 11, you are to describe what has happened in some such way as this: *Either* 'I have made a mistake in my counting' *or* 'Someone has played a practical joke and abstracted one of the objects when I was not looking' *or* 'Two of the objects have coalesced' *or* 'One of the objects has disappeared', etc.

This, I think, is the truth that is in the various 'conventionalist' theories of mathematics. Only, unfortunately, the formulae expressing such theories are usually misleading and incorrect. For example, to say that: 'a mathematical proposition merely expresses the speaker's or writer's determination to use symbols in a certain way', is obviously untrue. For if it were true, and if I decided to use the symbol '+' in such a way that 5 + 7 = 35, I would then be speaking truly if I said '5 + 7 = 35'. But this proposition is not true. The truth of any mathematical proposition does not depend on my decision or determination. It is independent of my will. This formula neglects the 'public' or 'over-individual' character of mathematics.

Or, consider the formula: 'A mathematical proposition is really an empirical statement describing the way people commonly use certain symbols'. This, I think, is nearer. But it is open to the following obvious objection: If '7 + 5 = 12' were really an assertion about the common usage of symbols, then it would follow that 7 + 5 would not equal 12 if people had a different symbolic convention. But even if people did use symbols in a way quite different from the present one, the fact which we now express by '7 + 5 = 12' would still be true. No change in our language-habits would ever make this false.

This objection is, I think, sufficient to show that the suggested formula is untrue, as it stands. But we should be blind to its merits if we did not see *why* it is that no change in our language-habits would make the proposition '7 + 5 = 12' untrue. The reason is this: As we use symbols at present, this proposition is incorrigible—one which we maintain to be true whatever happens in the world, and never admit to be false under any circumstances. Imagine a world where the symbolic conventions are totally different—say on Mars. How shall we *translate* our incorrigible proposition into the Martian symbols? If our translation is to be correct—if the proposition in the Martian language is to mean the same as our '7 + 5 = 12', it *too* must be incorrigible—otherwise we should not call it a correct translation. Thus a correct Martian translation of our '7 + 5 = 12' must be a proposition which the Martians maintain to be true whatever happens. Thus '7 + 5 = 12', and any correct translation into any other symbolic convention will be incorrigible, i.e. true whatever happens. So its truth does, in a sense, depend on the empirical fact that people use symbols in certain ways. But it is an inaccurate way of stating this fact to say that it describes how people use symbols.

A better formulation is: 'A mathematical proposition really expresses a rule for the manipulation of symbols'. But this, too, is unsatisfactory, and for the following reason: To say that it is a 'rule for the manipulation of symbols' suggests that it is entirely arbitrary. A symbolic rule is something which we can decide to use or not, just as we wish. (We could easily use 'hice' as the plural of 'house', and get on as well as we do now.) But, it seems, we cannot just change our mathematical propositions at will, without getting into difficulties. An engineer, building a bridge, has to use the standard multiplication tables and no others, or else the bridge will collapse. Thus which mathematical system we use does not seem to be entirely arbitrary—one system works in practice, and another does not. Which system we are to use seems to depend in some way not on our decision, but on the nature of the world. To say that '7 + 5 = 12' really expresses a rule for the use of symbols, suggests that this proposition is just like ' "house" forms its plural by adding "s" '. But there *is* a difference between the two, and so the formula is misleading.

I want to conclude this paper by considering in some detail the objection that you cannot build bridges with any mathematics, and that therefore mathematics does depend on the nature of reality. Before doing so, however, I should like to mention the type of theory I called 'conservative'. We saw that the (radical) theory, that mathematical propositions are 'really' empirical propositions about the results of counting, is untrue. But there is a close connection between the two sorts of proposition, and therefore the 'empirical' theory, although untrue, has a point. It emphasizes the connection between mathematical propositions and our everyday practice of counting and calculation; thus it serves as a useful corrective to that type of theory which would make mathematics too abstract and pure—a matter of pure intellect and Platonic 'Forms', far from the mundane counting of change. Similarly the various 'conventionalist' theories are also, strictly speaking, untrue, but they too have their point. Mathematical propositions in certain respects are *like* rules for the use of symbols, *like* empirical propositions about how symbols are used, *like* statements of intention to use symbols in certain ways. But conventionalist formulae are untrue because mathematical propositions are not *identical* with any of these. They are what they are; they function in the way they do, and not exactly like any other sort of proposition.

And this it is which makes that sort of theories I have called 'conservative' perfectly correct. Mathematical propositions are *sui generis*. But merely to say: 'They are what they are' is not very helpful. Nor is it any better if this is dressed up in learned language: e.g. 'Mathematical propositions state very general facts about the structure of reality; about the necessary and synthetic relations between the universals number, shape, size, and so on'. If you are inclined to think that such answers as this, to the question 'What are mathematical propositions about?', are informative and illuminating, ask yourself: 'How does my hearer come to understand the meaning of such phrases as "structure of reality", "necessary relations between universals", and so on? How were these phrases explained to him in the first place?' Surely he was told what was meant by 'necessary relation between universals', by being told, for example, that colour, shape, size, number, etc., are universals, and that an example of a necessary relation between universals would be 'everything that has shape has size', '$2 + 2 = 4$', 'two angles of an isosceles triangle are equal', and so on. These phrases, such as 'necessary relation between universals', are *introduced* into his language *via* or *by means of* such phrases as '$2 + 2 = 4$'; they are introduced *via* mathematical propositions, among others. To use an expression of John Wisdom's,[1] they are 'made to measure'. So to tell someone that mathematical propositions are 'so-and-so' does not help, if, in explaining what is meant by 'so-and-so', you have to introduce mathematical propositions, among others, as illustrative examples. Compare giving a 'conservative' answer to the question 'What are mathematical propositions?' with the following example: A child learns the meaning of the words 'see', 'can't see' 'blindfolded' etc., before he learns the meaning of the word 'blind'. The latter word is then introduced into his vocabulary by the explanation: 'A blind man is one who can't see in broad daylight even when not blindfolded'. If the child then asks of a blind man 'Why can't he see in broad daylight even when not blindfolded?', it is not much use answering 'Because he is blind'. Like the 'conservative' answer in philosophy, it may serve to stop any further questions, but it usually leaves a feeling of dissatisfaction.

Then what sort of answer *can* be given to one who is puzzled about the nature of mathematics? Mathematical propositions are what they are, so any radical answer equating them with something else, such as symbolic rules, or statements of the results of counting and measurement, or of common symbolic usage, will be untrue. Such answers will be untrue, because the two sides of the equation will have different meanings. Similarly conservative answers will be unhelpful, because the two sides of the equation will have the same meaning. The definiens will be useless, because it will contain terms which are introduced into the language *via* the definiendum, and can only be explained in terms of it. It is 'made to measure'. No simple formula will do. The only way of removing the puzzle is to describe the use and function of mathematical propositions in detail and with examples. I shall now try to do this, to some extent, in considering the natural objection to the strictly untrue but illuminating theory: 'Mathematical propositions express rules for the manipulation of symbols'. The objection is that symbolic rules are essentially arbitrary, whereas mathematics does, to some extent at least, depend not on our choice of symbolic con-

[1] My debt to the lectures of Wisdom and Wittgenstein, in writing this paper, is very great.

ventions, but on the nature of reality, because only our present system gives useful results when applied to the practical tasks of the world. Against this, I shall maintain that we could use *any* mathematical rules we liked, and still get on perfectly well in the business of life.

Example 1. 6 × 4, according to our current multiplication table, equals 24. You might argue: this cannot be merely a conventional rule for our use of symbols, for if it were we could use any other rule we liked, e.g. 6 × 4 = 12, and still get satisfactory results. But if you tried this alternative rule, you would, in fact, find your practical affairs going all wrong. A builder, for example, having measured a room to be paved with tiles, each one yard square, and having found the length of the sides to be 6 yards and 4 yards, could not use the alternative table. He could not say to himself: 'The room is 6 by 4; now 6 × 4 = 12, so I shall have to get 12 tiles for this job.' For, if he did, he would find he had not enough tiles to cover his floor.

But the builder could quite easily have used an arithmetic in which 6 × 4 = 12, and by measuring and counting could have paved his room perfectly well, with exactly the right number of tiles to cover the floor. How does he do it? Well, he:

(1) Measures the sides, and writes down '4' and '6'.
(2) Multiplies 4 by 6 according to a 'queer' multiplication table which gives 4 × 6 = 12.
(3) Counts out 12 tiles, lays them on the floor. And they fit perfectly.

The 'queer' multiplication table he uses gives 2 × 2 = 4, 2 × 4 = 6, 2 × 8 = 10, 4 × 4 = 9, 4 × 6 = 12, etc. The number found by multiplying a by b according to *his* table, is that which in *our* arithmetic we should get by the formula:

$$(a + 2) (b + 2) / 4$$

And he could pave any other size of floor, using the queer multiplication table described, and still always get the right number of tiles to cover it.

How is this possible? He measures the sides of the room

with a yardstick as follows: He lays his yardstick along the longer side, with the 'o' mark of the yardstick in the corner, and the other end of the stick, marked '36 inches', some distance along the stick. As he does this, he counts 'one'. He then pivots the yardstick on the 36 inches mark, and swings it round through two right angles, till it is once more lying along the side of the room—this time with the '36 inches' mark nearer to the corner from which he started, and the 'o' mark further along the side. As he does this, he counts 'two'. But now the direction of the stick has been reversed, and it is the convention for measuring that lengths should always be measured in the same direction. So he pivots the stick about its middle and swings it round so that the '36' mark is now where the 'o' mark was, and vice versa. As he does this, he counts 'three'. He then swings the stick round through two right angles, pivoting on the '36' mark, counting 'four'. He then reverses its direction, as before, counting 'five'. He swings it over again, counting 'six'. It now lies with its end in the corner, so he writes down the length of the side as 'six yards'. (If we had measured it in our way, we should have written its length down as four yards.) He then measures the shorter side in the same way, and finds the length (using his measuring technique) to be four yards. (We should have made it three.) He then multiplies 4 by 6, according to his table, making it 12, counts out 12 tiles, and lays them down. So long as he uses the technique described for measuring lengths, he will always get the right number of tiles for any room with his 'queer' multiplication table.

This example shows you that we use the method we do for multiplying lengths to get areas, because we use a certain method of measuring lengths. Our technique of calculating areas is relative to our technique of measuring lengths.

Here you might say: Admitting that this is true, it is still the case that mathematics is not arbitrary, for you could not use the method of measuring we do, *and* a different multiplication table, and *still* get the right number of tiles for our room. Can't we? Let's see.

Example 2. Suppose our 'queer' multiplication table gave 3 × 4 = 24. The builder measures the sides of a room exactly as we do, and finds that they are 3 yards and 4 yards, respectively. He then 'multiplies' 3 by 4, and gets 24. He counts out 24 tiles, places them on the floor, and they fit perfectly, with none over. How does he do it?

He measures the sides as we do, and writes down '3' and '4'. He 'multiplies' and gets 24. He then counts out 24 tiles as follows: He picks up a tile from his store, and counts 'one'. He puts the tile on to his truck and counts 'two'. He picks up another tile and counts 'three'. He puts it on his truck and counts 'four'. He goes on in this way until he reaches a count of 'twenty-four'. He then takes his 'twenty-four' tiles and paves the room, and they fit perfectly.

This example shows that our technique of calculating areas is relative both to a certain technique of measurement, *and* to a certain technique of counting.

At this stage you might make a further objection. You might say: Mathematics *does* tell you something about the world, and is not an arbitrary rule of symbolic usage. It tells you that *if* you both count and measure lengths in the way we do, you will not get the right number of tiles for a room unless you multiply the lengths according to our present table. It is not arbitrary, because if, for example, you measure the sides of a room as we do, and find them to be 4 and 3, and if you count tiles as we do, you would get the wrong number of tiles to pave your room if you used some other multiplication table—say one in which 3 × 4 = 24. I maintain, on the contrary, that we could quite well use such a 'queer' table, and count and measure as at present, and still get the right number of tiles. To help us to see what is involved here, let us consider a rather analogous case.

Example 3. Imagine that the following extraordinary thing happened. You measure a room normally, and find the sides to be 6 and 4. You multiply normally and get 24. You then count out 24 tiles in the normal way. (Each tile is 1 × 1.) But when you come to try and lay the tiles in the room, you find that you can only get 12 such tiles on to the floor of the room, and there are 12 tiles over. What should we say if this happened?

The first thing we should say would be: 'You must have made a mistake in your measuring' or 'You must have made a slip in multiplying' or 'You must have counted your tiles wrongly, somehow'. And we should immediately check again the measurements, calculations and counting. But suppose that, after the most careful checking and re-checking, by large numbers of highly qualified persons, *no* mistake at all of this sort can be found anywhere. Suppose, moreover, that this happened to everyone constantly, with all sorts of rooms and tiles. What should we say then? There are still a number of ways in which we might explain this curious phenomenon. I shall mention two conceivable hypotheses:

(1) Measuring rods do not, as we supposed, stay a constant length wherever they are put. They stay the same size when put against things the same length as themselves, and also when put against things larger than themselves running from north to south. But when put against things larger than themselves running east-west, they always contract to half their previous length (and this contraction happens so smoothly that we never notice it). Thus the room is in fact 6 by 2 yards, i.e. 12 square yards, and twelve tiles are needed. When the measuring rod is put along the north-south wall of six yards' length, it stays a yard long, and so we get a measurement of 6. When, however, it is put along the shorter east-west wall it contracts to half a yard in length, and can be put four times along the two-yard wall. If you now say the dimensions are 6 and 4, and multiply to get 24, you are overestimating the real area.

(2) An alternative hypothesis: When we measure the room our yardstick always stays a constant length, and thus the area of the room is really 24 square yards. But since we can only get 12 tiles in it, each tile being 1 yard square, it follows that the tiles must *expand*, on being put into the room, to double their area. It is just a curious *physical* law that objects put into a room double their area instantaneously. We do not see this expansion because it is instantaneous. And we can never measure it, by measuring the tiles, first out of the room and then inside, because our yardstick itself expands proportionately on being taken into the room.

This example (which might easily have been put in much more detail with *ad hoc* hypotheses to cover every discrepancy) shows that, however much the practical predictions of builders' requirements are upset when we use our present multiplication table, this need never cause us to alter our present rules for multiplication. Anomalies are accounted for by saying our knowledge of the relevant *physical* laws is defective, not by saying that the multiplication table is 'untrue'. If, when working things out in the usual way, we found that we had constantly 12 tiles too many, we should not say that we had been wrong in thinking that $6 \times 4 = 24$. We should rather say that we had been wrong in thinking that physical objects did not expand and contract in certain ways. If things go wrong, we always change our physics rather than our mathematics.

If we see, from Example 3, what we should do if things went wrong when we used our present arithmetic, we can now answer the objection it was intended to throw light on. The objection was this:

'It is wrong to say that we could use any arithmetic we liked and still get on perfectly well in our practical affairs. Mathematics is not a collection of arbitrary symbolic rules, therefore, and does tell us something about, and does depend on, the nature of reality. For if you *both* count and measure as we do, *and* use a "queer" multiplication table, you won't get the right number of tiles to pave a room. Thus the proposition "$3 \times 4 = 12$" tells you that for a room 3 yards by 4, measured normally, you need neither more nor less than 12 tiles, counted normally. Its truth depends on this fact about the world'.

But I deny this. I say we could have

(1) used our present technique of counting and measurement,

(2) multiplied according to the rule $3 \times 4 = 24$ (for example),

(3) and still have got exactly the right number of tiles to pave our room.

I therefore say that $3 \times 4 = 12$ depends on *no* fact about the world, other than some fact about the usage of symbols.

Example 4. Imagine that we did use a 'queer' arithmetic, in which $3 \times 4 = 24$. If this was our universally accepted and standard arithmetic, we should treat the proposition

'3 × 4 = 24' *exactly* as we now treat the proposition
'3 × 4 = 12' of our present standard arithmetic. That is to say,
if we did use this queer system, we should stick to the proposition '3 × 4 = 24' no matter *what* happened, and ascribe any
failure of prediction of builders' requirements, and so on, *always* to a mistaken view of the physical laws that apply to the
world, and *never* to the untruth of the formula '3 × 4 = 24'.
This latter proposition, if it *were* part of our mathematical system, would be *incorrigible*, exactly as '3 × 4 = 12' is
to us now.

In Example 3 we saw what would be done and said if
things went wrong in using '3 × 4 = 12'. Now *if* 3 × 4 = 24
were our rule, and incorrigible, and *if* in using it we found
ourselves getting the wrong practical results, we should do and
say exactly the same sort of thing as we did in Example 3.
Thus, assuming that our rule is 3 × 4 = 24, a builder measures his floor normally and writes down '3' and '4'. He multiplies according to his table and gets 24. He counts out 24 tiles
normally and tries to put them in the room. He finds that he
can only get 12 tiles in. What does he say? He *does not* say
'I have proved by experiment that 3 × 4 does not equal 24',
for his proposition '3 × 4 = 24' is *incorrigible*, and no event
in the world, however extraordinary, will ever lead him to
deny it, or be counted as relevant to its truth or falsity. What
he does say is something like this: 'The area of the room is
really 24 square yards. Since I can only get 12 yard square tiles
into it, it follows that the tiles must expand to double their
area on being put into the room'. (As we have seen, he might
use other hypotheses, e.g. about the behaviour of measuring
rods. But this is probably the most convenient.)

Thus we could easily have counted and measured as at
present, *and* used an arithmetic in which 3 × 4 = 24, *and*
have got perfectly satisfactory results. Only, of course, to get
satisfactory practical results, we should use a physics different
in some respects from our present one. Thus a builder having
found the area of a room to be 24 square yards would never
attempt to put 24 tiles in it, for he would have learnt in his
physics lessons at school that tiles put in a room double in

area. He would therefore argue: 'Since the tiles double in area, I must put half of 24 tiles, or 12 tiles, in the room'. He would count out 12 tiles and pave the room perfectly with them.

But even here an obstinate objector might admit all this, and still maintain that mathematics was not an arbitrary convention; that it did depend on certain facts about the world. He might say '"$3 \times 4 = 12$" is true, and it is true because of this fact about the world, namely that *if* tiles and rulers do not expand and contract (except slightly with changes in temperature), and if we measure and count normally, we need exactly 12 tiles, no more and no less, to pave a room that is 3 by 4. And "$3 \times 4 = 24$" is false, because of the "brute fact" that *if* tiles, etc., don't expand, and *if* you measure and count normally, 24 tiles are too many to pave a room that is 3 by 4'.

The point that is, I think, missed by this objection could be brought out by asking: 'How do we *find out* whether a tile or a yardstick has or has not expanded or contracted?' We normally have two ways of doing so. We can *watch* it growing bigger or smaller. Or we can *measure* it before and after.

Now in the case described in example 4, where our queer arithmetic gives $3 \times 4 = 24$, and things double in area on being put in a room, how do we find out that the things do expand? Not by watching them grow—*ex hypothesi* we do not observe this. Nor by measuring them before and after. For, since we assume that a measuring rod *also* expands on being taken into the room, the dimensions of the tile as measured by a yardstick outside the room are the same as its dimensions as measured by the same (now expanded) yardstick inside the room. In this case we find out that the tiles expand by *measuring, counting and calculating in a certain way*—by finding that the tiles each measure 1×1, that the room measures 3×4, or 24 square yards, and that we can only get 12 tiles in it. This is our sole *criterion* for saying that the tiles expand. That the tiles expand *follows from* our queer arithmetic. Similarly, as we do things at present, our criterion for saying that tiles do not expand, is that when 12 tiles measuring 1×1 are put into a room 3×4, or 12 square yards, they fit exactly. From our present arithmetic, it follows that tiles do not expand.

In Example 4, where we have a 'queer' arithmetic in which 3 × 4 = 24, and a 'queer' physics, it is a 'law of nature' that tiles expand on being put into a room. But it is not a 'law of nature' which describes what happens in the world. Rather is it a law 'by convention', analogous to that law of our present physics which says that when a body falls on the floor with a certain downward force, the floor itself exerts an equal force in the opposite direction. It is just put into the system to balance our calculations, not to describe anything that happens.

This last objection might have been put in a slightly different form. It might have been said: ' "3 × 4 = 12" does describe and depend on the nature of reality, because it entails a certain purely empirical proposition about what does and does not happen, namely the complex proposition: "It is not the case *both* that tiles do not expand *and* that we need less than 12 tiles to pave a floor measuring 3 by 4" '. But I should maintain that this complex proposition (of the form 'Not both p and q') is not empirical; that it does not describe anything that happens in the world, because it is incorrigible. Nothing whatsoever that we could imagine happening would ever lead us, if it happened, to deny this complex proposition. Therefore it does not tell us what happens in the world. The simple propositions which are elements in this complex one —the propositions 'Tiles do not expand' and 'We need less than 12 tiles to pave a 3 by 4 floor'—are both of them corrigible, and both describe the world (one of them falsely). But the complex proposition that they are not both true is incorrigible, and therefore, for the reasons given earlier, does not describe or depend on the nature of the world. There is nothing out of the ordinary about this. The propositions 'My curtains are now red over their whole surface', and 'My curtains are now green all over' are both of them corrigible propositions, descriptive of the world. (One is true, the other false, as a matter of fact.) But the complex proposition 'My curtains are not both red and green over their whole surface' is incorrigible, because nothing would ever make me deny it, and it is therefore not descriptive of the world.

I have talked, throughout the paper, as if mathematical propositions were completely incorrigible, in the sense that *whatever* queer things happened, we should *never* alter our mathematics, and always prefer to change our physics. This was a convenient over-simplification that must now be qualified. I maintain that we *need* never alter our mathematics. But it might happen that we found our physical laws getting very complicated indeed, and might discover that, by changing our mathematical system, we could effect a very great simplification in our physics. In such a case we might decide to use a different mathematical system. (So far as I can understand, this seems to be what has actually happened in certain branches of contemporary physics.) And mathematics does depend on and reflect the nature of the world at least to this extent, that we would find certain systems enormously inconvenient and difficult to use, and certain others relatively simple and handy. Using one sort of arithmetic or geometry, for example, we might find that our physics could be reduced to a logically neat and simple system, which is intellectually satisfying, whereas using different arithmetics and geometries, we should find our physics full of very complicated *ad hoc* hypotheses. But what we find neat, simple, easy, and intellectually satisfying surely depends rather on our psychological make-up, than on the behaviour of measuring rods, solids and fluids, electrical charges—the 'external world'.

XII

Theory Construction

J. J. C. SMART

In a monograph[1] published in 1939 Dr. J. H. Woodger puts forward some interesting views as to the ideal at which a scientific theory should aim, and illustrates some of the features of this ideal by putting forward a specimen theory which exemplifies them. As I think that Dr. Woodger's conceptions both of what a scientific theory is and of what it ought to be are mistaken, and as they are in some quarters very fashionable conceptions, I think that it is worth while to consider Dr. Woodger's monograph in some detail.

In the opening pages of the monograph Woodger puts forward reasons for inventing an artificial language for scientific purposes. He says that the richness of the vocabularies of natural languages such as English or French makes them unsuitable for scientific purposes, because 'the process of calculation is not possible in a natural language'. Another objection to the natural languages is that since 'we learn them during the most impressionable period of our lives, they become to such an extent part of ourselves that we come to use them without ever being aware of their conventional and arbitrary character, and thus of certain of their properties which are least admirable from the point of view of science' (p. 2). I shall try to argue that the whole conception of an artificial language is extremely confused; and that the reasons given by Woodger for constructing one are bad reasons; and that his programme acquires a specious plausibility on account of our liability to confuse it with a very different one which he

[1] *The Technique of Theory Construction*, by J. H. Woodger (International Encyclopedia of Unified Science, Vol. II, No. 5), University of Chicago, 1939.

mentions on p. 3. Here he says something which is true and important, namely that 'in so far as the *direction* of the development of mathematics has been given a bias by the special requirements of the problems of physics . . . it may, in some of its most fully developed branches, be unsuitable for the use of other sciences, e.g. for the biological sciences'. It is indeed possible that some parts of *Principia Mathematica*, such as the calculus of relations, or similar branches of mathematics, may turn out to be valuable in biological theory. 'We require a technique for constructing new kinds of mathematics as well as for constructing new languages for scientific purposes', says Woodger, and I do not in the least want to argue that new kinds of mathematics may not be highly desirable, though whether there could be a *technique* for producing them seems doubtful, for surely new branches of mathematics are the products of genius. What I want to object to is the alleged programme of constructing new *languages*. My argument will be in two parts. In the first place I shall try to point out that it is misleading to call the artificial language a 'language' at all. In the second place I shall argue that whatever it is, language or not a language, it is not a desirable thing to incorporate in a science.

It is logically possible that a person might know how to use a language without ever having been taught it. It is logically possible, though of course it never happens, that a baby might be born talking Latin or English. Nevertheless if we suppose that a language has been acquired by being *taught* it is a logical impossibility that certain expressions should have been learnt before certain other expressions have been learnt. A child cannot learn how to use 'or' as in 'my brother or my sister is crying' until it has learnt words like 'brother' and 'sister'. A consideration of how a language might be taught to a child thus sheds light on some of its logical features; it enables us to classify concepts in layers of sophistication. It is worth noting that the layers of sophistication have a bottom layer; this is equivalent to the platitude that it is possible to teach a natural language to someone, e.g. a baby, who knows no language whatsoever. Let us examine whether this feature is shared by Woodger's 'language'. This consists partly of various logical expressions such as 'not', 'and', 'or', 'asym'. Logical expressions, however, belong to a higher level of sophistication than certain non-logical ones; they can never form a bottom layer of sophistication. So we must look to Woodger's non-logical expressions. These are 'cell', 'part of', and 'before in time'. Let us concentrate on 'cell'. How could we teach a person how to use this word? A cell, we might say, is the smallest form of living thing. There would not be much precision in this. Can we precisely explain what is meant by 'living'? Perhaps 'cell' could be explained ostensively? Should we show the person a cell through a microscope? This by itself would hardly do. How would he know that we weren't trying to show him *protoplasm*, for example? Again, we should have to make it clear that he had to look through a microscope. This would involve teaching him something about optics, for clearly looking through a tube with flat plates of glass instead of lenses would not do. Again, suppose that he did look through a tube with flat plates of glass and saw a freak which looked just as a cell looks through a microscope. Is he to call *this* a cell? Should *we* call it a cell, a monstrously huge cell, but still a cell, or should we call it something else? We should have to observe it and see if its functioning was similar enough to that of cells to make it *convenient* to call it a cell. All sorts of considerations might be relevant. For example the word 'cell' as actually used by biologists gets much of its meaning from the role it plays in cell theory. Now if a cell were very large the ratio of its surface area to its volume would be very much less than for small cells. This might upset cell theory considerably and make us very reluctant to recognize very large cell-like things as cells. We see from all the above considerations that the use of a word like 'cell' is a complicated thing and that quite a lot of talk would be required to teach a person how to use the word.

Woodger would almost certainly agree that it would be impossible to teach his artificial language to a person who knew no language whatever. The explanation of the use of his language, he might say, would be done in a metalanguage, which would be the natural language of the person concerned. The trouble is that this sort of terminology misleads by suggesting that the artificial language and its metalanguage have the sort of independence which two real languages such as

English and French have. It tends to make us minimize or even totally ignore the extent to which the artificial language has its roots in ordinary language and to which it draws almost its whole life from ordinary language. In the monograph Woodger says hardly anything about how the use of the word 'cell' is to be explained, and yet if biology consisted entirely of his theory and the evidence for it then this explanation of the use of 'cell' would be the most important thing in biology. This shows how misleading it is to talk of 'a new language for scientific purposes', for the most important scientific purposes would be subserved by something outside the 'language'.

Woodger constructs his 'language' by introducing a few 'meaty' (or not purely logical) words into a logical calculus. Now a logical calculus is not a language but is part of the mathematical theory of languages, to which certain parts of actual languages more or less conform. Thus the axioms of the propositional calculus may be *interpreted* as a set of suggested rules (not quite the actual ones) for the use of words like 'and', 'or', 'not'. (They may also be given an *arithmetical* interpretation. To propound a paradox: there is nothing specially logical about logic.) Now the mathematical theory of languages no more lends itself to being turned into a language than the mathematical theory of games can be made into a game.

Physical theory makes use of various branches of mathematics, and similarly a biological theory might make use of a logical calculus. In neither case, however, would the branch of mathematics or the logical calculus be coextensive with the theory. Thus in a physical theory some of the mathematical expressions must correspond to measurable magnitudes, and it must be explicitly stated that they do. This correlation with measurable magnitudes must involve the description of processes of measurement, and hence a descent from the high language of theory to the often technical but nevertheless 'earthy' language of the laboratory. We must not say, therefore, that a theory can be written 'in mathematics' as you or I could write a story in English or French.

The thesis that an artificial language is desirable for scientific purposes, then, will not seem plausible even if we confuse 'scientific purposes' with 'theoretical purposes'. The thesis begins to take on quite a fantastic air when we pay attention to the great part of scientific literature which consists in reports of experimental and observational work. A great deal of the vocabulary of this part of the literature of science is technical, but a great deal, which is quite indispensable, is taken from the vocabulary of ordinary life. Consider this short extract from Millikan's *The Electron* (Cambridge University Press, 1935), p. 67, which is the beginning of a description of the experiment which proved the atomic nature of electricity: 'In order to compare the charges on different ions, the procedure adopted was to blow with an ordinary commercial atomizer an oil spray into the chamber C. The air with which this spray was blown was first rendered dust-free by passage through a tube containing glass wool. The minute droplets of oil constituting the spray . . .' Here we have homely words like 'oil', 'spray', 'chamber', 'air', 'dust', 'tube', 'glass', 'droplet'. What could be meant by saying that this sort of language is unsuitable for science? What could do the job better? There is nothing that could do the job better. Ordinary language just is something whose use cannot be distilled into strict rules, and experimenters, even in atomic physics, cannot get along without this sort of language. It is quite beside the point to say that here 'the process of calculation is not possible' or that the language is not completely precise. Whoever wanted to calculate in this instance? Again if the language is precise *enough* we do not want it to be any *more* precise. If we were not perfectly satisfied with Millikan's description we should ask for a *fuller* description. We should not ask him to stop writing in English.

Woodger might concede all this. He might agree that it is highly misleading to call his system 'a language', and that at some vital points it is rooted in ordinary language, and also that it is totally inapplicable to the experimental and observational literature of science. He might nevertheless stick to the assertion that *theories* would be much better if constructed according to his model. This is the assertion which we must now consider. Of course the theory which Woodger develops in the monograph is only meant to be an illustrative one, and we must not complain because it is not *in fact* a good or useful one. If on the other hand we consider as a specimen a theory which is admitted to be both well-established and fertile and we find that it contains features without which it could only be trivial and which an axiomatized theory just could not possess, and if we find that the axiomatic method conduces only to the development of those features which are of little value in a theory, then the matter will be quite different. For then there would be strong reason to suspect that not only the illustrative theory but *any* theory of the sort that Woodger tries to illustrate would be valueless. This is the point for which I shall argue, and the people I shall try to convert are logicians, for I shall be trying to point out certain features of language. I shall not be trying to convert scientists, for if biologists, for example, ever agree among themselves that a theory similar to Woodger's illustrative one is of genuine value, then there will clearly be something wrong, either by omission or commission, with what I say. It would be arrant scholasticism to lay down criteria for judging theories to a consensus of working biologists. Even if I show that there are errors in Woodger's conception of scientific language, this will not prove that there is not also something of positive value as well. All I want to do is to draw attention to what seem to me to be the errors.

In order to form a just estimate of the value of Woodger's method we must state his theory T as simply as possible, and consider what, if anything, is gained by stating it in his more detailed or 'rigorous' way. We must also see whether T has the characteristics of a good theory: we must see what, if anything, it is supposed to explain, and whether it is able to explain it. To do this I shall also state in outline another theory, which I shall call 'U'. This is the Kinetic Theory of Gases. It will be agreed that U is a good theory, for there are certain things (mainly the gas laws) which it was invented to explain, and it is successful in explaining them. We shall find that U is genuinely explanatory, while T is not, simply in virtue of certain features of U which could not be incorporated in a completely axiomatized theory.

Diagrammatic Version of the Theory T

Regard cells as 4-dimensional solids. (This corresponds to Woodger's propositions 1.1 to 3.13.)[2]

Then the situations in which two cells have a part in common[3] are (a) and (b), and (a) and (b) alone:

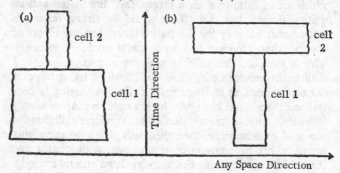

Corollary

The following do not represent possible situations:—

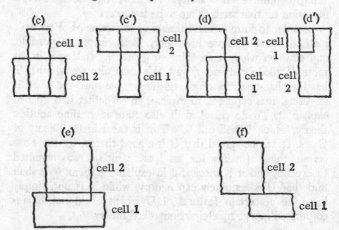

[2] *Technique of Theory Construction*, pp. 33–40.
[3] Woodger uses 'part' in such a way that being contiguous in time counts as having a part in common.

(a) and (b) constitute a picture mainly of Woodger's proposition 3.14.

In situation (a) we say that cell 2 is derived from cell 1 by division. In situation (b) we say that cell 2 is derived from cell 1 by fusion. (These are Woodger's propositions 3.5 and 3.6.)

(My diagrams look a little unnatural because they are designed to say neither more nor less than the propositions of the theory T. Thus we should expect a picture of division to look not like (a) but like (a¹):—

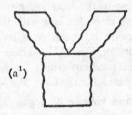

(a¹)

This, however, would be to state more than is actually contained in T. (a¹) is of course compatible with the theory but is not actually entailed by it. I have mentioned this point simply to remove possible misunderstanding; it is not in the least a criticism, for it is highly desirable that an illustrative theory should be simpler than it might have been.)

We can now 'read off' from the diagrams (a) and (b) any of the propositions about division and fusion in Woodger's theory and in particular—

3.52. The relation of division is one-many and asymmetrical.

3.62. The relation of fusion is many-one and asymmetrical.

3.71. No cell both divides and fuses with another cell.

3.72. No cell arises both by division and fusion.

This 'reading off' is very easy and involves no more than our simplest spatial intuitions. I cannot imagine two people ever disagreeing about whether 3.71, for example, can be 'read off' from the diagrams. Now one of the avowed aims of the axiomatic method is to avoid unnecessary controversy. If, however, there is likely to be no controversy, what is the point of stating 'rigorously' in 40 closely packed pages what can be put diagrammatically in about one page? If Woodger had invented a theory of complexity comparable to that of an actual biological theory it would have taken a whole library to state it according to his method, and his simple example, at any rate, has not shown that anything important would have been gained.

The next thing to note is this: most of the things we normally call 'theories' were invented in order to explain certain laws, and in the case of any such theory there would be no difficulty in pointing to the facts which were to be explained. This does not seem to be the case with the theory T. All its propositions appear to be much on a level. Let us contrast the Kinetic Theory of Gases, U.[4] There is no difficulty in pointing to the propositions which U is meant to explain. For example U explains Boyle's Law, '$P \propto \frac{1}{V}$', where P and V are the pressure and volume of a gas. The propositions of the theory itself involve some quite new ideas, for example that of a molecule or a gas particle. When we go from the experimental facts, such as that $P \propto \frac{1}{V}$, to the propositions of the theory, we rise to a totally new level of language. A word like 'molecule' cannot be strictly defined, and the properties of molecules are logically different from measurable properties. 'Find out the velocity of a molecule' makes no sense as does 'Find out the velocity of a billiard ball'. 'Velocity' as it occurs in 'velocity of a molecule' is logically different

---

[4] N. R. Campbell, in *Physics. The Elements* (Cambridge University Press, 1920), pp. 127 ff. discusses the Kinetic Theory of Gases as an instructive example of a physical theory, and what I shall say about it derives very largely from his ideas. Of course the element of *analogy* is present in varying degrees in different theories. In quantum mechanics, for example, Hamilton equations with operators are modelled on Hamilton equations in analogous systems in classical mechanics. In Newtonian dynamics itself there is very little of the element of analogy. I think, however, that it is possible to show that in the non-analogous type of theory also there is not a tight logical connection between propositions of theory and propositions of observation, that here also the theory and the statements of observational fact are on different levels of language.

from 'velocity' as it occurs in 'velocity of a billiard ball'. The latter is an empirical or measurable property, while the former is a purely theoretical concept. If we consider U we shall see how this fact, that the propositions of U are on a different level of language from the laws it is called upon to explain, is an indispensable condition of the fact that U *does* explain those laws, and also of something else which is hardly less important, that U suggests new experiments and new laws which it will explain. Let us therefore consider a very much simplified version of U and examine some of its logical features.

The Theory U

The laws to be explained are the following:

(1) At constant temperature $PV =$ constant, where P and V are the pressure and volume of a given mass of a gas. (Boyle's Law.)

(2) If several gases occupy a vessel of volume V then their combined pressure is equal to the sum of the pressures which each gas by itself (and at the same temperature) would have in a vessel of volume V. (Dalton's Law of Partial Pressures.)

It is also tempting to say that the theory should explain the law that if V is constant then $P \propto T$, where T is the absolute temperature, or to rewrite the law in the form '$PV = RT$', when R is a constant. This would be a mistake. The equation '$PV = RT$' does not state a law over and above Boyle's Law but *defines* the gas scale of temperature. We may reasonably expect of the kinetic theory of gases, however, that it should give a plausible physical meaning to 'temperature' as so defined, and this would be in some ways analogous to explanation of a law. We shall see that the theory does give a plausible physical meaning to 'temperature' as defined on the gas scale.

The situation is that we have some laws crying out for an explanation which cannot be given unless we move outside the limited range of ideas within which the laws are framed. Here the theory U differs considerably from T. In T we do not feel quite sure what explains what, and T never moves outside the range of the experiential ideas about cells which are its basis. In U we proceed to connect the gas laws with ideas, roughly speaking, of the behaviour of things like billiard balls. We introduce the quite new idea of a swarm of very minute perfectly elastic particles moving with very large velocities inside a box in accordance with the laws of dynamics. We investigate whether there would be anything in such a system analogous to the known behaviour of gases.

The following is an extremely simplified form of the investigation. It will make use only of the very easiest algebra and a correct presentation would of course be very much more complicated. It will, however, suffice to make clear the principles involved. (Also, in order to save space I shall only give that part of it which is the deduction of the analogue to Boyle's Law.)

Consider a box in the form of a cube of side l, three of whose edges lie along the axes OX, OY, OZ. Let ABCD and OEFG be the faces perpendicular to OX. Suppose that the box contains a very large number n of very minute per-

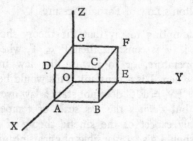

fectly elastic particles $P_1, P_2, \ldots P_n$, each being of mass M and let u_r, v_r, w_r be the components of the velocity of P_r. If we disregard the possibility of collisions between the particles, u_r, v_r, w_r will remain constant except that they will change sign when P_r hits the walls of the box perpendicular to OX, OY, OZ. (It is extremely plausible to suppose that our conclusions will remain unaffected if we disregard collisions between the particles, as any momentum lost by one of two colliding particles will be gained by the other, but the actual proof of this would involve us in more complicated considerations than are necessary for our present purposes.)

The time taken for the particle P_r to go from the wall ABCD to OEFG and back to ABCD again is obviously $\dfrac{2l}{u_r}$.

The change of momentum of P_r at each impact on ABCD is $2mu_r$

since it changes its velocity parallel to OX from u_r to $-u_r$

Hence the average rate of change of momentum of P_r at the face ABCD is $\dfrac{2mu_r}{\dfrac{2l}{u_r}} = \dfrac{1}{l}mu_r^2$

Hence the total rate of change of momentum on ABCD due to all the particles, and hence the force on ABCD is $\dfrac{m}{l}\sum\limits_{r=1}^{n}u_r^2$

By symmetry we may take it that

$$\sum_{r=1}^{n}u_r^2 = \sum_{r=1}^{n}v_r^2 = \sum_{r=1}^{n}w_r^2$$

So the force on ABCD is

$$\frac{1}{3}\frac{m}{l}\sum_{r=1}^{n}(u_r^2 + v_r^2 + w_r^2)$$

$$=\frac{1}{3}\frac{m}{l}\sum_{r=1}^{n}c_r^2$$

where c_r is the magnitude of the velocity of the particle P_r, that is,

$$\frac{1}{3}\frac{mn}{l}\overline{c^2}$$

where $\overline{c^2}$ is the mean square velocity of the particles.

The pressure P is clearly equal to the last quantity divided by the area of ABCD, which is l^2.

That is,

$$P = \frac{1}{3} \frac{mn}{l^3} \overline{c^2}$$

Now l^3 is the volume V of the box.

$$\text{So } P = \frac{1}{3} mn \, \overline{c^2} . \frac{1}{V}$$

$$\text{or } PV = \frac{1}{3} mn \, \overline{c^2}.$$

But $\frac{1}{2} mn \, \overline{c^2}$ is the total kinetic energy of the particles, and so

$$PV = \frac{2}{3} \times \text{total kinetic energy of the particles.}$$

If two gases are at the same temperature no heat flows between them. So if we identify the heat energy of the gas with the kinetic energy of our particles we may take it that if the temperature is constant the kinetic energy is constant, that is

PV = constant, which corresponds to Boyle's Law.

It is also very easy to derive a law corresponding to Dalton's Law of Partial Pressures, and also to give a plausible physical meaning to 'temperature' as defined by the gas scale of temperature (i.e. by the equation PV = RT), namely as corresponding to the average kinetic energy of a particle of the gas.

We see, then, that if we think of a gas as a swarm of particles the gas laws become more intelligible; we feel that they have been explained, for we see that the laws of the behaviour of a swarm of perfectly elastic particles would be similar. The theory is explanatory because it shows the analogy between a gas and a swarm of particles, and in putting forward the analogy it has created some entirely new ideas, such as that of a gas particle. It is important to see that this is the case and that if we use 'particle' in the sense of 'molecule' or 'gas-particle' and if we use it in the original dynamical sense (roughly speaking in such a sense as that in which we might call a billiard ball a particle), we are using language in two different ways, and have created a new systematic ambiguity[5] in the use of 'particle'. For example a billiard ball must be either white, black, coloured, or transparent, but it would be absolutely without sense to apply any of these predicates to a molecule. Again, when we talk of the mass or velocity of a billiard ball we are talking about an experimental magnitude which might be determined by weighing or by clocking, whereas 'mass' and 'velocity' as applied to a molecule only have meaning within the theory. If told to measure the velocity of a billiard ball I might say 'No, it's too difficult', but if you told me to measure the velocity of an air molecule I would not say that it was too difficult but that I did not know what you wanted me to do. Again, we can talk about the history and distinguishing marks of an individual billiard ball, but we have given no meaning to talk about an individual molecule. Such talk would be quite in the air and without possibility of test. If asked to measure the root mean square velocity of a set of billiard balls I might do it by measuring their individual velocities and taking the root mean square, whereas if asked to find out the root mean square velocity of the molecules of the air in this room I should do quite a different sort of thing, such as to measure the barometric pressure and the temperature and, by connecting my measurements up with the kinetic theory, say what the root mean square velocity was. 'Velocity of a billiard ball' is an experimental concept, a magnitude that can be determined prior to all theory whatsoever, whereas 'velocity of a molecule' is a theoretical concept which if connected up with experiment would be connected up *via* the theory to experimental magnitudes quite different from velocities. In these and other ways we can see that the logical grammar of 'molecule' differs in important respects from that of 'billiard ball'.

It thus follows that unless we recognize the difference of language level between the various uses of 'particle' it might be misleading to say that a gas consists of particles. On the other hand it would not do to retain the use of 'particle' for

[5] [See above, Second Series, Ch. I, pp. 232 ff. for an explanation of this expression.—EDITOR.]

things like billiard balls and to refuse to say that a gas consists of particles. How else can we bring out the analogy on which the explanatory power of the theory consists?

'All right', a semantic philosopher might say, 'we'll lay down a set of strict syntactical rules for "particle" = "molecule" and for "particle" = "billiard ball" and we will bring out the analogy[6] required for the theory by showing which rules are similar for the two cases, and also show where the analogy breaks down, by showing where the rules do not correspond'. This would not be a good idea, comforting though it is to our love for tidiness. *It would destroy the fertility of the theory.* All that it would be possible to derive from the theory would be the laws it was originally invented to explain.

In the first place *Avogadro's hypothesis* that all gases at the same temperature and pressure contain the same number of molecules in a given volume is a simple deduction from the theory if we identify his 'molecules' with the hypothetical gas particles of the kinetic theory. Avogadro's hypothesis was invented as an explanation of certain chemical facts, and the concept of a molecule was originally a chemical concept. We have now to attribute to our particles the property of being able to enter into combination with one another, a property quite unlike any property of a particle, in the sense in which a billiard ball is a particle. That is, we have to keep the logical grammar of an expression like 'gas particle' fairly fluid, so that we are ready to introduce modifications of the concept which will link our theory up with other theories and with laws of different sorts from those which it was first called upon to explain.

Secondly, it is eminently desirable to think in a fairly crude way and to press the analogy further than it will go. (The axiomatic method is expressly designed to prevent us from pressing analogies further than they will go.) The following example will show why this over-pressing of analogies may be

---

[6] If the theory is to be explanatory some device for bringing out the analogy is required, even though we do not wish to use the very convenient and (so long as we are aware of what we are doing) perfectly harmless one of systematic ambiguity.

a good thing. In the case of dynamical particles like small billiard balls the condition of perfect elasticity is never fulfilled, and some of the kinetic energy of the particles is not transferred on collision but is dissipated as heat and sound radiation and as internal vibration within the particles. The kinetic theory will not work if we attribute these properties to the gas particles. Why not? A logician whose ideal of a language is that it should everywhere proceed in accordance with rigid rules would have to say that from his point of view the question is a silly question, that 'particle' in the sense of 'billiard ball' and 'particle' in the sense of 'molecule' are two different words, and that some questions which, according to his rules, can be asked with the one, cannot, according to his rules, be asked with the other. I want to point out that a great deal of vital importance would be liable to be lost if we were to adopt such an attitude. Physicists rightly tried to press the analogy in the direction of asking why the energy of the gas particles was not dissipated in the way it could be expected to be on the analogy, and when it was eventually found that there were reasons, drawn from quantum theory (which itself was derived from a realm of observations quite different from those which led up to the kinetic theory of gases), why the analogy could not be expected to work in this respect, this constituted a triumph not only for the quantum theory of radiation but also for the kinetic theory of gases.

In the third place it is not true that we say that a theory has to be given up, or even 'modified', if its predictions are not always closely confirmed. A failure to fit the facts may in certain circumstances be additional reason for accepting the theory as being essentially sound. This is the case with the theory of gases, for at high pressures the laws predicted by the theory are not closely obeyed. Now on the analogy on which the theory was based we can see that we could have expected that this would be so. We failed to consider the *volumes* and the *mutual attractions* of the particles of the gas. Even without working the thing out in detail we can see from a general consideration of the rough outline of the kinetic theory that in cases where the particles are so near one another that the above two factors cannot be neglected the modification of Boyle's Law called 'Van der Waal's Equation' would be extremely plausible. Hence our confidence in the general soundness of the theory and the accuracy of its predictions in the cases in which we should expect it to work is not diminished but enhanced.

We may note some of the linguistic expressions which occurred in the last paragraph—'can be neglected', 'might have expected', 'failed to consider'. Such expressions are very characteristic of much actual scientific language but could find no place in a formalized language. Strict rules for 'what we might expect' cannot be laid down; we use such an expression when we are using our judgment.

It might be retorted that all this applies only to the growing stages of a theory, but that when a theory is in its final and perfect stage it can then be formalized. My reply to this would be that when a theory is in its final and perfect stage it is dead and of no further use, for, as I have tried to show, if a theory is to have any valuable explanatory, predictive, and unifying function, it must contain linguistic features which are present only in a living language, and which could not be present in a formalized system. It would be patently absurd to construct a 'language' for 'scientific purposes' if the only theories which could be put into the 'language' are fossilized theories, theories with no surviving scientific purpose.

Consideration of the above theory U, and comparison with theory T, have, I hope, shown that U possesses features which are indispensable and which no theory of the axiomatized sort could possess. It is perhaps superfluous, therefore, to claim that any of the supposed virtues of T are not really virtues, if it be agreed that T lacks an *indispensable* virtue. Nevertheless it may help to persuade a reader who is as yet unconvinced if I say a few words about what is supposed to be the chief virtue of T, namely *rigour*. I want to point out that 'rigour', in the sense in which it is pursued in pure mathematics is not an ideal in applied mathematics (or physics). The conception of 'rigour' involved in physics is that whereby it makes sense to say 'rigorous enough', and if enough *is* enough there is no point in making our proofs *more* rigorous. In any case rigour is not the all-important thing.[7]

Rigour, in the pure mathematician's sense of the word, is an ideal which only does apply to pure mathematics. Pure mathematics can be made into a calculus, and theorems may be derived from the axioms in accordance with strict rules. The axioms really are axioms (postulates), and they are not in any way to be tested by experience in the way that some of Woodger's 'postulates' are supposed to be. If a theorem can be proved it can be strictly proved, and if the proof is accepted there is no further question. Science is not like this. Even if the steps within a theory are formalized, the important steps, which are those from the theory to the experimental facts, are of quite a different sort. We saw this in the theory U when, for example, we identified the theoretical concept of the average pressure exerted by a swarm of minute particles with the empirical concept of the pressure we measure with a barometer tube. It is in this step from the theoretical to the empirical, and in the converse step from the empirical to the theoretical, that 'judgment' characteristically enters into science. An experimenter has often to judge, on the basis of his general 'feel' for the subject, whether a new phenomenon has entered into his experiments or whether something has just gone wrong. Thus Millikan's oil drop experiment might give results which at first sight might be thought to falsify the theory of discrete electronic charges, but then the anomalous way in which the rate of fall of an oil drop changed would be attributed by the experimenter to some such cause as the evaporation of the drop. It ought to be obvious that no strict rules can be invented for telling the experimenter what he ought to say in such cases; for one thing there is no finite set of types of experimental apparatus, and so there is no knowing from what range of experience the experimenter will have to extract his 'excuses' for an apparent

[7] In the preface to his 'Introduction to the Kinetic Theory of Gases' (Cambridge University Press, 1940) Sir James Jeans, who was a lover of pure theory if ever there was one, speaks of 'the physicist's need for clearness and directness of treatment rather than the mathematician's need for rigorous general proofs'.

anomaly. Again, it is often only genius, which works according to no rules, which spots the apparent anomaly which it is important to recognize as a real anomaly.

We thus see that the step from theory to fact is not like the step from one proposition to another in a calculus; roughly speaking, we may say that within a theory or within the description of fact we are on one level of language, but when we step from the level of theory to the level of fact or vice versa, we are in a region where expressions like 'make more plausible', 'lead us to expect that', or 'strongly suggest' apply, but where the logical relations of implication and contradiction do not strictly apply.[8] If, then, some of the most important and quite indispensable steps which a scientist makes cannot be reduced to strict rule, why bother about absolutely strict rules within a theory either? So long as our rules are strict enough to prevent us getting into trouble, or so long as we watch our step in those deductions where it is relatively easy to commit an important fallacy, why do any more towards making our theoretical deductions rigorous? To suggest that it is desirable to formalize a theory in the way that pure mathematics is formalized is like suggesting that holes in the side of a bottomless bucket should be stopped up. However carefully we seal the sides of the bucket it still will not hold water. (This analogy must not be taken too seriously, for I am far from wanting to suggest that science is somehow defective as a bottomless bucket would be. The ideal of a bucket with a bottom is not a logically absurd ideal, whereas the ideal of a science for which the canons of criticism are everywhere those of strict deduction is a logically absurd ideal.) As I have said, the conception of 'rigour' in physics is that in which it makes sense to say 'rigorous enough'. My statement of U, for example, would certainly not be regarded by physicists as

---

[8] I owe this idea to Dr. F. Waismann. As a rough analogy, compare the way in which one chess rule may be incompatible with another, or one move may be incompatible with another, but a move cannot contradict a rule, though it may be a breach of it. Logic, in the sense of *Principia Mathematica*, Dr. Waismann has said, is not coextensive with language, but at most with a given level of language. [See his *Language Strata*, above, Second Series, Ch. I.—EDITOR.]

rigorous enough. This does not mean, however, that the standard of rigour required is that of the pure mathematician.

My statement of Woodger's theory T, with the aid of diagrams, was not rigorous, i.e. not formalized, but surely it is
far easier to understand than Woodger's version, and it enables us to grasp the properties of cells which are described
(though not explained) by it. Rigour would only be useful to
the extent that it would prevent avoidable controversies, but
what controversy could there be about the conclusions of the
theory T?

In pure mathematics it is proved rigorously that if $f(x)$ is a
continuous function which has a derivative $f^1(x)$ for all values
of x, then if $f(x) = 0$ for $x = a$ and $x = b$ then $f^1(\xi) = 0$
for some values ξ of x where $a < \xi < b$. This corresponds to
the proposition that if we draw a smooth curve which cuts
the line OX at two points A and B then there is some point
in between A and B where the tangent to the curve is parallel to OX. We get the feeling that if we were to connect up
the proposition about drawn curves with the proof of the
proposition in pure mathematics we would put the proposition about drawn curves on a sounder basis. This feeling is
quite wrong. It comes from the failure to see that the strict
idea of continuity which is applicable in mathematical analysis is quite inapplicable to the realm of talk about drawn
curves, trajectories of rifle bullets, and so on. For example if
$f(x)$ is a continuous function then between any two values of
$f(x)$ we can find a third, but when we say that a trajectory is
continuous we do not mean that between two points $\dfrac{1}{10^{10}}$
millimetres apart we could find a third. No possible measurement or observation would be in the least relevant to such an
assertion; no possible experiences could verify or falsify it,
and consequently it can do no work and is quite pointless.
Of course we do represent trajectories by continuous functions, e.g. by $y = x^2$, rather than by very subtly discontinuous
ones. It is clearly far more convenient to do so, for continuous
functions are easier to handle mathematically—for example
they can usually be differentiated. This, however, is all there

is to the matter, and should not blind us to the change in the use of 'continuous' which occurs when we pass from the use of this word in physics or in ordinary life to its use within pure mathematics. Even if the mathematical ideal of rigour were applicable to scientific language it would not be worth striving after. A physicist would be just silly if he were to put axioms about continuity, etc., into his talk about trajectories, so as to model his talk on rigorous pure mathematical talk about functions, quite apart from the fact that his axioms would have no physical meaning or possibility of test. What would be the good of constructing a strict derivation of the proposition that if a projectile moves in a smooth curve from A to B, where A and B are at sea-level, then at some point between A and B its motion will be momentarily in a horizontal direction? Who could doubt it? What controversy could there be? The ordinary crude ideas of continuity are good enough for physical purposes, nor is there anything better for those purposes, and the sort of activity the pure mathematician goes in for would have no point.

In any case it is worth asking ourselves, in the light of the actual development of science, just how true it is that by making our derivations more rigorous we shall materially reduce the chance of controversy about our theories.[9] Controversies in physics, at any rate, do not seem normally to hinge on the strict rigour of derivations. They hinge on other things, such as the satisfactoriness of the analogy displayed; for example on whether pressing the analogy further does not lead us to deduce all sorts of false laws, and as to whether anything can be said as to why the analogy should not be pressed in these directions. I suggest that Woodger in constructing his theory T is doing in biology what a physicist would be doing if he

[9] On p. 34 proposition 1.25 Woodger claims to have cleared up, or at least avoided, a controversy. He has defined 'sum' so that it becomes analytical to say that a thing is the sum of its parts. This, however, is to miss the point of the controversy in question, which is something like this: as to whether after doing sufficient experiments on the parts of an organism we can predict the laws of its behaviour as a whole. This is surely a real question, though it may also be a muddled one, and remains unaffected by Woodger's treatment.

included in a theory of ballistics proofs of things such as the proposition about trajectories discussed above, that are everywhere, outside pure mathematics where the position is different, quite rightly allowed to pass without question. His method conduces to what is misplaced in a theory, namely rigour (in the pure mathematician's sense) of derivations, and leaves out something which is incompatible with strict rigour (in this sense), namely the features of scientific language which are not present in a calculus and which give a theory the power to explain. The only language which can be used in an explanatory way is language with what Dr. Waismann has called 'a many-level structure'. Dr. Woodger's monograph is an ingenious and admirable exercise in pure logic, but as a contribution to the philosophy of science it seems to me to be one more case of the tendency, so common in modern philosophy, to carry over into other realms of language ideals and conceptions which have their place only in pure mathematics.

ANCHOR BOOKS

BIOGRAPHY, AUTOBIOGRAPHY AND LETTERS

ANDRADE, E. N. da C. Rutherford and the Nature of the Atom, S35
——— Sir Isaac Newton, S42
BEETHOVEN, LUDWIG VAN Beethoven: Letters, Journals and Conversations, trans. & ed. Hamburger, A206
BENDIX, REINHARD Max Weber: An Intellectual Portrait, A281
CASALIS, GEORGES Portrait of Karl Barth, A422
COLETTE My Mother's House *and* The Vagabond, A62
DE BEER, SIR GAVIN Charles Darwin, N41
DICKINSON, EMILY Selected Poems and Letters of Emily Dickinson, ed. Linscott, A192
ESSLIN, MARTIN Brecht: The Man and His Work, A245
FULLER, MARGARET Margaret Fuller: American Romantic—A Selection from Her Writings and Correspondence, ed. Miller, A356
GATHERU, R. MUGO Child of Two Worlds, A468
GEIRINGER, KARL Brahms: His Life and Work, A245
——— Haydn, A361
GRAVES, ROBERT Good-Bye to All That, A123
GREVILLE, CHARLES CAVENDISH FULKE The Great World: Portraits and Scenes from Greville's Memoirs, ed. Kronenberger, A409
JONES, ERNEST The Life and Work of Sigmund Freud, ed. & abr. in 1 vol. Trilling & Marcus, A340
KENDALL, PAUL MURRAY Richard the Third, A455
LEWIS, W. H. The Sunset of the Splendid Century: The Life and Times of Louis Auguste de Bourbon, Duc du Maine, 1670–1736, A355
MAC DONALD, D. K. C. Faraday, Maxwell and Kelvin, S33
NEALE, J. E. Queen Elizabeth I, A105
NEWMAN, JAMES R. Science and Sensibility, A357
SHATTUCK, ROGER The Banquet Years, A238
TAYLOR, A. E. Socrates, A9

LINGUISTICS AND LANGUAGE

HALL, ROBERT A., JR. Linguistics and Your Language, A201
JESPERSEN, OTTO Growth and Structure of the English Language, A46

ANCHOR BOOKS